Neo-Victorian Tropes of Trauma

The Politics of Bearing After-Witness
to Nineteenth-Century Suffering

D1797031

Neo-Victorian Series

The Neo-Victorian Series aims to analyse the complex revival, re-vision and recycling of the long nineteenth century in the cultural imaginary. This contemporary phenomenon will be examined in its diverse British and worldwide, postcolonial and neo-colonial contexts, as well as its manifold forms, including literature, the arts, film, television, and virtual media. To assess such simultaneous artistic regeneration and retrogressive innovation and to tackle the ethical debate and ideological consequences of these re-appropriations will constitute the main challenges of this series.

Series Editors
Marie-Luise Kohlke
Christian Gutleben

Volume 1

Neo-Victorian Tropes of Trauma

The Politics of Bearing After-Witness
to Nineteenth-Century Suffering

Edited by

Marie-Luise Kohlke and Christian Gutleben

Amsterdam - New York, NY 2010

Cover image and design: © Marie-Luise Kohlke

Central image features a model of the clipper Cutty Sark.

The paper on which this book is printed meets the requirements of "ISO 9706:1994, Information and documentation - Paper for documents - Requirements for permanence".

ISBN: 978-90-420-3230-9
E-Book ISBN: 978-90-420-3231-6
© Editions Rodopi B.V., Amsterdam - New York, NY 2010
Printed in the Netherlands

Contents

Introduction:
Bearing After-Witness to the Nineteenth Century

Marie-Luise Kohlke and Christian Gutleben

Abstract:
Increasingly, the nineteenth century has become a significant locus of investigations into historical trauma, in terms of the retrospective analysis of actual catastrophic events and their long term after-effects, as well as their fictional re-experience and belated 'working through' in literature. The neo-Victorian phenomenon both reflects and contributes to crucial developments in trauma discourse and cultural memory, both at national and global levels, constructing competing versions of the past that continue to inform the present. Crucially, the neo-Victorian also problematises the politicisation and appropriation of trauma and resulting ethical dilemmas vis-à-vis the suffering other, especially relating to the notion of trauma's unrepresentability and the figurative language used to convey the central paradox of the unspeakable.

Keywords: cultural memory, ethics, memory politics, neo-Victorian, the other, trauma, unrepresentability, violence, witness.

*****

1.   The Ages of Trauma Then and Now

Although trauma studies as an academic discipline or, more accurately, a strand of cultural and memory studies indebted to psychoanalytical, poststructuralist, and postcolonial, as well as literary theory, only came fully into its own in the 1990s, its origins and antecedents stretch back much further than the twentieth-century limit events that promoted the theoretical interest in trauma as the defining condition of modernity and present-day subjectivity, as well as a transhistorical phenomenon. Long before World War I, the Holocaust, Hiroshima, and the Vietnam War, nineteenth-century artists and scientists had speculated about altered states of consciousness, split selves, and disturbed psyches produced by situations of existential crisis and extremity. These disrupted states of being complicated notions of the autonomous Cartesian subject founded on reason and self-knowledge by conversely highlighting the mind's vulnerability to life's varied shocks and its radical fragility and self-estrangement when confronted with bodily suffering and the threat of extinction. From the study of hysteria to 'railway spine' to neurasthenia and the US Civil War disorder of 'soldier's heart' (also known as Da Costa's syndrome) prefiguring the later concept of shellshock, the pathological private self, its existence disrupted by symptomatic obsessions, ritualistic repetitions, and inexplicable aberrations, became as much a focus of interest as the rational public self, the standard bearer of enlightened political, economic, and intellectual progress that supposedly undergirded nineteenth-century social reform and nation and empire building. In a sense, the nineteenth-century hysteric or otherwise disturbed and decentred personality, the object of scientific investigation and analysis, stands as the harbinger of the omnipresent traumatised and (self-)alienated subject of postmodernity – a subject radically 'othered' and 'other' even to itself.

To some extent the cradle, then, of contemporary trauma studies and notions of subjectivity, the nineteenth century has become a prominent focal point for literary investigations into and fictional re-enactments of historical trauma from contemporary perspectives. The double temporal consciousness typical of the emergent subgenre of historical fiction commonly referred to as the neo-Victorian novel lends itself especially well to such explorations.[1] For it could be said to mimic the double temporality of traumatic consciousness, whereby the subject occupies, at one and the same time, both the interminable present moment of the catastrophe which, continuously re-lived, refuses to be relegated to the past, and the post-traumatic present that seems to come after but is paradoxically coterminous. This is not so

---

[1] In some novels, this consciousness is rendered explicit either by the juxtaposition of dual plot-lines set in the nineteenth century and the present day, or linguistic markers, such as paratext (especially epigraphs and footnotes), deliberate anachronism, and metafictional or authorial interventions. In others, the duality remains implicit, inscribed more circuitously at the linguistic or structural level, dependent on readers' registration of divergences between nineteenth-century and current word usage, as in the case of a term such as 'queer', or their recognition of revisionist uses of intertextuality that highlight ideological blind spots (for example in relation to race or gender) in canonical nineteenth-century works.

much "an erasure of temporality", as Rosemary Gates Winslow suggests, rendering thought "without-time-ness" (Winslow 2004: 630), but more a superimposition of conflicting temporalities, in which consciousness operates simultaneously within multiple incompatible time-zones of being. As such, the neo-Victorian novel – used in this collection in a generic sense of literature re-imagining and engaging the nineteenth century in global terms, not necessarily confined to only British or Britain's colonial contexts – may function as a belated abreaction or 'working-through' of nineteenth-century traumas, as well as those of our own times, albeit more obliquely. Frequently, neo-Victorian fiction highlights interconnections between acts of aggravated historical violence and their long-term cultural and political aftershocks still resonating well into the twentieth and twenty-first centuries. Yet it also plays out more insidious personal kinds of trauma linked to individual crises (of personal identity, family, belief, and inheritance) as much as collective catastrophe. In many cases these narratives too resonate uncannily with contemporary concerns, as evident in today's keen interest in – and ready market for – confessional literature of abject pain and suffering, for instance on the themes of child and sexual abuse. Neo-Victorian literature thus both reflects and actively contributes to the prevailing present-day trauma discourse operating at personal and public, individual and collective, national and global levels, as myriad past and present traumas jostle and compete for our attention.

Whereas the disturbed nineteenth-century psyche constituted the exception, however, the traumatised subject now assumes the position of the contemporary norm. It functions as a veritable paradigm of modern subjectivity in the context of our so-called 'trauma culture', as all individuals become (at least *in potentia*) 'lost' and traumatised others-to-themselves. Far from being an isolated diagnosis, then, Nancy K. Miller and Jason Tougaw's assertion that "[i]f every age has its symptoms, ours appears to be the age of trauma" finds numerous echoes in other contemporary analyses (Miller and Tougaw 2002: 1).[2] Trying to explain the origins of this

---

[2] In his thorough and useful synthesis of works on trauma, Roger Luckhurst quotes several theorists who hold trauma to be "responsive to and constitutive of 'modernity'" (Micale and Lerner 2001: 10, qtd. Luckhurst 2008: 20) and who consider that "the modern subject has become inseparable from the categories of shock and trauma" (Seltzer 1997: 18, qtd. Luckhurst 2008: 20). Luckhurst himself

"true age of anxiety" (Bracken 2002: 181), critics and theoreticians commonly evoke the unprecedented scale of the mass destruction of World War II and the Shoah,[3] together with later deadly conflicts, genocides, and acts of terrorism, such as 9/11. Yet besides these historical roots in 'real' events, the ubiquitous sense of trauma arguably has an epistemological component: the knowledge of the relativity or impossibility of all knowledge, the fraught certainty of the uncertainty of any cognitive system, and the insistence on the aporetic nature of signification all help nurture our culture of loss and dispossession. As Ana Douglass and Thomas A. Vogler argue:

> Driven underground in the poststructuralist moment, the "real" has returned to mainstream discourse like the Freudian repressed, this time as the traumatic event [... which] bears a striking similarity to the always absent signified or referent of the poststructuralist discourse, an object that can by definition only be constructed retroactively, never observed directly.[4] Even so, this elusive object now serves as paradigm for the indexical signified real of much of our historical and ethical commentary. (Douglass and Vogler 2003: 5)

In these terms, the very historical traumas that neo-Victorian writers attempt to bear witness to must inevitably remain indeterminate and

---

asserts at the very beginning of his analysis that the "trauma paradigm [...] has come to pervade the understanding of subjectivity and experience in the advanced industrial world" (Luckhurst 2008: 1). Winslow similarly stresses the importance of engaging with trauma narratives "[a]s one century that has often been called 'the century of trauma' passes into another like it, but compounded so far by the fear that it may also be a century of terror" (Winslow 2004: 607). Paul Crosthwaite meanwhile contends that the whole postmodern culture is "convergent with the post-traumatic" (Crosthwaite 2009: 13).
[3] Crosthwaite goes as far as saying that all "Anglo-American postmodernist fiction" shows "the pervasiveness of the war's [WWII's] legacy" (Crosthwaite 2009: 1).
[4] Gene Ray, drawing on Jacques Lacan, resonantly describes trauma as the "'missed encounter' with the real": "Overpowered, lacking the means to confront and interpret the hit as experience, the subject misses the appointment." Even when retrospectively reconstructed, Ray argues, "[t]he encounter happens, belatedly, but remains missed. What is assimilated is the miss itself" (Ray 2005: 1).

abstruse, even as these traumas' traces, left on individual and social bodies and psyches, paradoxically become the new dominant 'real'.

2.   Trauma, Power and Politics

Increasingly, the mark of trauma as an ineradicable disabling rupture in psychological-cum-bodily integrity has also become a contrary means of empowerment, political currency, and wider cultural capital, if often ambiguously so. While today trauma confers visibility and publicity, often eliciting political activism on behalf of, monetary support for, and public commemoration of victims/survivors, the traumatised subjects themselves are often deemed unable to render their suffering intelligible without the specialist aid of interlocutors in the form of analysts, therapists, and advocates. This applies even more so in the case of historical trauma that lies beyond living memory. The fact that no sufferers remain to offer personal testimony necessitates a reconstruction of events from intermediary texts and images, which, even when records of actual first-hand experiences, require analytical commentary, (re-)interpretation, and translation for today's general public, characterised by short-term memory and brief concentration spans, as well as an ever loosening grasp of history in what Janet Walker calls "our historically amnesiac age" (Walker 1997: 805). Trauma has a limited 'life-span' with regards to both collective remembrance and a shared vocabulary, whether linguistic or visual, denotive or figurative. Hence, as Susan Sontag suggested, "one day, captions will be needed, of course" even for images of 9/11 (Sontag 2004: 26). However striking the visual (or literary) images encapsulating and producing/preserving particular cultural memories of suffering, they may ultimately become emptied of their specific historical referents and unique meanings:

> Eventually, the specificity of the photographs' accusations will fade; the denunciation of a particular conflict and attribution of specific crimes will become a denunciation of human cruelty, human savagery as such. (Sontag 2004: 109)

Some day even such 'unmistakable' iconic images as Huỳnh Công 'Nick' Út's Pulitzer Prize winning photo of the napalm covered, nine-year-old, Vietnamese Kim Phúc Phan Thị, or Richard Drew's 'The

Falling Man' or, indeed, pictures of Auschwitz, will require explanatory contextual notes to be accurately identifiable or attributable by future viewers/witnesses.[5]

Hence the *power of trauma* as a cultural force – of memory, of justice, of claim-staking to specific rights, of demands for reparation, of political utility – displays a curious tendency to reside elsewhere than only, or even primarily, with the sufferers and hence the primary witnesses. In some cases, it may even be claimed by the very agents who inflicted the trauma or their direct descendents. The historic 2008 apology by the Australian Prime Minister Kevin Rudd may serve as a case in point, made on behalf of the Australian government and nation to the country's aboriginal peoples for the victimisation inflicted on them in the course of two centuries of British dominated settlement and colonisation. Both before and since Rudd's apology, the predominantly white government of Australia has held and continues to claim the power to grant or withhold national recognition of indigenous suffering, to accept or deny historical accountability, and to determine the nature and kinds of reparation, which have remained largely symbolic.[6] As discussed by Kate Mitchell's chapter in this volume, the result is a divisive, still on-going power struggle over Australian memory politics and about how aboriginal trauma might best be incorporated into communal narratives of national identity. Indeed, it could be argued that, as much as being intended as a form of restitution, Rudd's apology was aimed at conveniently diffusing 'white' guilt via transmutation into a shared 'national' trauma, appropriating aboriginal suffering for a discourse of new beginnings and the transcendence of the past, which reflects the interests of the establishment and status quo rather more than those of the indigenes.

---

[5] Sontag pertinently notes that, since "photographs echo photographs", the images of "emaciated Bosnian prisoners at Omarska, the Serb death camp created in northern Bosnia in 1992" inevitably "recall[ed] the photographs taken in the Nazi death camps in 1945" (Sontag 2004: 75). Whether the average viewer of the future will still be able to differentiate the two groups of victims at all remains uncertain.

[6] In contrast to the Aboriginal Tent Embassy in Canberra, Rudd's apology strategically evaded any reference to still on-going landclaims or to practical measures aimed at ensuring the aboriginal people's full representation and involvement as equal partners in the country's political processes.

Such ambiguous calibration of acknowledgement and appropriation focalises an ethical dilemma, which we consider typical of neo-Victorian attempts to bear what we call 'after-witness'. We differentiate *secondary witnessing*, in the sense of bearing witness to a victim or survivor's actual first-hand testimony of trauma via empathic listening, viewing, or reading, from *after-witness*, in the sense of the fictional re-creation of trauma that both testifies to and stands in for inadequate, missing, or impossible acts of primary witness-bearing to historical trauma. Even when motivated by the best of intentions, the after-witness cannot help but appropriate trauma to some extent, since the critical distance of "empathic unsettlement" – the virtual participation in another's trauma *without* taking the sufferer's place (LaCapra 2001: 41-42, 78-79) – must give way to vicarious identification involved in the re-enactment or re-living of the other's suffering from the inside out by assuming *the discursively empty or unfilled place* of the sufferer.[7] Especially where historical trauma has been or continues to be denied, or attempts are made to obliterate its residual traces, the presumed authority to name and speak trauma remains both contentious and unequally distributed.[8]

Perhaps on account of after-witnessing's more acceptable appropriation – since it attempts to fill a lacuna rather than seize an already occupied space of enunciation – there is something strangely appealing about the nineteenth-century traumatised subject, inhabiting the ghostly liminal space between historical and living memory. As Sally Shuttleworth pointed out in her keynote speech to the 2010 *Fashioning the Neo-Victorian* conference in Erlangen-Nürnberg, Germany, analogous to the passing of the last WWI veterans, just about now, as the first decade of the new millennium draws to a close, the very last of the Victorians (or, more generally, any nation's citizens still born in the nineteenth century) are dying out, so that the

---

[7] In one sense, then, after-witness resembles the act of a primary witness who testifies *in the place of* those who perished and therefore cannot ever speak for themselves, those whom Primo Levi called "the drowned" and the only complete or "true witnesses" (Levi 1998: 63-64). As James Hatley explains, in such a case, "[t]he text is the voice of one who would witness for the sake of an other who remains voiceless even as he or she is witnessed" (Hatley 2000: 20).

[8] Consider the Armenian 'Genocide', which is still officially refused that designation not only by the Turkish government but also by numerous European states intent on appeasing, or at least not antagonising, a strategically important political partner.

las: remaining "sense of immediate connection is being lost" (Shuttleworth 2010). The shift from one sort of memory-work and commemorative practice to another, as we need to find different ways of relating to and maintaining a dynamic connection with the period, may facilitate a greater creative freedom in recreating this particular past. Yet it also carries a risk of turning historical trauma into spectacle at a reassuring temporal remove, which conveniently renders impossible any actual intervention – beyond the purely symbolic and mnemonic compensatory functions of narrative – thereby absolving complacent readers of any ethical obligations to take action, disconnecting the act of witnessing from subsequent political engagement.

Put differently, narrative identification and 'involvement' may take the place of concrete activism, although of course literature's literal effects on readers, their lives, and future conduct are in any case virtually impossible to quantify. On the other hand, 'doing' history, whether in theoretical or literary terms, is *always* political, since it constitutes a form of public discourse, disseminating implicit ideological judgements as to what is – and is not – worth recording and remembering *as* history in the first place, thereby determining the shape of the past for the future. Along these lines, James E. Young argues that "historical inquiry" is a two-pronged activity, combining "the study of both *what happened* and *how it is passed down to us*" (Young 2003: 283, original emphasis), to which Douglass and Vogler add a third essential element, namely "*what we are doing with it now*" (Douglass and Vogler 2003: 1, original emphasis). As will be seen from the range of novels discussed in the chapters to follow, neo-Victorian literature actively engages in this tri-partite enquiry, repeatedly reflecting on and problematising its own uses (and abuses) of the agencies of representation and after-witness.

If neo-Victorian fiction thrives on the sensational aspects of suffering, the issue of spectacle, of course, equally haunts our obsession with contemporary trauma, which is fostered, entertained and exploited by the omnipotent media. Wars, catastrophes, atrocities, crimes, and accidents are constantly circulated on the web, exhibited on television, displayed by the cinema, highlighted by newspapers, and harnessed by the publishing and museum industries, as well as permanently inscribed on the cultural landscape by memorials, monuments, and public rituals of commemoration. Re-mediated in-between different realms of cultural discourse, the resulting trauma saturation not only renders trauma everyone's constant close companion or 'secret sharer', but also produces any number of potential secondary trauma victims, traumatised not by their own experience of extreme events but by their witnessing of them at second hand. As Roger Luckhurst puts it, "Western cultures have convulsed around iconic trauma events" (Luckhurst 2008: 1), displaying a quasi fetishistic, perhaps even eroticised fascination with suffering. Miller and Tougaw put it more bluntly in economic terms of commodity markets and profits:

> In a culture of trauma, accounts of extreme situations sell books. Narratives of illness, sexual abuse, torture, or the death of loved ones have come to rival the classic, heroic adventures as a test of limits that offers the reader the suspicious thrill of borrowed emotion. (Miller and Tougaw 2002: 2)

Once again, though, the nineteenth century arrived before us at much the same point, or one near enough to invite outright comparison. For such bloody conflicts as the Crimean War (1853-56), as well as the 'Indian Mutiny' (1857-59), and the later Boer Wars (1880-81 and 1899-1902), were also highly mediatised and re-mediated events. The press pandered to news-hungry publics back home and abroad, manipulating opinion via first-hand survivor testimonies and dramatic war correspondents' reports from the frontlines.[9] These conflicts also employed photography to unprecedented extents, especially following the invention of mass produced, increasingly portable cameras which, during the second Boer War in particular, enabled amateurs as well as professionals to become active witnesses to atrocity (see Morgan 2002: 9). Two decades earlier, the Sepoy Rebellion – or the First Indian War of Independence as it is now often called – had precipitated a frenzied production of survivor memoirs, campaign histories, and so-called 'Mutiny fiction', including numerous sensation novels, a flood that

[9] Frances Rappaport notes of the Crimean conflict that "it was a war that established the power of the press and the newspaper reporter and which saw the average daily circulation of *The Times* leap by a third, from 42,500 when war broke out in 1854, to 58,500 within the year" (Rappaport 2007: 2).

did not abate until the next century. Shortly before that conflict, the Crimean War had not only introduced the first war artists and photographers and 'live' war reporting via electric telegraph, but also one of the earliest instances of modern 'battlefield tourism',[10] with civilians, including army wives, taking outings to the best vantage points along the front, equipped with telescopes and opera glasses to watch the death and dying up close and personal. In light of such vicarious spectatorship of horrific events, Miller and Tougaw's "suspicious thrill of borrowed emotion" can hardly be termed a particularly modern phenomenon. As Richard Beeston notes in the context of his own present-day battlefield tourism to the Crimea in the footsteps of William Howard Russell, war correspondent to *The Times* during the conflict, so-called "TGs" or "Travelling gentlemen" commonly "came out with the army on what must have been the Victorian equivalent of an adventure holiday" (Beeston 2007). Similarly, in the decades after the war, battlefield tours, akin to the more organised ones offered by tour operators today, appear to have rapidly gained popularity. Major resort developments took place along the Black Sea coast, and new hotels and boarding houses sprang up at Yalta and elsewhere to accommodate those eager visitors, among others, "who wanted to explore the battlegrounds of the Crimean War"; ironically, due to the horrendous medical conditions and Florence Nightingale's nursing reforms in the treatment of injured soldiers, "[t]he war had provided the dramatic connection between health and history, two of tourism's most important elements" up to the present day (McReynolds 2003: 176).[11]

Already in the nineteenth century, then, the fetishisation of extremity and survival against all odds, of heroism and abjection in

---

[10] Tourism to sites of conflict and suffering has become a profitable business, with places such as US Civil War, WWI and WWII battlefields, Auschwitz and other concentration camps, the Cambodian killing fields, the Cu Chi tunnels of the Vietnamese resistance forces, or one-time secret service prisons and torture cells in former Communist countries attracting large numbers of visitors, some of whom arguably come for the thrill of horror rather than a history lesson in inhumanity. Both the industry and the visits to such sites are also referred to as 'trauma tourism' or 'atrocity tourism'.

[11] McReynolds further points out that John Murray's popular 1888 guidebook, *Handbook for Travellers to Russia, Poland, and Finland, including the Crimea, Caucasus, Siberia, and Central Asia*, 4th ed., "devoted its longest section to the Crimean War" (McReynolds 2003: 176, fn. 106).

equal measure, served capitalist enterprise and what might be described as an emergent heritage industry linked to leisure and entertainment. Put differently, even if 'trauma culture' still lay in the future, the 'traumatic marketplace', appropriating, commodifying, and adulterating trauma, was already open for business. As discussed by Vanessa Guignery's contribution to this collection, even the photographic record of the Crimean War – and, indeed, many later hostilities – could not be relied upon to bear 'authentic' witness to the conflict's traumas, since pictures were often opportunistically 'staged' rather than 'found', fabricating the 'real' for ulterior motives, including propaganda and marketability (see also Sontag 2004: 48-51). Hence Victorian representations of trauma, even when seemingly grounded in the incontrovertible reality of suffering and dead bodies,[12] pre-empted the crisis of truth often highlighted by today's trauma theory and trauma narratives.

As such, neo-Victorian treatments of nineteenth-century trauma, situating themselves *ipso facto* in a historical and/or epistemological perspective, are hardly as distant or estranged from our own time as they may initially seem. Even though most of the neo-Victorian novels under consideration in this volume do not address the major traumas of the twentieth and twenty-first centuries directly,[13] writers clearly intend readers to make crucial connections between the earlier period and our own.[14] Indeed, many

---

[12] Douglass and Vogler pertinently note that, within trauma theory and witness discourse, the body has progressively assumed an equal, sometimes even greater significance than the psyche as "the visible – and representable – site of trauma" because, crucially, "[t]he body can signify even in, or by, its absence, like the infamous 'disappearing' signifier in Latin America's regimes, or the even more spectacular non-body count of the 1991 non-war with Iraq" (Douglass and Vogler 2003: 13).

[13] Graham Swift's *Ever After* (1992) may appear as an exception here since it does evoke World War II and fleetingly refers to Hiroshima, but these allusions remain peripheral, as if dreaded or repressed. Similarly, David Mitchell's *Cloud Atlas* (2004) employs distinct Holocaust imagery but only applied to historical periods other than the 1940s (see Wallhead and Kohlke, this volume: 227-232). David Cowart appropriately notes that, for the novelist's art not to be overwhelmed, "the more proximate the history, [...] the more obliquely the author must treat it" (Cowart 1989: 120-121).

[14] Many historical novelists, Suzanne Keen notes, "enthusiastically adopt historical settings and characters in order to address a wide range of present-day concerns" (Keen 2006: 176). However, this shared feature is arguably more pronounced in neo-

fictionalisations of specific historical traumas stand for indirect representations of, or analogical commentaries on, contemporary shocks and disasters. How could one fail to see that the shameless appropriation and misrepresentation of the Crimean War, critiqued by Vanessa Guignery, sheds a disturbing light on the role played by today's media in the (often highly selective) coverage of much more recent and current armed conflicts? Or fail to note that the ideological oppositions between oriental and occidental cultures, which inform the novels on the Indian Mutiny discussed by Marie-Luise Kohlke, continue to fuel international hostilities and global terrorism in the present? Just as surely the breach of trust implicit in the incest trope, examined in Mark Llewellyn's essay, resonates forcefully and uncannily with the child abuse scandals involving the Roman Catholic Church that repeatedly dominate our news headlines. Similarly, one might consider the extent to which revisiting the brutal truths of the Irish Famine, addressed in Ann Heilmann's chapter, implicitly denounces the ongoing scandal of today's world famines and the unequal access of the world's poor not only to crucial resources, but also to legal protections and basic human rights. Again, one can hardly miss that re-envisionings of colonial horrors in Africa, Canada, Australia, and the Chatham Islands, respectively discussed in Lies Wesseling's, Elodie Rousselot's, Kate Mitchell's, and Celia Wallhead and Marie-Luise Kohlke's contributions, constitutes an apt reflection of – and on – the neo-colonialism of today's superpowers, developed capitalist nations, and global corporate players. More overtly, Western nations' historical 'exportation' of trauma beyond their own borders, highlighted in Dianne F. Sadoff's chapter, clearly ensures that the legacies of imperialism, with its expedient disregard of others' humanity on account of differences of race, religion, or ideology, continue to engender conflict in postcolonial contexts.

Victorian as opposed to other historical fiction or historiographic metafiction: firstly, because of the nineteenth century's relative proximity to our own, which permits fairly direct discernments of causes and after-effects, what Gene Ray terms "the historical backgrounds to current global emergencies" (Ray 2005: 17); and secondly, because of the period's function as the mainspring of modernity, establishing many of the economic, political, legal, and ideological frameworks that continue to structure the world we inhabit. Furthermore, the neo-Victorian may transform the requisite 'belatedness' vis-à-vis current traumas into a fictional projection backwards in time, so as to facilitate an earlier working through and (albeit always partial) 'healing' or closure than would be possible otherwise.

Moving further into the epistemological realm, much neo-Victorian fiction focalises post-Darwinian anxieties and the on-going contest for the moral high ground between religious and secular worldviews, which Catherine Pesso-Miquel's essay explores. Other texts, still in the wake of Darwin's theories, focus on redefinitions of the limits between mind and body, matter and life, and hence on the traumatic understanding of the unclear boundaries of the human, as addressed by Georges Letissier's chapter. If the biological sciences of life seem to seriously threaten the possibility of transcendence, the sciences of language and meaning seem to precipitate a profound crisis of subjectivity. The teachings of poststructuralism and deconstruction, often presented in simplified form in neo-Victorian fiction, insist on a sense of loss (of meaning, of subjectivity, of teleology), precipitating an anxiety of absence, as analysed by Christian Gutleben and Julian Wolfreys' joint contribution to this collection. Arguably, it is this deep sense of deprivation that explains the contemporary novel's turn to the past in an attempt to retrieve the solace of meaning, causality, and sheer joy in traditional narrative.

Yet neo-Victorian fiction, it must be stressed, does not present tradition as a direct source of nostalgic refreshment or palliation. The epistemological disruption, "the weariness, the fever and the fret" (Keats 1973: 346, l.23), clearly already torment the nineteenth-century characters of neo-Victorian fiction. Accordingly, the trauma of doubt and uncertainty is presented as a unifying device of the multi-layered temporality of the neo-Victorian novel rather than a differentiating (post)modern characteristic, which divides and 'others' us from our nineteenth-century predecessors. The comprehension of historical traumas as interactive foils or mirrors of present-day traumas forestalls any such facile distinctions, underlining trauma's transgenerational repercussions.[15] At the same time, it invites a sympathetic, if not empathic, understanding of the former suffering of those who stand in our place just as readily as we might project ourselves backwards through time into theirs. The neo-Victorian novel, we want to propose, does not dramatise an opposition between (post)modern self and Victorian other, so much as the *self-as-other*.

---

[15] As Miller and Tougaw expound, "trauma often unfolds intergenerationally; its aftermath lives on in the family – but no less pervasively in the culture at large" (Miller and Tougaw 2002: 9).

The traumatised subject of modernity pre/rediscovers *itself* in its manifold nineteenth-century others.

3.   The Ethical Debate: Voicing Others' Trauma

The self-as-other takes various forms in the neo-Victorian novel: the racially, ethnically, gender or sexually discriminated; the physically disabled or mentally ill; the socially marginalised, economically exploited or otherwise persecuted, including the poor, prostitutes, prisoners, slaves, and victims of war and genocide. Yet the neo-Victorian self-as-other is not limited to traumatised victims, but also includes primary and secondary witnesses as well as bystanders, collaborators, and perpetrators implicated in historical violence and atrocity. This complicates the issues of fictional testimony and of how to meet the ethical appeal of the suffering historical subject, which confronts us in all its naked radical fragility, stripped of modern legal protections, human rights laws, and welfare systems that, in principle at least, provide some sort of rudimentary safety net in today's developed nations, intended to safeguard our humanity and existence. Ironically, while living in comparatively much safer and more secure environments than did most citizens of the nineteenth century, we nonetheless claim that *we*, not they, are the ones who live permanently under threat, inhabiting a 'trauma culture' even in developed occidental societies. This again raises the spectre of self-centred misrepresentation and appropriation of historical trauma, already alluded to earlier.

Yet over and over again, philosophers and critics have not merely questioned *how* we represent trauma, but the ethical right to represent trauma per se. Cathy Caruth's work has been especially influential in conceptualising trauma as essentially beyond language: unsayable, unspeakable, incommunicable, and consequently unrepresentable.[16] The impossibility to tell the Holocaust in particular has been a major concern of writers such as Theodor Adorno, Primo Levi, and Emmanuel Levinas. This ethical problem has not ceased to spur contemporary thinkers' passionate arguments, as evident from Jean-François Lyotard's 1988 statement:

---

[16] Ruth Leys asserts that "what is new in [Caruth's] work, to begin with, is a fascination with, almost a relishing of, the currently modish idea that the domain of trauma is the unspeakable and unrepresentable" (Leys 2000: 304).

> To represent "Auschwitz" in images, in words, is a
> way of forgetting it. I'm not just thinking here of B
> movies and soap opera series and pulp novels or
> testimonies. I'm also thinking of those representations
> which can and could best make us not forget by virtue
> of their exactness or severity. Even such efforts
> represent what should remain unrepresentable in order
> not to be forgotten precisely as forgotten. (Lyotard,
> qtd. Kearney 1999: 17)

Even Adorno, however, modified his famous 1949 declaration that
"To write poetry after Auschwitz is barbaric" (Adorno 1981: 34),
eventually conceding that to deny the attempt at representation, that is,
the very attempt at literature, would be equally barbaric. Similarly,
other theorists' ethical condemnations of the artistic representations of
trauma have been systematically qualified. Lyotard, for instance,
restores the prerogatives of art by stating: "What art can do is bear
witness [...] to this aporia of art and to its pain. It does not say the
unsayable, but says that it cannot say it" (Lyotard 1990: 47). If not
exactly advocating speechlessness – art still "says" – Lyotard's
formulation nonetheless ends in silence, since as Ludwig Wittgenstein
put it, "'*Wovon man nicht sprechen kann, darüber muß man
schweigen.*' ('About that of which one cannot speak, one must keep
silent.')" (Wittgenstein 1963: 115, qtd. Ray 2005: 145).

It should be stressed, though, that this interminable circling
around an impenetrable nucleus of unspeakability and unknowability,
with trauma situated as a core of epistemological and (ethically)
necessary failure,[17] is hardly radical or new, nor restricted to our own
age. Yet again the Victorians anticipated this aspect of trauma
discourse, when commenting on the catastrophes of their own time.
During the Great Irish Famine, for instance, witnesses repeatedly
stressed the failure of language in the face of extreme suffering; in one
correspondent's words: "No language is adequate to give the true, the
real picture; one look of the eye into the daily scenes there witnessed
would overpower what any pen, however graphic, any tongue,
however eloquent, could portray" (Asenath Nicholson 1850: 9, qtd.

---

[17] Julian Wolfreys accordingly calls this "[t]he aporia *of responsibility*" (Wolfreys
2002: 131, emphasis added).

Douglass and Vogler 2003: 32). As Douglass and Vogler extrapolate from this example, "[a]n event that defies all representation will best be represented by a failure of representation" – in effect by the lacuna of saying nothing – "and this is in fact one of the oldest tropes of Western writing, what Kant called the negative or non-presentation of the idea of horror in the sublime" (Douglas and Vogler 2003: 32).

This can end up resembling a get out clause to witnessing. One does not need to bear to look too closely, since one will not be able to render subsequent witness through telling in any case; hence one might as well look away or not look/speak at all. As Jenny Edkins remarks with regards to the Holocaust, "[w]hat survivors have witnessed has long been recognised as 'unimaginable' and 'unspeakable', although these epithets have often served as an excuse for neither imagining it nor speaking about it" or , alternatively, for deeming oneself "excused from further enquiry" (Edkins 2003: 2, 176). But can one even *be* a meaningful witness without *bearing* witness, that is, without bringing forth some sort of evidence and testimony to events, without engaging in some sort of meaning production? In acquiescing to the representational hiatus of the subliminal horror, what Gene Ray calls "a permanent ghastly latency" (Ray 2005: 5), one risks becoming a meaning*less non*-witness, like the trauma victim her/himself while still in the midst of the overwhelming (non-)experience.[18] Hence Primo Levi, for instance, insisted that "silence, the absence of signals, is itself a signal, but an ambiguous one", warning that such "ambiguity generates anxiety and suspicion" rather than truthfulness to trauma: "To say that it is impossible to communicate is false; one always can" (Levi 1988: 83).[19]

---

[18] Maurice Blanchot defines trauma as "the disaster, unexperienced. It is what escapes the very possibility of experience – it is the limit of writing. This must be repeated: the disaster de-scribes." Nonetheless, Blanchot situates the disaster as intra- rather than extra-textual, however not as the represented object of the text but rather as the "force of writing" (Blanchot 1995: 7, qtd. Edkins 2003: 38).

[19] In any case, the unspeakable character of trauma concerns the *direct victim* of trauma, who is overwhelmed by the event so that it cannot be registered at the time of its occurrence, and consequently "emerges as a non-experience, causing conventional epistemologies to falter" (Whitehead 2004: 5). Neo-Victorian fiction writers – since not direct victims of the nineteenth-century traumas they narrate – can only re-experience them indirectly, so that the rule of unrepresentability need not apply. In trying to 'realistically' portray trauma's missed encounter with the real, *both* fictional representations *and* non-representations of trauma can only ever be marks of

To privilege unspeakability may paradoxically prove as *un*ethical as the disparaged 'falsifying' representation in place of the supposedly 'authentic' non-representation. For since "[m]odern historical writing sublimates moral judgment into the narrative form it employs", non-presentation avoids the necessity of moral judgement, which Robert Braun argues is implicit "in all [...] cases of historical representation" – hence evading the "conflict between the moral authority of the narrator" (as moral witness/interpreter of trauma) and "the supposed moral authority of the [unrepresentable] past 'itself'" (Braun 1994: 182). It also complicates matters for those who nevertheless *want* to attempt to make visible the full horror, whether literally or figuratively, placing them in the invidious position of the insensitive, disrespectful, or even immoral participant/observer. Levinas, for instance, asserted that representing the face of the traumatised other pertains to a form of immodesty (Levinas 1974: 139), since representing the other's suffering erases that suffering, so that it becomes associated with "immorality itself" (Levinas 1982: 164). In spite of acknowledging the power of the imagination and of the "living word", Levinas held that this power inevitably "turns [experience] into a creature" (Levinas 1989: 148)[20] – in effect closing off/closing down the rawness of trauma and curtailing the secondary witness' openness to the other's humanity, hence de-humanising the victim once more.

The ethical debate revolving around the representation of trauma, then, appears aporetic. Questioning the legitimacy of voicing the other's trauma in art naturally leads to questioning the freedom of art and, of course, denying that freedom can hardly be called an ethical duty. Furthermore, to reject representations of trauma outright would mean silencing trauma or, in the case of unrecorded or inadequately acknowledged historical traumas addressed in neo-Victorian fiction, silencing trauma *anew*, replicating the actions of

---

attempted verisimilitude, which in itself is only a *semblance* of truth. Indeed, Walker, drawing on Hayden White's work, contends that traumatic events may only be "unrepresentable *in the realist mode*" (Walker 1997: 812, original emphasis), but not necessarily in fantasy formations, involved in both memory and fiction writing.

[20] Note that for Levinas the living word is essentially found in the forms of avant-garde art, while much neo-Victorian fiction opts for a more traditional realist mode, though often spliced with metafictional elements.

perpetrators and victimisers.[21] Again this diverges from the ethical duty to bear witness to suffering and critique/contest the violence that engenders it. The case of fiction, however, stands in a still more complex relation to this ethical problem. Where (f)actual witness discourse is concerned, telling the other's trauma may indeed represent a form of second dispossession and even of renewed betrayal, cheating the other of her or his own words and forcing upon the victim/survivor a form of linguistic violence that "leads to the annihilation of the autonomy of the other, to domination and oppression" (Bauman 1993: 11). As previously indicated, however, historical fiction primarily seeks to fill vacant spaces of enunciation rather than usurp prior subjects' voices.[22] Hence, both the represented suffering and the words used to describe it are the result of fictional production, of creation rather than theft, with trauma conveyed primarily via invented images and metaphors, rather than these being used to embellish or supplement actual witness narratives so as to bridge comprehension between ordinary and traumatic worlds. Neo-Victorian fictions do not pretend to be 'real' first-hand or secondary witness statements, but only re-imagined acts of after-witness. As works of imagination, neo-Victorian trauma fictions might therefore possess what Richard Rorty calls "the imaginative ability to see strange people as fellow sufferers" (Rorty 1989: xvi). Put differently, they facilitate a cultivation of empathy that sees ourselves *in* (rather than *in place of*) the suffering victim and reciprocally encounters the self-as-other and the other-as-self by acknowledging our own vulnerability to traumatisation. James Hatley, drawing on Levinas,

---

[21] Edkins pertinently notes that "[t]he concept of trauma oscillates between victimhood and protest and can be linked with or articulated to either" (Edkins 2003: 9). Ironically, the refusal of silence, that is, the representation of the 'unimaginable', likewise risks accusations of betrayal. Discussing the Holocaust, James Hatley argues that "we are called upon to pose the issue of how our very affirmation of the other's suffering might yet again betray the extremity of that suffering" (Hatley 2000: 2).

[22] 'Biofiction' or fictional biography/autobiography is an exception, re-imagining as it does actual historical individuals, most commonly prominent cultural figures, to reveal more intimate aspects of their personality or, often irreverently, expose their secret lives and hidden vices. Neo-Victorian examples include Margaret Forster's *Lady's Maid* (1990), which views Elizabeth Barrett-Browning and Robert Browning through the eyes of the poetess' maidservant, Lynne Truss' *Tennyson's Gift* (1996) and more recently, David Lodge's *Author Author: A Novel* (2004) and Colm Tóibín's *The Master* (2004), both about Henry James.

calls this the inadvertent "exposure of being exposed" (Hatley 2000: 85), which in neo-Victorian fiction, however, also involves a volitional anticipation or *preparedness* to expose oneself to otherness.[23] Such an attitude seems to embody

> the possibility of imagination recovering its hermeneutic power to speak-for-the-other and to listen to the powerless cry of the stranger, the widow and the orphan – a cry which, in demanding that I respond and speak to the unseen other (*le tiers*) is already a demand for justice. (Baudrillard 1983: 215)

This is a very different kind of "speak[ing]-for-the-other" to one that seeks to appropriate, silence, or take the place of another's trauma.

How does neo-Victorian fiction answer Baudrillard's "demand for justice"? Although it does at times play on the trope of unrepresentability, it refuses to countenance the imperative of non-representation vis-à-vis horror, actively seeking out exactly such traumatic elisions, blind spots, and figurative black holes in the historical record to in-fill them imaginatively. This comparative greater freedom of invention exercised by writers, as opposed to historians, ensures that, as David Cowart claims, "one finds the past often less accessible to history than to historical fiction" (Cowart 1989: 1). Neo-Victorian literature lends a voice to the voiceless, speaks for the speechless, where historians can only speculate as to what such persons *might* have said or sounded like, emphasising the purely theoretical nature of their representations. Nor is neo-Victorian fiction obliged to present a measured view or depict both sides of a conflict objectively; with unashamedly partisan outrage, it can denounce the suffering of the forgotten of history – the excluded, the outcast, the downtrodden, the marginalised, the colonised. For instance, few individuals outside New Zealand, apart from anthropologists and historians specialising in the southern Pacific,

---

[23] Hatley explains Levinas' notion of trauma as follows: "one is not only capable of being traumatized but also has already been traumatized by the other's capability of being traumatized, of suffering. For Levinas, trauma involves how the face of the other [...] already brings one into the scene of suffering that is not one's own" (Hatley 2000: 93). On the witnessing subject's pre-empted volition in this process – "the other's address constitutes us [...] against out will" – see Butler 2006b: 130.

would likely have heard of the genocide of the Moriori before David Mitchell's best-selling *Cloud Atlas* (2004). Telling the tales of the pariahs of history means revealing – or, more accurately, *reconstructing* – neglected or unheard-of stories of stifled suffering.[24] In this way, neo-Victorian rewritings of nineteenth-century traumas acquire the capacity "to speak-for-the-other". This opening to and concern for the various forms of the other correspond closely to Levinas's conception of ethics as *an ethics of alterity*, in which (or through which) the self – in the case of neo-Victorian fiction the contemporary self – is enlarged and enriched by the other and transcends its own egoistic limits.

Clearly, this form of an ethics of alterity coincides with an ethics of justice, or more specifically an ethics of acknowledging past *injustices*: the doubled injustices of literal acts of violence that inflicted untold suffering on others, and the subsequent symbolic violence, repeating the offence, of sidelining the trauma or consigning it to outright historical oblivion. Hence, neo-Victorian fiction can be said to answer Paul Ricoeur's call at the millennial turn for

> a parallel history of, let us says, victimisation, which would counter the history of success and victory. To memorise the victims of history – the sufferers, the humiliated, the forgotten – should be a task for all of us at the end of this century. (Ricoeur 1999: 10-11)

Here ethics and politics dramatically coincide. For as Edkins points out, "[t]he memory of [victims'] past struggles", even where such struggles proved fruitless and ended in defeat or extinction, can nonetheless "be disruptive of power", by "contest[ing] power relations" that perpetuate trauma and iniquity indefinitely (Edkins 2003: 59).[25] On the topic of belated or unfinished historical justice,

---

[24] Again, it must be noted that the focus on marginal voices constitutes a feature equally common to other kinds of historical fiction and historiographic metafiction, which "may participate in historiographical arguments by offering neglected perspectives or focusing on places whose history has been ignored" or which aim "to redress perceived injustices", impulses that also pervade feminist revisionist writing and postcolonial literature (Keen 2006: 176).
[25] "What has been forgotten – subjugated knowledges – like the memory of past traumas, returns to haunt the structures of power that instigated the violence in the

always following *after* the history written by the victors, Ricoeur propounds an argument of crucial relevance for the stakes of neo-Victorian fiction. The focus on traumatic events from a time beyond living memory is sometimes deemed retrograde, because "[i]t is far easier, even seductive, to memorialize past injustice, to weep over human crimes of another era, than to take responsibility for what's before our eyes" (Miller and Tougaw 2002: 5). In contrast, Ricoeur insists on the *prospective* quality of a parallel history of suffering, explaining that it addresses

> [a]n ethico-political problem because it has to do with the construction of the future: that is, the duty to remember consists not only in having a deep concern for the past, but in transmitting the meaning of past events to the next generation. The duty, therefore, is one which concerns the future; it is an imperative directed towards the future, which is exactly the opposite side of the traumatic character of the humiliations and wounds of history. It is a duty, thus, to tell. (Ricoeur 1999: 9-10)[26]

Similarly, David W. Price asserts the importance of what he terms "speculative novels of poietic history" for our ability to "imagine new possibilities for the future" (Price 1992: 3-4). Such historical fictions, which "focus on the formation of values" that inform individual and collective historical action, are not just recreations of the past, but of past subjects' constructions of their own futures and thence, at least in part, their constructions of our present also:

---

first place. Trauma is that which refuses to take its place in history as done and finished with" (Edkins 2003: 59).

[26] For Michael Rothberg it is "by virtue of its performative address to a post-traumatic context [that] this kind of writing possesses a future orientation." He explains that the project of recording the traumas of the past "is not an attempt to reflect the event mimetically, but to *produce* it as an object of knowledge, and to *transform* its readers so that they are forced to acknowledge their relationship to post-traumatic culture" (Rothberg 2002: 67, original emphases). Gene Ray links the strands of futurity and otherness via Jacques Derrida's work: "The obligation to receive and transform the ghastly, traumatic legacies of history and tradition is, with Derrida, turned toward the future in the form of an obligation to make hospitable spaces and openings that invite the arrival of the radically other or new" (Ray 2005: 17).

every act we commit is a projection of a figured future. A recreation of the past, therefore, would be the projection of the future in the past. In other words, to comprehend fully the reality of the past, we must participate in the processes whereby individuals, peoples, and entire cultures and societies *figured* their futures through imaginative projections of their wills. (Price 1999: 4, 3, original emphasis)

Because of its "metahistorical consciousness" (Elias 2000: xii),[27] the contemporary novel not only narrates history but also interprets how and why the past was played out as it was – and how it continues to be re-worked, legitimated, and preserved for posterity. In fulfilling this hermeneutic task, neo-Victorian fiction arguably avoids the nostalgic imprisonment in the past and performs its ethico-political duty for the future.

Our argument so far asserts that representing the other's trauma is *not* unethical in itself and that neo-Victorian fiction *can* assume an ethical function in 'speaking-for-the-other'. This is not to claim, however, that all neo-Victorian fiction necessarily meets, or strives to meet, the afore-mentioned ethical demands and objectives. By focusing on the trauma of the other, neo-Victorian fiction can also be accused of a superficial 'fashion consciousness', so to speak. Commenting on how trauma discourse has pervaded all strata of contemporary culture, Douglass and Vogler note the inevitable baggage of "opportunism and excess, and the opportunity for trivialization" (Douglass and Vogler 2003: 13). When all modern subjects claim traumatisation, trauma risks becoming a badge of conformity rather than of exception. Correspondingly, Lyotard denounces the alterity business, claiming that otherness has become a profitable market and that the generalised exploitation of the other leads to consensus, that is, the erasure of difference and otherness (Lyotard 1993: 171). Although there are doubtless still many untold tales of the nineteenth century to be written and many of its silenced voices to be made to speak, and although it remains an ethical duty to

---

[27] It s Amy J. Elias's main contention that post-1960s fiction has "a metahistorical consciousness [which] models itself as post-traumatic consciousness" (Elias 2001: xii).

bear after-witness to past atrocities in fiction, it must also be admitted that certain neo-Victorian perspectives – the nineteenth-century fallen woman, medium, or homosexual, for instance – have become rather over-used, tired, and hackneyed, to the point where it becomes difficult to view them any longer as embodiments of an ethics of alterity.[28] Banalised through repetition, 'revealing' only what has already been disclosed before, such characters' traumatic experiences can no longer muster the ethical force of denunciation evoked by the suffering of their neo-Victorian fictional predecessors.

Fictionalising trauma can also lead to sensationalism, exhibitionism, garishness, trivialisation, cynicism, coarseness or obscenity, which raises the delicate question of the ethical value of the very forms of literature. Yet it is not the fact of representing trauma that can be unethical, but rather the *way* of representing it, not the topic and referent but the stylistic excesses with which these are treated by writers. If ethics can be reduced to a question of style, then the ethical problem is necessarily individual to each novel instead of generic. In the last resort, the ethics of representing trauma in neo-Victorian fiction depends on the art of specific practitioners. Concerning the vicarious presentations of trauma, it may be individual authors' sense of restraint, their art of ellipsis and suggestion rather than spectacle and exhibitionism, their handling of metaphorical as well as literal narrative, which may best succeed in fulfilling the ethical task of bearing after-witness without abjecting the traumatised subject or its trauma into an object of graphic monstration.[29] Thus ethics can also be a question of poetics.[30]

---

[28] It should be noted, however, that such over-exposure is partly a result of the disproportionate attention some perspectives have received due to the popularity of feminist and queer theory in neo-Victorian criticism. Crucial differences are easily overlooked; for example, the representation of male homosexual trauma, as opposed to that of lesbians, is far less prevalent in neo-Victorian literature, and while Sarah Waters' *Tipping the Velvet* (1998) has attracted numerous commentaries, there is no comparable work on one of her novel's acknowledged inspirations, Chris Hunt's neo-Victorian, male homosexual Bildungsroman *Street Lavender* (1988).

[29] Fittingly, Wolfreys urges that "the trace of trauma" be understood "as a figure of catachresis, the absolutely monstrous trope without discernible or otherwise accessible relation to its source or origin" (Wolfreys 2002: 140).

[30] Richard Kearney pithily expresses this relationship between ethics and poetics: "Ethics needs poetics to be reminded that its responsibility to the other includes the possibility of play, freedom and pleasure. Just as poetics needs ethics to be reminded that play, freedom and pleasure are never self-sufficient but originate in, and aim

4.   Troping Trauma

The question of poetics brings us back to the title of our collection, namely to the actual process of translating or 'troping' trauma. The figurative language here invoked, however, proves another contentious issue with regards to testimonial writing and witness bearing. As Hatley explains, some critics, including Berel Lang and Lawrence Langer, have argued strongly against the use of figurative language, believing that testimony "must free itself from any influence that would stand between the reader and the event itself" (Hatley 2000: 108). This may include such features as metaphors, irony, repetition, *mise en abyme*, fantasy, symbols and, of course, tropes, which draw undue attention to themselves and to the writer's deliberate formulation of her or his discourse, thereby creating "a *literary* as opposed to *historical* space of representation" (Hatley 2000: 108, original emphasis).

Since neo-Victorian after-witness evidently and necessarily operates within a literary space, such reservations do not actually apply. Yet two problems with this critical position must be briefly signalled. Firstly, "the event itself" does not exist prior to or outside of language, which is always in some sense figurative due to the gap/substitution between sign and referent. Secondly, it can be argued that whatever facilitates the communication of trauma must be ethically justifiable. Drawing on Samuel R. Levin's *Metaphoric Worlds* (1988), Winslow proposes that "[i]n the absence of already-made language" for the survivor/victim to articulate her/his experience, new figures of speech may be the *only* way to be able to begin to conceive or "think *of* the experience" (Winslow 2004: 610, original emphasis) – as opposed to conceiving/thinking the experience itself, which always remains beyond her/his full apprehension – and also for listeners/readers to be able to gain 'privileged' (since otherwise impossible) access to the sufferer's wholly alien world. Narrative ethics relies *on the potentiality at least* of entering into dialogue, of sharing thoughts "*of* the experience", however impaired or faltering such an interchange may prove to be. Arguably, such potentiality is dependent on the construction of some kind of linguistic bridges, so as to re-establish the very inter-responsive connectivity

---

towards, an experience of the other-than-self, of being-foroneanother" (Kearney 1999: 23)

with the collective social world that trauma severed. Hatley comes to an analogous conclusion: "one can also argue that the figurative space opened up in literary writing might articulate a particular sense of the ethical that is actually covered over in critical or historical prose" (Hatley 2000: 116).

We previously stressed the paradox at the heart of trauma narrative, namely that, although often deemed unrepresentable and unspeakable, trauma must be represented and spoken nonetheless. Or as Julian Wolfreys puts it: "How does one verbalize or visualize where there is nothing present as such, and yet where there is a non-material reality and its material effects?" (Wolfreys 2002: 136) Perhaps more accurately, trauma must be spoken not in spite of but *because of* its very unrepresentability as an event/experience *in itself*. As Shoshana Felman and Dori Laub point out with regards to Claude Lanzmann's epic *Shoah* (1985): "The *necessity of testimony* [...] derives [...] from the *impossibility of testimony*" (Felman and Laub 1992: 224, original emphases). How do neo-Victorian narratives of trauma set about meeting this challenge, which they share with testimonial discourse?

Considering the variety of neo-Victorian novels discussed in this volume and bearing in mind that the language of fiction varies according to cultural contexts, the heterogeneity of fictionalisations of nineteenth-century trauma comes as no surprise. Novelistic tactics, for instance, will tend to differ according to whether authors adopt postcolonial or ex-colonial perspectives to work through historical trauma. So too, their respective figurative strategies will be qualified by their choice of protagonists from among the range of available subject positions, including history's 'drowned', victims/survivors, nineteenth-century secondary witnesses, bystanders, and even perpetrators, or after-witnesses in the present,. Nevertheless, the novels in general tend to share certain rhetorical and figurative strategies, which may be deemed typical of neo-Victorian trauma narratives.

One such strategy consists of the encapsulation of the referential trauma in an object or work within the novel itself, functioning as a sort of *mise en abyme*. This affords a means to convey both the irrepressible urge for testimony and the possibility of confiding and communicating trauma. Thus, the manuscript containing the apostatic confessions of a Darwinian surveyor (see

Pesso-Miquel), the diary of a reluctant colonial caught up in the horror of genocide (see Wallhead and Kohlke), the legal documents recording the violent betrayals within an Irish household during the Famine (see Heilmann), and the sculptured pots revealing a potter's incestuous practice (see Llewellyn), all become metaphorical tropes inasmuch as they serve as quasi archival 'texts' offering themselves for decoding and analysis. Crucially, their reception and interpretation are systematically delayed in time (both structurally within each novel's own temporality and chronologically in the context of narrated historical and/or reading time), so that they acquire a multiple temporality, linking past and present and potentially extending into the future. Graham Swift's *Ever After* (1992), for instance, suggests that the present-day protagonist Bill Unwin is likely the first person ever to have read his Victorian ancestor Mathew Pearce's diary about his loss of faith and marital breakdown, the journal having been kept but apparently left unread by his predecessor's deserted wife. The diary is revealed to the reader haphazardly and piecemeal over the course of the novel, as Unwin gradually works his way through it extracting possible meanings. Eventually the diary itself is passed on to his colleague's wife for a future use, which remains unspecified but extends the temporal repercussions of the document into the future. Similarly, in *Cloud Atlas*, the nineteenth-century Adam Ewing's diary, which constitutes the novel's frame, is discovered by chance and read by Robert Frobisher, the 1930's protagonist of the following section. Yet Ewing's journal is also abruptly interrupted halfway through, literally curtailing further interpretation, permanently in Frobisher's case and, for Mitchell's extra-textual readers, deferring further decoding until the closing section of the novel. What makes these literal and metaphorical texts such relevant tropes of trauma is exactly such temporal elasticity and connectivity, as well as their outright function as transmittable property, passed on between generations.

Just as significantly, however, such works may be produced not only by those undergoing trauma but also those inflicting it, compulsively revealing their implication in the suffering of others. The potter's hidden collection of graphic vessels in A.S. Byatt's *The Children's Book* (2009), for example, obsessively displays the violated bodies of his daughters, thus rendering visible secret sexual acts never actually represented in the novel. Accordingly, some encapsulating objects stand not so much for the necessity of and/or the witnessing act enabling the trauma's transmission – via disclosure, dissemination, and bequeathal to those who come after – as for trauma's unrepresentability, its forcible silencing and deliberate occlusion. In Kate Grenville's *The Secret River* (2005), for instance, the white settler's fortress-like house, built atop an Australian aboriginal stone carving on the indigenes' ancestral land, emptied of its original inhabitants, renders its master deeply disturbed and insecure; he exists in a permanent state of heightened vigilance anticipating an invisible threat, effectively the return of the repressed violence and suffering of colonialism itself (see Mitchell). Here the object, namely the house – literally overwriting another sign – becomes a trace of the very trauma it seeks to deny, encoded or incorporated in the building's own construction.

A further significant method of troping trauma in neo-Victorian fiction can be discerned in the genre's quasi-systematic representation of actual acts of narrating or writing, on the one hand, and of reading or listening, on the other. So often the object of a metafictional embedding strategy, the narrative situation may itself be considered as a trope. The *mise en abyme* of written or oral testimonies highlights the verbalisation of trauma as the central act of the novelistic apparatus. Occurring by necessity after the related events, the testimonies possess the main characteristic of trauma narratives, namely *Nachträglichkeit*, a Freudian concept translated variously as belatedness, deferred action, or delayed response. Thus Swift's Matthew Pearce, for instance, only commences writing his diary some ten years after the traumatic crisis. By self-consciously duplicating the mechanism of *Nachträglichkeit*, the embedded trauma narrative not only reflects the principle of anachronism but also reproduces the process of re-living/re-imagining past events via reading/re-reading, itself akin to that found in historiographic metafiction, which highlights "the paradox of the *reality* of the past but its (only) *textualised* accessibility to us today" (Hutcheon 1996: 483, original emphases). Furthermore, since the retroactive (re)construction of the past is also the manifest principle of rewriting the nineteenth century, scenes of trauma narratives *in production*, as it were, also constitute embedded images of the neo-Victorian project itself. Recreated by an altered subject in another temporality, neo-Victorian trauma narratives thus effectuate a return to history in which history is acknowledged as a narrative and linguistic construct, a discursively constituted object of 'facts' moulded from archival "textual traces" of concrete (but inaccessible) 'events', thus "problematiz[ing] the very possibility of historical knowledge" (Hutcheon 1996: 490, 475), while conversely insisting on the reality of past suffering and the importance of *making it known*. With its ambiguous status in relation to the real, trauma allows a roundabout way out of the poststructuralist impasse, enabling a return to the real while at the same time maintaining the idea of its slipperiness and ungraspable nature (see Douglass and Vogler 2003: 5; Foster 1996: 168).

In a third, closely linked strategy, the ostentatious (f)act of narration becomes the visible trope of a self-generated healing. Narrating trauma is essentially performative, because the trauma – and consequently the possibility of recovery and of the ruptured subject's reintegration – only come into existence *with* and *through* the production of speech and/or narrative during the act of witnessing the self's and/or others' suffering: "knowledge or self-knowledge […] can only happen through the testimony" (Felman and Laub 1992: 51). The embedded trauma narrative, then, is not only a verbal exchange; it also constitutes an act of generation, begetting the (however partial) understanding, transmission, and healing of trauma. Narrative appears as a metaphor of reciprocal communion, foregrounding what might be termed its 'addressive' quality, particularly through the fictionalisation of the act of decoding – as a complement to the act of encoding. By staging the addressees' responses to the trauma narratives, by representing – and performing – the sympathy and the community of suffering thus created, neo-Victorian fiction indirectly addresses its own readers in order to try and create an analogous community of feeling. The circulation of trauma described within the novel is meant to generate a wider circulation of trauma outside of/beyond the world of the text. This emotional and ethical involvement of contemporary readers of neo-Victorian fiction serves as another means of securing a continuity between nineteenth-century traumas and contemporary experience. Narrative thus perceived transforms the unrepresentability of trauma into an experience of cooperation and solidarity. As David Wood puts it: "Narrative heels aporia" (Wood 1991: 4).

In its endeavour to represent trauma, neo-Victorian fiction troubles itself not only with the devices in the novel but also with the novel as device. The very structures of the novels can be seen as metaphors signifying or imitating the features or symptoms of trauma. The layered nature of neo-Victorian narratives in particular evokes the well-known trope of the palimpsest, a trope that seems crucial inasmuch as it suggests the superposition of interrelated traumas – and especially the porous strata of Victorian and contemporary texts, situations, and traumas, permeating one another. Being composed of heterogeneous temporalities, the contemporary revisions of the Victorian era unravel several narrative strands, a presentation of plurality left deliberately fragmented in spite of efforts by various narrators to make them coalesce into some sort of coherent whole. In Nuala O'Faolain's *My Dream of You* (2001), for instance, the travel writer Kathleen de Burca tries to work through the trauma of the death of a close friend by interweaving the story of a nineteenth-century victim of marital and legal abuse, her own and her mother's life stories of failed relationships, Ireland's collective national trauma of the Great Famine, and a grand romance into a neo-Victorian novel, which, unsurprisingly, is never completed (see Heilmann). Inherited from the modernists,[31] novelistic fragmentation reproduces on the textual surface and in the deeper narrative structure the breaches produced by and etymologically constitutive of trauma. As Anne Whitehead contends, "in representing trauma, many writers have mimicked its symptomatology at a formal level" (Whitehead 2004: 161). Pervasive internal narrative gaps and elisions, as when Swift's modern-day narrator repeatedly leaves out words (indicated by empty quotation marks), as well as instances of irresolution and lack of closure, further demonstrate that any purely linear, chronological, or teleological account of trauma would be false, misrepresenting traumatic experience, as well as traumatic memory and the struggle of conscious recall.

   In addition to seeking metaphorical equivalences of trauma and its symptoms, neo-Victorian fiction can be said to adhere to a metonymic principle. Rather than trying to formulate didactic generalisations, neo-Victorian novels prefer to particularise trauma by depicting specific victims, with the particular example standing for a whole class or people, and possibly even a whole new conception of

---

[31] That the principle of novelistic fragmentation became generalised after the First World War is certainly not coincidental, and interestingly it could be argued that this formal fragmentation already constituted an attempt at representing the fundamental ruptures caused by such a major trauma.

history, namely the parallel history of victimisation described by
Ricoeur. As Diane Sadoff points out, the individual victim of trauma
represents "a metonymy for a repressed/repressive, national,
historical, imperial project" (this volume: 180) – and for the suffering
engendered by it, which, however collectively undergone, is
nonetheless always experienced *singularly*. As Winslow stresses:

> Although a traumatic event may happen to large
> groups of people, it always happens to each person –
> to each body, mind, and spirit. It is felt and thought in
> individuals, in each body and mind, even if many are
> physically together. (Winslow 2004: 608-609)

Hence, the metonymic mechanism clearly at work in neo-Victorian
fiction contradicts Miller and Tougaw's diagnostic of trauma theory's
tendency "to universalize suffering with little attention paid to the
singularity of the experience" (Miller and Tougaw 2002: 6). In *Cloud
Atlas*, for instance, the flayed body of the Moriori Autua, the only
individuated representation of his decimated and enslaved people,
functions as a Christ-like figure, standing not only for his kind,
sacrificed to colonialist expediency, but also as a sign of mankind's
inhumanity to the other. Eventually he saves the life of 'Adam' (that
is, 'everyman') Ewing, after the white man protected the Moriori's
life, having been compelled to recognise not only their common
humanity but also the other's human singularity. By privileging
metonymic micro-narratives over totalising macro-narratives, neo-
Victorian fiction also manifests the distrust it shares with
postmodernism of all grand narratives and heuristic explanations. In
the field of neo-Victorian trauma narratives, any bid for absolute truth
or essentialism is shown to be deceptively partial and local rather than
genuinely global and universal. Put differently, the historical other's
trauma only becomes accessible by investing it with the unique
suffering individuality (or in Levinas' terms, the 'face') that History
writ large has *effaced* and consigned to the anonymous oblivion of
non-representation.

  From a rhetorical point of view, what neo-Victorian fiction
mainly does is to lend a voice to the dead, that is, to resort to the
principle of prosopopoeia, eloquently summed up in *Ever After*: "it is
a prodigious, a presumptuous task: to take the skeletal remains of a

single life and attempt to breathe into them their former actuality" (Swift 1992: 90). Yet rather than a question of resurrection or reconstitution, we want to propose, contemporary rewritings of nineteenth-century trauma involve actual creation. More often than not, the characters brought to life in neo-Victorian novels are those whom fiction or historiography has forgotten, those who have never had a proper voice, story, or discursive existence in literature. In human rights terms, they are what Judith Butler calls "not established, disestablished, or yet to be established" subjects (Butler 2006a: 1659). By speaking for these speechless characters, recording their unrecorded thoughts, telling their untold stories, asserting their human rights to be recognised, to be given back a face, to have their suffering affirmed, contemporary fiction does not repeat the already said, but rather gives birth to what has never been able to be born. It gives historical non-subjects a future by restoring their traumatic pasts to cultural memory.[32]

Since this act of creation concerns not only generalised stories and previously encountered subjectivities but also new individual voices, particularly those of the ex-centric, the marginalised and/or the deviant – that is, voices *previously unheard/unheard of* rather than an effect of discursive repetition – neo-Victorian fiction manages to perform a labour of regeneration from both an ideological/ethical and stylistic/aesthetic point of view. It is this fictional and poetic type of prosopopoeia that constitutes the hallmark of contemporary revisions of the nineteenth century. The after-witness that begets unheard – and often discordant – voices from history constitutes neo-Victorian fiction's way of innovating while reverting to the past.

Bibliography

Adorno, Theodor. 1981. *Prisms* (tr. E.B. Ashton). London and New York: Routledge.
Baudrillard, Jean. 1983. *Simulations* (tr. Paul Foss, Paul Patton and Philip Beitchman). New York: Semiotext(e).
Bauman, Zygmunt. 1993. *Postmodern Ethics*. Oxford: Blackwell.
Beeston, Richard. 2007. 'The original war reporter in the Crimea: On the path of William Howard Russell, the Times correspondent whose dispatches from Crimea set the nation alight', *Times Online* (10 November). Online at:

---

[32] As Butler appropriately queries, "is it possible that human rights do not so much presuppose the human as conjecture or posit its future possibility?" (Butler 2006a: 1659)

http://www.timesonline.co.uk/tol/travel/holiday_type/history_and_travel/art icle2840108.ece.

Blanchot, Maurice. 1995. *The Writing of Disaster: l'écriture du désastre* (trans. Ann Smock). New edn. Lincoln and London: University of Nebraska Press.

Bracken, Patrick. 2002. *Trauma: Culture, Meaning and Philosophy*. London and Philadelphia: Whurr.

Braun, Robert. 1994. 'The Holocaust and Problems of Historical Representation', *History and Theory* 33(2) (May): 172-197.

Butler, Judith. 2006a. 'Afterword', *PMLA* 121(5) (Oct.): 1658-1661.

—— 2006b. *Precarious Life: The Powers of Mourning and Violence* [2004]. London: Verso.

Cowart, David. 1989. *History and the Contemporary Novel*. Carbondale: Southern Illinois University Press. [GOOGLE Books]

Crosthwaite, Paul. 2009. *Trauma, Postmodernism, and the Aftermath of World War II*. Basingstoke: Palgrave Macmillan.

Douglass, Ana, and Thomas A. Vogler (eds.). 2003. 'Introduction' in *Witness and Trauma: The Discourse of Trauma*. New York and London: Routledge: 1-53.

Edkins, Jenny. 2003. *Trauma and the Memory of Politics*. Cambridge and New York: Cambridge University Press.

Elias, Amy, J. 2001. *Sublime Desire: History and Post-1960s Fiction*. Baltimore, Maryland: The Johns Hopkins University Press.

Felman, Shoshana and Dori Laub. 1992. *Testimony: Crises of Witnessing in Literature, Psychoanalysis, and History*. New York and London: Routledge.

Foster, Hal. 1996. *The Return of the Real: The Avant-Garde at the End of the Century*. Cambridge, Massachusetts: The MIT Press.

Hatley, James. 2000. *Suffering Witness: The Quandary of Responsibility after the Irreparable*. Albany, New York: State University of New York Press.

Hutcheon, Linda. 1996. '"The Pastime of Past Time: Fiction, History, Historiographical [sic] Metafiction', in Hoffman, Michael J., and Patrick D. Murphy (eds.), *Essentials of the Theory of Fiction*. London: Leceister University Press: 473-495.

Kearney, Richard. 1999. 'The Crisis of the Image: Levinas's Ethical Response' in Madison, Gary B., and Marty Fairbairn (eds.), *Current Trends in Continental Thought*. Evanston, Illinois: Northwestern University Press: 12-23.

Keats, John. 1973. *The Complete Poems* [1819]. Harmondsworth: Penguin.

Keen, Suzanne. 2006. 'The Historical Turn in British Fiction', in English, James F. (ed.), *A Concise Companion to Contemporary British Fiction*. Malden, Massachusetts and Oxford: Blackwell Publishing: 167-187.

LaCapra, Dominick. 1994. *Representing the Holocaust: History, Theory, Trauma*. Ithaca: Cornell University Press.

—. 2001. *Writing History, Writing Trauma*. Baltimore & London: The Johns Hopkins University Press.

Levi, Primo. 1988. *The Drowned and the Saved* (tr. Raymond Rosenthal). New York: Vintage.

Levin, Samuel R. *Metaphoric Worlds: Conceptions of Romantic Nature*. New Haven: Yale University Press, 1988.

Levinas, Emmanuel. 1974. *Autrement qu'être ou au-delà de l'essence*. Paris: Martinus Nishoff.

——.   1982. 'Useless Suffering' in Bernasconi, Robert (ed.), *The Provocation of Emmanuel Levinas: Rethinking the Other*. London & New York: Routledge: 156-167.

——.   1989. 'The Transcendence of Words' in Hand, Sean (ed.), *The Levinas Reader*. Oxford: Basil Blackwell: 144-149.

Leys, Ruth. 2000. *Trauma: A Genealogy*. Chicago: The University of Chicago Press.

Luckhurst, Roger. 2008. *The Trauma Question*. London & New York: Routledge.

Lyotard, Jean-François. 1990. *Heidegger and 'the Jews'* (tr. A. Michel and M. Roberts). Minneapolis: University of Minnesota Press.

——.   1993. *Moralités postmodernes*. Paris: Galilée.

——.   1988. *The Differend: phrases in dispute* (tr. Georges van den Abbeele). Minneapolis: University of Minnesota Press.

McReynolds, Louise. 2003. *Russia at Play: Leisure Activities at the End of the Tsarist Era*. New York: Cornell University Press. [GOOGLE Books]

Micale, Mark S., and Paul Frederick Lerner. 2001. *Traumatic Pasts: History, Psychiatry and Trauma in the Modern Age 1870-1930*. Cambridge: Cambridge University Press.

Miller, Nancy K., and Jason Tougaw (eds.). 2002. *Extremities: Trauma, Testimony, and Community*. Urbana and Chicago: University of Illinois Press.

——.   2002. 'Introduction' in Miller and Tougaw (2002): 1-21.

Morgan, Kenneth O. 2002. 'The Boer War and the Media (1899-1902)', *Twentieth Century British History* 13(1) (March): 1-16.

Rappaport, Helen. 2007. *No Place for Ladies: The Untold Story of Women in the Crimean War*. London: Aurum Press.

Ray, Gene. 2005. *Terror and the Sublime in Art and Critical Theory: From Auschwitz to Hiroshima to September 11*. New York and Houndmills, Basingstoke: Palgrave MacMillan.

Ricoeur, Paul. 1999. 'Memory and Forgetting' in Kearney, Richard, and Mark Dooley (eds.), *Questioning Ethics: Contemporary Debates in Philosophy*. London and New York: Routledge: 5-11.

Rorty, Richard. 1989. *Contingency, Irony, and Solidarity*. Cambridge: Cambridge University Press.

Rothberg, Michael. 2002. 'Between the Extreme and the Everyday: Ruth Klüger's Traumatic Realism' in Miller and Tougaw (2002): 55-70.

Seltzer, Mark. 1997. 'Wound Culture: Trauma in the Pathological Public Sphere', *October* 80: 3-26.

Shuttleworth, Sally. 2010. 'Retro- or Neo-Victorian Fiction and Beyond: Fearful Symmetries'. Keynote lecture presented at *Fashioning the Neo-Victorian: Iterations of the Nineteenth Century in Contemporary Literature and Culture* (University of Erlangen-Nürnberg, 8-10 April 2010).

Sontag, Susan. 2004. *Regarding the Pain of Others* [2003]. London: Penguin.

Swift, Graham. 1992. *Ever After*. London: Picador.

Walker, Janet. 1997. 'The Traumatic Paradox: Documentary Films, Historical Fictions, and Cataclysmic Past Events', *Signs* 22(4) (Summer): 803-825.

Whitehead, Anne. 2004. *Trauma Fiction*. Edinburgh: Edinburgh University Press.

Winslow, Rosemary (Gates). 2004. 'Troping Trauma: Conceiving (of) Experiences of
          Speechless Terror', *JAC* [*The Journal of Advanced Composition*], Special
          Issue, Part 2: Trauma and Rhetoric 24(3): 607-633.
Wittgenstein, Ludwig. 1963. *Tractatus logico-philosophicus/Logisch-philosophische
          Abhandlung* [1921]. Frankfurt am Main: Suhrkamp Verlag.
Wolfreys, Julian. 2002. 'Trauma, Testimony, Criticism: Witnessing Memory and
          Responsibility', in Wolfreys, Julian (ed.), *Introducing Criticism at the 21st
          Century*. Edinburgh: Edinburgh University Press: 126-148.
Wood, David (ed.). 1991. 'Introduction: Interpreting Narrative' in *On Paul Ricoeur.
          Narrative and Interpretation.* London and New York: Routledge: 1-19.
Young, James E. 2003. 'Between History and Memory: The Voice of the
          Eyewitness', in Douglass and Vogler (2003): 275-283.

Part I

Poethics and Existential Extremity:

Crises of Faith, Identity, and Sexuality

Postmodernism Revisited : The Ethical Drive of Postmodern Trauma in Neo-Victorian Fiction

Christian Gutleben and Julian Wolfreys

Abstract:
This chapter sets out to explore the correspondences between Victorian and postmodern situations of trauma. Through its refutation of Enlightenment values postmodernism gave rise to a traumatic sense of loss, which in turn created a need to find sources of solace and also of comparison – since trauma invites compassion for other forms of trauma, just as specific victims are more likely to feel compassion for other types of victim. And because the Victorian (rather than the modernist) period represents, phantasmally and mistakenly of course, the period before the fragmentation of the self and of the novel, it is toward the Victorian tradition that postmodernism turns as a source of comfort. Alternatively, it might be because the imperial losses and crises of Victorianism are still acute today that the contemporary arts ceaselessly return to and work through these unfinished traumas. Whatever the preferred explanation, the (re)integration of a historical comparative paradigm entails a return to ethics in the sense that the self constantly extends to the other. The rediscovery of the historical other as part of the contemporary self creates a sense of exhilaration, which conveys a new vitality to a new ethical form of postmodernism.

Keywords: bearing witness, entanglement, ethics, incredulity, jubilation, neo-Victorian fiction, postmodernism, trauma.

*****

Maybe we're symptomatic of whole flocks of exhausted scholars and theorists. (A.S. Byatt, *Possession*, 1990)

1.   Introduction: Postmodernism and Preconceptions

When put in its novelistic context the introductory quotation might be taken as nothing less than an aphoristic self-definition of neo-Victorian fiction. What seems fascinating in this proclamation is that its late twentieth-century fictional academic author establishes the link between the causes of the contemporary exhaustion in question, namely the repercussions of an education based on postmodern theories, and its consequences, namely a retroactive interest in Victorian culture and concepts. In the logic of this conception postmodernism appears very much as a destructive and inhibiting force, whereas Victorian culture is presented as a source of comfort and regeneration – and it is of course no coincidence that at the end of Byatt's novel the protagonist reinvents himself as a poet. Yet the neo-Victorian *modus operandi* does not reside in an excessively clear-cut opposition between postmodern trauma and Victorian solace but rather, we dare to believe, in a labour of comparison which qualifies the perceptions of both eras and their respective ethos. Since we wish to analyse the relationships between the traumatic legacy of postmodernism and the (often false) promises of Victorian palliation, it seems appropriate to start by exploring the reasons why postmodernism might be perceived as traumatic.

Ventriloquising the academic, the novelist seeks an affirmation of a 'pure' novelistic discourse, through the implicit critique of theoretical language embodied in the postmodern mode of arch-auto-referentiality. Tilting at windmills, the author refuses her death, the death that is the inevitable condition of all writers, once the text has travelled beyond its inscription, to be taken up and read. Presuming, or at least seeking to abrogate to herself novelistic and discursive 'purity' in what might be termed a moment of historical and generic chauvinism, as if the idea of the novel were itself sacrosanct, not to be contaminated by the belated attention of critical discourse, Byatt advocates the belief in the idea of an unsullied narrative mode. In seeking to maintain her authority, the novelist attempts to maintain the fiction of the author as originary source; for Byatt, it is as if the Victorian novel were not – as it always already is – hybrid, heterogeneous, self-referential, and the novelist were merely a conduit or medium. In this amnesiac or myopic dream, the trauma of fiction's inescapable heritage manifests itself, declaring, with all the force of a haunting figure, that the Victorian voice remains at work, and will not be denied by the assumption of loss, mourning, and melancholia. Are we being Victorian enough yet? Are we not the other Victorians, all the more Victorian for seeking to announce separation and loss, rupture from a previous generation? There appears to be an encryption of Byatt's desire here, traumatised by critical intervention, and seeking to reconstitute an historical and cultural moment 'before' criticism.

Roland Michell and Maud Bailey's exchange about their distinctly postmodern identities in *Possession* seems a good starting point to clarify certain implications of postmodern theories. Just before the excerpt that serves as the epigraph, the contemporary scholars try to take stock of their own situation:

> We are very knowing. We know all sorts of other things, too – about how there isn't a unitary ego – how we're made up of conflicting, interacting systems of things – and I suppose we *believe* that? We know we are driven by desire, but we can't see it as they [the Victorian poets] did, can we? (Byatt 1990: 267)

Echoes of discourse inform this passage. They serve to promote the reading of the previous epoch for the postmodern and, therefore, for postmodern identity. The traces of these discourses are marked, on the one hand, by the knowledge that "we are driven by desire" and, on the other hand, that "we can't see it as they did". Between psychoanalysis and the dawning of phenomenology, we might argue, or between Lacan and Kant: here, then, are the knowing parameters of postmodern subjectivity, borders which mark the subject both temporally and spatially. But the question is raised, and so another postmodern frame introduced: for whom is this knowing? Roland and Maud? The narrator who frames the discourse of the novel, or the novelist who fills her characters' heads with knowing-unknowing thoughts, haunted in this citational resonance? The main ideas contained in this passage, to wit the fragmentation and contradictory nature of the self, are manifest echoes of the postmodern conception of subjectivity, as it is usefully summarised by Stuart Sim:

> [for] postmodernists, the subject is a fragmented being who has no essential core of identity, and is to be regarded as a process in a continual state of dissolution rather than a fixed identity or self that endures unchanged over time. (Sim 2001: 367)

What seems relevant here is that Byatt borrows two set ideas about a topic which has much more complex ramifications. As the work of Lyotard proves, postmodern subjectivity is not restricted to disruption or insolvable conflicts. Admittedly in *The Inhuman* Lyotard stresses the idea – which he had already developed in *The Postmodern Condition* (Lyotard 1984: 63) – that the subject produced by contemporary capitalism is dehumanised, or, in his own term, inhuman. But in the same work he also identifies another sense of the inhuman which he calls "admirable" and which he defines as a site of resistance because of the transformative possibilities and ontological nuances of its infinite strangeness:

> what else remains as 'politics' except resistance to this inhuman [system]? And what else is left to resist with but the debt which each soul has contracted with the miserable and admirable indetermination from which it was born and does not cease to be born? [...]
> It is the task of writing, thinking, literature, arts, to venture to bear witness to it. (Lyotard 1991: 7)

The use of the phrase "to bear witness to" is distinctly reminiscent of the labour of overcoming trauma. It is in this critical and creative sense that Lyotard's constructive – and not only deconstructive – conception of postmodernism can be discerned. Indeed, Lyotard's implication of affirmative survival, given voice in that act of attestation, takes up the burden of a knowing-unknowing subjectivity, which writes, thinks, paints and so forth – and, by extension, engages in the endless act of reading – in order, simultaneously, to admit this fragmentary and "continual state of dissolution", while also structuring fragments of memory as the post-traumatic act of witness. He certainly professes the demise of the fantasised stability of the humanist subject, but he also, paradoxically, celebrates "the Idea of humanity in our subject" in the very forms of the inhuman, multiple, uncanny and thought-provoking as those may be (Lyotard 1988: 170). This paradoxical humanity that emerges out of the opening, and with that the destabilisation of the humanist subject, is made possible, and indeed takes place, as the haunting, spectral post-traumatic articulation of the self. In this rupture we come to read the traces of a culture not only driven, but riven, rent violently, by desire and phenomenological apperception, affirmed through postmodern self-referentiality and literary allusion.

When neo-Victorian fiction tackles the topic of postmodern subjectivity, it provides various illustrations of the striking eponymous notion of the inhuman, but it never probes into the complex qualifications of Lyotard's arguments. Hence, when *Possession*'s academics restrict the postmodern subject to the loss of a "unitary ego", their discourse proves to be quite typical of the (mis-) representation of postmodernism which is subjected to ample negative stereotyping. Still on the subject of identity and subjectivity, the children of postmodern theories have much more to say in Byatt's exemplary novel. Here are the heroine's musings on the topic: "Narcissism, the unstable self, the fractured ego, Maud thought, who am I? A matrix for a susurration of texts and codes?" (Byatt 1990: 251) Matrix: organic and mechanical, human and inhuman, mother and machine – in these implied choices, none of which can be decided upon in any of the available contexts of this rhetorical question, Maud marks herself as both producer and produced. More than this, her selfhood is divided, doubled, and placed as the projection of something hybrid and cyborg in condition. Written upon as much as self-inscribing, the unstable subject dissolves into, as much as it is generated out of, and in response to, that whispering or murmuring. Human doubt arrives as the traumatic reaction to inhuman encoding and moulding (matrix referring also to the mould in which printing type or a vinyl record is cast or shaped), whereby the subject is subject to tele-technological rendering. And in a clear echo, the hero reflects how he

> had learned to see himself, theoretically, as a crossing-place for a number of systems, all loosely connected. He had been trained to see his idea of his 'self' as an illusion, to be replaced by a discontinuous machinery and electrical message-network of various desires, ideological beliefs and responses, language-forms and hormones and pheromones. (Byatt 1990: 424)

This echo transforms Roland. His subjectivity is inscribed as a matrix of sorts, and, with that, his gender is written as having been transformed. As a 'matrix', becoming and apprehending himself as that locus, that 'crossing-place', he is simultaneously re-inscribed and reinscribes himself. On the one hand, like his reading of himself, Roland's identity is placed, under erasure, where the crossing place signifies both the sign of the X that threatens (self-)cancellation and that which retains, even in its crossing out, the worn-out signifier of his identity – Roland remains as the trace of himself, and yet no longer, fully, himself. On the other hand, in being made this "crossing-place", Roland becomes a matrix; he becomes the seed-bed for the reproduction of ideas in an academic and discursive feminisation. Of course these quotations take place in a context of anti-academic satire, and both the sexual metaphors in the first case and the scientific tropes in the second must be likened to parodic devices mimicking postmodern jargon,[1] but the point is precisely that postmodernism is systematically the butt of satire and hence of distortion.

2.   The Postmodernist Sense of Trauma

Because postmodernism is experienced as a cause of loss, a loss which is evident in the unfavourable comparison between the postmodernists' lot and that of the Victorians ("we can't see it as they did, can we?"), it is also experienced as a cause of trauma. In this context trauma has to be redefined, seeing that it is unrelated to the catastrophes, shocks and concrete violence usually associated with the term. Nonetheless, the effects of the loss of a unified self mirror those of the more conventional senses of trauma, which likewise produce a radical disjuncture in selfhood, between the self before and after, with intrusive flashbacks, nightmares, and involuntary body memories resisting any subsequent regained sense of wholeness and integration. The "accident model" evoked – and condemned – by Nancy Van Styvendale (2008: 207) has then to be given up and, as in the case of postcolonial trauma, postmodern trauma likewise makes blatant "the need to supplement the event-based model of trauma that has become dominant over the past fifteen years" (Rothberg 2008: 226).[2] The

---

[1] The main hypotextual source and butt is here of course Lacan's conception of the empty subject defined as a site of multiple interactions, a crossroads of infinite and conflicting functions and networks (Lacan 1977: 112 and *passim*).

[2] Of course, we are not dismissing collective traumas undergone in the postmodern era, precipitated by conflict or natural disasters, but are arguing for alternative and

trauma we are talking about, i.e., the ubiquitous sense of deprivation derived from and heralded by (a simplified version of) postmodern theories, cannot be accounted for by classical trauma theories, because the main components of other kinds of traumatic situations (the triggering events, the victim/survivor, the will to forget, the necessity to bear witness) are absent. So the trauma in question cannot be individual; it cannot be located in any specific time or place. On the contrary, trauma becomes collective, circumstantial and global. Additionally, postmodern trauma is understood to be inscribed as a recognition of the loss of self and as a condition of reflective perception generated from within a given epoch, which constitutes the conditions for crisis and trauma. Global, however, does not mean universal, and it must indeed be specified that the phenomenon of postmodernism has left many (and possibly most) people in many (and possibly most) places indifferent. On the other hand, this phenomenon cannot have failed to affect the intellectuals and artists of the world, including the writers of neo-Victorian fiction who are, almost by definition, on the look-out for diachronic evolutions and historical landmarks and watersheds. So what is it in postmodernism that can be and has been perceived as traumatic? In other words, to pursue the analysis of *Possession*'s postmodern dystopia, what is it that explains the contemporary scholars' weariness and disenchantment?

As Patricia Waugh has convincingly argued, postmodernism covers at least three different conceptual fields, broadly corresponding

---

more inclusive models that also take into account what Dominick LaCapra terms "structural" as opposed to "historical" traumas, that is, traumas related not to specific events and sufferers, but to "transhistorical absence" that can affect anyone in any society – a sense of separation or alienation that may take various forms and is often associated with the "the notion of a fall from a putative state of grace, at-homeness, unity, or community" (LaCapra 1991: 76-77). Hence, "it may not be possible to locate or localize the experience of trauma that is not dated or, in a sense, punctual" (LaCapra 1991: 81). Structural trauma is thus similar to insidious trauma, which is occasioned by long-term conditions of crisis and anxiety produced not only by *actual* but also *potential* suffering, usually attributable to inequitable socio-political and economic systems and involving forms of harm that need not be conspicuous (such as disease, discrimination, poverty, sexual abuse, restricted freedom of expression or movement, political disenfranchisement, etc.). This chapter limits itself to exploring the structural and insidious trauma of the (perceived) postmodern condition which, like all collective traumas, is nonetheless experienced on an individual basis also.

to three terminological variations: the postmodern, postmodernism
and postmodernity. Waugh therefore defines it

> firstly as a mood or style of thought which privileges
> aesthetic modes over those of logic or method;
> secondly as an aesthetic practice with an
> accompanying body of commentary upon it; and
> thirdly as a concept designating a cultural epoch
> which has facilitated the rise to prominence of such
> theoretical and aesthetic styles and which may or may
> not constitute a break with previous structures of
> modernity. (Waugh 1992: 7)

Although the differences between the theoretical, aesthetic and
historical concepts are quite considerable in the actual discussions and
debates about postmodernism, the various meanings of the term are
often so mixed and mingled that the negative analyses of the period
concept are also (and mistakenly) applied to the literary works. The
amalgamating generalisations therefore tend to be understood as
applying to the whole contemporary scene – and not only to the sole
philosophical branch, the artistic production or the cultural *Zeitgeist*.
One such amalgamating practice can be traced in the deathly rhetoric
used by postmodern thinkers and artists and misconstrued as
apocalyptic announcements. That sense of apocalyptic revelation is
measured in those remarks of Maud and Roland, already cited,
wherein trauma is marked as the experience of an inhuman dissolution
of stability, and character appears to itself in this knowingness, as if it
were dead. Being only the productive, and reproductive matrix, the
death of the stable subject is the pre-condition for the performative
referentiality of the postmodern subject, knowing itself, or appearing
to itself, as the sum of its inscriptions and its projections. After Roland
Barthes's famous statement about "the death of the author" (Barthes
1977: 142), Frederic Jameson proclaimed "the death of the subject
itself" (Jameson 1991: 15) and Jean Baudrillard "the true end of
history" (Baudrillard 1994: 22), while all the time the controversy
about the death of the novel was kept alive by Gore Vidal, Barthes,
John Barth and Ronald Sukenick (who wrote a short story called 'The
Death of the Novel' in 1969). The theorists' endism is summed up in

Derrida's significantly titled paper 'Of an Apocalyptic Tone in Recent Philosophy':

> It is not the end of this here but also of that there, the end of history, the end of the class struggle, the end of philosophy, the death of God, the end of religions, the end of Christianity and morals [...] the end of the subject, the end of man, the end of the West, the end of Oedipus, the end of the Earth, Apocalypse now. (Derrida 1984: 29)[3]

If one takes the trouble to look at the context of these statements, one quickly realises that the emphasis is not necessarily necrological – on the contrary. Barthes proclaims "the death of the author" only to celebrate "the birth of the reader" and the freedom of multiple interpretations. Similarly "the death of the subject itself' in fact constitutes "the end of the bourgeois monad or ego or individual" (Jameson 1991: 15). So it is really the idea of a unified self or a coherent identity that is negated, and there is no reason why the plurality of the postmodern subject that replaces the old "bourgeois monad" should necessarily be distressing or depressing. In this different light, the staged anxiety of reflexive knowing-unknowing articulated by Roland and Maud marks them both, as they remark themselves, with the signs of postmodern subjectivity's historicity. Moreover, given the context of *Possession*'s Tennysonian resonances, Maude's 'authorisation' as a consciousness constituted through fragments of sensate apprehension echoes Tennyson's poem from which her name is taken. Not knowing grounds the self as subject to its moment, while referentiality gives to that ground a historical trajectory within the epoch, which trajectory is not to be understood as a grand narrative, but the 'sussuration' of haunting, recurrent myths of subjectivity. Even Baudrillard, in spite of his uncompromising condemnation of the postmodern destruction of the indispensable distance between the real and the rational, propounds

---

[3] To this death roll could be added Lyotard's statements about the "terminal exhaustion of philosophy" (qtd. Norris 1990: 246).

> an anagrammatic history (where meaning is
> dismembered and scattered to the winds…), rhyming
> forms of political action or events which can be read
> in either direction […]. Such would be the enchanted
> alternative to the linearity of history, the poetic
> alternative to the disenchanted confusion. (Baudrillard
> 1994: 122, unbracketed ellipses in the original)

And even if he does not explain what these forms of poetic histories
might consist in, he does pave the way for writers to imagine
alternative versions of postmodern history. As for the debate about the
death of the novel which occurred in the context of the French
Nouveau Roman and American Surfiction, it seems manifest
retrospectively, since the debate generated a new kind of fiction, that
the death in question concerned only a certain type of novel – a type
of realist and/or naturalist novel that had in great part already been
discredited by the modernists.

In view of the preceding outline, it should be clear that
postmodernism's deathly rhetoric is precisely that, just rhetorics
encapsulated in striking apophthegms, and that the actual texts of
postmodernist criticism are far from apocalyptic.[4] Nevertheless, this
type of alarming discourse has had a powerful impact on the collective
imagination of contemporary artists; thus, according to Stef Craps,
"insofar as postmodernity is committed to living with loss and
uncertainty as a permanent condition, its dominant mode is mourning"
(Craps 2005: 19). So the theoretical rhetoric of death seems to
correspond to a fictional mode of mourning. To illustrate his point
Craps cites Graham Swift's work, because it "manages to evoke the
cultural pathologies of an entire nation, an empire or even an era"
(Craps 2005: 18). Such pathology, it can be argued, is to be found
already at work in Victorian sensibility, as a constituent element in the
traumatic perception of one's collective subjectivity, that which Tim
Armstrong has described as the Victorian trauma of becoming
historical. Tim Armstrong has described the Victorian subject's "entry
into history, the trauma of *becoming-historical* which is central to
nineteenth-century conceptions of the historical" (Armstrong 2000: 2),

---

[4] Derrida's paper itself is full of irony at the expense of the apocalyptic mood of
contemporary philosophy (see Callus and Herbrechter 2004).

and it may be argued that neo-Victorian postmodern (so-called) trauma replays in postmodern registers the very same condition, albeit a 'translated' manifestation of the same, of an entry into history as the constituent condition of the dissolution and death of narratives of stable subject-positions. As a translation of the dystopian perception of the phenomenon of postmodernism *Ever After* (1992) is indeed a case in point, but any of Byatt's neo-Victorian novels and novellas, D.M. Thomas's *Charlotte* (2000), Emma Tennant's *Tess* (1993), or even John Fowles's *The French Lieutenant's Woman* (1969) would be equally suitable to reflect the postmodern sense of loss.[5]

3.   Generalised Incredulity

The sense of traumatic crisis instigated by the advent of postmodernism is not only a consequence of the necrological tendency of some of the theoreticians' rhetorical catch-phrases; it also derives from the fundamental scepticism of postmodernism's messengers, starting with its forerunner, Jean-François Lyotard. The central statement of Lyotard's pioneering work, "I define *postmodern* as incredulity toward metanarratives" (Lyotard 1984: xxiv), has considerable consequences, because it implies a radical break with the preceding values of truth, knowledge and progress. As Simon Malpas explains, what is definitely forsaken is "the idea of the development of knowledge as a progress towards universal enlightenment and freedom" (Malpas 2005: 38). Instead, knowledge – the main concern of Lyotard's report because its evolution under the forces of capitalism proves emblematic of the postmodern – has become a commodity ruled by the laws of profit in a world market.

> The postmodern condition is thus one in which the demands of capitalist economics rule supreme, and all developments of knowledge are determined by the pragmatic logic of the markets rather than the overarching dream of a universal good. (Malpas 2005: 39)

---

[5] For the contemporary repercussions of the specifically Darwinian sense of loss see Georges Letissier's and Catherine Pesso-Miquel's chapters in this volume.

According to Lyotard, the imperative necessity of efficiency, of being operational, "necessarily entails a certain level of terror" (Lyotard 1984: xxiv). Lyotard's message is not always alarmist; he has much more to say about postmodernism, and he even finds arguments "to supply the proof that humanity is constantly progressing toward the better" (Lyotard 1988: 170).[6] Yet his association of the postmodern with loss and terror becomes the overriding principle henceforth attached to postmodernism *per se*.[7] The tyranny of efficiency and the perversion of the quest for knowledge became dominant traumatic motifs that informed the work of artists concerned by these transformations.

One might read D.M. Thomas's *Charlotte* (2000) as a work reflecting the loss of faith in any form of progress. Although loosely chronological, the contemporary section of the novel clearly illustrates the idea of senselessness, with the various episodes concerning the first-person narrator showing no progression whatsoever. If, before the advent of postmodernism, a narrative was to reach a certain goal or reveal a certain understanding, then *Charlotte*'s un- or anti-teleological structure is the most blatant feature betraying the postmodern negation of progress. The protagonist's various adventures, mainly of a sexual nature, do not lead to any revelation or any betterment; they simply record moments of perplexity, anxiety or distress. In this novel, anxiety is made manifest as the lack of lack, to paraphrase Lacan (Lacan 2008: 57). Because the narrator's sanity is emphatically questionable and because she confesses to a propensity for lying and fabulation, it is in fact the reliability of the whole narrative discourse that becomes doubtful. There is thus an analogy implicitly drawn between the impossibility of desire's fulfilment and narrative resolution. Yet because sanity is put into question, notions of epistemological rationality are called into question as suitable or dominant modes of narration for subjectivity. Not only is truth never

---

[6] Waugh cites another constructive program on the part of Lyotard, the one he propounds against terror: "Let us wage a war on totality; let us be witnesses to the unpresentable; let us activate the differences and save the honour of the name" (qtd. Waugh 1992: 30).
[7] David Mitchell's *Cloud Atlas*, which Celia Wallhead and Marie-Luise Kohlke analyse in detail in this volume, could be said to constitute an ideal example of a novel "mimicking postmodernity's trauma of the loss of metanarratives" (this volume: 218).

the object of the narrator's quest but its very possibility is refuted, or one might say deconstructed, by the very situation of enunciation. What Lyotard called the Grand Narratives of truth, love, and progress are all missing in Thomas's heroine's life, and because of these lacks she is an annihilated subject. Her shock – and shocked – statement, "I died a long time ago" (Thomas 2000: 72) recalls another resonant confession of a traumatised first-person narrator, the postmodern version of one of the living dead: "These are, I should warn you, the words of a dead man" (Swift 1992: 1). Swift's *Ever After*, like Thomas's novel, is bereft of and even opposed to a teleological progression, which is made obvious in the structural principle – or lack thereof. The novel's extreme fragmentation, the confusion of its temporal sequence that cannot be unravelled, and the absence of logical links between the various chapters all highlight the order of disorder that prevails and conveys the idea of a dominating chaos, both moral and metaphysical. In "this random universe" (Swift 1992: 224), the metanarratives are indeed invalidated, and the title constitutes the first indication that in Swift's novel generic and moral models are subverted. By using the concluding words of a traditional fairy tale as the introductory words of a postmodern novel, Swift at once signals that the world of the fairy tale and its moral edification is already past. The end of the tale becomes the beginning of the novel, which means that the novel does not move towards but away from happiness: it is an exploration of the disillusioned era of lost innocence and post-happiness. Its logic is not that of a progressive construction but that of a radical deconstruction. Happiness and the soothing Grand Narratives are done away with as soon as the novel starts. In *Ever After* the hopeful universe of the fairy tale is presented as a possibility of the past, while the present is always already dystopian and dysphoric, always already a witness to the demise of "*grandes histoires*" (Lyotard 1984: xxiv). [8]

Postmodernism's breaking up of previously structuring concepts like truth and meaning finds an echo in the theories of deconstruction such as they are (often wrongly) accounted for by

---

[8] For a detailed analysis of Swift's "incredulity toward metanarratives" see Craps, whose central thesis is that Swift's "texts are quite vocal in their condemnation of redemptive, totalising narratives, which they expose as dangerous forms of reality-denial" (Craps 2005: 3). For a specific study of trauma in Swift's novel see Catherine Pesso-Miquel's chapter in this volume.

critics and, alas, fiction writers. John Ellis, for example, takes an explicitly hostile stance in *Against Deconstruction* when he declares that "now deconstruction, an intensified expression of these [*laissez-faire*] tendencies, has attempted to seize the mantle of theory in order to pursue [an] anti-theoretical program" (Ellis 1989: 159). For Ellis deconstruction means a sort of hermeneutic licentiousness, an interpretive activity with no scientific rule or purpose. As Christopher Norris convincingly demonstrates, deconstruction is often reduced "to an endless dissemination of meaning, speech-acts and conventions", which leads to the central aporetic notion that "there is no possibility of meaning what one says or effectively saying what one means" (Norris 1990: 143-144). The idea that the signifier is always floating free of the signified, in other words that meaning is always indeterminate, inevitably produces linguistic anxiety and even what Peter Barry calls "terminal anxieties about the possibility of achieving *any* form of knowledge through language" (Barry 2002: 64). Similarly, Derrida's "axial proposition [...] that there is nothing outside the text" (Derrida 1976: 163) seems to cast an ontological doubt on the very notion of referentiality. Derrida later amply qualified this aphoristic statement,[9] explaining that it applied to the forms of archival reality that are only available in discursive guise, but his provocative claim has doubtlessly created a sense of crisis in the comprehension of reference and reality.

Byatt's neo-Victorian novels seem quite representative of the negative stereotypes of deconstruction that find their way into contemporary fiction, where postmodern theory is systematically presented as harmful or useless or both. The male protagonists of both *Possession* (1990) and Byatt's later *The Biographer's Tale* (2000) have to learn to get "entirely freed from post-post-structuralist clutter" before they can hope to reach personal fulfilment (Byatt 2000: 165). Because they "had been taught that language was essentially

[9] In *Limited Inc*, for example, Derrida explains that "the concept of text or of context which guides me embraces and does not exclude the world, reality, history." And he further clarifies his position: the text "does not suspend reference – to history, to reality, to being, and especially not to the other since to say of history, of the world, of reality, that they always appear in an experience, hence in a movement of interpretation which contextualizes them according to a network of differences and hence of referral to the other, is surely to recall that alterity (difference) is irreducible. *Différance* is a reference and vice versa" (Derrida 1989: 137).

inadequate, that it could never speak what was there, that is only spoke itself" (Byatt 1990: 473) and because they resent "the disagreeable amount of imposing that went on in it [deconstructionism]" (Byatt 2000: 144), the children of postmodernism feel stifled by the theories of their era. This fact is most blatant in the case of Maud Bailey, whose theoretical self-awareness blocks her writing and her emotional involvement. It is remarkable that all these characters find their inspiration to resolve the traumatic inhibitions arising from their deconstructionist education within Victorian literature – a fact on which we shall have more to say anon. Derrida's epigones are further discredited in neo-Victorian fiction because they are the specific butts of satire, as in the case of Fergus Wolff in *Possession* and Robyn Penrose in David Lodge's *Nice Work* (1988). Robyn's Derridean creed –"il n'y a pas de hors-texte, there is nothing outside the text" (Lodge 1988: 40) – is pitilessly debunked when she has to face the social reality of a factory strike, thus pinpointing the limits of her linguistic conception of the world, although of course Derrida's theory is situated on an altogether different plane from social reality. Of course, all this points to, yet again, is a failure to comprehend Derrida's statement and the difficulties of translation. Saying that there is no outside-the-text admits not to the absence of referentiality but rather to an endlessness of the same – and also to the fact that every statement to do with subjectivity is always instituted through, and authorised by, structures of meaning, whether these be linguistic or 'real', as in the case of Lodge's factory strike, an event which emerges from out of various discursive and practical matrices.

The crisis concerning the concept of reference and reality initially stirred up by misreadings of Derrida's deconstruction is brought to a climax by another theoretician of postmodernism: Baudrillard. Baudrillard is not interested in the linguistic accessibility of the real; his much more radical purpose is to negate the pertinence of the concept of the real and to announce 'the loss of the real'. In the postmodern world of images (produced by advertising, computers, films and television) Baudrillard contends that the rules of representation are overturned, so that the model precedes the real and the copy prevails over the referent, resulting in what he calls "the order of simulation" or "the precession of simulacra", whereby what is produced is "hyperreality", i.e., "the generation by models of a real without origin or reality (Baudrillard 1983: 2). In this postmodern world of hyperreality the guiding principle is performativity; hence, if it works, it is good. When the efficiency of the strategies of simulation is declared paramount, the question of ethics and ideology becomes automatically redundant. Baudrillard's position represents, therefore,

> the furthest stage yet reached in th[e] widespread disenchantment [...] with 'theory' in just about every shape and form and the most radical stance with regard to the obsolescence of truth, the non-availability of rational grounds and the need to break with all the forms of 'enlightened' conceptual critique. (Norris 1990: 186-187)

Postmodernism as simulacrum is of course a reductive simplification and generalisation,[10] but it is an idea that certainly inspired contemporary writers – probably because of its very outrageousness.

In David Mitchell's *Cloud Atlas* (2004), which interweaves several stories reaching from the Victorian epoch to an unspecified post-apocalyptic future, a character set in the 1970s remarks that the virtual past is "malleable, ever-brightening" and that "symmetry demands [a] virtual future too", before raising the crucial following question: "Is there a meaningful distinction between one simulacrum [...] the actual past – from another such simulacrum – the actual future?" (Mitchell 2004: 408-409) Considering that the novel is entirely constituted of more or less distant pasts and futures, the rhetorical question seems to have a self-reflexive scope that defines the novel itself as an exercise in various forms of simulacra. Additionally, in so far as the various simulacra only *seem* temporally discrete – there is, after all, a common thread between different historical moments and cultural identities represented – and that they re-mark history as difference without order (order coming into focus only in the belated act of reading), the implication is that the present is itself a simulacrum. The present is without presence in the novel. The virtual quality of Mitchell's temporal explorations is not hidden but becomes part and parcel of the novel's ontological relativism and

---

[10] For a criticism of Baudrillard's theories see Norris 1990, particularly chapter 4: 'Lost in the Funhouse: Baudrillard and the Politics of Postmodernism': 164-192.

metafictional transparency. Mitchell's choice of the term "simulacrum" is evidently inspired by Baudrillard and so is his presentation of the future where "no originals remain", only "molecule-for-molecule copies of the original" (Mitchell 2004: 227). Of course, in writing postmodern pastiches of different historical moments and their narratives, Mitchell structures a world not only of simulacra, but also of derivative narratives and, with that, the subjectivities by which such narratives are formed. The catastrophic nature of this world deprived of originals manifests itself in the motif of the exploitation of human clones, which links up with the scandal of the slaves exposed in the Victorian strand of the narrative and shows the regressive and anti-humanist value of a hyperreality *à la* Baudrillard.

To a certain extent D.M. Thomas's vision of the contemporary world can also be considered as a reflection of the predominance of simulation, since the main production of the protagonist Miranda is a perverted version of a Victorian canonical novel. Obsessed with the sexual perversions of the Victorian characters never intimated in *Jane Eyre* (1847), Miranda's pastiche of Charlotte Brontë's text does not rely on any 'original' as such, be it referential or fictional. So here the postmodern copy ostentatiously flaunts its status as a copy, as a simulacrum once again, and this logic of simulation finds expression in a pervasive sense of deprivation, nowhere more evident than in the protagonist's utter loss of bearings. What is true of Miranda is even more pertinent for Bill Unwin, the protagonist of Swift's *Ever After* who, helplessly and hopelessly, witnesses the triumph of the civilisation of the fake. The plastic industry and its "polymerization of the world" constitute the novel's central metaphorical network (Swift 1992: 7), testifying to the precedence of simulacra. Bill's quest for the real thing is an ordeal leading him from disappointment to failure; it is also fraught with intertextual irony since Tom Stoppard's play *The Real Thing* (1982) is precisely about infidelity and the undermining of the eponymous notion. *Ever After*'s protagonist thus ends up realising that the sham prevails not only in his postmodern civilisation but also in the field of epistemology, of personal relations and even of love. He is forced to acknowledge the supremacy of the order of simulation or, to borrow Umberto Eco's highly rhetorical phrase, the order of *Faith in Fakes*

(1987), which is meant to encapsulate the spirit of postmodernism in a perspective close to Baudrillard's.

Let us take stock of the arguments examined so far. What is striking is that postmodernism has come to be associated with a sense of crisis and deprivation, moral, emotional, and spiritual: such fundamental values and notions as knowledge, meaning, truth and even referentiality are deemed irretrievably lost.[11] And since postmodernism encompasses not only philosophical or theoretical precepts but also a historical and political reality, it arouses (and supposedly consists in) a disenchantment with a whole civilisation. We want to suggest that contemporary fiction turns away from the present scene of trauma and reverts to other situations and chronotopes predating that trauma exactly to escape this postmodern sense of crisis, loss and disenchantment. Via this structural apotropaism, which amounts to a kind of 'turning away' or 'warding off' of 'evil', contemporary fiction narrates the historical and haunting traces of trauma through an indirect attestation. Contemporary fiction engages in an act of speaking indirectly, saying otherwise and in other words. In bearing witness to that which it cannot speak of directly (th s is the condition of all historical narrative), it must find for itself a mode of presentation commensurate or analogous with the experience, to which it can only gesture indirectly. This is made a necessity in the face of loss, lack, and the reiterated confrontation of limits, fiction only bearing witness indirectly to its own loss, lack and trauma, following the loss of access to any Grand Narrative. The losses proclaimed by the harbingers of postmodernism are inevitably what the practitioners of postmodernism wish to retrieve. In the field of fiction when a contemporary artist retreats to a time before the sense of crisis, he or she cannot choose the modernist epoch, since the crisis of the novel was already acute for the modernists. As Waugh has successfully argued, postmodernism includes modernism not only from a terminological point of view but also because the former is a

---

[11] The theorists and philosophers who propound these principles never actually consider any concrete works of art. In sharp contrast, the critics who also examine postmodern art, be it in architecture for Charles Jencks (*The Language of Post-Modern Architecture* [1977]; *What Is Postmodernism?* [1986]) or in literature for Patricia Waugh (*Practising Postmodernism, Reading Modernism* [1992]) and Linda Hutcheon (*A Poetics of Postmodernism* [1988]), always present more qualified views, stressing postmodernism's ambiguity and regenerative virtues.

continuation of the challenges undertaken by the latter in the field of epistemology, psychology and ethics (Waugh 1992: 19-24).[12] On the basis of the theories of Freud, Einstein and Saussure the notions of subjectivity, truth and meaning were already greatly unsettled and modernist novels reflect these shattering doubts. So for postmodernists the first (imagined) model of stability, the first era before the fragmentation of the self and the novel, is the closest pre-modernist period, i.e., the Victorian period. The time before the losses incurred by postmodernists is Victorian time (not modernist time); it is naturally toward that time that the traumatised contemporary writers turn when they want to come to terms with their dispossession.

4.   The Revival of Ethics

There is another way of reaching the same conclusion. The postmodern theories that gave birth to the crises of knowledge, meaning and referentiality all date from the 1970s and 1980s. After that two things happened. The theoreticians (bar Baudrillard) grew impatient with the negative perception and simplification of their ideas and opened up the study of ethics in order to show that their theories were not nihilistic. As J. Hillis Miller explains in the introduction to *Black Holes*, he turned to "the notion of the other, or rather of 'others'" as something new after deconstruction, something which allows him to show that his theory does not reject "the referentiality of language" (Miller 1999: xi; 83).[13] Miller's work constantly examines an ethics beyond the ethics of reading and witnessing, not only through the idea of the other, but also through performative speech acts, and through the reading of the work of various classical rhetorical tropes such as parabasis and apophasis, as a means of destabilising stable identities and certainties of narrative articulation. (To digress briefly: an ethics beyond ethics involves one in not judging ahead of a reading, or prejudging through the imposition of a critical model. Every text is completely and wholly

---

[12] The continuities stressed by Waugh do not exclude discontinuities and, indeed, for questions like the sacredness and autonomy of art or the conception of ontological strata the divergences prove considerable; see Waugh 1992 and Brian McHale's *Postmodernist Fiction* (1987).

[13] His interest in ethics does not mean that Miller turns his back on deconstruction (for he never does so); it is just a means to clarify and defend the precepts of Derrida's school of thought.

other from every other text. Therefore, as far as possible, without the
imposition of conceptual frameworks such as 'postmodernism',
'deconstruction' or some other critical chimera – which critics such as
Derrida and Miller would refute and reject – one must remain open to
the text as an other, seeking to mitigate the violence of reading – the
limiting of the play of difference through the determination of
meaning – and thereby engaging in a reading which is also a response,
and thus, it is to be hoped, a countersignature to that which the text
imposes on one.) Concurrently "[t]rauma theory emerged in the
United States in the early 1990s and sought to elaborate on the
cultural and ethical implications of trauma" (Whitehead 2004: 4).
Trauma studies is inextricably linked with an ethical concern for the
other for, as Cathy Caruth, one of the pioneer theorists of the field,
expounds, "it opens up and challenges us to a new kind of listening,
the witnessing, precisely, of impossibility" (Caruth 1995: 10). More
lately, theorists like Jennifer Geddes have claimed something similar
for postmodernism's critical role in the recovery of and the renewed
turn to ethics:

> the very delegitimizing of grand narratives by
> postmodern thought opened up space that allowed and
> encouraged the particular narratives of those not in
> power to be told and heard, but […] in doing so, this
> 'delegitimizing' gesture has brought forth narratives
> that describe, express, and protest a range of
> suffering, injustice, and evil that postmodernism has
> been ill equipped to respond to – hence its turn to
> questions of ethics. (Geddes 2007: 73)

So the early postmodern theories of loss brought about the return of a
concern for ethics and particularly a concern for the other, which
necessarily finds expression in an investigation of alternative
subjectivities. Between the modernist and the postmodernist subjects
there are more similarities than differences; the closest available form
of the other for postmodernism thus becomes the Victorian other.
Postmodernism's interest in Victorianism can therefore be seen as an
expression of the return of an ethical concern for otherness.
      If Neo-Victorian fiction thrived in the wake of trauma studies,
however, it had already started to develop much earlier. And if fiction

illustrating the omnipresent and transhistorical nature of trauma predated the formal theorisation of trauma,[14] it is conceivable that trauma theory developed in the wake of neo-Victorian fictional practices, or wider historical fictional and historiographic metafictional practices,[15] rather than vice versa.[16] To explain the anticipatory quality of neo-Victorian fiction several factors seem relevant. It is plainly the very function of art to perceive, reflect and interpret the spirit of its times, and in the 1980s, when neo-Victorian fiction started to expand significantly (before the appearance of trauma studies as a quasi separate academic discipline), that spirit was one of anxiety in the face of an epoch and ethos dominated by the concept of entropy.[17] Equally, it can be argued that one reason for the rise and proliferation of neo-Victorian fiction and Victorian pastiche in the 1980s was, in the UK at least, an indirect reaction against Margaret Thatcher's neo-liberalism, particularly in its *laissez-faire* and free market economics, themselves echoes of much Victorian economic policy and the ideologies that it mediated and was mediated by. The global fiction of the 1980s can also be considered as a reaction to and against postmodern theories of crisis (thus again anticipating trauma studies), which may explain how much of this

---

[14] As Nancy Van Stevendale explains, "the concept of trans/historical trauma has the potential to make a crucial intervention in trauma theory invested as this concept is in an 'event' that refuses historical location at the same time as it insists on being multiply lodged" (Van Stevendale 2008: 220).

[15] Neo-Victorian fiction does not occupy a privileged position per se amongst these literary practices; indeed many historical fiction writers, such as Peter Ackroyd, work both within neo-Victorian and alternative historical settings. Yet the neo-Victorian engagement with the nineteenth century, which laid the groundwork for so many of postmodernity's socio-political and economic configurations, on both a UK national and international basis, arguably makes the interplay between past-time and presentism within neo-Victorian fiction both more readily discernible and directly relevant to our current condition.

[16] The development of trauma studies, of course, was also responding to the wider ethical turn occurring in the 1970s and 1980s in related disciplines, such as literary theory, moral philosophy, and cultural studies, reflecting a dissatisfaction with deconstructionist relativism and a search for more appropriate critical tools to deal with the complex legacies of cultural memory as explored in emerging fictional and testimonial literature on the two World Wars and the Shoah.

[17] In his study which takes stock of the latest theoretical and scientific developments at the end of the 1980s, Patrick O'Neil suggests "the notion of entropy as a metaphor for the crumbling of ordered systems, the breakdown of traditional perceptions of reality, the erosion of certainty" (O'Neil 1990: 8).

literature incorporates both the sense of loss and a possible after-effect or solution, i.e., the opening up to otherness. Finally, it must not be forgotten that while the postmodern defeat of meaning and referentiality entailed an occultation of ethical concerns, Emmanuel Levinas never ceased to argue for the overwhelming role of ethics. As early as 1961 (1964 for the English translation) Levinas claimed that ethics was more important than epistemology (Levinas 1964: 31 and *passim*), thus refuting in anticipation Lyotard's theory of knowledge. In the same work Levinas attacks the contemporary ascendancy of the show and the spectacle as a dangerous counterforce to the imperative of ethics, thus refuting in anticipation Baudrillard's theory of simulation. Levinas' persistent interest in the ethical importance of the other finds a sort of crystallisation in his concept of excendance, as first articulated in *De l'évasion* (1935).[18] According to Andrew Gibson, who paraphrases Levinas, the concept of excendance represents "the spontaneous and immediate desire to escape the limits of the self, a desire generated as those limits are experienced in their narrowness, even their sheer absurdity" (Gibson 1999: 37). Excendance, then, represents an exodus from oneself: "it turns us incessantly elsewhere, outside: not towards death, the timeless or supernatural (this would be the drive to *transcendence*, not *excendance*) but towards the other" (Gibson 1999: 37). By reviving a comparative approach to the present and the past, the known and the imagined, the self and the other, neo-Victorian fiction can be said to have answered Levinas's call for excendance. To put this another way neo-Victorian traumatic narrative exceeds and overflows the stable self implicit in Victorian realist fiction, in order to offer a countersignature to its nineteenth-century forebears, and thereby confront Victorian anxiety in the face of becoming historical, as Tim Armstrong has it, of knowing oneself to be separated by history from any myth of continuity, with an anxiety of influence writ large onto the supposedly postmodern subject. Such a subject is thereby revealed as an uncanny subjectivity, traced in its contours by particular phantasms, phantasms that are referential in that they evoke and invoke an historical 'real' that is all too material in its forces and effects. The phantasm or revenant refigures the 'real' violence enacted

---

[18] For the relevance of this concept in neo-Victorian fiction see Gutleben 2009/2010: 150-152.

on human bodies, but the material effects are not limited to corporeal transgression; material effects are left in cultural organisation, ideological orientation, and so forth, so that the immaterial, that which, strictly speaking, is neither something nor nothing, neither real nor unreal, continues to produce material conditions.

5.   The Conjunction of Postmodernism and Neo-Victorianism

Because ours is "the true age of anxiety" (Bracken 2002: 181), "a catastrophic age" (Caruth 1995: 11), a "post-auratic, decathected, depthless" age (Maltby 2007: 44), the fictional return to the Victorian age represents both a sidestep and a quest for solace. This is double-edged, though, because, not being a one-way street, the return to a mystified Victorian age also implies a return of the Victorian other, a traumatic return of what might be described as a 'familial repressed', a family romance of spectral indebtedness. To put this in another fashion, that 'quest for solace' is rooted in a mis-recognition of a past moment – and the narratives of that past – as essentially, solidly and materially homogeneous. We read the past in a simple, undifferentiated manner, as though its identity were fixed and untroubled. In this misreading, our contemporary anxiety is revealed as the driving force. Having 'forgotten', as it were, the true histories of Victorian identity, we seek a return of, as well as to, an age apparently untroubled by catastrophe and not yet having undergone cathexis. (Catastrophes are of course all too real; yet the reconstruction of a history, a fable, nostalgic for another time as preferable to the real catastrophes of its present, reconstitutes fictions of the past, as though the catastrophes of moment were of little consequence.) What this fails to read, what it cannot interpret, is the violence of cultural repression undergone in the name of Victorianism, the legacy of which returns to haunt us, on the one hand, in our contemporary anxieties and traumatic loss of identity, and, on the other, in all that remains unread and yet shared epochally. (To go into detail concerning that which is shared epochally is unnecessary, because to detail everything that is shared would be, in effect, to attempt the impossible, to recreate the entirety of all that is shared – hence the use of the term epoch.) Because ours are the times of incredulity and hyperreality, the "essentially post-historical" times (Kugelman 1996: 199), the exploration of Victorian history represents a labour of comparison, an attempt at discovering a world that predates the sense of an endist crisis.

What do neo-Victorian writers find out at the end of their exploration? (For it must not be forgotten that these novelists conduct thorough research into their Victorian subjects, as the quasi-systematic acknowledgement of paratextual sources clearly indicates.) Strikingly, the recreation of Victorian microcosms more often than not shows splintered worlds, suffering subjects, individual or collective traumas. As the extreme variety of examples discussed in this volume demonstrates, neo-Victorian fiction focuses on the dramatic effects of sexual and religious intolerance, social conflicts and tragedies, and the horrors of wars and colonisation. Hence, to explore Victorianism as a counterpoint – and possibly counterforce – to postmodernism is to discover the always already prevalent precedence of trauma. It is also to discover that the "original state of harmony [before] fragmentation" for which postmodernism is deemed nostalgic (Waugh 1992: 13) – what Lyotard calls "the nostalgia of the whole and the one" (Lyotard 1984: 82) – has always already been lost and that the values of Enlightenment, supposedly shattered by postmodernism, have always already been darkened by social and historical realities. In such discoveries can be found convincing arguments for a relativist conception of the despondent (self-)definitions of postmodernism.

Trying to find a common point between the various situations of trauma described in contemporary fictional reconstitutions, one may think of the deregulations of the crumbling Empire and its axiological system. And considering the ongoing repetitiveness of accounts stressing the failures of the British Empire, the possibility cannot be excluded that the neo-Victorian phenomenon represents a response to that Victorian trauma – as opposed to postmodern trauma. As Marie-Luise Kohlke perceptively foresaw,

> [t]he analysis of the nineteenth century as a harbinger of our own trauma culture is currently gaining critical mass as another neo-Victorian concern with evident political implications. Increasingly, the period is configured as a temporal convergence of multiple historical traumas still awaiting appropriate commemoration and full working-through. (Kohlke 2008: 7)

So the ceaseless return to Victorian traumas in contemporary historical fiction focused on the nineteenth century might well represent the trace of the collective, historical and unresolved shock of an irretrievable loss, the loss of an expanding world, the loss of a time before loss. The Victorian era could then be the "still present past" of the traumatised (collective) subject,[19] and the tardiness of the concrete, textualised response may correspond to the dormancy of trauma, the labour of working through which

> is effected belatedly through repetition, for the numbingly traumatic event does not register at the time of its occurrence but only after a temporal gap or period of latency, at which time it is immediately repressed, split off, or disavowed. (LaCapra 1994: vii, 174)

To avow the disavowed certainly seems to be on the agenda of neo-Victorian fiction, particularly if one thinks of its emphasis on colonial contexts. In that respect one cannot strictly speak of a belated response or a return of the repressed because, both for the descendents of the former colonisers and the colonised, the guilt and the anger, the shame and the revolt are still acutely present – as can be perceived in the numerous accounts (from both perspectives) of the evils of colonisation and the suffering it produced. Yet neo-Victorian narrative does figure the return of the repressed in another manner; for it presents that which the Victorians could not articulate about themselves, as we have already suggested above, not because they were ashamed but because theirs was also a material and historical condition of historicised traumatism, and thus a communal mutism,

---

[19] Let us specify that the ever acute potency of the Victorian past is equally valid for the Western, post-imperial subject traumatised by historical guilt and for the non-Western subject haunted by the colonial suffering of its ancestors. Haunting and spectrality are crucial neo-Victorian tropes as Kohlke clearly explains: "spectrality links to the neo-Victorian's preoccupation with liberating lost voices and repressed histories of minorities left out of the public record and, hence, with imagining more viable ways of living with one another in the future. It is no coincidence that Jacques Derrida's deliberations on hauntology should begin with Karl Marx, that great nineteenth-century would-be liberator of the oppressed working classes. Derrida's hauntology too evinces a simultaneous retrospective and future orientation" (Kohlke 2008: 9).

wh_ch it is the burden of the postmodern to bear witness to. To explain this further, any moment of traumatism, culturally speaking, takes place as part of the epochal events that condition and make it possible. It thus bears the signs of its own historicity, and yet, because the traumatic event becomes repressed as such, its traces – those traces wh ch are also the signs of the times, as it were – only return belatedly, remaining to be decrypted, and frequently misread, mistranslated. Neo-Victorian narrative lays bare the traumatisation of our cultural others and, in showing the trauma, returns to us the signs of its historicity. At the same time, though, in revealing that which the Victorians themselves could not necessarily read, or even see, about themselves, given that they were 'in the moment' as it were, then that insight which the neo-Victorian text offers is also structured by a concomitant and inescapable blindness about its own historical moment of inscription and interpretation.

So two hermeneutic assumptions can be formulated to try and understand the genesis of the neo-Victorian phenomenon. Either one can put forward the traumatic sense of loss and utter faithlessness of the postmodern condition's "radical and pervasive state of disenchantment" (Maltby 2007: 42), and the quest for a frame of reference supposedly predating and avoiding the modern sense of cris s, fragmentation and disintegration. Or one can argue for the lingering trauma embodied by the catastrophic failure of the Victorian imperial era, which found a fertile ground in the challenging of grand narratives of early postmodernism and in the ethical revival of late postmodernism. As Dianne Sadoff explains elsewhere in this collection, neo-Victorianism allows us "to view Victorian writing itself as informed by a traumatic sense of national experience which, repressed and un-cognised at the time, continues to haunt us in the modern world" (this volume: 163-164). A third, and possibly more convincing, hypothesis comes inevitably to mind: the decisive factor may be the echo, similitude and conjunction of the two types of trauma and the two situations of deprivation. The shattering of the Victorian imperial world may be said to find its apotheosis in the axiological atomisation effected within the postmodern sphere. Similarly, the postmodern tendency towards epistemological, ontological and ethical doubt, if not outright nihilism, may have its origins in the Darwinian crisis and the Victorian religious and ideological upheavals.[20]

6.   Entanglement and the Ethics of Bearing Witness

Trauma, then, is not only the *cause* of postmodernism's regressive quest in time, it is also the *common point* between the contemporary and the Victorian periods. As Caruth perceptively points out,

> in a catastrophic age [...] trauma itself may provide the very link between cultures: not as a simple understanding of the pasts of others but rather, within the traumas of contemporary history, as our ability to listen through the departures we have all taken from ourselves. (Caruth 1995: 11)

Caruth insists on the connective propensity of trauma by underlining "the way in which one's own trauma is tied up with the trauma of another" and by contending "that history, like trauma, is never simply one's own, that history is precisely the way we are implicated in each other's traumas" (Caruth 1996: 8; 24). As these quotations show, trauma – or rather the reflection upon trauma – has in itself an ethical virtue, since it entails an exodus from oneself and an openness to the traumas of others. In his review of Caruth's work, Petar Ramadanovic stresses the ethical and adjunctive quality of trauma that "chart[s] a history of the modern subject as a history of implication" (Ramadanovic 1998: 55). According to Ramadanovic, entanglement constitutes the main trope of trauma, and not only in Caruth's approach to the topic. The notion of entanglement has a clear ethical dimension, since "my trauma is (tied to) the trauma of another", as well as a historical dimension, since "the past is repeated and reversed in the present, and the present is projected back onto the past" (Ramadanovic 1998: 62). It also represents "a vantage point from which to define the modern predicament of mutually entangled histories, communities and writings" (Jacobus 1998: 3). Entanglement thus defined, it seems to us, is equally operative in neo-Victorian

---

[20] This last argument ties up with Dianne F. Sadoff and John Kucich's main thesis that "the cultural matrix of nineteenth-century England joined various and possible stories about cultural rupture that, taken together, overdetermine the period's availability for the postmodern exploration of cultural emergence" (Sadoff and Kucich 2000: xv).

fiction, with the contemporary insistence on the Victorians' predicaments – arguably a reflection (or a projection) of our own predicaments. Are the explorations of neo-Victorianism, employing the tools and cultural contexts of postmodernism, not an obvious means to suggest and encourage a dialectic comparison between the past and the present? The entanglement inherent in trauma is then also inherent in neo-Victorian fiction, a concurrence which seems to further bind neo-Victorian fiction to trauma.

What Ramadanovic also clarifies is that entanglement, the inextricable tie between the traumatised self and the traumatised other, "summons us – 'us' – to responsibility", a responsibility that "consists of an overturning of the I so that the other is revealed", a responsibility that marks "the advent of the other and of the 'we' as other to itself" (Ramadanovic 1998: 63). The discovery of the self in the other and of the other in the self is very much the experience of neo-Victorian fiction, which goes beyond the trauma of postmodernism and accepts the responsibility to account for the (Victorian) other: in this, neo-Victorian fiction corresponds to Ann E. Kaplan's "ethics of witnessing", i.e., the obligation "to expose the structure of injustice and to invite viewers to take responsibility for related specific injustice" (Kaplan 2005: 135). In this ethical responsibility there is also the implication of the ultimate ethical position and subjective atomisation, expressed epigrammatically by Jacques Derrida in the phrase, "*tout autre est tout autre*", implying "every other is completely (wholly and completely) other" (Derrida 1995: 82). As a result, I must do justice to each and every other, and yet this is impossible; I cannot. In recognising this atomisation of subjectivity, there has to be admitted the traumatic realisation of an ever-extendible horizon of infinite and absolute responsibility. My duty is non-negotiable, but in attending to that responsibility to an other, I must sacrifice others. And every time I do justice to the other, bear witness, or take responsibility, I reconstruct implicitly the sacrifice of an other or others. Note that this ethical task does not derive from the experience of trauma but from the reconstruction of trauma. Because trauma is not registered at the moment of its occurrence, it is only its reconstruction in narrative form that actually constitutes the registration of trauma and the beginning of coming to terms with it. The trauma narrative, then, is essentially performative, because "the knowledge [of the trauma] *does not exist*, it can only *happen* through the testimony" (Felman and Laub 1992: 51). To follow this logic through, bearing witness to an other causes the reconstruction of trauma to take place through attestation. Similarly, it could be argued that the entanglement with the other is first created by the discursive projection into the individualised past(s). Hence the ethical function of neo-Victorian fiction is likewise performative.

By embracing an ethics of witnessing, neo-Victorian fiction

> requires a highly collaborative relationship between speaker and listener. The listener bears a dual responsibility: to receive the testimony but also to avoid appropriating the story as his or her own. A fragile balance is engendered between the necessity to witness sympathetically that which testimonial writing cannot fully represent and a simultaneous respect for the otherness of the experience. (Whitehead 2004: 7)

By shifting its perspective from the self to the other, or by integrating the other's perspective into the perspective of the self, neo-Victorian fiction (as a phenomenon of postmodernism) "readjusts the relationship between reader and text, so that reading is restored as an ethical practice" (Whitehead 2004: 8). Far from being delegitimated as an axiological trace of Enlightenment, ethics, then, is restored to the central place of the narrative apparatus in neo-Victorian fiction, doubly so in contemporary narratives of trauma.

7.   An Ethics of Truths
"To bear witness" is also "to take responsibility for truth" (Felman and Laub 1992: 204). Superficially, to assume the responsibility for truth in works of fiction might seem paradoxical. However, as soon as one considers the fictional dimension of testimonies (and of history) in parallel with the testimonial (and historical) dimension of fiction, it becomes clear that the purpose of testimony, as defined by Felman and Laub, can also be the purpose of fiction. Rather than dwell on the documentary aspect of neo-Victorian fiction and its common use of historical information and data, we want to focus on the equally common practice of pastiche, considered as a narrative and discursive form devoted to retrieving the lost truth of a singular voice. Pastiche is

not only the reproduction of a linguistic code but also of a referential and cultural context. When Byatt tries to reconstruct the testimony of an erotophobic housewife in *Possession*, when Swift imagines the intimate reflections of an honest apostate in *Ever After*, when Patricia Duncker projects herself into the thought-process of a cross-dressed colonial doctor in *James Miranda Barry* (1999), when Emma Tennant strives to conjure up the recollections of the victim of incestuous rapes in *Tess* (1993), they all seek to come as close as possible to the truth of a particular language and experience at a particular moment in history. Each instance of pastiche represents a quest for a fragment of individual truth, so it should be clear that the truth which is at stake here is not an absolute concept but a relative and plural one. The use of truth, yet another Enlightenment value, is typical of neo-Victorian fiction's postmodernist principle: it rehabilitates the concept but at the same time redefines it and broadens its epistemological horizons. By deconstructing and reconstructing truth as a plural concept neo-Victorian fiction complies with Alain Badiou's "ethics of truths", considered as "processes of truths" (Badiou 2001: 28), which can only always be particularised – never abstracted or rendered absolute.

Bearing in mind that in Greek, *a-letheia*, which is the very name of truth, also means non-forgetting (Davoine and Gaudillère 2005: 36), the refusal to forget, implicit in the neo-Victorian quest for truths, reveals a thoroughly ethical character. So pastiche, seen in the light of a discursive attempt to capture glimpses of truth, can be said to invalidate Jameson's accusation of "the necessary failure of [postmodern] art and the aesthetic, […] the imprisonment in the past" (Jameson 1985: 116). On the contrary, pastiche embodies a communion with the past, an ethical contiguity with the historical other. Inasmuch as the practice of pastiche implies an attempt at understanding, synthesising and reproducing another's way of speaking and thinking, it undeniably stands for a form of empathy, what Levinas describes as "the new modality of faith today" (qtd. Cohen 2001: 277). The neo-Victorian's vocation, then, appears to be a movement favouring pastiche to look for an empathic, and hence ethical, concurrence with the other.

8.   The Unpresentable, the Sublime and at Last Jubilation
As contended by Andrew Gibson, one of postmodernism's privileged tropes is monstrosity, for "postmodern aesthetics […] is in large

measure an aesthetics of the monstrous" (Gibson 1996: 244). Gibson proceeds to argue that

> the monstrous is that which is exiled by the normative judgements, [...] epistemic illegitimacy understood as outrage in or against nature, [...] the otherness that undermines any concept of man as unitary, knowable being. (Gibson 1996: 238-239)

Hence, the monstrous represents not only an epistemological and ontological challenge to the humanity of the human but also an ethical reminder of the potential othernesses of the human. In its fascination with monsters, neo-Victorian fiction once again follows the postmodernist trend and raises the ethical question of the limits of the human. Neo-Victorian monsters include the criminal, as in Peter Ackroyd's *Dan Leno and the Limehouse Golem* (1994), Matthew Kneale's *English Passengers* (2000), Julie Myerson's *Laura Blundy* (2000) or Margaret Atwood's *Alias Grace* (1996), the sexual 'deviant', as in James Buxton's *Pity* (1997), Emma Tennant's *Tess* (1993), or A.S. Byatt's *Angels and Insects* (1992), and the freakish products of evolutionary mysteries, whether actual, as in Liz Jensen's *Ark Baby* (1998) and Graham Swift's *Ever After* (1992), or possible products of con-artistry, as in Angela Carter's *Nights at the Circus* (1984). When David Mitchell extends the notion of the monstrous and narratively links nineteenth-century aboriginals – "just one rung up from the great apes" (Mitchell 2004: 507) – to post-apocalyptic clones, he illustrates the very postmodern conception of monsters as "theorized and fabricated hybrids of machine and organism" (Haraway 1991: 150), concrete manifestations of the ever-evolving and ever-problematic conceptualisation of the human. To know how different the other can be also means to question how different 'I' can be and therefore to open oneself up to various forms of otherness. Since the monstrous incarnates a form of mystery, those probing the mystery also commit themselves to an ethical task. Indeed, as Elena Andonova-Kalapsazova explains, "[t]he surrendering to this mystery" – i.e. the mystery of the other's irreducibility to predetermined moulds – "which signals the event of re-enchantment of the impersonal space, is for Levinas part of the process in which the ethical subject is constituted" (Andonova-Kalapsazova 2007: 15).

Equally crucial is that "the idea of the monstrous is linked to and partly interchangeable with that of the unnameable" (Gibson 1996: 242), a quality which cannot but recall trauma itself. Indeed, over and over again, trauma is described in its "essential incomprehensibility" (Caruth 1995: 154), as "the unspeakable" (Herman 1992: 175), "the unsayable" (Edkins 2003: 7), a case of "unrepresentability" (Kaplan 2005: 37), and of "unspeakableness" (Lloyd 2000: 214).[21] This linguistic and conceptual impossibility affects the victims of trauma in particular, because their experience "demands not just an amnesic response but actually denies the very existence of a subject that could remember" (Lloyd 2000: 214). The situation is quite different for the subjects of a non-event-based type of trauma, such as the postmodern sense of deprivation, and even more so for the literary witnesses or novelistic spokespersons of vicarious trauma, such as neo-Victorian novelists. For the latter, it must be admitted, trauma has an extraordinary narrative potential, in addition to the ethical pathways it provides. The dramatic circumstances surrounding the catastrophe, the narrative tension preceding the shock, the powerful affects that are brought into play, all of these convey a sort of tragic intensity to the account and favour strategies of narrative deferral, targeted descriptions and discursive diversification (in order to capture the moments of emotional upheavals). So the unspeakableness of trauma is paradoxically what arouses and encourages speech in the fictional restitutions of the topic. To speak the unspeakable, to say the unsayable, then, becomes neo-Victorian fiction's specifically poetic task in the sense of a fictional attempt at a linguistic re-creation of trauma.

To represent the unrepresentable inevitably also recalls Lyotard's conception of the sublime as that which "puts forward the unpresentable in presentation itself" (Lyotard 1984: 81). If one takes into consideration Lyotard's staunch rejection of "the solace of good forms" and his defence of "an aesthetics of silence and negation [which] must remain in a sphere resistant to conceptual understanding" (Waugh 1992: 31), then it becomes clear that neo-Victorian fiction's treatment of the unpresentable cannot correspond

---

[21] The same aspect is underlined in the French studies of the topic. Arnaud Tellier in particular evokes "l'indicible", "l'ineffable", "l'inimaginable", "ce qui échappe à être dit" (Tellier 1998: 15, 89) – which could be translated as "the unsayable", "the ineffable", "the unimaginable", "what evades telling".

to Lyotard's sublime, bent as it is on breaking the silences of trauma and on rehabilitating "conceptual understanding". On the other hand, since the sublime also "indicates a mixed feeling of pleasure and pain: simultaneous attraction and repulsion, awe and terror" (Malpas 2005: 29), it can hardly be said to be absent from the ambiguous process of writing trauma with its painful evocation of shock (of an empathic or personal nature) and its exhilarating process of narrative transfiguration. Hence, we would argue that with its emphasis on the awe-inspiring experiences of trauma, its numerous attempts at presenting the unpresentable, and its revelation of atrocity and resilience, neo-Victorian fiction cultivates a form of the sublime, not of a Lyotardian kind but of a kind that reveals the infinite possibilities of suffering humanity. Moreover, in trying to come to terms with the traumas of empire, an entire period, or even two entire periods (the Victorian and the postmodern), this form of the sublime assumed an epic dimension. Through the retrieval of this epic dimension, the neo-Victorian movement has acquired what could be called a post-imperial scope, which holds a wide-ranging appeal for writers and readers alike.

Undeniably then, there can be "thriving in the wake of trauma" to borrow the title of Thema Bryant-Davis's work. Thriving "requires empowerment", "regaining" or "actually finding one's voice" (Bryant-Davis 2005: 6), or restoring others' one-time silenced voices, and writing, narrating or presenting trauma manifestly represents such a form of empowerment. Ramadanovic goes further still to suggest that "the possibility of the transmission of the repetition of trauma, may function as a strategy of prolonging compulsion repetition and of guaranteeing *jouissance*" (Ramadanovic 2001: 117). The jubilation in question does not, or at least does not only ensure the repetitive re-consideration of trauma; in other words it not only constitutes an enjoyment of one's symptom. It also stems from the overcoming of the symptom, from the exodus from the self, from the gift of transmission. The transcription of trauma in general and in neo-Victorian fiction in particular is always an overt or covert celebration of resilience, a gratifying act of transformation from passivity to agency, from affliction to production, from withdrawal to opening up, from possible annihilation to actual creation, from a sense of loss to a sense of enrichment. The postmodern trauma of loss, which constitutes the origin of the neo-Victorian movement, is simultaneously the cause of its testimonial jubilation. By opening up to the Victorian other and by voicing Victorian traumas as harbingers/echoes of, and foils for, postmodern suffering, neo-Victorian fiction establishes a novelistic principle that is always comparative, bi-historical and ambi-cultural. It manages not only to rehabilitate ethics but also to combine ethics and aesthetics, a combination that heralds a form of postmodernism revisited.

Bibliography

Andonova-Kalapsazova, Elena. 2007. 'Shakespeare's Pastoral Romance *The Tempest* and the Levinasian Component in the Ethics of John Fowles's *The Magus*'. In Onega and Ganteau (2007): 10-30.

Antze, Paul, and Michael Lambek (eds.). 2006. *Tense Past: Cultural Essays in Trauma and Memory*. London & New York: Routledge.

Armstrong, Tim. 2000. *Haunted Hardy: Poetry, History, Memory*. Basingstoke: Palgrave.

Badiou, Alain. 2001. *Ethics: An Essay on the Understanding of Evil (Wo Es War)* (tr. Peter Hallward). London & New York: Verso.

Barry, Peter. 2002. *Beginning Theory: An Introduction to Literary and Cultural Theory*. Manchester: Manchester University Press.

Barthes, Roland. 1997. *Image – Music – Text* (tr. and ed. Stephen Heath). London: Fontana Cape.

Baudrillard, Jean. 1983. *Simulations* (tr. Paul Foss, Paul Patton and Philip Beitchman). New York: Semiotext(e).

——. 1994. *The Illusion of the End* (tr. Chris Turner). Cambridge: Polity Press.

Bracken, Patrick. 2002. *Trauma: Culture, Meaning and Philosophy*. London & Philadelphia: Whurr.

Bryant-Davis, Thema. 2005. *Thriving in the Wake of Trauma: A Multicultural Guide*. Westport, Connecticut: Praeger.

Byatt A.S. 1990. *Possession: A Romance*. London: Chatto & Windus.

——. 2000. *The Biographer's Tale*. London: Chatto & Windus.

Callus, Ivan, and Stefan Herbrechter. 2004. 'The Latecoming of the Posthuman, Or Why "We" Do the Apocalypse Differently Now', *Reconstruction: A Journal of Interdisciplinary Culture* 4(3): (s.p.).

Caruth, Cathy (ed.). 1995. *Trauma: Explorations in Memory*. Baltimore, Maryland: The Johns Hopkins University Press.

——. 1996. *Unclaimed Experience: Trauma, Narrative, and History*. Baltimore, Maryland: The Johns Hopkins University Press.

Cohen, Richard. 2001. *Ethics, Exegesis and Philosophy. Interpretation after Levinas*. Cambridge: Cambridge University Press.

Craps Stef. 2005. *Trauma and Ethics in the Novels of Graham Swift: No Short-Cuts to Salvation*. Brighton, Portland: Sussex Academic Press.

Davoine, Françoise, and Jean-Max Gaudillère. 2006. *Histoire et Trauma : La folie des guerres*. Paris: Stock.

Derrida, Jacques. 1976. *Of Grammatology* (tr. Gayatri Chakravorty Spivak). Baltimore, Maryland: The Johns Hopkins University Press.

——. 1984. 'Of an Apocalyptic Tone in Recent Philosophy' (tr. John P. Leavey), *Oxford Literary Review* 6(2): 3-37.

——. 1989. *Limited Inc* (ed. Gerald Graff, tr. Samuel Weber). 2nd edn. Evanston: Northwestern University Press.

——. 2008. *The Gift of Death. Second Edition. Literature in Secret* [1995] (tr. David Wills). Chicago: University of Chicago Press.

Eco, Umberto. 1987. *Faith in Fakes: Travels in Hyperreality.* London: Picador.

Edkins, Jenny. 2003. *Trauma and the Memory of Politics.* Cambridge: Cambridge University Press.

Ellis, John M. 1989. *Against Deconstruction.* Princeton, New Jersey: Princeton University Press.

Felman, Shoshana and Dori Laub (eds.). 1992. *Testimony: Crises of Witnessing in Literature, Psychoanalysis, and History.* New York and London: Routledge.

Foster, Hal (ed.). 1983. *The Anti-Aesthetics: Essays on Postmodern Culture.* Port Townsend, Washington: Bay Press.

Geddes, Jennifer. 2007. 'Attending the Suffering in / at the Wake of Postmodernism', in Brooks, Neil, and Josh Toth (eds.), *The Mourning After: Attending the Wake of Postmodernism.* Amsterdam and New York: Rodopi: 65-78.

Gibson, Andrew. 1996. *Towards a postmodern theory of narrative.* Edinburgh: Edinburgh University Press.

——. 1999. *Postmodernity, ethics and the novel: From Leavis to Levinas.* London & New York: Routledge.

Gutleben, Christian. 2009/2010. 'Shock Tactics: The Art of Linking and Transcending Victorian and Postmodern Traumas in Graham Swift's *Ever After*', *Neo-Victorian Studies* 2(2) (Winter 2009/2010): 137-156.

Haraway, Donna. 1991. *Simians, Cyborgs, and Women: The Reinvention of Nature.* London: Free Association Books.

Herman, Judith Lewis. 1992. *Trauma and Recovery.* New York: Basic Books.

Jacobus, Mary. 1998. 'Preface'. *Diacritics* 28(4): 3-4.

Jameson, Frederic. 1983. 'Postmodernism and Consumer Society', in Foster (1983): 111-125.

——. 1991. *Postmodernism, or the Cultural Logic of Late Capitalism.* London: Verso.

Kaplan, Ann E. 2005. *Trauma Culture: The Politics of Terror and Loss in Media and Literature.* New Brunswick, New Jersey & London: Rutgers University Press.

Kohlke, Marie-Luise. 2008. 'Introduction: Speculations in and on the Neo-Victorian Encounter', *Neo-Victorian Studies* 1(1) (Autumn): 1-18.

Kugelman, Jack. 1996. 'Missions to the Past. Poland in Contemporary Jewish Thought', in Antze and Lambek (eds.) (1996): 199-214.

Lacan, Jacques. 1977. *Ecrits. A Selection* (tr. Alan Sheridan). New York: Norton.

LaCapra, Dominick. 1994. *Representing the Holocaust: History, Theory, Trauma.* Ithaca: Cornell University Press.

——. 2001. *Writing History, Writing Trauma.* Baltimore & London: The Johns Hopkins University Press.

Levinas, Emmanuel. 1964. *Totality and Infinity* (tr. Alphonso Lingis). Pittsburgh: Duquesne University Press.

Lloyd, David. 2000. 'Colonial Trauma / Postcolonial Recovery?' *Interventions* 2(2): 212-228.

Lodge, David. 1989. *Nice Work.* Harmondsworth: Penguin.

Lyotard, Jean-François. 1984. *The Postmodern Condition: A Report on Knowledge* (tr. Geoffrey Bennington and Bian Massumi). Manchester: Manchester University Press.

——. 1988. *The Differend: phrases in dispute* (tr. Georges van den Abbeele). Minneapolis: University of Minnesota Press.

——. 1991. *The Inhuman: Reflections on Time* (tr. Geoffrey Bennington and Rachel Bowlby). Cambridge: Polity Press.

Malpas, Simon. 2005. *The Postmodern.* The New Critical Idiom. London and New York: Routledge.

Maltby, Paul. 2007. 'Postmodernism in a Fundamentalist Arena', in Brooks, Neil, and Josh Toth (eds.), *The Mourning After: Attending the Wake of Postmodernism.* Amsterdam and New York: Rodopi: 16-51.

Miller, J. Hillis / Asensi, Manuel. 1999. *Black Holes / J. Hillis Miller; or, Bloustrophedonic Reading.* Stanford, California: Stanford University Press.

Mitchell, David. 2004. *Cloud Atlas.* London: Sceptre.

Norris, Christopher. 1990. *What's Wrong with Postmodernism: Critical Theory and the Ends of Philosophy.* New York: Harvester Wheatsheaf.

O'Neil, Patrick. 1990. *The Comedy of Entropy: Humour / Narrative / Reading.* Toronto: University of Toronto Press.

Onega, Susana and Jean-Michel Ganteau (eds.). 2007. *The Ethical Component in Experimental British Fiction since the 1960's.* Newcastle: Cambridge Scholars Publishing.

Ramadanovic, Petar. 1998. 'When *"To Die In Freedom"* Is Written in English'. *Diacritics* 28(4): 54-67.

Rothberg, Michael. 2008. 'Decolonizing Trauma Studies: A Response'. *Studies in the Novel* 40(1-2) (Spring & Summer): 224-234.

Sadoff, Dianne F., and John Kucich (eds). 2000. 'Introduction: Histories of the Present', in Kucich, John, and Dianne F. Sadoff (eds.), *Victorian Afterlife: Postmodern Culture Rewrites the Nineteenth Century.* Minneapolis: University of Minnesota Press: ix-xxx.

Sim, Stuart (ed.). 2001. *The Routledge Companion to Postmodernism.* London: Routledge.

Tellier, Arnaud. 1998. *Expériences traumatiques et écriture.* Paris: Anthropos.

Swift, Graham. 1992. *Ever After.* London: Picador.

Thomas, D.M. 2000. *Charlotte.* London: Duck Editions.

Van Styvendale, Nancy. 2008. 'The Trans/Historicity of Trauma in Jeanette Armstrong's *Slash* and Sherman Alexis's *Indian Killer'*, *Studies in the Novel* 40(1-2) (Spring & Summer): 203-223.

Waugh, Patricia. 1992. *Practising Postmodernism Reading Modernism.* London: Edward Arnold.

Whitehead, Anne. 2004. *Trauma Fiction.* Edinburgh: Edinburgh University Press.

Trauma by Proxy in the "Age of Testimony": Paradoxes of Darwinism in the Neo-Victorian Novel

Georges Letissier

Abstract:
This paper assesses the appropriation of the Darwinian legacy by neo-Victorian novelists. It argues that the subjective, affective consequences of potentially traumatising scientific discoveries are what such novels investigate. Darwinian science, by providing an accessible discourse to the non-initiates, and by raising fundamental existential questions, appeal to contemporary twenty-first-century readers. Instead of responding to the latest scientific changes, neo-Victorian fictions opt for a form of temporal distancing which in fact could already be observed in the Victorian era. From individual narcissistic wound to postcolonial trauma, the impact of Darwinism on neo-Victorian novels is wide-ranging. The approaches are equally varied, covering a whole spectrum from the frustration or despair of those who saw the collapse of all their values (FitzRoy and Covington) to the commitment of those who saw in evolution the possibility of founding a new humanism (*Human Traces*).

Keywords: catastrophic imagery, crisis of faith, Darwinism, freedom, postcolonial mimicry, schizophrenia, *second order* loss, testimony, witnessing.

*****

Through its concern for Darwinian science the neo-Victorian novel shows its commitment to contemporary issues and escapes charges of "decadent sentimentalism, nostalgia or spurious liberalism" (Kohlke 2008: 9). The chief question raised by the nineteenth-century Darwinian revolution was how to found moral values in a world deprived of any transcendent ruling principle – a question more pertinent than ever in the "Age of Testimony" (Felman 1992: 53). Darwinian evolution and its many contemporary developments, such as population genetics, teleology, or evolutionary biology, have triggered many ethical debates in their wake, frequently echoed in neo-Victorian fictions. The shock encounter with prehistoric skeletons

– n itself emblematic of man's sudden confrontation with
des abilising, scientific data – has been treated as trauma in a novel
like Graham Swift's *Ever After* (1992). Other neo-Victorian texts
evince an overlap with the postcolonial trauma subgenre, as in
Matthew Kneale's *English Passengers* (2000), which relates the
Darwinian question to warped racial theories.

Turning to the question of the Darwinian influence on neo-
Victorian fiction inevitably leads to historicising trauma.[1] Indeed, the
two previously mentioned novels, and others like Roger McDonald's
Mr Darwin's Shooter (1998), Harry Thompson's *This Thing of
Darkness* (2005), or Sebastian Faulks's *Human Traces* (2005), do not
so much seek to come to grips with the latest, potentially disturbing –
when not utterly traumatising – developments of twenty-first-century
science, as they attempt to recreate the historic circumstances of the
deeply unsettling discoveries of the past, conjuring up what Sally
Shuttleworth presents as trauma at one remove, i.e. *second order
trauma*, or trauma by proxy (Shuttleworth 1998: 260). The reception
of contemporary science broaches bio-ethical issues entailed by
biotechnology, in vitro fertilization (IVF), reproductive cloning and
the attendant questions of life's beginnings, through embryology to
the end of life, euthanasia, brain death, and physician-assisted suicide
(see Hull and Ruse 2007). Neo-Victorian fiction, however, transposes
these existential debates on to a more metaphysical plane, for example
by reviving the conflict between natural theologians and evolutionists
(in John Fowles's *The French Lieutenant's Woman* (1969), *Ever
After*, A.S. Byatt's 'Morpho Eugenia' (1992), or *This Thing of
Darkness* among others), or by setting the current interrogation on
human origins within the historical context of late nineteenth-century
anthropological investigations in a novel like *Human Traces*. The
result is what Shuttleworth perceptively diagnosed as "a displacement
of current fears", not just "concerning the indivisibility of man and
machine" (Shuttleworth 1998: 259), but also bearing on other crucial,
aporetic concerns about identity, the self, and the human. At a time
when bio-medicine redefines the boundary lines of what may fall

---

[1] Historicising trauma is also a matter of concern for Victorian scholarship; see for
example the recent article by Jill L. Matus, 'Historicizing Trauma: The Genealogy of
Psychic Shock in *Daniel Deronda*' (Matus 2008: 59-78).

under the category of *life*, mind and body (or spirit and flesh) oppositions become an area of riddling, unsolvable contradiction.[2]

The central question is therefore how the return to Darwin's writings and, more widely, to Darwin's scientific and cultural context, relays present preoccupations amongst contemporary readers. Does this historicising of a traumatic historical moment – roughly from the 1859 publication of *On the Origin of Species* to the 1871 appearance of *The Descent of Man, and Selection in Relation to Sex* – blunt the impact of the epistemological earthquake that occurred then, or are history-bound scientific discourses but an alibi for a literary treatment of a form of trauma that is actually more relevant to twentieth- and twenty-first-century readers?

1.   Darwinism and the Individual Crisis of Faith

The history of the neo-Victorian novel started with Jean Rhys's *Wide Sargasso Sea* (1966), which does not deal with scientific subjects, but with Fowles's *The French Lieutenant's Woman* in 1969 a new current was set up. Indeed, according to Byatt, this landmark fiction initiated a trend by being "one of the first [texts] of what is almost a genre", whose concern went far beyond fossil-hunting expeditions of Victorian gentlemen in Lyme Regis (Byatt 2000: 78). Fowles actually introduced two topics that were taken up by a number of subsequent neo-Victorian fictions, namely the crisis of faith induced by the Development Hypothesis and the possibility of human freedom in a nature indifferent to man's purpose. Fowles's double temporal perspective, combining a nineteenth-century protagonist and an overtly twentieth-century narrator, allows both the insertion of passages from Darwin's *On the Origin of Species* as epigraphs, and the inclusion of what a contemporary novelist imagines their effects to have been on the consciousness of a prototypical Victorian gentleman, named Charles Smithson. Arguably, this process of displacement is in itself consistent with the logic of belatedness that is inherent in trauma (Caruth 1996: 17), as is shown by Dianne F. Sadoff through the concept of *Nachträglichkeit* in this volume. The three citations from *On the Origin of Species* inserted in *The French Lieutenant's Woman* raise seminal questions that are frequently re-encountered in later neo-

---

[2] New perspectives can be opened, for instance, by starting the investigation from the close proximity with a mentally-ill character, as Faulks convincingly does with Olivier in *Human Traces*.

Victorian fictions: the deterministic influence of inheritance (Chapter Three); the ruthless Malthusian law of the gap between population growth and food increase, and the advantage that adaptive capacities confer upon some chosen individuals (Chapter Nineteen); and finally how natural selection leads to the formation of new species, alongside the extinction of others, and how those who are the closest to changing improving specimens suffer the most (Chapter Fifty). Fowles's novel clearly highlights the way in which the new intellectual paradigms devised by evolutionary biology led to a revised perception of the self. This is done both by establishing the inner division of the formerly unified subject and by presenting freedom as a hard-won and traumatising experience. It is hinted that Charles has not quite fathomed the import of the new theory which he has recently espoused: "Charles called himself a Darwinist, and yet he had not really understood Darwin. But then, nor had Darwin himself" (Fowles 1982: 47; see also Jackson 1997: 221). The novel thus opens on an experience of self-alienation, with both the amateur geologist and the originator of a revolutionary theory figured as in a sense being intellectually dispossessed, i.e. not quite able to correlate the principles of evolution with their common daily perception of the world surrounding them. Charles knows for a fact that the Linnaean theory of a fixed creation, where everything could be meticulously itemised and classified and where "*nulla species nova:* a new species cannot enter the world" (Fowles 1982: 47), is sheer nonsense. Yet he cannot refrain from seeing in Lyme's liassic cliffs a proof of the edifice of time, governed by inexorable laws. What Fowles demonstrates is the psychic split induced by the emergence of new theories. The heated debates in which Smithson engages with his future father-in-law only serve to turn the reader's attention away from the essential fact that the clash of ideas is first and foremost an inner mental form of self-estrangement. It is lodged within Smithson's own mind, so that the bravura sallies he addresses to his creationist challengers are, to some extent, a pose. The self-estranging consequence of such a crisis of truth, when the intellect grasps what the mind, steeped in habits, refuses to acknowledge, is precisely what neo-Victorian novels like *Ever After* or *This Thing of Darkness* foreground. In a way, such texts stage a variation on the narcissistic wound, as the subject finds himself punished by the knowledge he has acquired and by his inability to reconcile his private intellectual self with his social conventional self. By the forces of circumstance, this results in Charles being progressively self-ostracised from the rest of the community. Metaphorically, he becomes the stock character of the Victorian novel, namely the orphan. In *Ever After*, after becoming convinced of the scientific validity of the struggle for existence theory, the Victorian Matthew Pearce is reduced to merely going through the motions of conversations with his nearest and dearest – haunting his own life as if he were a ghost:

> It is his conscience which causes Matthew to question his faith on the basis of his readings of Lyell and Darwin, and to face the consequences of his apostasy. He even professes "to have a conscience about having a conscience"; that is concerned not to worry his wife unduly by revealing the full extent of his spiritual torment, he decided to keep his religious doubts to himself in the years leading up to the final showdown. (Craps 2005: 139)

As is clear from Matthew Pearce's predicament in *Ever After*, Darwinian science confronts the solitary individual with a dilemma between pretending to go on with one's life as if no radical change had upset one's psyche – thus opting for what Swift designates as "make belief" (Swift 1992: 101), that is sham and pretence – and bracing oneself for the final showdown and the likelihood of social exclusion in its aftermath. In the neo-Victorian novel, the callous eliminatory laws that rule the species in the biological world are shown to apply equally to those who make the rash decision to act according to their newly-acquired conviction. In other words, following the dictates of one's conscience, being true to oneself and making use of one's free will in a Darwinian world – which is by definition ever-changing, fluid and metamorphic – is fraught with dire personal consequences. This is why Fowles resorted to Sartrean existentialism in his attempt at defining the plight of the Darwinian and post-Darwinian man, for whom freedom is of necessity always exerted at some cost:

> He [Charles] had not the benefit of existentialist terminology; but what he felt was really a very clear

> case of the anxiety of freedom – that is, the realization
> that one *is* free and the realization that being free is a
> situation of terror. (Fowles 1982: 296, original
> emphasis)

In Chapter Forty-Eight, Charles's decision to break off the
constraining bonds of inheritance is treated as an inverted Damascus
epiphany. In the solitude of an empty church where he has locked
himself, Charles perceives as a revelation the fact that the purpose of
the crucifixion does not lie in the sacrifice made for the benefit of
mankind. He further interprets the necessity to uncrucify Jesus, nailed
on his cross, as an imperious call of conscience. Tennyson's fifty-first
canto from *In Memoriam* (1851) is quoted, only to be spurned: "*There
must be wisdom with great Death; the dead shall look me thro' and
thro*'" (qtd. Fowles 1982: 316, original emphasis). In this agonising
episode, in which Charles does not want to forego his faith, though
rejecting the morbid pressure of religion that forces one to fear the
judgment of the dead, Fowles summons up a highly Darwinian
moment. Indeed, the main protagonist is caught up between the
hecatomb of past generations of deceased, the "[w]orn names and
dates, last fossil remains of other lives", and the unknown future of the
species, or "one's unborn sons" (Fowles 1982: 312, 316). At this
crossroads between past and future, Charles is about to take a leap into
the unknown by throwing off "the ghostly presence of the past
condemn[ing] him [...] to a life in the grave" (Fowles 1982: 316).
Significantly, he experiences a blasphemous vision of Sarah
Woodruff, the French lieutenant's woman, standing in for the cross on
which he feels himself destined to be crucified. In this passage, the
"decisive crisis of faith" and "the ecstatic agony of indecision", which
Shuttleworth saw as the emblematic tokens of the retro-Victorian
novel, are meticulously rendered by deploying blatant trauma
symptoms (Fowles 1998: 260). Charles finds himself assailed by an
upsurge of conflicting emotions, "pac[ing] up and down, his eyes on
the paving stones" (Fowles 1982: 316). His sense of self is blurred, as
his brain can no longer channel and process the onslaught of images
confusingly summoning up an uncertain future: "A cascade of
concrete visions [...] poured through his mind" (Fowles 1982: 316).
Typically, the state of emotional turmoil is suggested through a highly
connoted Victorian trope: the split self. Charles is both staring at the

cross and fantasising that he himself is hanging on the crucifix. Paradoxically, Sarah is now pointing the way towards uncrucifixion (see Fawkner 1984: 81-85).

A somewhat perplexing dialogue begins to form between his better and his worse selves, which may involve Christ's voice too. The enunciation process further complicates the situation, as the voice addressing Charles can be his own better self, a mental projection of Jesus addressing the distraught sinner, or the narrator lecturing the character directly. All in all, the scene stages an unresolved crisis of faith, as the character is prompted to relinquish his former beliefs while remaining enmeshed in insurmountable inner contradictions. The aporetic moment – in the etymological sense of an impassable path – is illustrated by Charles's last-minute impulse, just before leaving the church: "He turned then and went back to his pew; and did something very irrational, since he knelt and prayed, though very briefly" (Fowles 1982: 317). Fowles therefore testifies to the traumatic experience of attempting to exert one's freedom, granted that any such attempt necessarily entails terror. The figure of Sarah in this conscience-rending episode stands for "the pure essence of cruel but necessary (if we are to survive – and yes, still today) freedom" (Fowles 1982: 317). That Fowles intends this traumatic moment set in the nineteenth century to be meaningful – by proxy – to the contemporary reader is clear from the parenthetical narrator's interjection.

2.   Unhealed Rifts and Black Holes

In neo-Victorian fiction, the conflict of ideas triggered by Darwin's theory is often treated as a dual confrontation between two emblematic characters, i.e. the creationist and the evolutionist. Far from being confined to the intellectual plane, such exchanges are bound to have deep emotional and affective repercussions, so that the epistemological aspect is arguably eclipsed by the psychological internalisation of ideological dissension. This face-to-face argument tends to be staged in two types of context, either during the Beagle expedition, as in *Mr Darwin's Shooter* and *This Thing of Darkness*, or in the privacy of the English household, as in 'Morpho Eugenia' and *Ever After*. In both cases, the potential side-and-after effects of these emotionally-laden conversations are brought to the fore.

This Thing of Darkness is an over-documented piece of fiction packed with meticulously collected data, whose main literary interest probably resides in its subtle nuanced rendering of the inner contradictions of its two main protagonists, fictionalised versions of respectively Darwin and Robert FitzRoy, the Tory aristocratic captain of the Beagle. FitzRoy is shown pathetically clinging to his creationist convictions to the very end. Whereas McDonald in *Mr Darwin's Shooter* derives poetic effects from the silences and failed acts of communication of his main protagonist, Syms Covington (in many respects Darwin's factotum), Thompson, for his part, presents two fully articulate characters, never at a loss for an argument. The overwhelming personal need to come to grips with the world through new grids of analysis is probably what stays most in the reader's mind.

The novels' titles indicate an undeniable link between the sheer anonymity of a silenced witness of history – a shooter who happened to be at the service of a certain Mr Darwin – and the dark shadow cast by an expedition originally meant to collect specimens to expand people's knowledge. "This Thing of Darkness", as shown in the epigraph, is Prospero's way of referring to Caliban, in the same breath dismissing and acknowledging as part of himself the semi-devil (*The Tempest*, V.i. l. 276). What is underscored is less the adventurous side of the voyage, let alone the scientific finds that it afforded, than the metaphysical anxiety and existential crisis that it entailed. In retrospect, the journey to the antipodes is viewed in terms of a black hole – FitzRoy's act of suicide in the coda. Syms Covington in *Mr Darwin's Shooter*, has, for his part, nursed resentment for having seen his efforts on behalf of his master unrecognised. He has been consigned to the metaphorical black hole of natural history as a lesser being, whose voice does not survive in the official record. The novel dramatises a scene in which an expectant Covington is being read pages from *On the Origin of Species* to realise that his name is not even mentioned once: "A name may be written in there. Doubtless in small print but writ there all the same, in acknowledgement of my existence […] *Your name is not there*. He gave his friend a beseeching, apologetic look" (McDonald 1998: 220-221). Worse still, in Thompson's novel, the shame of having one's achievements ignored is given a further perverse twist. At the end of his life, FitzRoy who has craved recognition for pioneering weather forecast contraptions to warn of coming storms, only hears his name perfunctorily mentioned on account of his former association with Darwin. The only accolade granted him is precisely for "this thing of darkness" that has remained a haunting gnawing obsession for the remainder of his life. For the ageing admiral the fact of having his name cited with that of Darwin, as if he had merely assisted the naturalist in shaping his theory, is a betrayal of all FitzRoy has held dear throughout his life. In near Shakespearean mode, the novel closes on the suicide of an old man bidding farewell to a new age, which he fails to understand and in which he has no viable part.

Novels like *Mr Darwin's Shooter* and *This Thing of Darkness* express the culpability, or at least the retrospective angst, occasioned by being, somewhat unwillingly, dragged into a chain of historical events. Both Covington and FitzRoy have been, to varying degrees, reluctant participants in the process of uncovering scientific troves that went on to shake the very foundations of their visions of the universe. Covington, born in Bedford, also Bunyan's birthplace through a freak of fate, finds himself embarked upon a modern, pre-Victorian avatar of the pilgrimage, i.e. a quest, whose purpose he does not quite fathom. His relationship with Darwin is akin to a "marriage of convenience", with the naturalist portrayed as an emotional cripple: "Darwin's technique with his underling was more suited to making a plan or sketch in botany or geology than in human dealings" (McDonald 1998: 240, 246). As a counterpoint to Darwin's growing materialism and religious scepticism, both neo-Victorian writers choose to introduce characters with staunch religious beliefs, even if their approaches differ. Through rhetorical fireworks, FitzRoy attempts to adduce each and every new geological or paleontological find in the antipodes to substantiate the thesis of the Flood and Noah's Ark. He adheres to the Mosaic chronology, postulating that the world was created in 4004 BC, and opposes catastrophist arguments to Darwin's uniformitarianism. Thompson barely conceals his empathy for FitzRoy who, in his many discussions with the naturalist, succeeds in holding his own with finely-chiselled arguments. Significantly, FitzRoy's final defeat does not so much stem from any flaw in his reasoning as in the forced silence ruthlessly imposed on him. In a poignant scene of humiliation, the omniscient narrator depicts an ageing diminished admiral unable to make himself heard amidst the general roar of approval for Darwin. The narrative records the repression of strong emotions that cannot be articulated:

> The students were chanting Darwin's name, as if to summon him up from behind his iron-age fortress of earthen banks. FitzRoy was surrounded by primitive, drunken braying, as ignorant as the yells of any crowd of natives on a Fuegian shore. His frustration boiled over. The rush of arguments in his head became a landslide, an avalanche, each irrefutable fact tumbling incoherently over the others. The inability of natural selection to account for the origin of life itself. The unsatisfactory reduction of the aesthetic, the emotional and the spiritual to mere epiphenomena. The falsity of Darwin's fossil narrative, which had been constructed on foundations that were geologically poles apart. (Thompson 2005: 708)

The unuttered flurry of objections leaves no tangible trace of this counter-manifesto to *On the Origin of Species*, yet the inner storm is raging within the old man: "*Nemo senex metuit Iouem* – An old man ought to be fearful of God"(Thompson 2005: 696, original emphasis). The evolutionary terminology is sardonically appropriated to heighten pathos: "a tiny spark of self-preservation remained. It told him to get out, and leave now, before something unimaginably awful happened" (Thompson 2005: 709). Through such psycho-narration, Thompson strives to convey the extreme frustration of the silenced antagonist, who in the midst of all the cheers of support for his adversary cannot get a word in edgeways and slinks towards the exit in total discomfiture. Thompson makes use of such extremes of emotions, which Darwin's theory aroused in his contemporaries, to nostalgically conjure up the riddling figure of the loser, fighting through to the end for his deep-seated beliefs, and dying as a result. The well-documented references to science help build up the tragic stature of the solitary character who, like Shakespeare's Lear, allegorically stands for old age surrendering to a new order: "He had lived his life long enough, he realized, to begin feeling the disappointment wrought by change. *An illusion that softens the prick of death*" (Thompson 2005: 727, original emphasis).

In sharp contrast, McDonald's Covington is a man of few words, whose conversation soon tails off, when he reflects on "Darwin and his manner of always making him feel unfinished and rough" (McDonald 1998: 247). For all his inarticulateness, the shooter's close involvement in an undertaking far exceeding his grasp shakes his rock-solid faith. McDonald, like Thompson, extrapolates graphic scenes from Darwin's Punta Alta episode in *The Voyage of the Beagle*: "We passed the night in Punta Alta, and I employed myself in searching for fossil bones; this point being a perfect catacomb for monsters of extinct races" (Darwin 2006: 92). The novel's adaptation of this seminal Darwinian episode conjures a sense of a quasi-Darwinian sublime. Covington is shown:

> standing on the beach where bits of worn skeleton rolled around in the waves […] the very brain itself breaking in half trying to understand what was in these problematical shapes that the living and the dead brought forward. The place was like a great slaughtering yard. (McDonald 1998: 281-282)

As Jay Clayton has aptly argued, McDonald suggests the insidious way in which Covington's natural faith is subtly eroded through his serving Darwin. The menial tasks he carries out for his master lead to his exposure to "the dizzy vistas of time that an evolutionary perspective opened before him" (Clayton 2003: 175). Clayton conceptualises this phenomenological experience of confronting the spatial and temporal infinite as "genome time", i.e. "the knowledge that all pasts and all futures lie coiled within the present moment" (Clayton 2003: 175). Such epiphanic episodes are conducive to a loss of certainties about hitherto firmly held beliefs. Covington, hardly the man to confess his feelings, comes close to acknowledging that his erstwhile religious beliefs are growing increasingly out of touch with the present moment: "There is something you don't know about me […] I have been shy to show it to you, lest I seem a relic like a mammoth or the sabre-toothed tiger. I am a natural religious man" (McDonald 1998: 219). As the novel progresses, in spite of his once unshakeable commitment to the Congregationalist denomination, Covington finds himself striving to grapple with "what Darwin set out to prove – that limitless time made all things possible" (McDonald

1998: 350). Fittingly enough, the last chapter shows the shooter in the
throes of death, being subjected to hallucinatory visions in which
various episodes from his past life mingle in total chronological
disorder, until he fantasises some improbable – and, at the reader's
level, parodic – reconciliation between religion and science: "He saw
Darwin on his knees, and there was no difference between prayer and
pulling a worm from the grass. As for Mr Covington, he prayed in the
usual way. It was the last of anything he knew" (McDonald 1998:
361).

        With Byatt's 'Morpho Eugenia' and Swift's *Ever After*, the
clash of ideas between the creationist and the evolutionist is brought
within the family sphere. In her novella, Byatt reports learned
conversations between William Adamson, the anthropologist-cum-
entomologist, shortly returned from Amazonia, and Harald Alabaster,
the *pater familias* and eventual father-in-law to Adamson, who
proposes to write the impossible book that would prove the presence
of a divine creator, or designer. The discussions between the two
scholars testify to the essential solitude that has become the plight of
the post-Darwinian man. In a sense, they offer a variation upon
Tennyson's famous lines in canto 54 of *In Memoriam*: "[…] but what
am I?/ An infant crying in the night/ An infant crying for the light/
And with no language but a cry" (Tennyson 1973: 34). Alabaster, with
his mineral patronymic, is caught in an intellectual quandary. Having
relinquished "his father's religion of torment, suffering and promised
bliss with a sigh of relief" (Byatt 1993: 57), like Bunyan's Christian,
he now finds himself trapped in a conceptual slough of despond.
Alabaster's ambition to justify Divine Design through the new
discourse of science proves a solipsistic fallacy, no more than a way
of searching the mirror of his own mind in the workings of nature.
Alabaster's inability to gain a hold on the surrounding world arguably
corresponds to his powerlessness to exert any control whatever over
his household. As a Victorian patriarch, he appears as no more and no
less than the superannuated embodiment of an obsolescent institution.
Holding no sway over his womenfolk and his offspring, he is very
much the "*deus absconditas*" of his domestic sphere (Byatt 1993: 76).
However, Byatt demonstrates that within the confines of this entropic
Victorian household, William Adamson, the explorer convert to the
new-fangled ideas of evolutionary science, hardly fares better than the
master of the house. Ironically, for a novella that goes to great lengths

to establish the community instinct of insects, Adamson's solitude is on a par with that of his host. To his former cultural estrangement amongst the Amazonian natives now corresponds his present state of exile from his own family and the attendant irony of having his presumed children sired through his wife's incestuous ties with her own brother. Such revelations of inbreeding anticipate late Victorian theories of degeneracy, and Byatt dramatises the traumatic experience of the outsider progressively discovering, at his own expense, a well-hidden family secret. Yet, the novella ends on an optimistic note with William Adamson setting out for Amazonia with Matty Crompton, the children's nurse. Far from the confining estate of Bredely Hall, the young couple, on the ship heading for the Amazon shore, bears the promise of a revitalisation of the species: "William's brown hand grips her brown wrist on the rail. They breathe salt air, and hope, and their blood swims with the excitement of the future" (Byatt 1993: 160).

Finally, the confrontation between the creationist and the evolutionist eludes all attempts at representation in *Ever After*, where the black hole of trauma turns into textual ellipsis. Bill Unwin, the contemporary narrator, strives to reconstruct the final showdown between Matthew Pearce, his Victorian ancestor, and the Reverend Hunt, Matthew's father-in-law, from erratic jottings in a notebook. However, the crucial banishment scene, when the clergyman voices his outrage at his son-in-law's denunciation of Natural Theology as a sham, cannot be felicitously rendered by the twentieth-century narrator. The defeat of mimesis bears witness to the reverberating, after-effects of the traumatic incident. Having first tried prose narrative focalised by the rector's wife, Bill Unwin then sets out to test another form – the television script – which turns out to be equally unsatisfactory. Experimenting with narrative forms to dismiss them as tentative and at best approximate is Swift's way of hinting at the traumatism that follows Pearce's decision to take up an ideological stance countering the teachings of religion. From many respects, Pearce's apostasy, his desertion of his family, and the silence that follows his momentous decision present a challenge to narratorial discourse. The character's ensuing mutism foreshadows the "not telling" phenomenon observed amongst the victims of tragedies on a much wider scale in the twentieth century:

> The 'not telling' of the story serves as a perpetuation
> of its tyranny. The events become more and more
> distorted in their silent retention and pervasively
> invade and contaminate the survivor's daily life. The
> longer the story remains untold, the more distorted it
> becomes in the survivor's conception of it, so much
> so that the survivor doubts the reality of the actual
> events. (Laub 1992: 79)

Interestingly, Swift preserves this gaping hole of the unsaid, or the
unsayable, by having his contemporary narrator exerting himself to
explore diverse strategies to set about telling the momentous
confrontation, only to admit the task's unfeasibility: "But I do not
know, I cannot even invent [...] I falter in my script-writing" (Swift
1992: 187). This failure to speak in the name of the actual witness is
proof of the *living* persistence of a traumatic Victorian moment in our
own Age of Testimony:

> The impossibility of speaking and, in fact of listening,
> otherwise than through this silence, otherwise than
> through this black hole both of knowledge and of
> words, corresponds to the impossibility of
> remembering and of forgetting [...] otherwise than
> through this 'hole of memory'. (Laub 1992: 65)

Even granting the vast gap between a twentieth-century Holocaust
victim and a Victorian apostate, the question remains how best to
address the likely effect of what is basically a narrative ploy on the
twenty-first-century reader of neo-Victorian fiction.

3.   Trauma and Origins

Odd as it may seem, the question of the origin of life is hardly ever
broached in the whole Darwinian theory, a fact which is jocularly
rendered in a recent study by Michael Ruse, by parodying one of
Sherlock Holmes's famous rejoinders in the story 'Silver Blaze'
(1892):

> 'But Darwin didn't discuss the origin of life
> in the *Origin of Species* [sic].'

> 'Precisely!' He knew he had no answer and
> that getting into a discussion of the topic would lead
> only to tears, so he stayed away from it altogether.
> (Ruse 2006: 53)

Precisely! What the scientist shuns, appeals to the fiction writer, and two neo-Victorian novels deal with the tantalising issue of the origin from totally different perspectives: Matthew Kneale's *English Passengers* and the more recent *Human Traces* by Sebastian Faulks. In either case, the question of trauma is crucial: respectively trauma linked to genocide in a postcolonial perspective, a subject that is addressed in both Elisabeth Wesseling's and Celia Wallhead and Marie-Luise Kohlke's essays in this volume, or trauma connected to mental illness, evoking the Greek etymological meaning of trauma as a cut and wound (Caruth 1996: 3) – in the case of Faulks's novel a lesion in the cerebellum.

In both novels what sets the plot in motion is a decision to return to the origin to find an answer to present cultural debates. In Kneale's fiction, an expedition to Tasmania aims to reveal the exact location of the Garden of Eden. Though Darwin's text is not referred to explicitly, the epistemological context of the evolutionary theory proves central. In particular, the Reverend Geoffrey Wilson intends disproving James Hutton's and Charles Lyell's uniformitarian conceptions of deep time via the maverick notion of divine refrigeration. According to staunch creationists such as Wilson, the earth in its primal burning, melting state would have cooled in no more time than allowed for the age of the universe in the Scriptures, i.e. four thousand years. The Darwinian background is also clearly called up through the corrupted version of the ship surgeon Dr Thomas Potter's theory of development, since his racialist treatise, titled "Destiny of Nations", is a fictitious variation on Robert Knox's genuine *The Races of Men, A Fragment* (1850), as Kneale points out (Kneale 2001: 456). It should be noted here that Darwin himself only very occasionally cited Knox – for example on certain minor aspects of human physiology, such as the humerus of man, in *The Descent* (Darwin 2006: 793). However, the Victorians often reinterpreted the evolutionary scale thesis to support warped notions of racial superiority, which is precisely what happens in Kneale's novel, in which Potter constructs elaborate racial hierarchies that place the

Tasmanian aborigines firmly on the lowest rung and explain their near-extinction as the fate of an unviable 'species'. The satirical thrust in *English Passengers* thus stems from the fact that through an expedition prompted by religious dogma, self-professed Christians find themselves complicit in trauma on an unprecedented scale by condoning, when not justifying, the extermination of the aborigines.

From many respects, *English Passengers* and *Human Traces* adopt diametrically opposed perspectives in their fictitious treatment of the notion of origin. For the former, the travel to the antipodes, supposedly the cradle of Christianity through the putative Garden of Eden, aims at substantiating a scale of the evolution of nations, whereby some populations are reduced to the level of subhuman brutes. For Faulks's novel, the dawn of the human species, going as far back as Lucy, the *Australopithecus afarensis*, more than three million years ago (see Johanson and Edey 1981), would provide the clinching argument to assert the essential *human* nature of a whole class of excluded, marginalised people, namely the mentally ill.

In *Human Traces*, the quest for the origin comes as an incidental development to one of the character's chief aims in life, which is to establish "the meeting point of thought and flesh" or "[t]he way in which functions the mind of man" (Faulks 2006: 75). It is because Jacques Rebière, a Breton boy from a family of farmers, has grown up beside his elder brother, Olivier, who progressively develops a form of *dementia praecox*, that he decides to dedicate his whole life to the understanding of mental disease. In poignant passages, Faulks suggests the closeness of the bond between the two brothers, notwithstanding – or possibly all the more because of – the mental abnormality that stands between them:

> In Olivier's skin and veins had been particles of inheritance that they had shared with no one else, and that had been the nature of their existence and its challenge: to make of their lives whatever they could, beginning in their narrow Breton world. (Faulks 2006: 537)

In the course of his scientific formation, Jacques makes friends with a young Englishman, Thomas Midwinter, who advises him to take Darwin's *On the Origin of Species* into account in his exploration of the human brain, because a crucial aspect of such investigation must be to establish the particular point the human being has already reached in the course of his evolutionary progress.

What Faulks's novel establishes, through a wide range of sources acknowledged in final notes, is that mental illness would have first entered into mankind at the moment when pre-humans had evolved into *Homo Sapiens*. Madness would have played a part in whatever transmutation occurred in East Africa, millions of years ago, when the early humanoids, or proto-humans, transformed into the first identifiable humans. Faulks, through the character of Midwinter, extracts from Darwin's monogenism – the belief that "all the races of men are descended from a single primitive stock" (Darwin 2006: 907) – some elements to argue that lunacy must have been endemic in the first humans on the African continent before the great human diaspora. This would account for there being roughly the same proportion of mentally afflicted populations on each continent, regardless of race or ethnic criteria. Midwinter then further complicates the argument by establishing that, if madness is inherently human and what differentiates humans from all other species, it is, in a sense, the price humans have to pay for their mental superiority. There cannot be humanity without psychosis, as the same genes that drive some people mad are the ones that make people human, the difference between the sane and the insane being very slight, possibly only a mere matter of the combination of those genes, even if the consequences are disastrous for those afflicted. This 'natural' injustice demands that those who have been spared, as it were, should make it their duty to look after and alleviate the plight of the mentally ill. They should be prompted to act protectively on account of their very humanity, i.e. what defines them as humans as opposed to lower species. Darwin theorised this form of altruism as an instinct of sympathy, pushing the more evolved species to tend to the weaker and more vulnerable amongst themselves: "the first foundation or origin of the moral sense lies in the social instincts, including sympathy; and these instincts no doubt were primarily gained, as in the case of lower animals, through natural selection" (Darwin 2006: 1242).

Human Traces describes a double movement towards the origin. Midwinter joins an expedition to Africa to track down the first human trail, and Jacques Rebière attends the dissection of his brother Olivier's brain. Both investigations aim at accounting for the mysteries of cerebral activities and the attendant question of mental disorder. From the heartland of the African continent, Midwinter propounds that the split from the line of apes, leading to the emergence of the human species, was caused not so much by the attainment of an upright posture as by a chance mutation in the chemistry of the brain. An extra neural connection somewhere between Broca's and Wernicker's areas in the brain would thus have transformed mere one-time grunts into articulated sounds, making possible words and language. Precisely, Olivier's pathology, the fact that his sense of self dissolves due to his constantly hearing inner voices that he wrongly construes as coming from outside himself, can be explained in terms of cerebral malfunctioning. It is the improper communication between the left and right hemispheres of the brain that explains why thoughts are experienced as though they were external voices. Through natural selection's preservation of only what is useful, the human characteristic of voice-hearing consciousness was progressively phased out as a consequence of the development of writing. Psychotic patients, more precisely those suffering from schizophrenia, are voice-hearers; their inner minds are in a state of perpetual cacophony – they are chaotic, Babel-like echo-chambers. Much as Faulkner allows the reader to penetrate Benjy's distorted consciousness in *The Sound and the Fury* (1931), Faulks has a whole passage filtered through Olivier's mentally perturbed psyche. In the reader this disconcerting narrative fragment elicits both unease and tension as a response to Olivier's stress at never being able to cope appropriately with outside situations:

> There are too many seen-people in this room, this hall. There is all this noise of wooden spoons on bowls, the clattering, the shouting, hurling, banging, outdoor horses, spades on stone, the people asking me, asking me questions. I want the waterfall that will drown their noise. I want the quiet.
> 'Come on, Olivier. Do as Daisy says. Just eat a little bread and tea. Then it's time for your appointment with Dr Midwinter. It's Wednesday. You like talking to him, don't you?'
> They are always asking me these questions.
> (Faulks 2006: 521-522)

Olivier's subsequent leap to death is focalised from the personal hell of his traumatised consciousness; his last ramblings are no more than the "*obiter dicta* of a broken mind" (Faulks 2006: 538). Later, the post-mortem discloses literal, tangible signs of his traumatic condition: the sulci, or fissures between the brain's convolutions, are more enlarged than normal. In the last resort, the exploration into the realm of madness – both geographical and physiological – sets up the foundations for a larger form of humanism. This is all the more remarkable as the novel is situated at a time when research into insanity, through accumulated inheritance, was to take a totally different direction towards "degeneration", with Henry Maudsley following in the footsteps of Bénédict Augustin Morel (Faulks 2006: 643). Such anachronistic appropriation of late Victorian scientific theory with the deliberate intention to adopt a positive, humanitarian stance is symptomatic of what Christian Gutleben and Julian Wolfreys describe as the neo-Victorian's vocation to use pastiche for an empathic and ethical concurrence with the other (this volume: 65-66).

After *Sweet Thames* (1992), his first neo-Victorian novel set in the London of the 1840s, Matthew Kneale wanted to show how the Victorians could be wrong-headed overseas with *English Passengers*.[3] Whereas Faulks's novel is linear and teleologically-oriented, leading up to World War I – a period the novelist has written about extensively – Kneale's text unfolds alternatively on two temporal levels and has been praised for its efficient use of polyphony.[4] These two narrative ploys – both the storm of voices and the double historical contexts – participate in the poetics of the postcolonial trauma novel, by eschewing any notion of a 'March towards Progress'. In a sense, this is a regressive fiction, in so far as it evokes a nostalgic quest towards a fantasised 'Garden of Innocence', by rejecting the teachings of modern science and by showing the destructiveness of the colonial adventure. The montage of all sorts of written sources, ranging from official reports to diary entries,

---

[3] "My first interest was in the craziness of the Victorian British mind. I had written about Victorians being disastrously wrong-headed at home (in London) and so it seemed only right to see them being disastrously wrong-headed overseas" (Kneale, qtd. in McDonald n.d.).

[4] Kneale provides a broader perspective on the historical process by interweaving two plot sequences, one starting in the 1820s, the other in 1857. The two levels eventually coalesce through the chronicle of the half-aboriginal Peevay.

journalism and essay, highlights shifting perspectives and irreconcilable, ideologically-biased testimonies on an apocalyptic historical moment. The juxtaposition of voices contributes to a crisis of witnessing, testifying to all manners of psychopathologies in a riven colonial society. From the colonist's wife, articulating her mixed fears and pity towards the natives, to the social reformer bent on Christianising the black aborigines in the name of progress, what Kneale depicts is an angst-ridden, insecure community of settlers torn by contradictions. The process of decline is all-pervasive, and the pastoral ideal of an Edenic virgin land yields to the harsh realities of a terrestrial Gehenna. The ineluctable eradication of the aboriginal natives is mercilessly recorded and their number dwindles as they are displaced from Van Diemen's Land, to the Flinders Island settlement, and ultimately to the Oyster Cove camp, where a mere eleven survive. Through the extermination of the aboriginals, Kneale grapples with extreme historical situations, of the Holocaust-type, setting a challenge to discursive representation. The paradoxes of the impossibility of testimony have been extensively investigated in the aftermath of the Shoah. Shoshana Felman, for instance, assesses the impact of Claude Lanzmann's film in the following terms:

> *Shoah* is a film about testimony, then, in an infinitely more abysmal, paradoxical and problematic way than it seems: *the necessity of testimony* it affirms in reality derives, paradoxically enough, from the *impossibility of testimony* that the film at the same time dramatizes. [...] In its enactment of the Holocaust as the *event-without-a witness*, as the ungraspable *primal scene* which erases both its witness and its witnessing, *Shoah* explores the very boundaries of testimony by exploring, at the same time, the historical impossibility of witnessing and the historical impossibility of *escaping* being – and of having to become – a witness. (Felman 1992: 224, original emphases)

As a historical novel revisiting the colonial epic from a postcolonial perspective, *English Passengers* hinges on the boundary line between parody and fictionalised testimony. The motley crew of the Manxmen on board their smuggling vessel falls under the first category; the sheer discomfiture of their return to England is an index of Kneale's irony. The traumatising consequences of the convicts' transportation in the opposite direction, however, calls for both memory and mourning works (see Ricœur 2000: 105-111), a point which Kneale himself underscores in the epilogue:

> All the major events of the Tasmanian strand of the novel follow real occurrences, from the stealing of aboriginal women by sealers to the massacre on the cliff, the bizarre cruelties of the convict system, the fiasco of the Black Line, and the terrible farce of Flinders Island. (Kneale 2001: 455)

First-hand testimonies of aboriginals being non-existent, the novelist lends them voices in his fiction, whilst pointing out that their non-fictitious, historical counterparts invariably met with tragic destinies, notably Tayaleah, re-christened George Vandiemen, a math prodigy, who died soon after his return to Tasmania and fell into oblivion. However, the fictitious status of these natives, who are included amongst the novel's cast through ventriloquism, never fills the historical void into which their original models were precipitated. The reader is all the more willing to accept this distortion of history, as it is felt to be a very minor compensation for these natives' almost total erasure from archival records. The fictionalisation process, notably through the romantic treatment of Peevay, the half-caste aborigine and product of rape, never competes with historical truth *per se*. Peevay is renamed Cromwell not so much to suggest any historical correspondences with the former English ruler as to deprive the native of his singularity: "Kneale's aborigines are depersonalised by being renamed. The insensitivity of the process is brought home by the sniggering jocularity of the name choices" (Ross 2006: 252). Indeed, a "title" is bound to conceal "some clever sting in its tail" (Kneale 2001: 248), which is perceptible to the coloniser only. Thus the name Cromwell, with its sombre, macabre connotations when referring to the Butcher of Ireland, belies Peevay's joviality. Given the absence – or in Felman's terms the *impossibility* – of an aboriginal witness, there can be no attempt at a genuine testimony. This is why, through the emblematic, highly fictitious character of Peevay/Cromwell, the past is revisited as farce, through mimicry, as if it were the only way not to betray destinies bound to remain beyond the reach of mimetic record: "Cromwell, being a notorious maker of trouble, [...] had learned to mimic the ways of an Englishman just well enough to be a perfect nuisance" (Kneale 2001: 312).

Traumatic history can only be reconstructed through the mode of parodic reversal. When it comes to the extermination proper, Kneale has thought up an ingenious answer to obviate the risk of falsification by a white English writer's usurpation of the ungraspable aboriginals' past. The whole process of decimation of the indigenes is encapsulated in a primal, paradigmatic scene of Nativity that is celebrated just as the emblematic figure of the old aboriginal mother in the novel is passing away. At this stage, Kneale resorts to the counterpoint technique with great efficiency. On Christmas Day 1857, the wife of the governor of Tasmania gives a party, to which she invites the few surviving aborigines, as she wishes to have their daguerreotypes taken to keep them as relics of a soon-to-be extinct race. The Nativity Drama turns sour though, as just when the actors begin performing in the crèche around the baby Jesus, a crash and a cry are heard. The commotion is caused by Peevay's own mother, an aboriginal woman named Walyeric, based on Walyer an authentic native, reputed to have been a formidable warrior.[5] In Kneale's novel, Peevay's mother had been baptised Mary, albeit in mocking reference to 'Bloody Queen Mary' (Kneale 2001: 248) rather than the Blessed Virgin. So Mary, the aboriginal, dies on the night when another Mary – or at least whoever is playing the part – is pretending to give birth. This reversal lends itself to multiple interpretations, from tragic irony to callous re-appropriation of the postcolonial mimicry trope. Of course, the native has no access to the crèche, where the Redeemer of mankind lies in his swaddling clothes. She is relegated to the room next door, to have her image taken to serve, with those of others of her

---

[5] "[S]ome of the characters are closely based on people of the time, including Robson, the various governors and their wives, and also Mother (Walyeric). She was inspired by a formidable woman named Walyer, who fought the whites and was greatly feared by them. She knew how to use firearms, was reputed to have cut a new path through the bush to facilitate her campaigns, and would swear fluently in English as she launched her attacks. She was eventually captured by the British in late 1831, and at once began trying to organize fellow aboriginals in a rebellion. She died not long afterwards" (Kneale 2001: 455).

kind, as a memorial, a process in which she significantly refuses to participate. Later, her corpse will be cut up by Potter, who purloins her bones intending to carry them back to England to be displayed in museums celebrating the glory of the British Empire. Yet this turns out to be a failed endeavour as Peevay retrieves his mother's remains, which he subsequently burns on a pyre in a private scene of improvised commemoration. In Kneale's novel, therefore, the Christmas Nativity becomes an apt symbolical substitute for a traumatic history that cannot be signified, a history that refuses representation.

4.   Conclusion

By investigating a sample of neo-Victorian novels that show a blatant concern with Darwinism, this essay has endeavoured to stress the sheer diversity of approaches, whilst insisting upon the prevalence of the traumatic element in each case. Neo-Victorian novelists are interested in the way in which human consciousnesses, individually or collectively, respond to epistemological challenges. The main advantage of drawing from Darwinian science resides in the accessibility afforded by a relatively straightforward type of discourse. To put it bluntly, Darwin's analyses are far more reader-friendly than (post)modern relativity or chaos theories, and not coincidentally, Darwin is sometimes studied for his own literary merits, regardless of scientific contents. Recent criticism has also emphasised the visual dimension of the reception of Darwinian science in Victorian England (see, e.g., Smith 2006). Central to this importance of the material and visual mediation of science was the prevalence of catastrophic imagery. In a recent article dedicated to Dickens, Adelene Buckland shows how "[t]ogether, Owen and Hawkins invented the image of the dinosaur for a whole generation of Victorians" (Buckland 2007: 683), emblematic of the always threatening extinction and supersession of dominant species. Returning to Shuttleworth's argument that the Darwinian moment in the neo-Victorian novel exemplifies *second order* loss, or catastrophe at one remove, it could be objected that this process of temporal distancing already existed in the Victorian age:

> All over London, then, visual and material cultures pictured a prehistoric world characterized by spectacular monsters, and the natural world as

> intrinsically catastrophic: size, spectacle, and the
> pleasures of fear in the face of calamitous disasters
> and gigantic creatures turned nature into performance,
> familiarizing their crowds with exaggerated versions
> of popular science. (Buckland 2007: 683)

If neo-Victorian novels revive this tradition of adapting science to the lay man/woman who, at the beginning of the twenty-first century, is likely to have easy access to various cultural media, it may be partly to address metaphysical and ethical issues and anxieties, first raised by Darwinism (life's origins, teleology, phylogenetics, evolution) but still of crucial relevance to current epistemological debates. Fully understanding that such questions are potentially traumatic, affecting as they do the most intimate part of individual and collective lives, neo-Victorian novelists opt for a subjective, profoundly personal response to science. Finally, it should be noted that some aspects of Darwin's thinking remain as contentious today, especially his theory of sexual selection. Oddly enough, the neo-Victorian fictions, which in the wake of Michel Foucault's edition of *Herculine Barbin* (1978) tackled the delicate subject of hermaphrodism, as in Patricia Duncker's *James Miranda Barry* (1999) and Wesley Stace's *Misfortune* (2005), did not relate to the Darwinian background, whereas on the other side of the Atlantic, Darwin's theory of sexual selection is subjected to complete rethinking, notably by the transgendered biologist Joan Roughgarden. This may be seen as yet another paradox in the neo-Victorian novel's return to Darwin and his very present legacy.

Bibliography

Buckland, Adelene. 2007. '"The Poetry of Science": Charles Dickens, Geology, and Visual and Material Culture in Victorian London', *Victorian Literature and Culture* 35: 679-694.
Byatt, A.S. 1993. 'Morpho Eugenia' in *Angels & Insects* [1992]. London: Vintage.
——. 2000. *On Histories and Stories: Selected Essays*. London: Chatto and Windus.
Caruth, Cathy. 1996. *Unclaimed Experience, Trauma, Narrative, and History*. Baltimore, Maryland: The Johns Hopkins University Press.
Clayton, Jay. 2003. *Charles Dickens in Cyberspace: The Afterlife of the Nineteenth Century in Postmodern Culture*. Oxford: Oxford University Press.

Craps, Stef. 2005. *Trauma and Ethics in the Novels of Graham Swift: No Short-Cuts to Salvation*. Brighton: Sussex Academic Press.

Darwin, Charles. 2006. *The Voyage of the Beagle* in *From So Simple a Beginning: Darwin's Four Great Books* [1845] (ed. Edward O. Wilson). New York & London: Norton & Company: 28-432.

——. 2006. *On the Origin of Species by Means of Natural Selection, or the Preservation of Favoured Races in the Struggle for Life*, in *From So Simple a Beginning: Darwin's Four Great Books* [1859] (ed. Edward O. Wilson). New York & London: Norton & Company: 449-760.

——. 2006. *The Descent of Man, And Selection in Relation to Sex* in *From So Simple a Beginning: Darwin's Four Great Books* [1871] (ed. Edward O. Wilson). New York & London: Norton & Company: 777-1248.

Duncker, Patricia. 1999. *James Miranda Barry*. London: Serpent's Tail.

Faulkner, William. 1977. *The Sound and the Fury* [1931]. Harmondsworth: Penguin Classics.

Faulks, Sebastian. 2006. *Human Traces* [2005]. London: Vintage.

Fawkner, H.W. 1984. *The Timescapes of John Fowles*. Rutherford: Fairleigh Dickinson University Press.

Felman, Shoshana, and Dori Laub. 1992. *Testimony: Crises of Witnessing in Literature, Psychoanalysis, and History*. New York & London: Routledge.

Foucault, Michel (ed.). 1978. *Herculine Barbin, dite Alexina B.* Paris: "Les Vies Parallèles" Gallimard.

Fowles, John. 1982. *The French Lieutenant's Woman* [1969]. Bungay, Suffolk: Triad.

Hull, David L., and Michael Ruse (eds.). 2007. *The Cambridge Companion to the Philosophy of Biology*. Cambridge: Cambridge University Press.

Jackson, Tony E. 1997. 'Charles and the Hopeful Monster: Postmodern Evolutionary Theory in *The French Lieutenant's Woman*', *Twentieth Century Literature*, 43(2) (Summer): 221-242.

Johanson, Donald C, and Maitland Edey. 1981. *Lucy: The Beginnings of Humankind*. New York: Simon & Schuster.

Kneale, Matthew. 2001. *Sweet Thames* [1992].London: Penguin Books.

——. 2001. *English Passengers* [2000].London: Penguin Books.

Kohlke, Marie-Luise. 2008. 'Introduction: Speculations in and on the Neo-Victorian Encounter', *Neo-Victorian Studies* 1(1) (Autumn): 1-18.

Matus, Jill L. 2008. 'Historicizing Trauma: The Genealogy of Psychic Shock in *Daniel Deronda*', *Victorian Literature and Culture* 36: 59-78.

McDonald, Roger. 1998. *Mr Darwin's Shooter*. New York: Grove Press.

McDonald, Sean. n.d. 'Interview: A Conversation with Matthew Kneale'. Online at: http://www.randomhouse.com/boldtype/0400/kneale/interview.html (consulted 29.12.2009).

Rhys, Jean. 1997. *Wide Sargasso Sea* [1966].London: Penguin Books.

Ricœur, Paul. 2000. *La Mémoire, l'histoire, l'oubli*. Paris: Seuil.

Ross, Michael L. 2006. *Race Riots: Comedy and Ethnicity in Modern British Fiction*. McGill-Queen's University Press.

Roughgarden, Joan. 2004. *Evolution's Rainbow: Diversity, Gender, and Sexuality in Nature and People*. Berkeley & Los Angeles: University of California Press.

Ruse, Michael. 2006. *Darwinism and Its Discontents*. Cambridge: Cambridge University Press.

Shakespeare, William. 2006. *The Tempest* (ed. D. Lindley) (The New Cambridge Shakespeare). Cambridge: Cambridge University Press.

Shuttleworth, Sally. 1998. 'Natural History: The Retro-Victorian Novel', in Shaffer, Elinor S. (ed.), *The Third Culture: Literature and Science*. Berlin, New York: Walter de Gruyter: 253-268.

Smith, Jonathan. 2006. *Charles Darwin and Victorian Visual Culture*. Cambridge: Cambridge University Press.

Stace, Wesley. 2006. *Misfortune*[2005]. New York: Back Bay.

Swift, Graham. 1992. *Ever After*. London: Pan Macmillan.

Tennyson, Alfred (Lord). 1973. *In Memoriam* [1851].New York & London: A Norton Critical Edition.

Thompson, Harry. 2006. *This Thing of Darkness* [2005].London: Headline Review.

Apes and Grandfathers:
Traumas of Apostasy and Exclusion in John Fowles's *The French Lieutenant's Woman* and Graham Swift's *Ever After*

Catherine Pesso-Miquel

Abstract:

This paper examines the narrative and aesthetic strategies of John Fowles and Graham Swift as they deal with the theme of post-Darwinian anxiety and loss of faith, Darwinism being used both in its literal meaning and as a metaphor for social evolution. The contention is that Swift's literary treatment allows for the creation of a trauma narrative conducive to reader empathy and identification, while Fowles precludes any possibility of empathy through the use of postmodernist distancing and frame-breaking. Other neo-Victorian novelists are evoked for purposes of comparison, notably A.S. Byatt, Liz Jensen, and A.N. Wilson, whose novels are characterised by a mainly ludic and comic tone. The essay analyses the specific effects created by the insertion of rare moments of sombre sobriety devoted to the telling of trauma within ironic and/or parodic neo-Victorian works.

Keywords: creationism, Darwinism, *Ever After*, John Fowles, *The French Lieutenant's Woman*, Liz Jensen, Graham Swift, trauma narrative, A.N. Wilson.

*****

Question: What is the opposite of faith? Not disbelief. Too final, certain, closed. Itself a kind of belief. Doubt. (Salman Rushdie)

As the narrative voice in Liz Jensen's *Ark Baby* (1998) unemotionally states, "1859 was the year that Charles Darwin's book, *Origin of Species* [sic], was published, and it was a date which also marked the decline into melancholy and madness of many a theologian" (Jensen 1998: 139). Nineteenth-century reactions to Darwin's theories seem to obsess neo-Victorian novelists, as if no attempt to fictionally capture the essence of the Victorian age could be complete without the staging of this particular trauma. Being faced with the brutal realisation that the world was not an ordered, meaningful place regulated by a just and benevolent God, but a place of randomness, chance, meaninglessness and emptiness was a deeply depressing ordeal for many a Victorian. This essay will attempt to show how, in the case of John Fowles and Graham Swift, different narrative strategies produce different effects on the reader, in other words a different reception of the trauma narrative. Indeed, it remains to be seen whether *The French Lieutenant's Woman* (1969) is to be considered at all as a 'trauma narrative', while Graham Swift's work seems inseparable from that very concept.

How can fiction capture the essence and characteristics of the traumatic experience and cause readers to understand, and suffer with, characters undergoing fictional traumas? Laurie Vickroy explains that

> traumatic experience can produce a sometimes indelible effect on the human psyche that can change the nature of an individual's memory, self recognition and relational life. […] The memory of one particular event comes to taint all other experiences, spoiling appreciation of the present. This tyranny of the past interferes with the ability to pay attention to both new and familiar situations. When people come to concentrate selectively on reminders of their past, life tends to become colorless, and contemporary experience ceases to be a teacher. (Vickroy 2002: 11-12)

Dwelling on Sigmund Freud's accounts of repetitive nightmares in *Beyond the Pleasure Principle*, Cathy Caruth comes to a similar conclusion, namely that

> the survival of trauma is not the fortunate passage beyond a violent event, a passage that is accidentally interrupted by reminders of it, but rather the endless *inherent necessity* of repetition, which ultimately may lead to destruction. (Caruth 1996: 62-63, original emphasis)

The fiction of Graham Swift could be read as an illustration of this theory of an intrusive, endlessly re-enacted, and potentially destructive past. In *Waterland* (1983), Swift's first neo-Victorian novel, the plot creates a collusion between the trauma of incest and the trauma of the war, between Tommies back from the First World War, whose psyche is deeply damaged and whose "life ha[s] stopped, though they must go on living", and a young girl who feels trapped "because when fathers love daughters […] it's like tying up into a knot the thread that runs into the future" (Swift 1984: 197). A different character in the same novel, the victim of a traumatic, botched abortion, becomes another such walking wounded or living dead: "[her] life came to a kind of stop when she was only sixteen, though she had to go on living" (Swift 1984: 106). Appropriately, one of the epigraphs of *Waterland* is borrowed from *Great Expectations* (1861), a novel that has provided British literature with the archetypal figure of the traumatised living dead, the living oxymoron of the white-haired, shrivelled, deserted bride, Miss Havisham.

In *Ever After* (1992), the second of Graham Swift's two neo-Victorian novels, the intrusion of the past into the present is less brutal. In *Ever After* the main characters are doomed *not* to live 'happily ever after'; their intense marital happiness is cut off at its height, but in one case the culprit is not death, illness, or war, but Darwinism, which leads to loss of faith in God and everlasting life. With this novel, Swift implicitly paid homage to John Fowles, one of the pioneer novelists who launched the modern neo-Victorian genre with the publication of *The French Lieutenant's Woman*. Fowles's protagonist Charles Smithson, a would-be progressive thinker and defender of the theory of evolution, is likewise assailed by a crisis of faith when confronted with his own inability to adapt to a rapidly changing society, which looks set to render his 'genus' of gentleman of leisure rapidly extinct. Swift was thus playfully adding several layers to a work that is itself a complex palimpsest, incorporating innumerable intertextual allusions.

The treatment of the Darwinian motif in neo-Victorian fiction seems to rely on a series of recurrent *topoï*. These include palaeontology and scenes located around Lyme Regis, with references to Mary Anning and ichthyosaurs, as well as dramatised conflicts between the Church and Science as embodied by a number of showdowns between clergymen and doctors, or else naturalists, eager to ascertain whether Man was or was not 'descended from apes', a statement that the prudent, wary Charles Darwin himself never wrote or uttered.[1] Neo-Victorian novelists insist on the fact that Darwin's theories were at once ludicrously simplified and drastically misrepresented, partly because Darwin's contemporaries preferred to distort and ridicule his ideas rather than seriously engage with their implications. Indeed, Darwin never included the human species in *On the Origin of Species* and would wait until 1871 before publishing *The Descent of Man*. Darwin himself was very much amused by the innumerable caricatures that turned him into an ape or a monkey and enjoyed collecting them.

Paradoxically, although the Darwin-linked trauma is mostly associated with loss of faith, racking doubt and even descents into madness, the *treatment* of the motif in the neo-Victorian novel is more often than not playful and comic (the comic potential of madness, for instance, is well-known). Thus *The French Lieutenant's Woman* opens in March of 1867, in Lyme Regis, and as early as the second chapter, the name of Darwin is introduced within a flippant conversation between the hero and his fiancée Ernestina Freeman. Charles admits to her that he has had "a small philosophical disagreement" with his father-in-law to be:

> Your father ventured the opinion that Mr Darwin
> should be exhibited in a cage in the zoological
> gardens. In the monkey-house. I tried to explain some
> of the scientific arguments behind the Darwinian
> position. I was unsuccessful. (Fowles 1987: 11)

Later Doctor Grogan and Charles cautiously ascertain that they are both "Darwinian[s]", acting, ironically, like early Christians wary of persecution, or civilised men threatened by superstitious natives: "Grogan then seized his hand and gripped it; as if he were Crusoe, and Charles, Man Friday" (Fowles 1987: 141). The narrator insists, again ironically, on the revolutionary dimension of their position, calling them "our two *carbonari* of the mind", who "knew they were like two

---

[1] Darwin contended that apes and humans have a common ancestor, no fossil of which was ever found, so that it remains the mysterious 'missing link' of his theory.

grains of salt in a vast tureen of insipid broth" (Fowles 1987: 141). When Grogan tells Charles he will not betray his confidence, he "la[ys] his hand, as if swearing on a Bible, on *The Origins of Species* [sic]" (Fowles 1987: 192).

In A.S. Byatt's novella 'Morpho Eugenia' (1992), the hero, ironically named 'Adamson', is a naturalist who moves gradually away from a belief in the Book of Genesis and "the wonders of divine Design" towards "atheistic materialism" (Byatt 1992: 10, 33). He too engages in lively debates with his father-in-law, a parson who likes to fly to the defence of faith and God, much like Swift's "good-hearted Rector" in *Ever After*, published in the same year, who hopes to find in his son-in-law a "vigorous whetstone to his own blunted faculties" (Swift 1992: 125). In Byatt's novella the father-in-law disappears gradually from the picture, leaving the hero to enjoy his moral and intellectual superiority over a decadent family of 'insects', in which his own wife, his conventional 'domestic angel', has revealed her true nature as a monstrously fat and immobile Queen ant (much like her mother). In contrast, in Swift's novel, the clergyman becomes a wrathful, vindictive figure of doom, precipitating the apostasy of the protagonist's Victorian ancestor Matthew Pearce. The same theme thus receives radically different literary treatments.

It should also be noted that Swift's twentieth-century protagonist Bill Unwin, the bumbling, mediocre literary critic, is no scientist and his ideas about Darwinism are the product of widespread misconceptions, as his musings show: "It is true (we know now) that we are descended from the apes" (Swift 1992: 233). He also uses the controversial, misleading phrase coined by Herbert Spencer to vulgarise Darwinism – "survival of the fittest" (Swift 1992: 2) – which Darwin would reluctantly adopt in later editions of his *On the Origin of Species*. In comparison, Matthew's agonised reflections on natural selection are precise and incisive, particularly in the diary entry of 6 January 1858, (see Swift 1992: 141-143), in which Swift pastiches scientific thought, letting questions, answers and objections follow each other in a rational, methodical way. Nevertheless, one could argue that Swift's literary interest in words tends to supersede scientific considerations. Matthew, for instance, remarks on the fact that, because human beings are never the same, "reproduction [...] belie[s] its name", and stresses that "special" is a "misnomer" in the phrase "to feel 'special'" (Swift 1992: 142, 143), since it opposes singularity and resemblance within a species.

Matthew Kneale, the author of *English Passengers* (2000), chose to end his plot in 1859, before the publication of *On the Origin of Species,* yet this text too allows for a dramatic confrontation between the Reverend Geoffrey Wilson, who duly (but comically) loses his wits at the end, and the sinister Dr Potter, modelled on Robert Knox, who in 1850 published the racist pseudo-scientific tract *The Races of Man, a Fragment.* In *Ark Baby*, however, Liz Jensen goes one step further, by placing Charles Darwin himself on stage in her novel: Parson Phelps represents the beleaguered clergy, while on the side of 'science' stand the taxidermist (who goes by the unlikely name of Ivanhoe Scrapie), his Belgian cook, Jacques-Yves Cabillaud,[2] who once went on a long voyage aboard the *Beagle*, where he experimented with fish and fowl for the benefit of Darwin's palate, and Darwin himself, who appears towards the end as a special guest of Queen Victoria alias the "Royal Hippo" (Jensen 1998: 306-307). Also included in the cast of characters is "the Gentleman Monkey", Jensen's ingenious version of Darwin's 'missing link'. Jensen's book is undoubtedly neo-Victorian, but also belongs to the genre of science fiction, since the plot contains dystopic scenes set in 2005, which manage to be at once sinister (sterility has struck Britain) and hilarious. Graham Swift does not resort to anything so fanciful, but, more academically, his character Bill quotes at length from a letter written by Charles Darwin to his wife in 1858 (see Swift 1992: 225-226).

Therefore, if the trauma linked to Darwinism is often given a comic, whimsical literary treatment, when and why does the playful reconstruction of a historical period and its intellectual debates give way to the tragic depiction of damaging experience and trauma? Both Fowles's and Swift's fictions include a highly self-reflexive dimension, and both clearly, if implicitly, ask the question of how fiction, the child of invention and imagination, can represent the intensely personal, painful and unutterable experience of deep trauma. Both writers are faced with the dilemma of accounting for the *privacy*

---

[2] In obvious parody of the famous French navigator, Jacques-Yves Cousteau; *cabillaud* means 'cod'.

and unique quality of suffering, on the one hand, and for a collective, even cultural, trauma within a wider historical context, on the other.

In her analysis of how trauma can be narrated and written, Cathy Caruth traces a number of "key figures" within "the textual itinerary of insistently recurring words or figures" present in trauma texts:

> The key figures my analysis uncovers and highlights – the figures of "departure," "falling," "burning," or "awakening" – in their insistence, here engender stories that in fact emerge out of the rhetorical potential and the literary resonance of these figures, a literary dimension that cannot be reduced to the thematic content of the text or to what the theory encodes, and that, beyond what we can know or theorize about it, stubbornly persists in bearing witness to some forgotten wound. (Caruth 1996: 5)

The figure of the falling body becomes particularly relevant in the fourth chapter of Caruth's *Unclaimed Experience*, entitled 'The Falling Body and the Impact of Reference (de Man, Kant, Kleist)'. Discussing Paul de Man and his 1982 essay 'The Resistance to Theory', Caruth explains that after Newton "the world of motion became, quite literally, a world of falling", and she suggests "that the history of philosophy after Newton could be thought of as a series of confrontations with the question of how to talk about falling" (Caruth 1996: 75-76). This same figure proves central to the narration of Matthew's traumatic experience in *Ever After*. As a young man of twenty-five in the summer of 1844, he first undergoes an encounter with the fossil of an ichthyosaur, not, like Bill Unwin, in the safe surroundings of a Museum, but *in situ*, in Lyme Regis, in the very place where the death of the creature had occurred, as mentioned obliquely, in a very Swiftian way, through the device of aposiopesis: "here, still trapped in the rock […], was the thing itself. Here, in the very spot where – Here. Now. Then" (Swift 1992: 100-101). Thus the narrative of the encounter with the ichthyosaur is twice mediated, since before this imaginative commentary by Bill Unwin, it first appears in the novel in a diary entry written by Matthew ten years after the event itself, as a memory triggered anew by the loss of an infant son (Swift 1992: 99-100). This is quite in keeping with Caruth's theory of trauma as possession, as adopted by Anne Whitehead:

> Insufficiently grasped at the time of its occurrence, trauma does not lie in the possession of the individual, to be recounted at will, but rather acts as a haunting or possessive influence which not only insistently and intrusively returns but is, moreover, experienced for the first time only in its belated repetition. (Whitehead 2004: 5)

And yet the figure of falling is not used by Matthew himself when he narrates the incident in his diary (see Swift 1992: 99-100) but by his descendant Bill, when the latter tries to "picture the scene",[3] to capture precisely what could have happened and how and the likely effect of the encounter on Matthew at the time. Bill uses the image of falling as an immediate, dreadful experience: "I see him lurching, slipping, fleeing down that wet path towards the beach" (Swift 1992: 89). Somewhat later Bill again reverts to the trope:

> He feels something open up inside him, so that he is vaster and emptier than he ever imagined, and feels himself starting to fall, and fall, through himself. He lurches on to the path, as if outward movement will stop this inward feeling. He passes a startled young woman, who has fallen also, but less than her own length and on to solid ground. [...] Everything is lost and confused – sea, rocks, cliffs, sand – in swamping greyness. (Swift 1992: 101-102)

Bill insists on the isolating intensity and the private quality of a holiday turned into "an experience from which he must recover, slowly convalesce", with no one to "help or nurse him" (Swift 1992: 102-103).

---

[3] Swift's narrators often use the phrase "You have to picture the scene", and not only in *Ever After* (see Swift 1992: 101,185, 260).

The young woman, who has fallen "on to solid ground",[4] provides a tragic parallel, the better to dramatise what Matthew has suddenly lost: the ground beneath his feet, the order and stability of a God-governed world as offered in Matthew's mother's Bible, which a few years before had still been for him "the literal and immutable truth", "the basis" of the world (Swift 1992: 92). This experience rocks Matthew's world and makes it fall apart: what happens to him is the contrary of an 'epiphany', in its literal sense, i.e. the revelation of a divine reality, since what 'manifests' itself here is only absence. Man, alone in a vast empty world, is himself a hollow void, inhabited by doubt and absence, doomed to dissolve into nothingness. Georges Letissier has drawn the contours of what he calls "une esthétique du vertige darwinien" – an aesthetics of Darwinian vertigo – in Swift's *Ever After*, by insisting on Swift's discontinuous treatment of novelistic time (inspired by Polonius's praise of "indirection" in *Hamlet*) and on the 'Darwinian structure' of Swift's novel (see Letissier 2001: 288).

Matthew Pearce falls "through himself" into an inner abyss, the desolation of which is matched by the stormy, misty and dramatic landscape of "swamping greyness" dissolving all certainty, all security, all landmarks. For the reader familiar with Swift's work, this objective correlative is reminiscent of the aesthetics of *Waterland,* in which Mary is "gone, still here but gone, somewhere inside [her]self", and in which the grey flatness both of land and water symbolises the "coming of things to their limits", the "invasion by Nothing of the fragile islands of life" (Swift 1984: 101, 296). In Bill's dramatised version of Matthew's trauma, the trope of the falling body is used both

---

[4] Daniel Lea underlines the intertextual link with Jane Austen's *Persuasion* (1818), "particularly in regard to the injured ankle that features in both narratives" (Lea 2005: 136). But Lea is a little imprecise here, since in *Persuasion* Louisa Musgrove falls from the high part of the Cobb onto the lower part, badly injuring not her ankle but her head. There is, however, a twisted ankle in *The French Lieutenant's Woman*, with Sarah Woodruff falsely claiming to have injured herself by falling down the stairs of her boarding house, but this happens in Exeter, not Lyme Regis (even if, ironically, Charles had always feared that she might hurt her ankles on the steep paths of the Undercliff). This detail is a good example of the way in which Swift exploits and mixes previous texts, not as nostalgic and sycophantic reiteration, but as a form of subversive innovation. The nineteenth-century novel has inspired in both Fowles and Swift what Christian Gutleben aptly calls "a spirit of new creation out of old forms" (Gutleben 2001: 146).

to depict the experience of nothingness and the redeeming act of 'falling' in love with Elizabeth. Bill "chooses to believe" that being in love and getting married would have helped Matthew to keep the traumatic experience repressed altogether, or at least to hold it at bay, "that he would have felt himself falling, sinking, collapsing again, not with that fearful sense of falling into a void, but with a sense of miraculous, restoring gravitation" (Swift 1992: 103). The sight of his father, the clock-maker, at work in his workshop, might have helped him to cling to his belief in a meaningful world, ordered by the hand of a creating genius, until the death of Felix in 1854 thrust him back into doubt and chaos again.

In A.N. Wilson's *Who Was Oswald Fish?* (1981), the eponymous Victorian architect leaves behind him "the dark years of grief and selftormenting guilt" to adopt a blithe paganism, acknowledging that "since Darwin and others have shown the Bible not to be true", there are many reasons "for saying farewell to the Christian church", though in his case these are not so much "intellectual difficulties" as "the Church's infernal insistence on chastity" (Wilson 1981: 24). The use of the adjective "infernal" alone, in this context, betrays the playful treatment of the theme; yet alongside the comedy Wilson seriously points to the vanities and fears inherent to the human condition, using the trope of a fall into a bottomless abyss. It is not in the pastiches of Victorian diaries that Wilson's narrator situates this dread, but within the minds of his twentieth-century characters, the contemporary descendents of the Fish family. The tone is half serious, half playful, as Fanny and Fred, having made passionate love on a tomb in Kensal Green Cemetery, stare, Hamlet-like, at a "grinning skull", but the Darwinian heritage of agnosticism is undeniably present: "Is this what we are all hurtling towards?" asks Fred, "Is this where it all leads – just to damp and mould?", to which the usually jolly, boisterous and vulgar Fanny answers quietly: "Now you know what I mean about emptiness at the heart of the universe" (Wilson 1981: 185).[5] Matthew's anguish over the death of Felix in Swift's novel is echoed by Fanny, who, suddenly chastened at the sight of a child's tomb, asks: "How can people believe in a God who lets their children die, Prince Consort, how can

---

[5] The phrase is used recurrently, on pages 104, 135 and 185 of Wilson's novel, creating a comedy of repetition, but combined with a grim and chilling effect.

they?" (Wilson 1981: 186) As usual in Wilson's novel, the parodic intent, manifested here by the use of Fred's ridiculous nickname, goes hand in hand with a much more sombre mood; and it is one of the strong features of this novel that the narrative voice always manages to strike the right note and tone, while shifting so perilously between radically opposed poles and moods.

In 'Morpho Eugenia', Harald Alabaster rebels against the modern idea that "we make God in our image, because we cannot do otherwise": "I cannot believe that. [...] It opens the path to *a dark pit of horrors*" (Byatt 1995: 34, emphasis added). Logically, to depict nothingness, the clergyman uses well known tropes: loss of faith is pictured as a fall into an abyss of chaos, reminiscent of the language of the Bible when it evokes both the world before Creation and the bottomless pits of damnation. The same deliberate lexical contamination operates in *Ark Baby,* in which Jensen portrays the Victorian hero of her novel, Tobias Phelps, helplessly watching his father losing his mind as he rants in the pulpit, tearing Darwin's book to pieces. Tobias later wishes he "had pulled [his] father back from the edge of the abyss", and explains: "I had thought we were safe. But the world had begun to tilt" (Jensen 1998: 141). The impression of vertigo and instability created by the latter sentence is emphasised by the fact that it stands alone on one line on the page, a paragraph unto itself. Parson Phelps is then taken to a "Sanatorium for the Spiritually Disturbed", housing clergymen who have lost their faith (and their minds) because of Darwinism. "[H]igh on a hill overlooking the North Sea", the Sanatorium is "tall and stark and built of grey stone", "perched on the edge of a precipice, as though in sympathy with the mental state of its inmates" (Jensen 1998: 216). The intrusive heterodiegetic narrative voice enjoins its readers to "picture another landscape, the landscape of loss", and, in striking poetic idiom, hints at horrors without, echoed by greater horrors within the mind and the subconscious of the inmates:

> Herring gulls and guillemots, oblivious to the symbolic disjunction between land and water, belief and chaos, wheel in the sky overhead, jostled by the sharp salt wind, and screech their hoarse and plaintive cries. Ink-blue, the sea rolls far below, its surface dashed with the startling white of horses' tails on the

wave-crests. The looming shadows of giant squid,
patrolling the coast, lurk ten fathoms deep beneath in
an unknown world. (Jensen 1998: 216)

Once inside the sanatorium, we witness the apparently
nonsensical dialogue between the mad inmates and the rational
Principal, and yet Jensen manages to convey the tragic dimension of
those broken lives, through the simple description of a bemused
Parson Phelps who has lost his flesh and his *joie de vivre*, whose
"beliefs have been shattered by Darwinism", and whose "life's work"
has been "set at nought as a result" (Jensen 1998: 217). As the
Principal asserts, it all depends on "whether you choose to cling to the
solid rock of your already established belief, or to take that leap of
imagination and faith that will hurl you into an abyss of chaos and
wonder" (Jensen 1998: 217-218). The fact that Parson Phelps is
forlornly knitting dark red wool, "the colour of Christ's blood"
(Jensen 1998: 216), adds to the sobering poignancy of the scene.
Unlike Wilson, who mixes moods frequently and subtly, Jensen has
only devoted a small parenthesis to the trauma narrative within a
novel that is mostly comic and light in its mood (even if the
implications and undertones can be sinister, for instance in the
dystopic 'science-fiction' scenes). But like Wilson, even within this
melancholic scene, Jensen pursues an original and paradoxical
interaction of comedy and tragedy, by building up a dialogue which is
not a conversation between two speakers but the juxtaposed, parallel
monologues of several clergymen who remain deaf to one another,
isolated in their madness:

> '*Our Father which art in Heaven,*' droned the
> blond-haired clergyman, doing something
> complicated and unsuccessful with the tangle of his
> fingers.
>   Parson Phelps asked in a croak, 'Did I do
> wrong?'
>   '*Thy Isambard Kingdom come,*' said the
> bearded clergyman. '*Thy Isambard rum-te-tum.*'
> (Jensen 1998: 220, original emphases)

The "bearded clergyman" is blasphemously punning on the name of an icon of his time, who also features prominently in *Ever After*, and whose work both Matthew Pearce and Bill Unwin admire, Isambard Kingdom Brunel. "To build a bridge! To span a void!" intones Bill, quoting Matthew's wistful enthusiasm: "To link *terra firma* with *terra firma*; to throw a path across a void" (Swift 1992: 203, 141). According to Bill, Brunel died just in time, since "only two months after his death, Darwin would publish (some come to fame by building, some by –) his *Origin of Species* [sic]" (Swift 1992: 203). Hence Brunel "would never know. Need never know"; he could remain, ever after, "[s]afe in his sunset glory. Safe within the limits of an old, safe world" (Swift 1992: 203).

Thus the trope of the falling body links to the Christian images of the Fall, of Hell as an abyss, as if apostasy, ironically, could find no other language to define and describe itself but the language of religion.[6] John Fowles places his own hero Charles in a position similar to Matthew Pearce's, but his use of the imagery of the falling body is much more ambiguous, applying both to apostasy and to blind, unimaginative faith in an established religion. In Chapter Forty-eight of *The French Lieutenant's Woman*, Charles, having just had sexual intercourse with Sarah, finds himself alone in a small redstone church in a shabby Exeter neighbourhood, desperately trying to pray, but unable to do so. He utters the Lord's Prayer without conviction: "The dark silence and emptiness welled back once the ritual words were said" (Fowles 1987: 311). Obsessed with Sarah's image, he finds himself unable to concentrate, an insistence taking the form of a chiasmus, as the narrative voice repeats his impressions: "How empty the church was, how silent" (Fowles 1987: 311). In his own house, God has become an absence and established religion an intolerable pretence: "[Charles] locked his fingers with a white violence, as if he would break his knuckles, staring, staring into the darkness" (Fowles 1987: 313). On the one hand, he is relieved to understand that his dread of the departed souls watching and judging him – "a whole dense congregation of others" – is pointless, that instead of the

---

[6] Salman Rushdie, a victim of contemporary religious bigotry, is particularly sensitive to the issue of religious discourse and imagery. In his novel *Shalimar the Clown*, the heroine, reflecting on Baudelaire's poem 'Harmonie du soir', notices that the poet has used a great number of religious similes, and realises that "[n]ew images urgently needed to be made. Images for a godless world" (Rushdie 2005: 19).

promise of an everlasting afterlife there are only "silent, empty pews" (Fowles 1987: 315). On the other hand, even if it implies exhilarating personal freedom, this blank *absence* is terrifying, and Charles cannot simply "leap into atheism" (Fowles 1987: 316). The narrator clearly sets Charles among the doubting, agonising, insufficiently emancipated atheists, commenting that "[i]n all but a very few Victorian atheists (that militant elite led by Bradlaugh) and agnostics there was a profound sense of exclusion, of a gift withdrawn" (Fowles 1987: 311). It is this sense of traumatic exclusion that Charles struggles with:

> Deep in his heart Charles did not wish to be an agnostic. Because he had never needed faith, he had quite happily learnt to do without it; and his reason, his knowledge of Lyell and Darwin, had told him he was right to do without its dogma. Yet here he was, not weeping for Sarah, but for his own inability to speak to God. He knew, in that dark church, that the wires were down. No communication was possible. (Fowles 1987: 312)

Charles is here reeling under the effect of a horror he had already felt earlier, while reading the story of M. de la Roncière: "life was a dark machine, a sinister astrology, a verdict at birth and without appeal, a zero over all"; "Life was a pit in Bedlam" (Fowles 1987: 204, 205). He needs to find buffers to place between himself and "the ultimate hell" of "infinite and empty space", between himself and "universal chaos, looming behind the fragile structure of human order" (Fowles 1987: 278, 209). However, in an ironic mirror effect, the void of unbelief is reflected in the pit of "iron certainties and rigid conventions", as Charles realises that his whole life so far has been an empty pretence, that "the vicious circle haunt[ing] him", the "vital flaw", have made of him "what he [is]":

> more an indecision than a reality, more a dream than a man, more a silence than a word, a bone than an action. And fossils!

> He had become, while still alive, as if dead.[7]
> It was like coming to a bottomless brink.
> (Fowles 1987: 315)

Fowles and Swift, as they weave their web of fossils, falls, and Lyme Regis seascapes, are both obliquely alluding to a Victorian hypotext, Thomas Hardy's *A Pair of Blue Eyes* (1873).[8] Georges Letissier develops the intertextual link between Hardy and Swift, noticing in both narratives the trope of the fall, but, he argues, in Hardy's novel Henry Knight is threatened with a literal fall whereas the fall that Matthew experiences is "strictement métaphysique", exclusively metaphysical (Letissier 2001: 295). Matthew's encounter with the ichthyosaur directly echoes an episode in Hardy's novel, in which Henry Knight, precariously suspended from a few tufts of grass on the cliff face, finds himself face to face with a fossil and threatened with immediate death. The encounter with the ichthyosaur remains the traumatic and intense experience that triggers terrible doubt, and Christian Gutleben has argued convincingly that the "aesthetics of doubt" in Swift's novel concerns Bill just as much as Matthew, Hiroshima as much as religious faith, marital faithfulness as well as religious faith, and that a striking "syntax of hesitation" (dashes, gaps, aposiopesis, etc.) characterises Swift's (or rather Bill Unwin's) style (Gutleben 2001: 147-148). Matthew Pearce's painful apostasy in 1860 puts an end to his habit of writing in his notebooks, which, as Bill Unwin phrases it, were "the record of his life as a fiction: 'the beginning of my make-belief'" (Swift 1992: 183). Bill is here quoting a passage that he had first copied out of context, without the diary entry from which he had extracted it, and which therefore stands out visibly from the page, framed by suspension dots: "… The moment of my unbelief. The beginning of my make-belief…" (Swift 1992: 101, original ellipses). The seamless transition from narrative to quotation, from the third person pronoun to the first person, and the use of the

---

[7] Uncharacteristically, Fowles is here using the idiom of a stopped life, a living death, which becomes, as previously argued, a favoured motif in Swift's fiction.

[8] See, for example, DeVitis and Palmer, who analyse the links between Fowles' novel and Hardy's *A Pair of Blue Eyes*, in an interesting study of the fossil imagery present in both works (DeVitis and Palmer 1974: 95-97), and Gutleben, who reads Swift's episode as an explicit development of what Hardy "could only hint at" (Gutleben 2001: 147).

possessive adjective "my" all contribute to blurring the boundaries between Bill's trauma and that of Matthew. The Darwin-linked trauma narrative is continued in another form in the context of the twentieth century; indeed the last sentence of the novel, with its binary rhythm, "he took his life, he took his life" is a direct echo to Bill's comment about Matthew: "He wished to disappear. And he did, he did" (Swift 1992: 220).[9] While ostensibly concerning Bill's father, the concluding sentence thus functions as a proleptic hint that Bill's traumatic experience has led him to the decision to take his life, a second time as it were, bearing out the opening declaration, "These are, I should warn you, the words of a dead man" (Swift 1992: 1).

For his part, Fowles often quotes Tennyson's *In Memoriam* (1850) in his novel, a poem which he describes in a footnote as "that celebrated anthology of after-life anxiety" (Fowles 1987: 30 fn). Tennyson, invoked by the omnipresent author-figure, also preys on the mind of the character, Charles, in the form of the four stanzas of part LI of the poem, quoted in the novel. Suddenly, presence becomes oppressive to Charles, and absence potentially liberating, as he rebels against the idea that the dead are watching him:

> *There must be wisdom with great Death; the dead shall look me thro' and thro'.* Charles's whole being rose up against those two foul propositions; against this macabre desire to go backwards into the future, mesmerized eyes on one's dead fathers instead of on one's unborn sons. (Fowles 1987: 316, original emphasis)

T.S. Eliot, a religious poet in his own right, devoted an essay to Tennyson's *In Memoriam*, in which he remarked that although the poem "antidates *The Origin of Species* [sic] by several years", it is "a poem of despair, but of despair of a religious kind", even if Tennyson's contemporaries, in Eliot's opinion, misunderstood it, taking it for "a message of hope and reassurance to their rather fading Christian faith" (Eliot 1975: 244, 245, 243). *In Memoriam*, he

---

[9] For a reading of this ambiguous ending, see Lea 2005: 150. I rather think that Swift is here echoing Hamlet's weary death wish, "You cannot, sir, take from me anything that I will not more willingly part withal – except my life, except my life, except my life" (*Hamlet* II.ii l. 215-217); see Pesso-Miquel 1999: 135.

suggests, "is not religious because of the quality of its faith, but because of the quality of its doubt. Its faith is a poor thing, but its doubt is a very intense experience" (Eliot 1975: 245).

In *Ever After* Matthew's intense experience of doubt, pictured as a fall into an abyss of emptiness and absence, is echoed years later by Bill Unwin's bereavement, felt to be a cosmic catastrophe, "since it was [Ruth], after all, who held things together for [him], who held [his] world together" (Swift 1992: 114). Bill shares with Matthew a feeling of helplessness, since he was raised in an anchorless world where his mother considered futile things to be essential, using religious words such as "heavenly", "divine", or "angel" to express her selfish, shallow emotions (Swift 1992, 16, 17), her adulterous sensuousness.

> That word [divine] had only to spring from her lips and I believed it to be so. [...] I thought *crêpes Suzette* and *tarte Tatin* were divine, and I thought oyster-grey silk camiknickers were divine, and I thought my mother's laughter, the sheer, vicious gaiety in her eyes, was divine. (Swift 1992: 17)

Elizabeth restored Matthew to a sense of gravity. Just like her, Ruth can "tug, like an anchor-chain" at Bill's heart, so that losing her means that the world falls apart again, and logically Ruth's imminent death is described in terms of inner vacuity similar to Matthew's "fall, through himself": "I knew then, [...] by the feeling that my body was like an empty sack, that she was going to die" (Swift 1992: 124, 113).

If the *nature* of the Victorian trauma linked to the death of God is clearly acknowledged and analysed, one cannot say that all neo-Victorian novelists are equally interested in communicating the intensity of this experience to the reader, through an awakening of the reader's capacity for empathy or, more problematically, by inviting outright identification, what Bill Unwin defines as "[such] a simple, unconscionable thing: to be another person" (Swift 1992: 101). Cathy Caruth insists a great deal on this quality of empathy, of being able to listen, to hear the voice crying out from the past, which enables her to suggest an interpretation of Tasso's story of Tancred, as reported by Freud in *Beyond the Pleasure Principle*:

> We can also read the address of the voice […] as the
> story of the way in which one's own trauma is tied up
> with the trauma of another, through the very
> possibility and surprise of listening to another's
> wound. (Caruth 1996: 8)

In Swift's novel Bill Unwin's trauma is thus deeply "tied up" with
Matthew's, and Bill is the first listener and empathic 'reader' of
Matthew's trauma, who in turn teaches the readers of Swift's novel to
see and listen, to *feel*, to understand and experience what it was "really
like" (Swift 1992: 42).[10] Christian Gutleben has shown how Bill's
reconstruction of Matthew "tallies with what [Dominick] LaCapra
defines as 'empathic unsettlement, a kind of virtual experience
through which one puts oneself in the other's position while
recognizing the difference of that position'" (LaCapra 2001: 78, qtd.
Gutleben 2009/2010: 145).

Bill Unwin constantly underlines his lack of real knowledge
and the constructed, mediatised nature of all the information he has
about Matthew, who had reported from memory, long after, the
ichthyosaur episode, which "scrupulous as Matthew's memory was,
might have been subject to a degree of narrative licence" (Swift 1992:
90) Bill insists on his lack of certainty, his distance, his
disengagement, as in his admission, "I don't understand him. I never
sought him out, I could do without him" (Swift 1992: 132). In a
passage akin to an essay, Bill underlines his insensitivity to the
Darwinian 'revolution' that caused so much soul-searching:

> I have dipped into Darwin. It's heavy-going. The
> prose thick, grey, and formidable, like porridge. It is
> hard to see in this sober stodge the bombshell which
> tore apart Matthew's life and horrified Victorian
> society. (Swift 1992: 223)

Paradoxically, this very scepticism is an *encouragement* for Swift's
readers to lose themselves imaginatively in the plight of the

---

[10] In a novel that takes palaeontology, i.e. the reconstruction of a skeleton from the
scattered bones, as its model, one is struck by the urgency of emotional re-enactment
conceived almost as an ethical duty: "what was it really like?" (Swift 1992: 42)

Victorians. Bill never stops emphasising the importance of fiction, of imagination, of "invention", in his own (and the reader's) dealings with Matthew: "I invent all this. I don't know that this is how it happened. It can't have been like this simply because I imagine it so" (Swift 1992: 109). Elsewhere, Bill reflects that "[i]f that scene ever really took place (I imagine. I invent), then how deluded the older man was" and asks himself, "So, have I got it all wrong? I invent. I imagine" (Swift 1992: 127, 212). The omnipresent world of the theatre (which, in spite of its supposedly illusory and ephemeral nature, gives Bill a satisfying sense of rootedness and belonging) contaminates Bill's narrative, as he "invent[s]" a highly dramatic scene of apostasy and anathema, watched from afar, "quite intently" by one spectator, Mrs Hunt, and, ironically by another, namely "God in the sky", so that Bill finally acknowledges reluctant defeat and "falter[s] in his script-writing" (Swift 1992: 184, 187).

Paradoxically, the more Bill protests his ignorance and asserts the fictitious nature of his narrative, the more convincing he sounds, so that the reader feels empathy for Matthew but also for Bill, who is aware of the strong materiality of the link between himself and his suffering ancestor. Indeed, like *Who Was Oswald Fish?* or *Ark Baby*, *Ever After* is a family saga stretching across the nineteenth and twentieth centuries, and the contemporary and Victorian characters share exactly the same degree of 'reality'; they are ontologically compatible. Moreover, the miraculous direct link with the past is foregrounded and materialised: in Wilson's novel Oswald Fish's diaries are found years later by his daughter Nana Owen, amazed to see the "little black and marbled notebooks" falling from the loft "like manna from heaven" (Wilson 1983: 20), while in Swift's novel Matthew's notebooks are found by Bill in "two old, rotting leather suitcases – one with its brass locks completely seized up", and when Bill opens them, he "touch[es] the pages that [Matthew] once touched" and "occup[ies], as it were, [Matthew's] phantom skin" (Swift 1992: 45, 46). Bill has inherited the clock that was Matthew's wedding gift from his father, and when Bill winds it, his hand "hold[s] the key once held by Matthew" (Swift 1992: 47).[11] This constant temptation to over-identify, this capacity to put himself in Matthew's

---

[11] Swift is here playing with intertextuality, since in Fowles' novel the winding of a watch is also linked closely to love and marriage, illusion and reality (Fowles 1987: 291).

shoes, makes Bill wonder, "What is he to me?", as he self-consciously echoes the actor in *Hamlet* who sheds real, bitter tears over the Trojan tragedy of old Hecuba:

> What was Darwin to him? What is Matthew to me?
> 'What's Hecuba to him or he to Hecuba?'
> 'Seems, Madam? Nay, it is; I know not "seems".'
> (Swift 1992: 49, 143)[12]

Matthew, like Hamlet, cannot live in pretence and dissimulation, and if Bill Unwin, who has identified with Hamlet since childhood, commits suicide, it is partly because he has lost Ruth, and because Katherine can only be for him a "substitoot", a word which, as the fate of his step-father Sam makes clear, rhymes with "prostitoot" (Swift 1992: 148). Ruth's face "was full of *life*" (Swift 1992: 118, original emphasis), whereas Katherine is not "the real thing", since she is only *lifelike*: "she *seems* to me […] *like* life itself. *Like* life itself" (Swift 1992: 87, emphasis added). Indeed, as Bill goes on to ask, "how can one person take the place of another?" (Swift 1992: 88) Later, as he narrates the ichthyosaur encounter, Bill cannot help alluding to Ruth yet again, and to the empathy necessary for good acting (see Swift 1992: 101).

Fowles's narrative strategies in *The French Lieutenant's Woman* are radically different, and my contention is that they are not nearly as efficient in enabling the reader to experience empathy. First of all, although the nineteenth and twentieth centuries sit comfortably side by side in the novel, Fowles has not chosen the genre of the family saga, and no descendants of Charles and Sarah appear on the scene. Therefore the two temporal frames are not ontologically compatible, since the only character contemporary to the reader is the author figure who interacts with Charles, a fictitious character, although he is supposed to belong to *our* 'reality'. Of course one could argue that the genre of the saga is present in the conventional ending in Chapter Forty-four, in which the narrator informs us that Charles's grandsons "today still control the great shop", but the siring of these descendants is treated so flippantly that they are dismissed as cardboard caricatures before they can spring to life: "[Charles and

---

[12] Bill is quoting *Hamlet* II.ii, l. 553 and I.ii, l. 75.

Ernestina] begat what shall it be − let us say seven children" (Fowles 1987: 292). Moreover, Fowles famously and playfully breaks the frame between ontological zones, between fiction and reality, in Chapter Thirteen, and most outrageously so in Chapter Forty-five, in which 'the author' travels in Charles's railway carriage; he also reverses the strategy by having Ernestina step over into 'our' world, when the narrator casually mentions that "she died on the day that Hitler invaded Poland" (Fowles 1987: 29).

Elsewhere, Fowles's narrator chides his *"hypocrite lecteur"* for not realising that 'real' characters turn their own lives into stories:

> You do not even think of your own past as quite real; you dress it up, you gild it or blacken it, censor it, tinker with it ... fictionalize it, in a word, and put it away on a shelf − your book, your romanced autobiography. We are all in flight from the real reality. That is a basic definition of *Homo Sapiens*.
> (Fowles 1987: 87, original ellipses)

Admittedly, Swift lends similar reflections to Bill and Matthew, but these are expressed in fictitious, autobiographical form, whereas the heterodiegetic narrator created by Fowles breaks the frame, and "can only smile" with a strong sense of superiority over both his readers and his characters (Fowles 1987: 87). Fowles does not hesitate to 'cheat' in order to mislead his readers, for instance when he asserts "the simple fact of the matter being that [Sarah] had not lodged with a female cousin at Weymouth" (Fowles 1987: 50). This shores up the lie on which the plot is built, i.e. Sarah's alleged affair with the titular French lieutenant, since we take the sentence as a euphemistic way of saying that she had lodged with the lieutenant. Such playfulness resists the readers' empathic recognition of existential 'trauma' as genuine suffering.

Fowles's insistence on control, on establishing a knowing dialogue with the reader over the helpless and hapless heads of his characters, seen from the outside, discussed, judged, contributes to the creation of a narrative voice that is often flippant and playful, deliberately preventing reader identification with the characters. In contrast, Swift's characters are empathic and encourage the reader to be so too, to see *with* the characters, to adopt their points of view, "to picture how the world might be – how it might fall apart or hold, incredibly, together – in the eyes of other people" (Swift 1992: 101).

Characteristically, when the reader gets to the crucial moment of Charles's crisis in the small church in Exeter, s/he is prevented from experiencing any imaginative understanding of Charles's plight by the narrator's shifts between inner and outer focalisations, as well as the juxtaposition of personal trauma narrative with the narrator's distanced, intellectual assessment of his Victorian characters, undertaken from the comfortable 'modern' standpoint of the 1960s. Swift's characters are eager to understand, from the inside as it were, "what was it like, what was it really like" (Swift 1992: 42); if Fowles's reader begins to *feel* what it was 'really' like for Charles, when his point of view is adopted (see Fowles 1987: 314-315), the narrator, as if dreading to be found guilty of pathos or sentimentality, takes care to break the spell and introduce sarcasm. Inner focalisation is cropped; Charles stops being a subject experiencing traumatic doubt to become once again the object of an ironic, condescending scrutiny. Outer focalisation ensures that we stop seeing *with* Charles in order to stare *at* him. The narrative voice resorts to jocularity, immediately debunking the hint of an epiphany by a return to trivial, mundane reality: "Charles was stopped – […] and there was a kind of radiance in his face. It may simply have been from the gaslight by the steps" (Fowles 1987: 317).

Fowles's novel was conceived not as a trauma narrative at all, but as a hybrid mixture, half story, half handbook on Victorian times, full of learned footnotes, precise statistics, rather condescending judgements, and moments of overdone, strained comedy, as when Dr Grogan remembers the young husband to whom it had to be hinted that "life is neither begotten nor born through the navel" (Fowles 1987: 190). This is, of course, part and parcel of what has made the novel so distinctive, experimental and famous as a model of metafictional postmodernism, but, viewed strictly in terms of a 'trauma narrative', Graham Swift's narrative strategies are much more conducive to empathy than those of Fowles. Where Fowles maintains an amused and caustic distance between an 'us' and a 'them', between author-narrator/reader and characters, between the 1960s and the 1860s, between naïve existential *angst* and cynical, sophisticated atheism laced with sexual savvy, Swift chooses to blur those boundaries. Indeed, with their distinctive typography and nineteenth-century idiom, Matthew's notebooks ought to be well isolated from Bill's narrative, and yet the two sets of texts constitute anything but watertight compartments. The framed narrative dissolves into the framing narrative; the notebooks leak into Bill's twentieth-century notes and musings, contaminating them, haunting them, in many different forms, as summaries, echoes, exegeses, questions, interpretations, constant dramatisations, metatextual criticism, or in the form of common points of reference or intertexts, such as *Hamlet*. Instead of the discrete juxtaposition of two separate worlds, the novel offers a fluid continuity, a fluctuating, unstable textual space, or postmodernist "zone", as Brian McHale would call it (McHale 1987: 60).

Both parts of the plot interact. Matthew's soul-searching is echoed in Bill's death wish and in Bill's father's qualms of conscience over Hiroshima, whereas Bill's jealous obsessions about cuckoldry leak into Matthew's notebooks and influence Bill's reading of the relationship between Matthew and his wife. Bill lends Matthew his own obsessions about the unreality of reality, and the vacuity and mutability of the self, as when he conjectures that Matthew, like him, "must have asked, many a time: [...] Am I this, or am I that?" (Swift 1992: 90) A good example of this constant flow and circulation of texts and meanings occurs when Matthew's apostasy, first reported directly in the notebooks, is re-imagined by Bill through filters and refracted perceptions, like the uncomprehending gaze of Emily, the rector's wife, who sees her husband "shaking with tears" without knowing why (Swift 1992: 189). Had those tears been evoked in a direct narrative, they would have run the risk of being perceived as maudlin and sentimental. Yet the imaginary tears move the reader much more effectively for being introduced into the narrative tentatively, obliquely even, as part of a moment reconstructed by both narrator and reader, "as patient palaeontologists reconstruct the anatomies of extinct beasts" (Swift 1992, 185). Put differently, Fowles claims to make fun of the omniscient heterodiegetic narrator of the Victorian novel with fastidious distaste, yet he also delights in his narrator's own postures of power and control, ironically staging the figure of the author/narrator as "omnipotent god" (Fowles 1987: 348). Swift's narrative strategies, for their part, illustrate the *absence* of any deity, the vacuity and uncertainty of the world, in which both Matthew and Bill have to grope their way blindly out of existential traumas.

One could argue that Fowles sets more store on self-conscious experimentation than on story and ethics, that he is above all interested in avoiding predictable plots and narrative forms, and in weaning the reader from lazy reading habits and expectations. As for Swift, although as a novelist he is a sophisticated craftsman, he never lets form get the upper hand. In their relationship to Victorians, they are also different: Fowles assumes an amused condescension towards them, even if he also enjoys going against the grain by envying the greater keenness of their sexual pleasure (Fowles 1987: 233-234). Swift's character Bill Unwin, on the other hand, tends to recognise in the Victorian 'Other' an image of himself, and Swift deliberately adopts an ethical stance that could come across as being at odds with his postmodernist narrative techniques. Katherine Tarbox chose to exploit the metaphor of evolution in her article on Fowles and Darwin, and she enthusiastically praises the way in which Fowles has made the genre of the novel "evolve" (Tarbox 1996: 101-102). Her work is a good example of the fact that Fowles' novel is much more often cited for its formal experimentations than for its ethical positions.

Apart from his spectacular authorial intrusions, such as the 'erasure' of events formerly presented as true, and the three discrete endings, Fowles predominantly maintains a classical heterodiegetic and chronological form for his narrative, quite representative of the fact that the narrator is constantly exercising his authority, that he has his fictional world 'under control', whereas Swift has chosen a completely fragmented, anti-linear form. This turning away from chronology and linearity, many critics argue, is characteristic of trauma narratives. Ann Whitehead draws on Caruth's work for this opinion:

> Caruth's conceptualisation of trauma [...] suggests that if trauma is at all susceptible to narrative formulation, then it requires a literary form which departs from conventional linear sequence. The irruption of one time into another is figured by Caruth as a form of possession or haunting. (Whitehead 2004: 6)

In Graham Swift's case, however, the fragmented, jigsaw-puzzle aesthetics is not limited to *Ever After* alone but is present in all his novels. One could argue that this is because his novels always have traumatised narrators, obsessively frozen in the past, caught up in the eternal present of a traumatic moment.[13]

Neo-Victorian novelists, then, treat Darwin-linked trauma in a whole gamut of moods, from the humorous and ironic to the tragic and empathic. Yet Darwinism, in another guise, also functions as a metaphor for traumas relating to one's position in society. In other words, 'social Darwinism' is used to explain, and sometimes to excuse, the brutal and traumatic exclusion of individuals from the social body. Again this leads novelists to use different treatments of the motif. Thus Christian Gutleben underlines the fact that social criticism in *Ever After* centres on the dire working conditions of miners in the copper mines, and is "carried out in the mode of social Darwinism using an extended analogy between miners, slaves and insects" (Gutleben 2009/2010: 143). The simile quoted by Gutleben is Matthew's, to which Bill adds his own conjectures about Rector Hunt's worried reactions to "that undermined world, waiting to collapse into infernal darkness" (Swift 1992: 218), couched in Christian similes of damnation that once more evoke the 'black hole' of trauma also.

Similarly, the motif of social evolution arguably differentiates the 'fossil' scenes as depicted by Thomas Hardy and Graham Swift. In *A Pair of Blue Eyes* (1873), Hardy describes a man, who, in the face of death, can only regret the life he might lose, a well-ordered life in which he is very much aware of hierarchies and of his privileged position. Henry Knight is a gentleman, whose name underlines his descent from the gallant knights of more chivalrous times, whereas the fossil is in his eyes an "underling", both physically close to him and infinitely distant from him, "*separated* by millions of years" (Hardy 1985: 209, original emphasis). This episode creates a resemblance between Knight and Charles Lyell, who, as a staunch Christian, tended to resist his friend Darwin's theory of natural selection (based on random chance), precisely because Lyell believed in a teleology, an 'evolution' of life forms progressing from lower to higher forms, from "uncouth shapes" and "sinister crocodilian outlines" towards the apex

---

[13] Swift's latest novel, *Tomorrow* (2008), although it departs abruptly from his other novels – firstly because it is a pleasurable bedtime story, and secondly because it is narrated by a heroine, not a hero – is nevertheless organised in the same rambling, associative, anti-linear fashion.

of the ladder, man himself, the ultimate purpose of Nature's minute changes over extended periods of time (Hardy 1985: 210). Knight is faced by a creature that belongs to "mean times" and is but a "relic", producing a sense of individual diminution: "he was to be with the small in his death" (Hardy 1985: 209). For Swift's Matthew Pearce, however, the encounter with the ichthyosaur shatters all his previous complacent certainties; far from being for him an inferior form of life, the fossil becomes an *alter ego,* and the millions of years do not *seperate* them but are rather a bridge linking them together. The gaze of the creature annihilates the distance between them: "the massive eye that stares *through* millions of years" (Swift 1992: 101, emphasis added). Moreover, if Knight thinks of his fiancée Elfride, whom he deems quite incapable of saving him, it is with protective condescension: "the mental picture of Elfride in the world, without himself to cherish her, smote his heart" (Hardy 1985: 210). His love for her will be sacrificed at the first hint that she might not be perfectly chaste, and the narrator acidly condemns his rejection of her "upon evidence [he] would be ashamed to admit in judging a dog" (Hardy 1985: 326). Knight jilts Elfride with the same implacable self-righteousness that animates Angel Clare's rejection of Tess in *Tess of the d'Urbervilles* (1891); Knight has no doubt concerning Man's privileged place in nature and his own privileged place within society. If Matthew, years later, decides to divorce his wife, it is not, like Henry Knight, on the altar of prejudice, convention and cant, but rather because of intellectual integrity. Fowles's character Charles similarly turns his back on Hardy's hero by choosing a woman he believes to be unchaste, thus sacrificing a marriage of convenience to Ernestina in favour of an exalting 'marriage of true minds'. However, according to Tony Jackson, Charles changes his views on Darwinism, from an optimistic reading of Darwinism as teleology (with evolution leading upwards, towards the higher, better human species) to a more postmodernist and existentialist reading of Darwinism as utter randomness, leading nowhere (Jackson 1997: 225-226).

Very early in *Ever After* the motif of social Darwinism is treated in a more humorous, flippant way, as Bill jokes about the inability of "desiccated, enfeebled" university dons, a.k.a. "dodos", to be the "fittest" and to survive, threatened as they are by uneducated, unemployed youths, "social scrap", "prowling, snarling lout[s], all tattoos and bared teeth" (Swift 1992: 2). Yet alongside the humorous, light touch, Swift is in fact introducing key themes and images, in particular the traumatic images of collapse and fall, in his account of "the 'real world'", outside the ancient walls of the college, a world which should be solid and reliable but is in fact "falling apart; its social fabric in tatters", "stricken, doomed" (Swift 1992: 2).

John Fowles also uses the theory of social Darwinism, of some social classes or individuals being 'fitter' than others, more capable of adapting to modern, industrial circumstances. This theory first propounded by Herbert Spencer in order to defend Darwinism, and later used by Darwin's enemies to discredit him, but in any case it remains a fanciful distortion of what Darwin had thought and written. In *The French Lieutenant's Woman*, Charles is flippant about the fact that his fiancée is not a gentleman's daughter, although he himself is a gentleman: "[Your father] did say that he would not let his daughter marry a man who considered his grandfather to be an ape. But I think on reflection he will recall that in my case it was a titled ape" (Fowles 1987: 11). The didactic narrative voice belabours the point, by underlining the fact that Tina's father "had been a draper", while "Charles's had been a baronet" (Fowles 1987: 11). At the beginning therefore, the theme is treated with amused detachment both by the protagonist and the narrator. Later, the metaphor of social Darwinism is exploited by the narrator, as Charles comes to realise that gentility, as he knows it, may soon be threatened with extinction:

> He felt that the enormous apparatus rank required a gentleman to erect around himself was like the massive armour that had been the death warrant of so many ancient saurian species. [...] He actually stopped, poor living fossil, as the brisker and fitter forms of life jostled busily before him. (Fowles 1987: 253)

Even Charles's prospective father-in-law, who protests that he will never be brought to agree "that we are all descended from monkeys" (Fowles 1987: 249), is willing to adopt the idea that a species must change in order to survive. Thus he attempts to overcome Charles's reluctance to 'fall' by working in trade, and he reawakens Charles's "doubts about the futility of his existence", making him feel "like a badly stitched sample napkin, in all ways a victim of evolution"

(Fowles 1987: 250). H.W. Fawkner, for his part, argues that Charles's attitude towards Freeman and capitalism is a deliberate and noble choice: "Charles's passiveness becomes noble refusal. He chooses not to adapt"; he is "not the feudal gentleman flinching at the vulgarities of bourgeois materialism, but the moral aristocrat nobly resisting time" (Fawkner 1984: 82).

Yet Charles embodies victimhood only relatively: Charles' situation, even when deprived of his prospects of inheriting his uncle's title, is still more than comfortable. The situation is very different for Sarah Woodruff, lost in the social jungle, where survival requires adaptability and new skills. Sarah Woodruff, explicitly called "the protagonist" by the narrator (Fowles 1987: 348), seems to adopt a suicidal attitude in this respect, since she deliberately invents a lover and a story of sinful seduction for herself, adopting the role of a fallen woman. Sarah is first a governess, and therefore a classless creature, neither master nor servant, condemned to loneliness. This traumatic exclusion, condemning governesses to a virtual non-existence as discreet ghosts on the fringes of other people's lives has often provided the subject of nineteenth-century art.[14] John Fowles takes up the theme, depicting Sarah's despair, when living with the Talbots, at being "allowed to live in paradise, but forbidden to enjoy it" (Fowles 1987: 148). But he goes one step further, imagining a heroine who can only feel real, alive and free by deliberately pretending to have 'fallen' and putting herself beyond the pale. There is a form of masochism evident in Sarah, and yet one could argue that Fowles's novel fails to convey to the reader a true 'inner' sense of the trauma of being a female outcast, a 'Jezebel', in Victorian society. By not giving Sarah a voice beyond a few stilted dialogues with Charles, by avoiding almost any introspection into Sarah's thoughts, Fowles prevents the reader from imaginatively entering this particular type of predicament. Since Fowles wants to keep her a cipher and an intriguing enigma, the scene showing Sarah tempted to jump out of the window is perceived only through the narrator's male viewpoint, with the incident treated lightly, even flippantly, in two brief, emotionless paragraphs (see Fowles 1987: 83-84).[15] Fowles does not dramatise Sarah, keeping her

---

[14] Charlotte Brontë's *Jane Eyre* (1847) comes to mind, but also Victorian painting, for instance *The Governess* (1854) by Rebecca Solomon.
[15] For a discussion of Sarah's possible existentialist self-awareness, see Jackson 2000: 230-231.

aloof and mysterious, as if he were a playwright refusing to write any monologues for the heroine.

   In *Who Was Oswald Fish?*, Wilson treats the problem of fallen women from the point of view of the male seducer, who was let off very easily in Victorian society, while the unmarried mother was usually turned out. Oswald Fish, an obscure Victorian artist leads rather a merry life, but his diaries reveal that his final years are marked by despair and madness, as he becomes obsessed with the idea of the cast-off son he begat but never knew, Toby Shakespeare. This theme is treated briefly and ambiguously by Wilson, as tragi-comedy, but he also chooses to construct a parallel with the traumatic ostracism of homosexuals in the twentieth century: one of his characters commits suicide because his beloved wife has just discovered his secret, guilty bisexuality and now considers him a monster. Unlike his flamboyant and foppish colleague Jeremy, who flaunts his homosexuality, David Matheson, like a badly adapted specimen within a mutating species, cannot survive. Here the portrayal of the experience of trauma is chilling and tragic, though rendered in an understated and unemotional way. As in the other neo-Victorian novels under scrutiny, the narrator resorts to the trope of a falling body, both literally, because the character throws himself under an underground train, and figuratively, since the victim first goes to the river Thames "to linger a moment from his purpose like a wanderer in the outer regions of hell before he plunged into the abyss" (Wilson 1983: 219).

   David remains a minor character, a tragic character trapped in an acerbic neo-Victorian comedy, and his trauma is given a remarkable literary treatment. Apart from an ironical self-reflexive detail, "ALL TRAINS GO TO VICTORIA read the sign. Not this one" (Wilson 1983: 220), the narrative voice never intrudes. Instead, the whole scene is focalised through the grim gaze of the man determined to put an end to his own life. The reader has an uncanny double feeling of recognition and affinity, on the one hand, and of distraction preventing empathy, on the other. This is no doubt due to the fascinating focus on minute, irrelevant external details, perceived by a mind that, instead of carrying on an agonised introspection, must continue to function under duress. He first has to find an answer for the bored ticket clerk at Westminster Station, and then he distractedly chooses a twenty-pence ticket rather than a destination, only to regret it:

> The machine did its work. The little piece of green
> card came slithering down the chute. Absurdly, he
> regretted the extravagance. He could have bought the
> cheapest sort of ticket. (Wilson 1983: 220)

Throughout, the style remains terse, matter-of-fact, and spare, as the character's body continues to function almost automatically. The less emotional the narrative is, the less direct its appeal to the reader's emotions and empathy, the more, paradoxically, the reader feels convinced of the truth and nature of the depicted trauma. The episode invites empathy and yet keeps readers at a distance, prevents them from drawing near, from getting involved. Wilson's idiosyncratic treatment of his character's predicament could be read as an illustration of Patricia Yaeger's arguments concerning the reception of trauma narratives. While discussing the issue of scale in thinking about trauma, and the reactions of "secondary witnesses", i.e. the readers of those narratives, Yaeger quotes Primo Levi, who insisted on the necessity of individualising trauma narratives, since "a single Anne Frank excites more emotion than the myriads who suffered as she did but whose image has remained in the shadows" (Levi 1989: 56, qtd. Yaeger 2006: 409). Yaeger contrasts Levi's opinion with that of Cynthia Ozick, who believes nobody ought to read Anne Frank's diary without being aware of the scale and magnitude of Nazi atrocities (see Yaeger 2006: 414). Yaeger also looks at how readers can be distracted by figures of speech that prevent intimacy, that force them "to shed [the] comforting illusion of empathy, to negate compassion's thrill" (Yaeger 2006: 410), but warns that "secondary witnesses" ought to resist falling off "those formal precipices":

> Even as this double defamiliarization feels like a
> violation of the etiquette of reading or listening, our
> only choice is to plunge down the precipice and then
> scramble back up again – into the next sentence, the
> next trial by fire. The failure to fall, the failure to try
> for entanglement, proximity, or painful intimacy with
> the Shoah's obscenities (that is, the failure to embrace

testimonial speech acts that both demand and deny identification) would mean that all these moments will be lost in time, like tears in rain. (Yaeger 2006: 422, emphasis added)[16]

In Fowles's novel Sarah is the prototypical victim of social ostracism, of the 'unfit', un-adapted specimen, and yet she is freed miraculously from having to face the consequences of her "long fall" (Fowles 1987: 87), allowed to escape the fate that should have been hers in Victorian society: eking out the small income of a prostitute. Fowles claims that his author-figure, his "impresario", as he calls him twice (Fowles 1987: 394, 395), suggests two different endings at the end, but in fact both are 'happy' endings for Sarah, improbably rescued and gentrified by Dante Gabriel Rossetti, with her vocabulary and accent 'refined' by London. Again Fowles is cheating, giving his heroine a miserable 'double' to increase the plausibility of the novel and lessen the 'Cinderella' effect of the end. The prostitute whom Charles hires because she reminds him of Sarah, in spite of her "too red" mouth "like a gash of blood", is called Sarah too, and the mirroring effect is emphasised when Charles, at the novel's end, soothes his own daughter with his watch, "as he had once before in a similar predicament", i.e. with the prostitute's baby (Fowles 1987: 267, 391, and see 277). The prostitute called Sarah bears the brunt of social ostracism; she is the dark shadow reminding us that, there, but for the grace of God, goes Sarah Woodruff; she is Fowles's apology for his wish-fulfilling plot, his concession to social realism.

Of course one could argue that Sarah Woodruff actually serves two functions. On the one hand, she reminds the reader of the ease with which a woman could 'fall', while on the other, she embodies an anachronistic version of the free, independent, artistic 'New Woman' at the fin-de-siècle. Fawkner insists that Fowles "very deliberately emphasizes the historical situation", the fact that March 1867 was the time of the "birth of feminism", and he argues that "Charles's partial awareness of the sexism of his time is more credible than Sarah's rather implausible feminine consciousness." According to him, Fowles gives his characters an ideological and allegorical

---

[16] Yaeger appears to view identification, so long as self-consciously enacted, as less ethically fraught than does LaCapra, who deems it a form of appropriation.

dimension: "he gives their private conflicts a wider human significance that allows us to see their struggle with themselves and each other in relation to feminism, socialism, and existentialism" (Fawkner 1984: 88). Mahmoud Salami shares this opinion: "[Sarah] represents the entire age of emancipation for women, a factor that is epitomized in the epigraph from Marx in the title page of the novel" (Salami 1992: 128).

In this anachronistic guise, Sarah attracts Charles and lures him away from Ernestina. Thus the 'love story' of Charles and Sarah could easily be read as an illustration of Charles Darwin's much less vulgarised theory of sexual selection, as propounded in *The Descent of Man*. However this double-weighted function mars the credibility of Sarah as a fictional character: portrayed in abandoned aesthetic poses, Sarah remains an object, onto which the male protagonist projects his fantasies, and she never really accedes to the status of subject. In comparison, Ruth in *Ever After* is not portrayed from the inside, nor is she given a direct presence, but for very different reasons, since she is already dead when the novel opens, and the elegiac mode in which she is treated, as well as the fact that she is not 'anachronistic' and 'new' like Sarah, contribute much better to the willing suspension of disbelief and identification on the part of the reader.

Perhaps we could tentatively conclude that to function as a 'trauma narrative' able to create empathic understanding in the reader, a literary text requires an insider's perspective and as little authoritative heterodiegetic narration as possible. The neo-Victorian novels discussed also show that the experience of trauma can be apprehended even within a mainly comic novel, where the Darwinian theme reminds us that evolution is not necessarily synonymous with progress and that societies can change for worse as well as for better. When Fowles began the fashion of revisiting both the Victorian novel and the *furore* over Darwin, he wrote from the secure standpoint of the sixties, with their atmosphere of defiance and sexual liberation. In the 1980s, when Salman Rushdie wrote *The Satanic Verses* (1988), he could still make fun of Christian Fundamentalists, Neo-Creationists all, by creating the character of Mr Dumsday. This American, whose name suggests a dumb harbinger of doomsday, once lectured to Indian audiences about the desperate young people of America, given, in their existential despair, to narcotics and sex. Mr Dumsday confides: "If I believed my great-granddaddy was a chimpanzee, why, I'd be pretty depressed myself" (Rushdie 1988: 76). A decade later, Rushdie explained that this fictitious episode had been inspired by a conference he had attended in Cochin, given by a ludicrous American creationist called Duane Gish,[17] who had "bellow[ed] on" much "like a dinosaur who hasn't noticed he's extinct" (Rushdie 2002: 280). Ten years on, Rushdie could only be appalled by the fierceness and the "unfunny" nature of anti-Darwin reactions within creationist circles (Rushdie 2002: 281). Contemporary literature in its neo-Victorian guise chooses Darwinism as a theme as rich in outrageously comic potentialities as it was laden with the tragic presence of trauma, but the opposition between science and Genesis has come to overstep the limits of fiction and history to leak into our present-day reality. John Fowles, the creator of one of the first modern neo-Victorian novels, took pains to stress the great distance between Victorian Britain and his own present, a time when "the Gentleman, in 1969 far more of a dying species than even Charles's pessimistic imagination might have foreseen", was mutating into "the modern gentleman, that breed we call scientists" (Fowles 1987: 256). Yet while he had the prescience to foresee new mutations ahead – "the scientist is but one more form, and will be superseded" (Fowles 1987: 257) – he did not specify by whom. By Creationists, we might conjecture, or perhaps by Bill Unwin's humorously nightmarish "snarling louts": "If the Vandals are coming, the Vandals are coming" (Swift 1992: 2). The doubt that racked the Victorians seems, in many people, to have been replaced by a staunch, intolerant, religious belief, often bordering on fanaticism; as Rushdie warns, "There are, once again, anathemas and persecutions" (Rushdie 2002: 281). There will always be new forms of cultural trauma, individual and collective. But by then the writers of neo-Victorian trauma narratives, or of literature more generally, might themselves have become an extinct species.

Bibliography

Byatt, A.S. 1995. *Angels and Insects* [1992]. London: Vintage.

---

[17] Duane Gish was also invited to a 'Creation Conference' in Turkey in 1992. Anti-Darwinism crosses religious and national boundaries; the Turkish Creationist campaign is financed both by Christian Fundamentalist funds and Islamist funds, and on its fringes gravitate controversial figures like Harun Yahya, who inundated European schools with glossy 'Atlases of creation'.

Caruth, Cathy. 1996. *Unclaimed Experience: Trauma, Narrative, and History.* Baltimore, Maryland: The Johns Hopkins University Press.

DeVitis, A., and William J. Palmer. 1974. 'A Pair of Blue Eyes Flash at *The French Lieutenant's Woman', Contemporary Literature*, 15(1) (Winter): 90-101.

Eliot, T.S. 'In Memoriam' (1936), in *Selected Prose of T.S. Eliot* (with notes and introduction by Frank Kermode). New York: Farrar, Straus and Giroux, 1975: 239-247.

Fawkner, H..W. 1984. *The Timescapes of John Fowles* (foreword by John Fowles). London and Toronto: Associated University Presses.

Fowles, John. 1987. *The French Lieutenant's Woman* [1969]. London: Pan Books.

Gutleben, Christian. 2001. *Nostalgic Postmodernism. The Victorian Tradition and the Contemporary British Novel.* Amsterdam & New York: Rodopi.

——— 2009/2010. 'Shock Tactics: The Art of Linking and Transcending Victorian and Postmodern Traumas in Graham Swift's *Ever After*', *Neo-Victorian Studies* 2(2) (Winter): 137-156.

Hardy, Thomas. 1985. *A Pair of Blue Eyes* [1873]. Oxford: Oxford World's Classics.

Jackson, Tony E. 1997. 'Charles and the Hopeful Monster: Postmodern Evolutionary Theory in *The French Lieutenant's Woman'*, *Twentieth Century Literature,* 43(2) (Summer): 221-242.

Jensen, Liz. 1998. *Ark Baby.* London: Bloomsbury.

Kneale, Matthew. 2001. *English Passengers* [2000]. London: Penguin Books.

LaCapra, Dominick. 2001. *Writing History, Writing Trauma.* Baltimore, Maryland: The Johns Hopkins University Press.

Lea, Daniel. 2005. *Graham Swift.* Manchester: Manchester University Press.

Letissier, Georges. 2001. '*Ever After* de Graham Swift: paléontologie, géologie, biologie, et fiction romanesque', *Études Anglaises* 54(3): 285-298.

Levi, Primo. 1989. *The Drowned and the Saved* (tr. Raymond Rosenthal). New York: Vintage.

Mc Hale, Brian. 1987. *Postmodernist Fiction.* New York & London: Methuen.

Pesso-Miquel, Catherine. 1999. '"Immortal Longings": la mort en représentation dans l'œuvre de Graham Swift', *ebc* 17 (décembre): 131-148.

Rushdie, Salman. 1988. *The Satanic Verses.* London: Viking.

———. 2005. *Shalimar the Clown.* London: Jonathan Cape.

———. 2002. 'September 1999: Darwin in Kansas' in *Step Across This Line: Collected Nonfiction 1992-2002.* New York: Random House: 280-282.

Salami, Mahmoud. 1992. *John Fowles's Fiction and the Poetics of Postmodernism.* London & Toronto: Associated University Presses.

Swift, Graham. 1984. *Waterland* [1983]. London: Picador.

———. 1992. *Ever After.* London: Picador.

Tarbox, Katherine. 1996. '*The French Lieutenant's Woman* and the Evolution of Narrative', *Twentieth Century Literature*, 42(1) (Spring): 88-102.

Vickroy, Laurie. 2002. *Trauma and Survival in Contemporary Fiction.* Charlottesville & London: University of Virginia Press.

Whitehead, Anne. 2004. *Trauma Fiction.* Edinburgh: Edinburgh University Press.

Wilson, A.N. 1983. *Who Was Oswald Fish?* [1981] Harmondsworth: Penguin.

Yaeger, Patricia. 2006. 'Testimony without Intimacy', *Poetics Today* 27(2) (Summer): 399-423.

'Perfectly innocent, natural, *playful*':
Incest in Neo-Victorian Women's Writing

Mark Llewellyn

Abstract:
Like her earlier novel *Possession: A Romance* (1990), A.S. Byatt's novella 'Morpho Eugenia' (1992), a tale of science and incest, has become a key item in the growing canon of neo-Victorian literature. This interests me because of my own work towards a monograph on the cultural history of incest in the nineteenth century. Between the 1835 Marriage Act and the 1908 Punishment of Incest Act, various sites of Victorian knowledge – politics, theology and religion, anthropology, classical studies, philosophy, economics, social commentary, eugenics, even visual arts and music, not to mention pornography – were the location of a heated debate around the issue of incest as a concept. This has received little sustained critical attention compared to the periods immediately preceding and following the Victorians. The fact that contemporary women writers should use the incest trope as part of the neo-Victorian aesthetic is intriguing, particularly in the varied and divergent approaches taken towards incest as trauma. In this essay, I discuss Byatt's novella and her more recent novel *The Children's Book* (2009) in order to suggest ways in which their metapoetics both make explicit and yet inadequately account for the Victorians' own traumatic pathology of incest. In the second part of the chapter, I bring these issues into a new reading of the trauma contained within Sarah Waters's novel *Affinity* (1999).

Keywords: aesthetics, affinity, 'anagrammatic trauma', anthropology, children's literature, consanguinity, ethics, father-daughter relationship, game, incest, law, 'scriptotherapy'.

*****

"A sociological riddle, a feminist issue and a category of law", writes Vikki Bell, "incest is all these things. But is 'incest' the same at each of these sites?" (Bell 1993: 1) In contemporary culture it might perhaps be considered easy to dismiss the significance (though not the outrage) associated with the incestuous by citing those public and seemingly rare cases such as that of Josef Fritzl,[1] which might figure as part of what Bell terms the "relations of power between groups: between men and women, and between men and children, particularly in the context of the institution of the family" (Bell 1993: 4). Yet alongside a feminist analysis about the power-dynamics often inherent within the context of incestuous acts, we must also recognise the prominence of the incest narrative in Western culture at the aesthetic level. Indeed, in one of the earliest pieces on the cultural significance of the Fritzl case, Ritchie Robertson argued in the *Times Literary Supplement* that "[l]ife in Austria seems to be competing with literature [...] to anyone familiar with Austrian literature it [the Fritzl case] calls up a host of literary reminiscences" (Robertson 2008: 3). To associate the incestuous with the literary or the cultural, however, is far from unproblematic. As Elizabeth Barnes noted, "critical work done on the subject [of incest] has been uneven", although it has also "become a central subject, and central concern, of the late twentieth century"; Barnes continues by remarking that "the narrativizing of incest reveals the ways in which discourses of sex, gender, class, race, desire, intimacy, family, domination, love, and violence inform, and have informed, understandings of personal, political, and cultural experience" in the same period (Barnes 2002: 3). It is through exploring the role of the incestuous within the specific historical revisionism afforded by neo-Victorianism at the end of the twentieth and beginning of the twenty-first centuries, and in particular the nature of such encounters in the work of A.S. Byatt and Sarah Waters, that this essay seeks to address how we might enhance our interpretation of the significance of incest for contemporary women writers in particular and the ways in which they attempt to interpret a revised understanding of the domestic, and desiring, spaces of the (neo-) Victorian family in the process.

The desire to ignore, or fear to understand and interpret, the incestuous has come to concern me from two different critical viewpoints: firstly, from my current research interest on nineteenth-century reconceptualisations of the incestuous across a range of discourses, and   secondly, from contemporary culture's continuing

---

[1] For further discussion of the Fritzl case and contemporary incest narratives see my forthcoming 'Incest and Literary Gender Studies' (Llewellyn 2011). See also Marsh and Pancevski 2009.

fascination with what perhaps still remains the final taboo. The presence of incest and incestuous narratives in the present perhaps relates more than we are initially prepared to admit to a continuity between incestuous ethics and incestuous aesthetics, which we have inherited from the conflicted theorisations of incest in the Victorian period. In my recent work on the nineteenth century, I have sought to conceptualise the ways in which the period between 1835 and 1908, from the Deceased Wife's Sister Act through to the Punishment of Incest Act,[2] can be divided into four decades where incest was a question of ethics,[3] morality and issues of legal (mis)conduct, followed by a further 30 or so years where the aesthetic possibilities of incest – as a structural, artistic and creative device or trope – played with, reinvented and reinterpreted these earlier ethical concerns. The advent of psychoanalysis and, of course, the deep indebtedness of Freudian diagnoses of primary desires, narcissism and Oedipal struggle to nineteenth-century psychologists intensified and crystallised what by the first publication of Freud's *Three Theories of Sexuality* in 1905 were already quasi-established understandings of the fraught nature of bloodlines and the incest taboo.[4] My argument in this chapter is that the structural and conceptual triangulation between ethics, aesthetics and psychoanalysis carries over into the tensions inherent in contemporary fiction's representation of incest, and that (re)interpretations of the primal taboo remain deeply divided, particularly in the case of neo-Victorian texts by contemporary women writers.

---

[2] For a summary of the legal issues around the Deceased Wife's Sister Act, see Anderson 1982 and Kuper 2009: 63-80. Information related to the Punishment of Incest Act can be found in Bailey and Blackburn 1979.

[3] My use of the term 'ethics' here requires further justification: by the ethical I do not imply that the incestuous comes under the definition of good or appropriate behaviour. Rather I seek to use 'ethical' as shorthand for the cultural, legal, moral, and social encoding of actions that form part of a collective understanding of acceptable and unacceptable action. Hence, the 'ethics' of incest here denotes the codification of prohibitions against incest, not an endorsement of its practice.

[4] The incest taboo as formulated in the late-Victorian period is to be found in a range of discourses, principally the legal, religious, and more particularly anthropological debates surrounding exogamy and endogamy to be found in texts such as John Lubbock's *Origin of Civilisation and the Primitive Condition of Man* (1870), J.G. Frazer's *Totemism* (1887), Ernest Crawley's 'Sexual Taboo' in the *Journal of the Royal Anthropological Institute* (1895), and Emile Durkheim's *Incest: The Nature and Origin of the Taboo* (1897).

Discussing the work of Virginia Woolf, Jen Shelton has commented that in general "[i]ncest works in the interstices between ind viduals and larger societies, presenting itself as a cultural phenomenon in other people's societies but a private problem within our own" (Shelton 2002: 226). While this has been the case in the past, particularly in the twentieth century since the legalistic prohibitions of incest have been increasingly codified, I want to argue that the works of contemporary women writers exhibit a feminist concern to negate part of this boundary creation between the cultural or anthropological (elsewhere) and the familial and doubly domestic (homely and here, rather than abroad), by acknowledging the differing ways to encode, make public, and revise aspects of a culturally incestuous history. Revision as a feminist concept is important, particularly when one traces the sense of incest as a foundational concept in Western culture. During the 'memory wars' of the 1990s, during which feminist activists and others sought to develop awareness of the everyday nature of 'trauma', Marina Warner commented that

> Incest has now become one of the dominant focuses
> of moral panic, flourishing virulently in fantasy as
> well as occurring, often tragically, in practice, while
> these old stories, which deal with it, and which offer
> the consolation of an image reflected back, of a wrong
> unmasked, of authority shaken and realigned, lie
> overlooked on the river-bed of contemporary
> consciousness, as a turbulent current of terror,
> suspicions and despair rushes by. Through its own
> form of riddling [... an incest narrative] encrypted
> emotional and social realities which helped its
> receivers at least to understand their situation a bit
> better. (Warner 2003: 132)

In the light of the recent Fritzl case, the media frenzy and the generation of "moral panic", one can see Warner's point. But one can also identify the importance of seeking to confront the incestuous as a social, cultural, familial and feminist problem within the present moment. The Fritzl case does this precisely by *not* being a fairytale or a fictionalised narrative, the dominant modes of questioning, exploring, and articulating such cultural fears and anxieties outside and alongside legal frameworks and moral prohibitions. Not coincidentally, in a seminal sociological study of incest in the US published in the 1980s, Judith Lewis Herman began her discussion with the Cinderella fairytale: "The Cinderella story warns little girls that it is dangerous to be left alone with a widowed father" (Herman 1981: 1). Such a warning carries over into twentieth- and twenty-first-century revisions of the fairytale, as signalled by the statement from Warner and, more recently, in Margo Lanagan's *Tender Morsels* (2009). A book for young adults, Lanagan's novel utilises magic realism to address in often bold and assertive terms the incestuous relationship and offspring produced by it. Within the first 50 pages, the central character Liga is subjected to sex with her father, has abortions induced by potions he purchases, and is impregnated again with the child to whom she will give birth after her father's mysterious death. Lanagan's rewriting of the 'Snow White and Rose Red' fairytale throughout the remainder of the book sees the story firmly rooted in the context of feminist revision of patriarchal narrative. But the real interest of the novel lies in its timelessness – disconnected from present, past and future through the construction of event and character as much as place and chronology, Lanagan's novel concerns the fundamental notion of identity formed within the trauma of an excessively close familial relationship. Such a relationship, the novel suggests, lies outside chronological specificity: it is timeless because repetitive, cyclical, and simultaneously reconstructive and deconstructive. As the narrator questions after Liga's father's death, "Without his voice and body to shape her, did she even exist?" (Lanagan 2009: 34) That the traumatic is here configured as part of the individual's development and core to her existence might be carried over into thinking about how the neo-Victorian itself is concerned with similar moments of conceptual questions around maternity, paternity and origins. It is this idea of identity formation, coupled with re-interpretations of the nature of incestuous desire, across aesthetic and ethical parameters, which I will focus on in the subsequent discussion. I begin with another book about children, reinvention, and storytelling.

1.   *The Children's Book* and 'Morpho Eugenia'

A.S. Byatt's most recent novel *The Children's Book* (2009) is an historical fiction covering the period from the 1890s to the First World War. Following the lives of a series of children and their parents, Byatt's text opens up a reading of the intellectual interactions, cultural exploration and experimentation, and period-dividing attitudes of the late-Victorian and Edwardian ages through the slippages, exchanges, and enclosures of the individual families whose relationships she describes. *The Children's Book* is also an incestuous text: in its narrative of (inter)relationships at levels of thought, emotion, and bodies, Byatt's novel engages with the three elements of the incestuous interpretative drive already mentioned: aesthetics, ethics, and psychoanalysis. As a text that consciously blurs fact and fiction, real figures and imagined identities, events which are verifiable and those which are dreamed, *The Children's Book* regularly reminds readers of its own artificiality, indeed artifice, alongside the more collective memory of an historical time-period obsessed with its own presentism, historical parentage and future. As readers would expect from Byatt, the text is full of playful games about its identity as a fiction, the nature of narrative coincidence and convenience, and the knowingness of the narrative voice; indeed, it might be seen to embody that sense of story, particularly one about families, as "riddling", to use Warner's word. Thus, we learn that one character, Etta Skinner, married to a social scientist interested in issues of inheritance, "was distantly related to the Darwins, the Wedgwoods and the Galtons, which […] must have been attractive to a specialist in heredity" (Byatt 2009: 40). But the neatness of these insider allusions is matched against the confusing, convoluted, and inherently contaminated lineages and heredity mapping of the other characters.[5] During the course of the narrative, the children who serve as the central protagonists of the novel and who live with the children's author Olive Wellwood and her husband Humphry, for example, turn out to be sometimes her children, sometimes his and hers, sometimes his but those of her sister, Violet, who also lives-in with the family, and so forth.

---

[5] For a discussion of the 'incestuous' interrelationships between leading individuals and families in this period, see Kuper 2009, especially 31-51.

The familial set-up at Todefright, Olive's apparently magical estate (from a child's viewpoint), blurs the boundaries between extended family and genetic trace, between bloodlines and kinship, between marital offspring and the results of adulterous liaisons, and between reality and fairytale or story. It also serves as an historical parody of the kinship between dead wives and their sisters, which prompted the Deceased Wife's Sister Act in 1835.[6] This is an incestuous household because blood relations and kinship, or consanguineous relations, are fractured. Byatt seems to lead us towards an understanding of relationships around the domestic, the heart of course of many a Victorian realist novel, which is fractured by the late-Victorian period's sense of decadence and regression. The novel focuses on the late-Victorian period as an age when all inhabitants of this intelligentsia, and the progenitors of new social movements and discourses, are themselves simultaneously adults and children, occupying both sides of the Alice in Wonderland looking-glass.[7] In a statement that itself plays with an incestuous intertextual echoing of Henry James's *Turn of the Screw* (1898), Julian Cain tells his cousin Tom, Olive's son, with whom Julian is in love, that the adults don't understand that they have knowledge of desire and sexuality:

> They think we don't know all these things. They ought to know you learn in school, just by being a boy. You learn them along with Greek and cricket and rowing and drawing. And sniggering and poking and

---

[6] More properly the Marriage Act of 1835, this law prohibited any marriage contract between a widower and his dead wife's sister after the date of the Act, although it legalised those marriages already contracted under the terms of canon law, which allowed such a union prior to 1835. The passing of the Marriage Act and the clauses relating to dead wives and their sisters caused political, religious, legal, and social debate for the next seventy years, until the law was overturned by the Deceased Wife's Sister's Marriage Act in 1907.

[7] There are frequent allusions throughout the text to children's texts of the Victorian period at an inter-layered level which is in some senses beyond the intertextual. The overtness of Byatt's references to children's writers, for example, such as Kenneth Graeme, and to figures associated with childhood, like Baden Powell, serve to portray the adults of the age as more naïve than the children they appear to lead. For a discussion of the glass metaphor and the idea of looking backwards in Byatt's novel see Heilmann and Llewellyn 2010: 156-163.

> passing messages. They ought to know we know.
> They must have known themselves. (Byatt 2009: 47)[8]

To this statement Tom, in many respects the key child of the novel, replies: "Grown-ups always think we don't know things they must have known themselves. They need to remember wrong, I think" (Byatt 2009: 48). It is these acts of misremembering by the parents, the dislocation from their own sense of childhood experience and yet their eternal longing to reach back to what Byatt elsewhere terms the "perfectly innocent, natural, *playful*" (Byatt 1992: 158) nature of sibling desire, which underscores her often cryptic family trees and extended relationships. For reasons of limited space,[9] I want to focus on just two significant instances of incest in the text, both rooted in the text's overall aesthetic but also divergent enough to represent separate cases within the narrative as a whole: firstly, Olive's relationship with her son Tom, and secondly the potter Benedict Fludd's relationship with his daughters. Both are cases of aesthetic or structural incest (that is the denoting of textual relationships within blurred familial boundaries), but the latter also comes under the category of the trauma of incest.

The love between Olive Wellwood and her son Tom is one of the narrative's key drive(r)s. Olive is a writer of children's stories at two levels: on the one hand she publishes quasi-fairytales for the reading public, and on the other she writes a series of children's books for each of the children in her home. These books, kept in a glass case at Todefright, are always in a state of revision, as Olive adds to each child's fabulistic narrative. Most important of these is Tom's story, which troubles Olive and to which she returns most often. As a private text between writer and reader, mother and child, the narrative

---

[8] Compare this to the statement from James's nameless narrator governess: "She [Flora, the young girl] had picked up a small flat piece of wood which happened to have in it a little hole that had evidently suggested to her the idea of sticking in another fragment that might figure as a mast and make the thing a boat. This second morsel, as I watched her, she was very markedly and intently attempting to tighten in its place. [...] I still hear myself cry as I fairly threw myself into [Mrs Grose's] arms: 'They *know* – it's too monstrous: they know, they know!'" (James 1995: 53-54)

[9] Byatt's novel is incredibly rich in incestuous allusions and details, from her use of the literature and visual arts of the 1890s through to her mythic framing intertexts. Interestingly, however, she does not make explicit reference to the legal acts surrounding incest legislation in the time period of the novel.

provides a kind of shared space where the desires between the two parties can be enacted. There is something erotic about Olive's relationship to Tom's book, although this is less discernible in Tom's own asexual attitudes for much of the first part of the novel. The crisis point in their relationship comes when Tom goes away to his cousin Julian's boarding school. Separated from the domestic homeland of Todefright and bullied and sexually abused by older boys at the school, Tom at first finds comfort in the updated versions of his story sent by Olive. But these secret missives are despoiled when discovered and destroyed by the bullies' ringleader, and Tom flees the school and goes missing only to return weeks later to Todefright. Up to this point Olive has always kept Tom's narrative secret, as a shared generational narrative between mother and son, but as the relationship between herself and Tom grows more distanced, Olive uses and appropriates Tom's narrative for public performance as part of a literary collaboration. This viewing of himself and his narrative outside of his relationship with his mother destroys Tom and subsequently leads to his suicide.

What we see here is the fundamental separation of the space between parents and children. As Byatt's narrator puts it: "The young desired to be free of the adults, and at the same time were prepared to resent any hint that the adults might desire to be free of them" (Byatt 2009: 227). The crux of the dilemma here is that which Tom and Olive undergo and interpret in different ways. In using his narrative in public form, it is Olive who 'grows up' and separates from her child rather than the other way round. That Tom's desires are located in the site of a childhood desire, which does not recognise bloodlines as dividing barriers, is clear not long before his death, when Olive encourages him not to dance with her at a ball but to find someone closer to his own age: "At that moment Tom danced jauntily past them, flashing a mild smile at his mother. He had found a partner who was indeed a young woman. She was also his sister" (Byatt 2009: 336). Replacing one female relative with another, Tom apparently seeks recognition of and reconnection to the bloodline identity such a kinship fosters and demands. While not strictly incestuous in a legal sense,[10] Byatt's narrative of Olive and Tom structures incestuous

---

[10] The legal definition of incest in both the Punishment of Incest Act 1908 and the Sexual Offences Act 1956, into which the law was consolidated, requires penetration of the female body by a male blood relative.

potentiality as a sublimated aesthetic sphere of mutual dependency and relation through proximity and the 'offspring' of (literary) art. The metaphorical and fictional serves as a space enabling the possibilities of a desire that expands beyond the everyday into the fairytale or fable. Yet when that creativity moves from the privacy of the domestic to the public sphere of a different kind of performativity, a literal/literary enactment of the space of desire, such freedom ceases to function.

While the relationship between Tom and Olive is such that it allows the often unformed desires between parent and child to be subsumed into a literary aesthetics of shared narrative space, one of the other incest narratives in Byatt's novel has a more physical and traumatic illustration, albeit still residing partly in the realm of the aesthetic. The 'truth' of the relationship between the potter Benedict Fludd, possibly based on the sculptor Eric Gill,[11] and his daughters Pomona and Imogen is discovered by the combined narratives of two other siblings, Fludd's apprentice Philip and his sister Elsie, who comes to join her brother at Fludd's rural home and studio midway through the novel. Philip has already become aware, quite early on in the narrative, of the queerness of relationships in the Fludd family. His first night in the Fludd household involves a nocturnal visitation by a seemingly sleepwalking, naked and pubescent Pomona creeping into his bed (Byatt 2009: 108). Only with Elsie's arrival, however, does the significance of this scene – as a clue to the sublimated father-daughter incest in the family home – become apparent. Elsie goes into the locked room of the artist Fludd, regarded by her as a Bluebeard-like figure, and discovers his private pottery collection:

> The pots were obscene chimaeras, half vessels, half human. They had a purity and clarity of line, and were contorted into every shape of human sexual display and congress. Slender girls clutched and displayed vase-like, intricate modellings of their own lower lips and canals. They lay on their backs, thrusting their pelvis up to be viewed. They sat in mute despair on

---

[11] The diaries of Gill (1882-1940) reveal that he sexually abused his children, committed incest with his sister, and engaged in acts of bestiality with his dog (see MacCarthy 1989).

the tips of towering jars, clutching their nipples defensively, their long hair falling over their cast-down faces. There were also clinical anatomical models – always elegant, always precise and economical, of the male and female sexual organs, separate and conjoined. There were pairs of figures, in strenuous possible and impossible embraces, gentle and terrible.

Some of them had Imogen's long face and drooping shoulders: some of them were plump Pomona. The males were faceless fantasms. Elsie crunched towards them over the destruction of other versions, and saw that the wavering arms and legs, the open mouths and clutching hands were not all the same age, went back years, into childishness. There were so many, Elsie thought they resembled a coral reef, thrusting out stony thickets underwater. It was hard for Elsie to look at them, in the state of bodily need which already possessed her. Something inside her own body responded to the opening up, the penetration, the visual shock of these. But under the sexual response, and stronger, was terror. Not terror, exactly, of what the girls had been made to do, or maybe only imagined as doing. Terror of the ferocious energy that had made so many, so many, compelled by a need she did not want to imagine. (Byatt 2009: 279)

Coming from the potteries herself – Elsie and her brother are from Burslem, the landscape and environs of the writer Arnold Bennett – she is used to the idea of incestuous relationships among the poverty around her,[12] "where someone's little brother or sister was generally thought to be really her child by her brother or father. They slept so close there, flesh to flesh" (Byatt 2009: 295). Here in the supposedly more refined society of an artist lauded by the aesthetic community, Elsie becomes witness to the ways in which such "flesh to flesh"

---

[12] Elsie's comments here fit with the narratives of social reformers from the Victorian period, who identified incest as part of a class/social issue related to confined living spaces and incest by familial proximity (see Wohl 1978).

desires reside just as much in the passionate intensity, "the ferocious energy", of a different class and creative instinct. Alongside the significance of Elsie's discovery of the artworks themselves, however, and the clues they provide to the behaviour of Pomona and Imogen both earlier and later in the novel, is the revelation of Elsie's fear and desire, the "sexual response" twinned with its own "terror". In this respect, Byatt's novel opens up, though it never resolves, the nature of the incest taboo as structured in this period. For Byatt's novel covers the moment at which cultural, social, and political models of the incest prohibition were beginning to change and develop into a more modern legalistic definition of incest as crime. The 1908 Punishment of Incest Act, for instance, serves as a statutory demarcation of the moment at which the twentieth-century definition of incestuous actions separated from the debates about consanguinity, deceased wives and their sisters, Darwinism, eugenics, and anthropological research that had marked the period from the 1830s onwards.[13] Although not referenced outright in Byatt's text, this Act's pivotal role in our interpretation of the something that seems to remain lost, (dis)remembered, unspoken in the novel's relationships between siblings and parents should not go unremarked, particularly as it relates so crucially to the connections between the aesthetic, the traumatic, and the domestic.

Discussing the writer Anäis Nin's relationship with her father, Suzette A. Henke suggests that it was through the configuration of the aesthetic that Nin forged a response to and ultimately experienced the trauma of father-daughter relationships. Henke makes reference to Nin's early experience with her subsequently absent father, what Henke terms the "pornographic photo sessions" (Henke 1998: 59).[14] As Henke comments, in relation to the photographic, the artistic, and the creative, from this point on "[t]he signature of the father marks the daughter, the photograph, and the iconic image that channels his libidinal drives into the framework of pornographic art" (Henke 1998: 59). The inherent duality of the conjoined creative-libidinal drives here is what connects one way of reading the relationships between

---

[13] For a summary of some of these issues across the nineteenth century, but specifically in relation to the bourgeois, see Corbett 2008: 1-29 and Kuper 2009: 52-105.

[14] As an aside connecting the experience of Nin with the Victorian period that provides the focus of this essay, it is worth noting that, as Henke points out, "Joaquin Nin shared some of the scopophilic obsessions of Lewis Carroll" (Henke 1998: 59).

Olive and Tom and Fludd and his daughters in Byatt's novel. That the trauma is performed through the aesthetic (writing; sculpture/pottery) might serve as a reflection on the dislocation of the aesthetic referents within the novel's space from their historical setting. This works at two levels: first, the characters are delineated as continuously aware of their own traumatic belatedness. As Byatt's narrative moves across the chronological separation of years and reigns, the narrator posits that this process was dual-time, reciprocal, unfixed:

> Backwards and forwards, both. The Edwardians knew they came *after* something. […] They looked back. They stared and glared backwards, in an intense, sometimes powerful nostalgia for an imagined Golden Age. (Byatt 2009: 391)

But in a second awareness of such "Backwards and forwards, both" stylistics the contemporary reader is confronted with the problematics involved in seeking to impose or deliberate over moral and ethical choices (even when associated with the traumatic) within this historical context from a perspective of both post and prior knowledge. We are aware that the Edwardian period ends in the cataclysm of the First World War, but one of the complex things that Byatt captures in her text is that the characters genuinely do not know. In spite of this unawareness of the future trauma, they are imbued with a nostalgia for the "Golden Age" that stands both for the seemingly greater stability and prosperity of the Victorians and, more generally, childhood itself. Byatt seems to challenge the preconceptions about the nature of incestuous acts, if they are deemed to be undertaken by adults who themselves have apparently regressed to a childish state of pre-moral self-gratification.[15] The narrative therefore represents a collective, rather than individual, trauma between what would today be regarded as perpetrators and victims, in which our judgement and concern over the domestic discontent prompting the incestuous is problematically reflected back to us as a kind of historical

---

[15] In this respect, the 'ethics' of Byatt's text prove more problematic in their re-enactment of Victorian debates around the differences between consequential, deontological and virtue ethics: see, for example, Henry Sidgwick *The Methods of Ethics* (1874), where the types of ethics are divided into the three categories egoism, intuitionism, utilitarianism (Chapter 1).

complacency. One might constitute both our reading of the novel and
Byatt's formulation of the 'innocence' of childhood disrupted by the
actions of the adults as part of what Henke calls a shared "pathological
configuration", in which

> traumatic memories constitute a kind of prenarrative
> that does not progress or develop in time, but remains
> stereotyped, repetitious and devoid of emotional
> content. Iconic and visual in form, these images
> relentlessly intrude on consciousness. (Henke 1998:
> xvii-xviii)

Moreover, for the children Tom and Pomona such "visual [...]
images" *are* their "consciousness", which causes the excision of
"emotional content" in Tom and the "repetitious" relationship-
formations in Pomona.

But the incestuous acts of Byatt's novel are not always what
they seem. Olive's husband Humphry, for example, attempts to seduce
his daughter Dorothy, who turns out not to be Violet's daughter by
Humphry but Olive's daughter by Anslem, the German puppet master
(Byatt 2009: 344-346). The grotesque and Gothic irony of Dorothy's
father being a man whose art and living derives from controlling
puppets enacting the Grimms' fairytales, those Ur-narratives of
familial discord and disunion, is self-evident. Similarly, while the
desire of Benedict Fludd for his daughters, as manifested in the
pottery viewed by Elsie, privileges the incestuous as an aesthetic act,
the attraction between Fludd's patron, Prosper Cain, and Fludd's
daughter raises further questions about the nature of sublimated cross-
generational desire. Here Byatt raises perhaps a wider concern, as true
of the Victorians and Edwardians as of now, about the nature of age in
relationships, about the potentially 'unnatural' or subversive (even
perverted?) desires judged so by a society that sees age difference
between partners, lovers, spouses, as itself immoral. Byatt may
summarise Freud, reminding us that his *Three Theories of Sexuality*
was published in 1905 as many of these issues come to a head for her
characters, and declare that "Children desired their mother or father,
wished to marry her or him, had fantasies of slaying the other parent"
(Byatt 2009: 396), but her own narrative indicates that these processes

are far more complicated. Thus the older man, Prosper Cain,[16] thinks of how the indefinable nature of his relationship to Fludd's daughter Imogen changes: "He had not expected his intense, quasi-fatherly affection and concern to become blind physical passion, but that had happened and he felt invigorated and renewed" (Byatt 2009: 435). As feminist critics have pointed out, fathers or father-substitutes often invoke the nature of their personal renewal through the relationship with a younger woman, but this in itself does not negate the nature of such relationships bordering on the order of child abuse or sexual exploitation (see Nelson 1988).

It is little wonder that Cain's own daughter Florence feels betrayed and confused, when the engagement of her father and Imogen is announced at the time when she wishes to make public her own marriage to Imogen's brother Geraint. As the scene suggests, this is a moment when the issues of kinship and friendship, companionship and consanguinity, come to the fore, as Florence points out:

> 'The relationships of the people round this table have suddenly become very confused.'
>
> She gave a sharp little laugh. She went on, staring darkly at her father across the silver and white.
>
> 'So Imogen is to become at once my sister and my mother. It is like a Greek myth. Or those things in the Prayer Book you aren't supposed to do.'
> (Byatt 2009: 454)

In her combination of the foundational myths of both Pagan and Judeo-Christian ritual and acceptability, Florence's statement serves as a reminder to readers of this cultural moment of the forbidden, for these are precisely the debates that were being rehearsed during the period 1903-1908 as the Incest Bill was debated, defeated, resurrected, debated again and eventually enacted.[17] The debate then, as perhaps now, revolved around what the specific crime of incest might be defined as involving. Religious law was too vast (as we are all

---

[16] The character's name indicates possible intertexts with Shakespeare's Prospero and his relationship with Miranda, as well as the Biblical Cain's jealousy.

[17] For a summary of the ways in which these parliamentary debates discussed, challenged, and reinforced ongoing cultural, social, medical and psychological discourses about incest, see Bell 1993: 126-149.

descendents of Adam all sexual relationships are incestuous) or too complex (any sexual act made you 'kin' within a wide degree of affinity to the relatives of the person with whom you slept), but legally what was (and is) the constitutive difference that makes *any* incest (even consensual between adults) a crime outside existing laws on rape, child, and sexual abuse? This is a question that has continued to vex legal and cultural theorists, including feminists, because in privileging the specificity of the crime we must also define the limitations of the statute that proscribes it. Byatt's revisionism is an attempt to 'get outside' of these limitations. Her novel reconsiders the close family and kinship bonds that fluctuate, cross-penetrate, embrace and divide her characters at the very historical moment at which cultural, political, and legal debates resurrected the very terms of incestuous relationships as sin and immorality, on the one hand, and social and scientific irrationality, on the other.

Byatt, of course, has had previous narrative engagement with issues related to incest. Her 1992 short story 'Morpho Eugenia' uses incest as a kind of ludic device, the game and pun of the insects in the text themselves intersecting with incest as a stylistic and aesthetic trick, but also at another level as a kind of anagrammatic trauma. By this term I am referring to the way in which Byatt uses textual play through the anagram (see below) to denote the nature of the childishness inherent in the familial (sexual) relationships within the text. For it is words which both reveal and conceal the nature of the traumatic in this novella, just as the words and meta-textual nature of *The Children's Book* are the locus of interaction between parents, children and siblings. The implication of the narrative in Byatt's novella dwells on the game itself in its biological formulation as a type of '*un*natural selection', a fact made clear in Eugenia's final speech to her now estranged husband William, following his discovery of her post-coitus with her brother Edgar:

> 'I *know* it was bad,' said Eugenia. 'I know it was bad,
> but you must understand it didn't *feel* bad – it grew
> little by little, out of perfectly innocent, natural,
> *playful* things – which no one thought wrong – I have
> never been able to speak to any other living soul of it,
> you must forgive me for speaking to you – I can see I
> have made you angry, though I tried to make you love

> me – if I could have spoken to anyone, I might have
> been brought to see how wrong it was. But – *he*
> thought it wasn't – he said – people like making rules
> and others like breaking them – he made me believe it
> was all perfectly *natural* and so it was, it was *natural*,
> nothing in us rose up and said – it was – unnatural.'
>
> 'Breeders know,' said William curtly, 'that
> even first-cousin marriages produce inherited
> defects.' (Byatt 1992: 158-159)

William's response is symptomatic of the scientific and
anthropological understanding of human relationships of mating and
ritual he has studied throughout the text. For William, there is no
recognition of the nature of desire as it might be experienced by blood
relatives, and as such he holds none of the imaginative capability of
Elsie, who sees her own desires stimulated by her knowledge of the
inner longings as displayed in the potteries. This is not to excuse or
eradicate the religious, moral, and social breeches of Eugenia and
Edgar's relationship; indeed, at this point in the novella we know that
this relationship has already caused the suicide of one man and throws
doubt on the paternity of William and Eugenia's brood. But the
novella also indicates an uneasy 'game' over the incestuous encoding
of desire. From the outset, William, himself an only child and orphan-
figure, has noted that his wife's family make "a charming and
homogenous group" (Byatt 1992: 4). His observations have been
marked by the fact that "he was, after all, a scientist and an observer"
in the line of Henry Walter Bates and Alfred Russell Wallace (Byatt
1992: 6, 10, 11). Both Bates and Wallace used their anthropological
works to explore the kinship relations of 'primitive' tribes and
communities, living outside of the inhibitions of Western civilisation's
legality, and as such their works reveal much about the incestuous
practices of such groups.[18] Such clues within the narrative framework
serve to underline a surprisingly intellectual and amoral, potentially
unethical, response to the incestuous act itself. The anagrammatic
trauma I have already mentioned comes to a culmination not in the

---

[18] For Alfred Russell Wallace's (1823-1913) work in this area see *Contributions to the
Theory of Natural Selection* (1870), *The Geographical Distribution of Animals* (1876)
and *Tropical Nature and Other Essays* (1878); for Henry Walter Bates (1825-1892)
see *The Naturalist on the River Amazons* (1863).

relationship between William and Eugenia, but in that between William and the family governess, Miss Matty (Matilda) Crompton. Eugenia's half-brother Edgar states to William that "I have noticed you know *nothing*", and this is seemingly proved true when he cannot decipher Miss Matty's encoding in her fairytale 'Things Are Not What They Seem' (Byatt 1992: 108, 119-140). As an aspiring children's writer, Matty serves as a prototype of *The Children's Book*'s Olive Wellwood, and it is "Miss Crompton [who ...] enlisted his support for a game of Anagrams" (Byatt 1992: 152). In the game, 'insect' is anagrammatised: "There it was, lying innocently in his hand. INCEST" (Byatt 1992: 153).[19] As Eugenia tells William, "It began as a game" (Byatt 1992: 150), and it is fitting that it ends in one too.

This reading of Byatt's two incest narratives acts as a challenge to Cora Kaplan's comments about *Possession*, which claim that

> Byatt's romantic investment is in good heterosexual sex [...] a symptom of her sexual conservatism which guides her selective use of feminism in her treatment of both present and past, a feminism happiest when it is most traditional. (Kaplan 2007: 110)

Both the Byatt texts discussed point toward the recognition of the turn away from incest narratives in the development and structuring of modernity. In *The Children's Book* the crisis is one of time: the narrative feels nostalgic for its own moment, it moves forward and backwards continually not in terms of structure but in the slippages between understandings of the world by the characters and readers. The return to childishness and childhood by both adults and adolescents alike is not sustainable, and it is the child-like unawareness of things outside of desire and attraction, and thought and body, which leaves this society unprepared for the harsh realities and traumatic consequences of war. Similarly, in 'Morpho Eugenia', science, eugenics, and modern anthropology are the looming concerns that turn what seemed "perfectly innocent, natural, *playful*" into the unnatural, the forbidden, and the unspeakable. In reasserting the

---

[19] See Kline 1996 for a discussion of the film adaptation of Byatt's novella and the incest theme.

incestuous slippages in desire and family relations in these texts, Byatt reminds us of a cultural moment in which such prohibitions are in the process of being codified, with the possibilities of slippage previously allowed being lost – or repressed – at the same time. This, I would argue, constitutes part of an unexpectedly feminist critique by Byatt of the stabilities of desire, of the strictures one might term a patriarchal code of performed sexuality, and instead invites an alternative understanding of the late-Victorian and Edwardian past that, in its move to domestic conformity, appears to surrender something that escapes or exceeds the legal parameters of desire. The Gothic and fairytale elements of Byatt's texts – she terms 'Morpho Eugenia' a "robust Gothic allegory" (Byatt 2000: 114) – are revisionist at an aesthetic level, coupled with a dual aesthetic and ethical reconsideration of the nature of families within this clash of tradition and modernity, fantasy and reality.

2.   Sarah Waters's Degrees of *Affinity*

Gothic spaces and the blurring of the intensity of the domestic with the public, the private and the incarcerated, are at the centre of Sarah Waters's *Affinity*. A significantly popular text with academics and critics, though perhaps less so with some readers compared to Waters's other novels, *Affinity* has not received sustained attention with reference to the incestuous possibility of transgressive and traumatic desire in this period.[20] The diary of Margaret Prior begins with the declaration: "Pa used to say that any piece of history might be made into a tale: it was only a question of deciding where the tale began, and where it ended. [...] I wish that Pa was with me now" (Waters 2000: 7). Indeed, in a novel so concerned with ghosts and spirits it becomes remarkably noticeable how often "Pa" is invoked in the first ten pages of Margaret's narrative. We learn about his style of history writing; his study; his reading; his presence in Margaret's life; even the comment that unlike Margaret he would "not have bothered with the detail of the skirts" in describing the prison matrons at Millbank (Waters 2000: 8). The simultaneous absence and presence of the father, which continues for so much of the narrative, constitutes the figure of George Prior, the historian, as a spectral and in some

---

[20] An important reference to the incestuous possibility in Waters's novel is made by Kohlke (2004: 161, 165).

ways sinister figure that has often been overlooked by critics of the
novel, who tend to focus instead on Margaret's relationship with her
mother. It is important that Margaret's illness, her hysteria and first
attempted suicide, all follow her father's death, likely even result
therefrom, and that even towards the end of the novel she implores her
father to bring the soul of her new lover, the imprisoned fraudulent
medium Selina, to her.[21]

In fact, in our readerly desire to unpick the clues of
Margaret's same-sex attraction towards Selina, we often forget the
ways in which the narrative signals the roots of her longing for contact
with the spirit world much earlier in the novel. Just as her diary entries
begin with an invocation of her father's writing spirit, so in an early
scene with Selina in her prison cell it is the figure of the father who
'appears' – or appears to communicate – through the spirit medium:

> Then her [Selina's] features gave another, stranger
> kind of shift, and she spoke, in a whisper. 'He is
> saying, *She has hung her care about her neck, and
> will not put it aside. Tell her she must lay it aside.*'
> She nodded. 'He is smiling. Was he clever, like you?
> He was! But he has learned many new things, now,
> and – oh! how he longs for you to be with him and
> learn them too! But what is he doing?' Her face
> changed again. 'He is shaking his head, he is
> weeping, he is saying, *Not that way! Oh! Peggy, that
> was not the way! You shall join me, you shall join me
> – but, not like that!*' (Waters 2000: 88, original
> emphases)

The fact that Selina hints towards Pa's condemnation of Margaret's
attempted suicide here should not prevent us from seeing that the

---

[21] "Father, if you see me now – if you see *her* searching for me through the gloom –
guide our two souls together! If you ever loved me, you may love me now by bringing
her whom *I* love to me" (Waters 2000: 317, original emphases). See also Margaret's
later recollection: "One time, two years ago, I took a draught of morphia, meaning to
end my life. My mother found me before the life was ended, the doctor drew the
poison from my stomach with a syringe, and when I woke, it was to the sound of my
own weeping. For I had hoped to open my eyes on Heaven, where my father was; and
they had only pulled me back to Hell" (Waters 2000: 321).

discourse of "join[ing]" between daughter and father also identifies the bonded and over(t)ly physical relationship between them. In Margaret's next diary entry after this scene, we read:

> I woke bewildered this morning, after a night of terrible dreams. I dreamt my father was alive – that I glanced from my window to see him leaning on the parapet of Albert Bridge, gazing bitterly at me. I ran out, and called to him: 'Good God, Pa, we thought you were dead!' 'Dead?' he answered. 'I have been two years at Millbank! They put me on the treadmill and my boots are worn to the flesh beneath – look here.' He lifted his leg, to show me his soleless shoes and his cracked and battered feet; and I thought, How strange, I don't believe I ever saw Pa's feet before...
>
> An absurd dream – and certainly very different to the dreams that used to torment me in the weeks after his death, in which I would find myself squatting at the side of his grave, calling to him through the newly-turned earth. I would open my eyes from those and seem to feel the soil still clinging to my fingers. (Waters 2000: 89-90, original ellipses)

At one level, this dream implies the blurring in Margaret's mind between the transmission of Pa's voice through Selina, the prison environment, and the events of the previous day. However, at another level, through the location of the prison, both these scenes insistently associate her father's identity with the idea of a criminal offence, arguably incest. It may be far from coincidental that the punishment for incest under the 1908 Act was three to seven years penal servitude or two years imprisonment.[22] Later, too, there are multiple ways of reading Margaret's statement that while viewing the pictures in the spiritualist archives, "I sat, and looked at Peter Quick's dark eyes. They seemed – how odd it sounds! – they seemed *familiar* to me, as if I might have gazed at them already – perhaps, in my dreams" (Waters 2000: 154). While this reference to the familiar eyes of Margaret's

---

[22] More pertinent to the novel's time frame, the Offences Against the Person Act 1875 prescribed two years imprisonment for carnal knowledge of a child under 13 (see Jackson 2000: 160, n. 62).

dream life may indicate her failure to recognise the eyes of her own
servant Ruth Vigers, the real figure of Peter Quick, as I have argued
elsewhere (Llewellyn 2004), it is also possible to view the recognition
as deriving from an earlier source in her memory, namely her father.

The same is true of the scene where Margaret believes she
recognises something about the plaster cast of Peter Quick's grasping
and materialistic hands. That Margaret continues to desire to see the
father, who is dead and lost to her, remains the case later into the
narrative too. As she pictures her own future, Margaret ponders in her
father's study:

> I went there, telling Mother I meant to begin to look
> through his letters; but I went only to think of him.
> The room is kept just as he left it, with his pen upon
> the blotter, his seal, the knife for his cigars, the
> looking-glass…
>   I remember him standing before that, two
> weeks after they first found the cancer in him, and
> turning his face from it with a ghastly smile. His
> nurse told him, when he was a boy, that invalids
> should not gaze at their own reflections, for fear their
> souls would fly into the glass and kill them.
>   Now I stood a long time before the mirror,
> looking for him in it – looking for anything in it from
> the days before he died. There was only myself.
> (Waters 2000: 201-202, original ellipses)

The scene suggests the ways in which Margaret's narrative longs for
the structural support of a paternal spectre in the looking-glass. The
father is potentially the vampiric undead. (One thinks of the mirror
scene between Harker and the vampire Count in *Dracula* [1897].) Yet
here the absence of paternal control in a primal site such as the mirror
phase raises speculation about the exact nature of the relationship
between Margaret's desire for contact with the spirits and the reader's
assumption that this inevitably represents the displacement of her
desire for another woman. Bloodlines, spirit-lines and lifelines are
merged in this text in ways that, coupled with its intertextual
referencing, should make us alert to possible affinities beyond those
we are most interested in exploring. It is perhaps not just its

relationship to the prison narrative that makes Dickens's *Little Dorrit* (1855-57) such an appropriate text for Margaret to read to her mother. It may constitute a coded signal to the relationship between older men and younger women, which also serves as a trope of power relations – spiritual and physical – in that novel. Thus when Margaret states "Mother and I are twenty chapters into *Little Dorrit*" (Waters 2000: 205), it is worth noting that chapter 19 of that novel ends with Amy Dorrit nursing her possessive father, after he has demonstrated his love, affection and favouritism towards her. The incestuous linkages between texts here (the overlapping of intertexts themselves producing a form of aesthetic kinship) becomes important at another level: Little Dorrit and Arthur Clenham's subsequent marriage in Dickens's novel configures the older man as a kind of father substitute. Just as Byatt invokes allusions to Freud, to Richard Strauss's *Elektra* (1909), and to numerous fairytales of bloodlines, so Waters, in bringing forward Dickens's novel as a text to be read inside the text of Margaret's diary, may be interpolating an additional layer of intellectual clues to our understanding of the father-daughter relationships in *Affinity* and Victorian pre-texts.

That such an encounter is figured at the level of reading and writing might also serve as an interesting context for returning to Henke's earlier cited work on trauma in father-daughter relations. In her discussion of a range of twentieth-century women writers, Henke proposes that writing provides an accessible medium, through which to demonstrate, articulate, and confront the trauma, which evades conscious experience when first undergone. Henke uses the term "scriptotherapy" to refer to "the process of writing out and writing through traumatic experience in the mode of therapeutic reenactment" (Henke 1998: xii). Waters's construction of Margaret's diary as a traumatic document, both in terms of its previous destruction following the failed relationship with Helen and its destruction in its current form following the discovery of Selina's betrayal, illuminates the possibility for reading her 'life-writing', her diaristic narrative of daily life, as part of a "reenactment" of and return towards a repetition of the repressed "traumatic experience" of incest. The visions she has of her father thus provide more than a recognition of her susceptibility to the promise of an afterlife and the world beyond death, as narrativised by Selina, instead reinforcing her relationship with her father in ways that suggest the roots of an earlier trauma. Selina here becomes the conduit not only for (tricked, faked) communication with the spirit of Margaret's father, but also an access point to the unspeakable trauma of Margaret's relationship with her father in life as well as in death. Thus, when Selina talks of the dead as unsexed and unclothed in the world beyond, Margaret's first thoughts turn to how this would impact on the visual representation of her hitherto 'hidden' relationship with her progenitor: "I tried to imagine the world she spoke of – the world she says has Pa in it. I imagined Pa, unclothed and sexless, and with myself beside him. – It was a terrible vision, that made me sweat" (Waters 2000: 210). Selina's follow-up statement is similarly enigmatic of transgression:

> we will all fly to someone, we will all return to that piece of shining matter from which our souls were torn with another, two halves of the same. [...] It may be someone she would never think to look to upon the earth, someone kept from her by some false boundary...' (Waters 2000: 210, unbracketed ellipses in the original)

It is worth remembering that both Margaret's relationships with Helen and later Selina were constrained by what we today would regard as just such a literal "false boundary"; the same might be said of Margaret's relationship with her father, at least assuming that such incest was consensual and conducted as adults. Indeed, immediately after this scene, Margaret mentions her "affinity" with her father and in her subsequent argument with her mother, she records:

> I said that I had always been wakeful, even before Pa died, even as a girl. That the wakefulness meant nothing – and that anyway, the medicine always cured it, and made me rest. She said, seizing on the one narrow point, that as a girl I had been indulged. She had left me *too much to the care of my father* and he had spoiled me. (Waters 2000: 221, 223, emphasis added)

Ultimately, what we do not see in this novel, the play and action we do not identify, is of as much importance in relation to

Margaret's father as it is in relation to Ruth/Vigers and Selina. For the novel's very title, in its potential allusion to the degrees of 'affinity', the strictures of the religious code of canon law that inscribed the prohibited relationships between those who became related via the marriage or intercourse of a relative of the same blood (i.e. kinship by marriage), is arguably a clue to more than we first imagine. In using a terminology that is open to subversion and its own encoding in the context of the multiple significance of a term like 'affinity' in the period, Waters might be signalling a deeper sense of sexual trauma – and forbidden desire, not least on the part of the 'victim' – than that identified upon first reading the text.[23] The parallel between Selina and Margaret is that both are controlled by the desires of paternal figures – in Margaret's case Pa, in Selina's Peter Quick alias Vigers. Thus the beginning of Margaret's diary narrative with the invocation of "Pa" and the concluding line of the novel from Selina's diary, quoting Vigers, "Remember whose girl you are" (Waters 2000: 352), have a neat symmetry to them that connects, and provides an additional affinity, between the two female narrators and their tales. For both women, the (quasi)paternal figure appears central to their identities, and it is the relationship between the male or masculinised parent (real or surrogate) that underscores the key aspects of the novel. Waters's negotiations of the potential trauma suffered by Margaret at the hands of two paternal figures, her own Pa and the spirit guide Peter Quick, must be taken into account in any thorough interpretation of the nature of (subversive) desire and sexual politics in the text.

3.   Concluding Speculation

What the novels explored in this chapter underline is the varied nature of neo-Victorian women writers' engagement with the incest theme. Byatt's overt discussion, or at least presentation, of narratives of incest, though frequently problematic in their seeming omission of traumatic responses, nevertheless invokes something of the Victorian period's own anxieties and concerns in relation to the domestic spaces of narrative and fairytale. In bringing such a theme to prominence in

---

[23] Inadvertently, the ludicrous insertion of Margaret's fiancé Theophilous in Andrew Davies's 2008 ITV adaptation of *Affinity*, and the character's attempted rape of the protagonist, apparently intended to provide a 'reason' for her desire for another woman, may have correctly identified sexual trauma between a male and female as crucial to Waters's original, albeit in a different constellation.

two very different texts, Byatt's neo-Victorianism is reflective of its
moment in a very precise (re)imagining of the unstable aesthetic and
moral parameters of Victorian/Edwardian familial relations, which to
some extent anticipate and reflect the often decried family breakdown
of our own time. Waters's novel, by the very inexplicit and unstated
nature of one aspect of its traumatic interpretation, serves as a
corollary to Byatt's unambiguous engagement with such a taboo topic.

Ultimately, both novelists indicate in their different ways that
for the neo-Victorian woman writer, incest might be a textual game,
but it remains one with undoubtable consequences for the Victorians
as for now. For just as the Victorians sought to define and redefine the
nature of the domestic family through issues of kinship, relation,
marriage and likeness, so the neo-Victorian novelist seeks to find both
similarity and difference in her reading of the nineteenth-century
domestic and writerly space. Byatt's novella in particular
demonstrates the intensity of Victorian speculations on the 'fitness'
(in terms of appropriateness but also physical, moral and aesthetic
appreciation) of such relationships. The longing for the similar, the
reassuring confidences of the familiar within a family setting, and
perhaps more importantly the language we use to tell of those bonds
and connections that run beyond bloodlines to textual encounters, lies
as much at the heart of our contemporary desire to see ourselves in the
Victorian and the Victorian in us. Such cultural narcissism, collapsing
the difference between self and other, into a unified conceptualisation
of self-love and self-pleasure, may serve to recognise that there is an
intellectual incest involved in thinking through such relations for the
contemporary writer. That this aspect of neo-Victorianism might be
read as a specific arena for the development of women writers could
be viewed as an essentialised position based on female identity and
family. However, what both writers demonstrate is rather a
conceptualisation of the possibilities for incestuous (re)reading of the
Victorians on the grounds of aesthetic and moral trauma.

Bibliography

Anderson, Nancy F. 1982. 'The Marriage with a Deceased Wife's Sister Bill
        Controversy: Incest Anxiety and the Defense of Family Purity in Victorian
        England', *Journal of British Studies,* 21: 67-86.
Bailey, Victor, and Sheila Blackburn. 1979. 'The Punishment of Incest Act 1908: A
        Case Study of Law Creation', *Criminal Law Review*: 708-718.

Barnes, Elizabeth (ed.). 2002. 'Introduction' in *Incest and the Literary Imagination*. Gainesville: University Press of Florida: 1-13.
Bell, Vikki. 1993. *Interrogating Incest: Feminism, Foucault and the Law*. London: Routledge.
Byatt, A.S. 1992. 'Morpho Eugenia', in *Angels and Insects*. London: Chatto & Windus: 1-160.
——. 2000. *On Histories and Stories: Selected Essays*. London: Chatto & Windus.
——. 2009. *The Children's Book*. London: Chatto & Windus.
Corbett, Mary Jean. 2008. *Family Likeness: Sex, Marriage and Incest from Jane Austen to Virginia Woolf*. Ithaca, Cornell University Press.
Heilmann, Ann, and Mark Llewellyn. 2010. *Neo-Victorianism: The Victorians in the Twenty-First Century, 1999-2009*. Basingstoke: Palgrave.
Henke, Suzette A. 1998. *Shattered Subjects: Trauma and Testimony in Women's Life-Writing*. Houndmills, Basingstoke: Macmillan.
Herman, Judith Lewis, with Lisa Hirschman. 1981. *Father-Daughter Incest*. Cambridge, Massachusetts: Harvard University Press.
Jackson, Louise A. 2000. *Child Sexual Abuse in Victorian England*. London: Routledge.
James, Henry. 1995. *The Turn of the Screw* [1898] (ed. Peter J. Beidler). Boston: Bedford Books.
Kaplan, Cora. 2007. *Victoriana: Histories, Fictions, Criticism*. Edinburgh: Edinburgh University Press.
Kline, T.J. 1996. 'Angels and Insects: Hass's Angle on Incest', *Psychoanalytic Review* 83: 777-780.
Kohlke, M[arie]-L[uise]. 2004. 'Into History through the Back Door: The "past historic" in *Nights at the Circus* and *Affinity*', *Women: A Cultural Review* 15(2): 153-166.
Kuper, Adam. 2009. *Incest & Influence: The Private Lives of Bourgeois England*. Cambridge, Massachusetts: Harvard University Press.
Lanagan, Margo. 2009. *Tender Morsels*. Oxford: David Fickling Books.
Llewellyn, Mark. 2004. '"Queer? I should say it is criminal!": Sarah Waters' *Affinity* (1999)', *Journal of Gender Studies* 13(3): 203-214.
——. (forthcoming 2011). 'Incest and Literary Gender Studies'. To appear in Ross, Karen (ed.), *Gender, Sexualities and Popular Culture*. Oxford: Blackwell.
MacCarthy, Fiona. 1989. *Eric Gill*. London: Faber and Faber.
Marsh, Stefanie, and Bojan Pancevski. 2009. *The Crimes of Josef Fritzl: Uncovering the Truth*. London: Harper Element.
Nelson, Sarah. 1988. *Incest: Fact and Myth*. Edinburgh: Stramullion Co-operative.
Robertson, Ritchie. 2008. 'Josef Fritzl's Fictive Forebears', *Times Literary Supplement* (14 May): 3.
Shelton, Jen. 2002. 'Speaking Incest in *The Voyage Out*', in Barnes (2002): 224-248.
Warner, Marina. 2003. 'The Virtue of Incest: Review of Marc Shell, *Elizabeth's Glass*' [1993], in *Signs & Wonders: Essays on Literature & Culture*. London: Chatto & Windus: 131-138.
Waters, Sarah. 1999. *Affinity*. London: Virago.

Wohl, Anthony S. 1978. 'Sex and the single room: incest among the Victorian working classes', in Whol, Anthony S. (ed.), *The Victorian Family: Structure and Stresses*. London: Croom Helm, 197-216.

Part II

History's Victims and Victors:

Crises of Truth and Memory

The Neo-Victorian Nation at Home and Abroad: Charles Dickens and Traumatic Rewriting

Dianne F. Sadoff

Abstract:

This essay investigates the usefulness of trauma theory for the study of neo-Victorian fiction. Historically, mid nineteenth-century England transported its traumas, first to the Americas and then the antipodes, to rid the nation of an increasingly criminalised working class, ignoring its colonial subjects' collective traumas. Yet Charles Dickens understood the Victorian individual's experience as fundamentally traumatic, and riddled with guilt and shame, like the protagonist of *Great Expectations* (1860-61), who is haunted by repressed psychic trauma. Lloyd Jones's and Peter Carey's postcolonial neo-Victorian rewritings of Dickens's novel represent trauma as a symptom of the real. *Mister Pip* (2007) and *Jack Maggs* (1997) immerse their readers in the colonial scene of trauma or the metropolitan scene of return; by deferred action, each submits readers to the hypnotic imitation of reading and forces them to bear affective and ethical witness to traumatic suffering.

Keywords: Australia, Peter Carey, colonial, criminal, Charles Dickens, Lloyd Jones, memory, New Zealand, postcolonial, trauma, wounding.

*****

The concept of trauma is "absolute[ly] indispensab[le]" for comprehending the "psychic harms" of certain central twentieth-century events, Ruth Leys rightly claims (Leys 2000: 2). What critics now call 'trauma culture', however, is normally associated with nations and national cultures that have survived revolution, genocide, or savage and deadly attacks during war; the Holocaust and Hiroshima may be our primary examples. Also, despite a large archive of work on trauma culture, theorists tend to locate their research in the twentieth century, for the most part. What would it mean, then, to call contemporary rewritings of nineteenth-century British fiction 'traumatic' responses to our Victorian past, or to view Victorian writing itself as informed by a traumatic sense of national experience which, repressed and un-cognised at the time, continues to haunt us in the modern world? Indeed, this doubly different perspective – the twentieth century as retrospectively reinventing the nineteenth; the Dominion nations writing back to the British Empire – necessitates revising trauma theory for a postcolonial case. Yet Charles Dickens, a writer immersed in the thematics of guilt and panic, understood Victorian experience as fundamentally traumatic well before he lived through and survived the disastrous railway accident near Staplehurst in 1865.[1] His fictional autobiography *Great Expectations* (1860-61) records this sense of trauma, inscribing its protagonist's haunting by repressed memories, repetition compulsion, acting out, and anxious dreams about or hallucinations of split off parts of himself and his unconscious others. Structured by the logic of trauma, *Great Expectations* reclaims a narratorial childhood and national past and, paradoxically, prepares its author, narrator, and reader for traumas ahead.

Neo-Victorian rewritings of Dickens's novel recuperate it as a textual past, often restoring to the fictive present aspects of psychic trauma repressed yet latent in *Great Expectations* itself. Peter Carey's *Jack Maggs* (1997) argues that Dickens neglected, forgot, or repressed the fact that his criminal, Magwitch, returned, only to be hunted down while fatally ill, from the imperial space of suffering and transportation, Australia, to haunt his gentlemanly adoptive son and so to require rescuing once more. Lloyd Jones's *Mister Pip* (2007), on the contrary, claims that Dickens's novel may alleviate not only psychic and physical trauma but national, imperial, and historical trauma as well. Whereas Carey challenges Dickens's novel's participation in Britain's ideology of overseas expansion and penal-colonisation of Australia, Jones subjects Australia's own discourses of colonisation to "powerful indictment", Jennifer Gribble notes,

---

[1] As Jill Matus notes, placing the railway "squarely within the history of trauma studies, [. . .] the railway accident was to Victorian psychology what World War I and shell shock were to Freudian." Moreover, Dickens's short story 'The Signalman', which he wrote shortly after the Stapleton accident, "signals" the "future discourse of trauma" as developed not by nineteenth-century psychology but by Freud (Matus 2003: 225, 231). Ralph Harrington identifies the railway accident as a specifically "*modern* phenomenon" (Harrington 2001: 35-36); Paul Lerner and Mark S. Micale view the expansion of the concept of trauma as linked to industrial, technological modernity per se (Lerner and Micale 2001: 10).

affirming as recuperative the postcolonial writing back by a dark-skinned, abjected female to the metropolitan reader (Gribble 2008: 183). My argument, like Leys's, is genealogical; it charts the oscillations between a mimetic and anti-mimetic theory of trauma within these Victorian and post-Victorian texts and in their historical relations. As Jones and Carey's novels implicitly do, I will argue that neo-Victorian reading and writing immerses us in the scene of trauma, submitting us to the "hypnotic imitation" of reading-as-suffering, even as they remind us that traumatic neurosis, memory, or mimesis is a kind of "fabrication or simulation" of the real (Leys 2000: 8, 10). Like Elizabeth Cowie, I claim that trauma is also a "symptom of the real" and that the subject awaits a "possible *future* wound" which, presented to a disordered memory by deferred action, becomes the "unrepresentable of anxiety" that splits off fragments of the subject, mimetically figuring the subject as other (Cowie 2003: 33, original emphasis).

Neo-Victorianism is currently reconstituting something like the 1930s "vogue of the Victorian age" that F.R. Leavis reviled, in *Scrutiny*'s pages and later in *The Great Tradition* (1948), as linked to the minor novel and to popular fiction (Leavis 1964: 1). Yet theories of neo-Victorianism's relation to its nineteenth-century predecessors have not, until now, addressed them as traumatic or as asking questions linked to trauma, an absence this volume seeks to redress. Some contemporary notions of the neo-Victorian's link to its predecessor century pointedly ignore trauma. In *Functions of Victorian Culture at the Present Time*, Christine Krueger proposes that unlike the modernists – Lytton Strachey, even Leavis – who sought to distance themselves from their Victorian predecessors, we later post-Victorians embrace their work to indulge our nostalgia for our own idealised pasts, or to misremember the past in the present; we adopt the literary critic's faith in authenticity and strongly adhere to fidelity aesthetics, especially in the realm of visual culture (Krueger 2002: xi-xx). Rejecting the neo-conservative and liberal attitudes toward the past that have dominated the current "vogue" for nineteenth-century culture and theoretically qualifying identitarian and postmodern views, Jay Clayton argues for the value of recovering the anachronistic and reclaiming the historical oddity as a form of knowledge for the post-Victorian (Clayton 2003: 39-40, 113-117). Cora Kaplan theorises neo-Victorianism as invoking an "historical imagination on the move" that is "permanently restless", "unsettled" and "out of place", and whose insistent a-chronicity identifies its power to constitute modernity even as it radically differs from and remains unassimilable to it (Kaplan 2007: 3, 6). None of these positions fully – or even successfully, in some cases – explains the cultural prominence of neo-Victorianism now or its often traumatic retrospective relation to nineteenth-century culture.

Simon Joyce, however, gains some purchase on the neo-Victorian mode's link to its nineteenth-century past by virtue of his retrospective reinterpretation of twentieth-century moments of anti- or pro-Victorianism. Joyce adopts and adapts John Kucich's and my proposal in *Victorian Afterlife* that postmodernism fetishises cultural emergence and rupture so as to posit multiple and overlapping stories of historical transition and influence – narratives of the uneven development of the contemporary present from Victorian past(s) (Sadoff and Kucich 2000). Viewing the present as a moment in which the Victorian past is constituted as a "condensation of contrary tendencies and oppositions" that constitute each other in a "form of dialectical spiral" throughout the twentieth century, Joyce advances our notion of the complex, historically situated links between nineteenth- and twentieth-century political and cultural projects (Joyce 2007: 7). Yet he imagines, even if implicitly, that from his millennial perspective, some version of "the historical whole" may be pictured, as though his own perception were not, like the others that address this problematic, limited, partial, or subject to the inevitable distortions of retrospection. Nevertheless, Joyce's take on our look back at the Victorians captures the historical dialectic I will also trace here, an oscillation between mimetic and anti-mimetic in the neo-Victorian fictional field and its genealogy. Psychoanalytic theory, itself linked to the historical emergence of trauma and theories of hysteria, among other conditions, may help us rethink the concepts of oddity, a-chronicity, and nostalgia with the tools of Freudian theory: repetition compulsion, the return of the repressed, and the deferred action that precipitates mimetic or anti-mimetic splitting and identification. Adding postcolonial notions to the mix leavens trauma theory into the cultural study of nation, narration, empire, and colonisation.

Nineteenth-century Britain, it would seem, experienced few major national disasters and disruptions at the heart of the empire that might easily be read as traumatic.[2] Yet during the late eighteenth century, Britain suffered the loss of its American colonies due to the patriot revolution; in the pre-Reform period, citizens coped with radical fervour, aristocratic insecurity, and status anxiety of all kinds as they sought to reshape the old hierarchy of ranks into a modern class system; during the 1840s, the political challenges and upheavals of Chartism and other labouring class movements questioned and contested the landed establishment's long-cherished rights and responsibilities in a deference culture; during the long Victorian period, the ordeal of bank panics, collapsing funds, and severe depressions, which alternated with periods of plenty, depleted individual savings and gross domestic product.[3] These traumas of a different, more psychological and economic kind shaped British psyches and experience during the long nineteenth century. Indeed, these traumas at home, if we can call them that, all involved Britain's place in the world: its wars with France and the attendant financial disturbances and strains accompanying rising prices and taxes; its position at the centre of the largest empire on earth.[4] Britain, we might say, exported its traumas, experiencing them at second hand, and located them far from the metropole, perhaps to attenuate their domestic and ignore their colonial harm. Nevertheless, Victorian fiction records individual, national, and historical traumas, and so induces us to repeat, remember, and act out in storytelling our own belated link to these long-dead predecessors.

Charles Dickens, the writer who most fully recorded the Victorian age, had a nose for guilt and panic. His formative personal trauma, as is well known, structured his narratives throughout his writing life and especially his fictional autobiographies. Jailed for debt when his son was a ten-year-old boy, John Dickens precipitated the traumatic experience described in the 'autobiographical fragment' that

---

[2] Even the Great Famine was seen largely as a trauma 'elsewhere', with Ireland and the Irish perceived as 'Other' to Englishness; in effect Ireland, even more than the other Celtic nations that are part of the United Kingdom, functioned as an internal colony. See Ann Heilmann's essay, in this volume, for discussion of the Famine's fictional narratives, Kate Grenville's for another take on Australia, and Marie-Luise Kohlke's on witnessing and the Indian Mutiny.

[3] I have, of course, condensed and summarised a great deal of historical research here; for further details on these aspects of British society, see Wahrman 1995: 223-272, 328-376; Mandler 1997: 153-173 and Mandler 1990: 13-40.

[4] On the impact of Anglo-French relations, see Colley 1992: 147-193.

John Forster included in his first biography of his friend and about
which he told not even his wife. Dickens's version of the 'family
romance' in this fragment and in his fiction is structured by this
oedipal trauma, a trauma in which the boy's suffering at Warren's
Blacking warehouse and his highly visible position in the factory's
window – immersed in the scene of trauma, his suffering witnessed by
others – marks an overdetermined moment of ambivalent
identification with, abjection by, and rage at the 'criminal' father. In
this phantasmatic and spectacular scenario, a son displaced and
replaced his own father, for, after his mother and siblings joined his
father in the Marshalsea, the boy became the only member of his
family living and working outside the prison (see Hutter 1977: 10,
Sadoff 1982: 22-26). Situating the sensitive boy amid labouring lads
and men, this trauma represented not only a betrayal by the father and
an abrogation of his responsibilities but, in addition, a "declassing"
(Solomon 1975: 125-153). "No words can express the secret agony of
my soul as I sunk into this companionship," Dickens wrote to Forster,
"of the shame I felt in my position." "My whole nature was so
penetrated with the grief and humiliation," he said, that "even now,
famous and caressed and happy, I often forget in my dreams that I
have a dear wife and children; even that I am a man; and wander
desolately back to that time of my life" (qtd. Forster 1966: 22-23).
Having quizzed Dickens about a report that, as a boy, he had been
seen at his "juvenile employment", Forster never again mentioned the
incident, "the recollection of which, at intervals, haunted [Dickens]
and made him miserable, [...] even to that hour" (Forster 1966: 19).
The celebrated author's inability to forget or to integrate into his
psyche the "emotions of terror and surprise" he clearly felt and which
he expresses in the autobiographical fragment, identify this as a
"disorder of memory": a haunting or possession by an "intrusive"
traumatic recollection that "refuses to be represented as past, but is
perpetually reexperienced in a painful, dissociated, traumatic present"
(Leys 2000: 2).

　　　Dickens re-presents this scenario of paternal abandonment and
neglect, repetition and haunting, at *Great Expectations*' opening. A
"small bundle of shivers growing afraid" among his family's
tombstones, Pip suddenly sees a man emerge from "among the
graves"; thrice "tilted" and "trembling", the "helpless" boy, rooted to
the tombstones by "powerful" eyes, watches the church "go head over

heels before me" (Dickens 1996: 24-25). In Pip's phantasmatic, spatially reconfigured scenario, the convict limps off toward the horizon's gibbet, "as if he were the pirate come to life, and come down, and going back to hook himself up again" (Dickens 1996: 27). "I was in mortal terror of the young man who wanted my heart and liver," the narrator recounts of Compeyson's effect on the boy; "I was in mortal terror of my interlocutor with the ironed leg; I was in mortal terror of myself, from whom an awful promise had been extracted" (Dickens 1996: 34). Dreaming or imagining himself as being hailed by the "ghostly pirate" on his own way to the Hulks, the young Pip identifies with the criminal for whom he robs food from his abusive sister's pantry and a file from his beloved Joe's forge. He identifies with the traumatic scenario that the boy, once become a gentleman, must forget and so remain haunted by. The novel's first scenes also link Joe, the man whom Pip imagines his equal yet to whom he looks up in his heart, as a brotherly figure who, like him, constantly experiences threats of oedipalised castration by Mrs. Joe's knives, pins, and forbidding apron. This scenario of ambivalent identification with blacksmith and convict links the Hulks as a space of criminality and potential transportation with a boy's robbing of the forge and with his own guilty knowledge that he has stolen from the sister who brought him up 'by hand' and has also implicitly lied about it. As retrospective autobiography, this scene deploys Magwitch and Mrs. Joe as stand-ins for the threatening, 'criminal' yet absent father in a scenario indelibly marked as at once mimetic and un-cognisable, as a traumatic memory that forecasts the intrication of guilt and criminality with declassing, with Pip's position as future apprentice to Joe at the forge.

　　　Pip's terrified, upside-down scenario refuses to be represented *as* past but is perpetually re-experienced as the adult narrator recounts – and so imaginatively repeats – the painful, dissociated, and trauma-laden past. Like the traumatic memory of a small boy whose spectacular humiliation identifies blacking as the mark of the inky substance around which the adult's career took shape, the forge also precipitates the fictional autobiographer's counterfeiting as central to his tale of declassing. Liar and storyteller, Pip's hallucinatory experiences recall, repeat, and seek to master but fail to integrate this trauma of declassing and abandonment into his psyche. He fabricates Miss Havisham's black velvet coach, immense dogs eating out of silver baskets, and niece eating cake from a gold plate at a coach window; feeling "peniten[t]", he confesses to Joe, who reproaches him with "lies is lies" that "come from the father of lies, and work round to the same" (Dickens 1996: 81-82). Fighting the pale young gentleman, who will become a benefactor better than he, Pip disavows his rage about his declassing and, at the same time, enacts threats of renewed declassing; "I never have been so surprised in my life", he claims, "as I was when I let out that first blow, and saw him lying on his back, looking up at me with a bloody nose and his face exceedingly foreshortened" (Dickens 1996: 100-101). The adult narrator again unconsciously discloses that devil-fathers, storytelling, and visual dislocation are linked in his disordered memory, that his dissociated, split off self undertakes acts of aggression and revenge against those upper-class figures he imagines humiliating him, whether in the churchyard, in Satis House's garden, or at the blacking warehouse of his author's childhood. He imagines that "the Law would avenge" his beating of Herbert Pocket:

> it was clear to me that village boys could not go stalking about the country, ravaging the houses of gentlefolks and pitching into the studious youth of England, without laying themselves open to severe punishment. (Dickens 1996: 102)

Although the boy did not yet understand it, the adult narrator knows the reality of this linking of class and trauma.

Throughout his tale, Pip's traumatic scene of past robbery and forgery, of dissociation and the terror of murder, returns to haunt him in the present of his storytelling, re-immersing him in the scene of trauma. The "cunning" man who stirs his drink at the Three Jolly Bargemen *with a file* represents a "turning up of my old misdeed and old acquaintance" (Dickens 1996: 88, original emphasis). Pip again sees the man when he takes a coach home and evades his responsibility to stay with Joe at the forge; now a convict on his way to the dockyards, the man who once "brought [him] down with an invisible gun," sits behind Pip, breathing on his head. Pip feels the sensation "all along [his] spine", as though he's been touched by "acid", which "sets [his] very teeth on edge" (Dickens 1996: 217-218). In this state of terror, Pip hears the convict tell Magwitch's –

and his own – graveyard rescue story; the reader now knows, even if the young Pip does not, that not Miss Havisham but Magwitch is his true benefactor. Pip's feeling of "great fear" and "dread" exceeded, he experiences "a painful or disagreeable recognition, [that] made me tremble." It was "the revival for a few minutes of the terror of childhood" (Dickens 1996: 220). Here, the convict, Compeyson, we will learn, represents a split-off and dissociated part of the boy, whose "rise in fortune" irretrievably separates him, he thinks, from his criminally implicated past (Dickens 1996: 151). Subsequently, of course, the "Lifer", whose story of transportation to Australia Compeyson recounts, literally returns from repression to act out what Dominick LaCapra would term an embodied form of repetition compulsion, an acting out that signifies a haunting or possession by, or an uncontrollable re-emergence of, traumatic scenes of suffering (LaCapra 2001: 21-22). The figure whose re-cognition Pip disavows returns to haunt him and heralds the return of 'his' convict, Magwitch, morphed into his benefactor, 'second father', and furthermore the real father of Pip's beloved and seemingly upper-class Estella.

This coach-riding convict represents Pip's struggle with the traumatic structure of *Nachträglichkeit* or 'belatedness'. His narrative builds into its temporal logic the traumatic perspective of deferred action, for Pip as narrator suffers a disorder of memory: a haunting or possession by an intrusive traumatic recollection that refuses to be represented as past. Throughout his story, Pip suffers from the "'afterwardness' of trauma whereby an event or experience becomes understood – translated [...] – traumatically through a subsequent experience", as Cowie notes. Quoting Jacques Lacan, Cowie identifies trauma as a "symptom of the real", as "the experience you are awaiting", a "possible *future* wound" that, re-presented to a disordered memory, "is the unrepresentable of anxiety" that makes the subject other, and turns the other into a split-off fragment or simulacra of the subject (Cowie 2003: 33, original emphasis). When Wemmick walks Pip by Newgate, the narrator reports on his young self as being "consumed [and] encompassed by all this taint of prison and crime", by his "first encounter" with and the twice "reappear[ance]" of his childhood brush with criminality which, "starting out like a stain that was faded but not gone", now equally pervades his "fortune and advancement" (Dickens 1996: 249). In a later parody of this unrepresentable and anxious haunting, the landlord of the inn where

Pip, Herbert, and Startop await the tide, which will carry Magwitch away from England, recounts Pip's own story to him, including the parodic figure of Uncle Pumblechook, the self-proclaimed benefactor who "made" Pip (Dickens 1996: 383).

Other split-off or dissociated figures for Pip and his criminality return from the repressed to haunt Dickens's fiction. All, moreover, circulate around the novel's obsession with a boy's rise in station or acquisition of fortune. Orlick, who emerges from the marsh's mist or primeval "ooze", thinks Pip will "displace" him at the forge and so masquerades plunging a red-hot bar into his enemy's gut; he fights with Joe as Mrs. Joe watches, a structural repetition of Estella's peeping at Pip's and Herbert's fistfight (Dickens 1996: 135, 119-121). Orlick later beats and silences the sister, who abused the brother she raised "by hand", using the leg iron cut from the convict's leg with Joe's file, stolen by Pip. If represented early in the tale, this attack would be apt to "shatter the victim's cognitive-perceptual capacities" and so make the "traumatic scene unavailable for a certain kind of recollection" (Leys 2000: 8-9). Thus, despite Pip's shadowy suspicions, soon forgotten or repressed, the attack remains unrepresented until the story's end. When Orlick tries to murder Pip at the limekiln, he insists of the attack on Mrs. Joe, "'It was you, villain; it warn't Old Orlick as did it; it was you. You was favoured, and he was bullied and beat. [...] Now you pays for it'" (Dickens 1996: 389). Biddy, who likewise suspects Orlick of Mrs. Joe's attack, later becomes Orlick's object of desire, in a parodic, metaleptic, and traumatic symptom of the real that foretells Orlick's attack on Pip, a possible future wound that, once again presented to a disordered memory by deferred action, the narrative reserves for belated representation. Here, a traumatic tale identifies Pip with Orlick, who acts out Pip's own aggression toward his sister; at the story's end, Orlick's displaced attack on Mrs. Joe seeks its true object, Pip.

Other parodic figures and fictions appear as split-off and dissociated parts of the traumatised Pip. Trabb's boy, who pantomimes the rise in fortune that enables him to purchase new clothes, later informs on Orlick and so rescues and saves Pip. Worsle's performance of *The London Merchant* tropes Pip as a possible prostitute-loving and uncle-murdering apprentice, who himself later becomes merchant and uncle to a figure for his innocent self, little Pip (Sadoff 1982: 32). Performing as Hamlet, Wopsle sees

Compeyson, seated behind Pip in the theatre, as "the ghost of a man's own father" and so becomes unwitting spectator of the ghost of Pip's traumatic criminal past (Sadoff 1982: 33-35). Declassing and sexualising a figure for Pip, parodying his rise and expectations, threatening him with an unforeseen yet impending re-wounding, these tales or scenes prepare for further violence and aggression. Pip's hallucination of Miss Havisham's hanging, for example, serves as a symptom of the real that forecasts her burning and rescue by Pip, his unconscious desire to take revenge for her failure to be his benefactor: another possible future wound whose representation still awaits (Dickens 1996: 367-369).

In *Great Expectations*, however, Dickens represses from his narrator's retrospective tale the British exportation of its criminal class and its colonial exploitation of the convicts it transported, first to the American colonies, then to Australia. Between 1614 and 1775, some 50,000 British citizens convicted, often of petty crimes, endured the transatlantic crossing to what would become Revolutionary America, especially Virginia and Maryland; the period between 1787 and 1868, saw more than threefold that number, some 162,000 residents of the Island home, transported to Australia (Brooke and Brandon 2005: 13, 20, Morgan and Rishton 2004: 38-51, Frost 1994: 110-143).[5] During the eighteenth century, the enclosure of commons land, the introduction of machinery to agricultural labour, and the redefining of landed-establishment property rights caused Parliament greatly to increase the number and kinds of capital crimes, especially rural crimes such as poaching and rustling. "Rushed through Parliament at the behest of the landowning class," Alan Brooke and David Brandon note, such acts provided the State with a "formidably comprehensive capital statute with which to attack the perceived menace of rural anarchy" (Brooke and Brandon 2005: 14). By the 1830s, industrial-agricultural innovation elicited rioting, imprisonment, and transportation. The 'Swing' Riots, which included acts of machine breaking, arson, and unlawful assembly, responded to the economic decline in the price of agricultural produce, to lower wages, to the

---

[5] Brooke and Brandon recreate the voyages, convict histories, personal statistics, and medical histories from the extensive records created by transportation; Morgan and Rushton do likewise, for the eighteenth century, and Frost for the First Fleet voyage (Brooke and Brandon 2005: 13, 20, Morgan and Rushton 2004: 38-51, Frost 1994: 110-143).

introduction of threshing machines, and to an influx of cheap Irish labour. Convicted and transported rioters were "the largest single group of protestors in Australia" (Hobsbawm and Rudé 1975: 265-280, Hughes 1987: 198).

In London, besieged by internal migration of the rural poor and of unskilled labourers, crime supported people hit by the century's economic downturns, slumps, and depressions. Criminal statutes were enforced by public hanging, against which Dickens would rally opinion in the mid-nineteenth century. Such practices had become "a form of mass entertainment", as the "grotesque spectacle" of mob abuse, cheering, and spectatorship accompanied to the gallows Britons convicted of crimes such as bigamy, concealing an illegitimate child's death, petty thefts such as shoplifting, and attacks on property (Brooke and Brandon 2005: 15). The prisons, such as the "notorious Newgate", were "incubators of crime" and places of "gross overcrowding, outbreaks of fever, attempted or successful riots and requests for assistance from the military" (Brooke and Brandon 2005: 14-15). The hulks, decayed ships moored on the Thames, housed convict labourers, both first-time, often youthful, offenders as well as recidivists. Adopted as the war with the American colonies commenced in 1775 and intended as a short-term measure only, the hulks became semi-permanent fixtures of the penal system, the population of which quadrupled in the early 1780s; the hulks enabled the "transitional" moment between the "two great phases of Britain's transportation" system (Frost: 1994: 40). In use until 1857 – virtually contemporary with Dickens's beginning of *Great Expectations* – the Hulks had by then, however, become a public "scandal" (Brooke and Brandon 2005: 31).

Suppressing the transported convicts' stories, as did Dickens, enabled Britons to ignore what historians have described as traumatic suffering. Yet the first convicts transported to Botany Bay, on the coast of New South Wales, had sailed as early as 1787, and, during the crossing, had endured the physical and emotional trauma of cramped quarters, confinement, and physical restraint (Hughes 1987: 129-157). Although few had died or grown ill, the second Fleet's convicts later bore the effects of starvation, beating, illness, and abuse. Only the outbreak of war with France – and a Home Office ruling that ensured payment for convicts healthy on arrival – stemmed the public outcry caused by the high death rate (Brooke and Brandon 2005: 55). Once in

Australia, convicts were manacled and flogged (often for minor offences, such as stealing food); many were incarcerated in coal mines or underground stone cells or were hospitalised with psychiatric conditions (Sweeney 1981: 93-111).

Although historians have identified these appalling conditions as traumatogenic, most contemporary trauma theory has attended as little to postcolonial suffering as did Dickens to Magwitch's presumed agony. Because, as earlier noted, trauma has been theorised as a particular, often individual, psychological event, as Dickens indeed represents it, the collective trauma undergone by groups of British citizens expelled from their homeland and relocated to colonial sites has been elided or gone largely unattended, at least in psychoanalytical studies (though some *have* focused on collective trauma with regards to displaced colonised subjects such as slaves or the Irish). As Michael Rothberg argues, theorists need now to "supplement the event-based model of trauma that has become dominant over the past fifteen years with a model that can account for ongoing, everyday forms of traumatizing violence" (Rothberg 2008: 226). As Stef Craps and Gert Buelens maintain, "colonial traumas such as dispossession, forced migration, diaspora, slavery, segregation, racism, political violence, and genocide" need to be considered (Craps and Buelens 2008: 3), not only because contemporary theory overlooks what Laura S. Brown calls the "insidious trauma" caused by the impact of horrific events or accidents, but also because the "traumatogenic effects of oppression" may also injure "soul and spirit" (Brown 1995: 107). For Brown, the ethnocentric perspective Europeans have brought to theories of trauma necessitates their reconsideration. As though in response, postcolonial narratives re-present chronic psychic suffering as well as violence perpetrated on transported bodies, in an effort to write back to the Empire and to right the representation of Dominion nations such as Australia, New Zealand, and Canada.

In *Jack Maggs* (1997), Peter Carey returns the 'transport' from the South Seas colony to the metropole. As correspondent to his 'son' Henry Phipps, the now wealthy Maggs writes back to the nineteenth-century nation from the perspective of colony and periphery. Carey's postcolonial reconstruction of Maggs's history gives Dickens's marginalised character a voice, enabling him to recount his own tale of orphanhood, urban poverty, adoption by criminals, tutorials in theft, and life of housebreaking. Thus Carey's neo-Victorian novel repeats and re-cognises Britain's repressed criminalised and criminalising past. The novel's multiple focalisers, its embedding of fictional autobiographical fragments as well as mash-ups of Charles Dickens's biography and *Oliver Twist*, enables the narrative to make visible and spectacular the second stage of trauma: the re-membering that identifies past suffering as traumatic. Thus, trauma becomes a symptom of the real, articulating not just a trace of past but also *future* suffering, presenting itself as the awaited, anticipated re-experience of pain – only ever postponed – that makes the unrepresentable capable of being expressed, albeit indirectly, for the first time. In this traumatic scenario, the subject's other returns from the repressed, and that same other, a split-off fragment of the subject, becomes worthy of embrace, of identificatory desire, even of emulation.

        Carey's neo-Victorian novel revises the official Victorian version of the convicts forced into transportation. Percy Buckle, the "owner of a gentleman's residence", who is "no more a gentleman" than is Jack Maggs, who breaks into his house disguised and posing as a footman, parodies Pip's rise in fortune and rank. However illogically, Buckle, formerly a "humble grocer", who has inherited a fortune from a "deceased stranger" apparently distantly related to him, voices the novel's recalling from repression the nation's "social *apartheid*" (Carey 1997: 12), its overseas transportation of its "unwanted excess population of felons" to colonial, penal space (Said 1994: xv). After Tobias Oates – thief-taker and writer, and so figure for the author, and like him, a devotee of mesmerism – first hypnotises Maggs, exposing the lash-scars on his body, Buckle accuses Oates of injustice. On his back, Buckle says, "we saw a page of his history. [...] Whatever his offence, anyone with half a heart can see that he has paid the bill. I could not send him back for more" (Carey 1997: 96). Oates's sister-in-law, Lizzie Warriner, pleads for Maggs's imprisonment; Buckle, however, who as a fried-fish monger and grocer experienced and witnessed the trials of working-class life and of the labouring poor, cautions Oates: "Did you never imagine yourself in his position? I *felt* that damned thing", referring to the double-cat lash (Carey 1997: 97, original emphasis). Having watched as an older sister, incarcerated in Newgate, was condemned to transportation, Buckle pleads with Oates to sympathise with another battered body, to identify with his suffering by projecting himself into an other's subject position. "Put yourself in [my sister's] place. [...] I never did forget that day [of judgment]. God help us all, that Mother England would do such a thing to one of her own" (Carey 1997: 98). When Mercy Larkin, the serving maid who discovers him housebreaking at the novel's opening, sees the lash scars on his neck at its end, Maggs tells her that "a cockney named Rudder, [a] soldier of the King", whipped him. "Then it were the King who lashed you," she insists, interpreting by metonymy and mimesis the crown's ultimate responsibility for the barbarities visited upon the bodies of impoverished criminals and exploited transports (Carey 1997: 346).

Maggs's embedded autobiographical fragment tells a typical tale of youthful Victorian criminal life. Abandoned when three days old, Jack is scrounged from the Thames's mudflats by Silas Smith, his 'benefactor', and brought home to Mary Britten, petty manufacturer of ladies' pills and receiver of stolen goods. Jack longs for Ma Britten (Mother England) to call him "*Son*," but Tom – "*he's the son*", Tom insists – despises his rival (Carey 1997: 102, 116, original emphasis). Thinking he will go to school, Jack is trained to the "*art*" of theft; he slithers down chimneys, and he and Silas's daughter, Sophina, scavenge luxury household items packed in sacks of soot (Carey 1997: 168, original emphasis). Tom, now Maggs's ally, turns Silas in to the police, and Sophina cries, "*Jack, they took my da. Who will take care of me now my da is gone?*" (Carey 1997: 171, original emphasis). Silas is the backstory's first imprisoned and transported convict, as well as abandoning father: Maggs and Oates have likewise abandoned or failed to rescue/save pregnant lovers, Sophina and Lizzie, and their sons. Indeed, at the climax of his embedded autobiographical tale, Maggs reports having been shamefully flogged by Ma Britten as Sophina watched, as Estella's and Mrs. Joe's peeping on fistfights haunts Carey's tale. Maggs also recounts having been forced by his surrogate Ma to look at the body of his and Sophina's aborted son, a reversal of the recuperative figure, little Pip, who revitalises Pip, a hard-working trader in the East – a specifically non-penal imperial space in Said's geo-political and imperial topography (Said 1994: xvi). Moreover, while Maggs pursues Phipps, Carey's version of Pip, across London, with the Thief-taker's help, Mercy, who guesses that the locks of hair he carries belong to his babes in Australia, repeatedly advises him, "They are waiting for you" (Carey 1997: 351). "You are their da," she insists; "I know what it is to lose a da" (Carey 1997: 340). At the novel's end, Maggs and Mercy return to New South Wales and become wealthy and respected citizens of the new nation; Mercy disciplines Maggs's two criminally minded sons and bears him five more children. Having endured the British landed establishment's harsh punishment of the criminalised labouring classes and the empire's exploitation of its excess underclass population, Maggs returns from repression in the cultural imaginary to re-cognise – and transfigure/transcend – his trauma through (re)writing.

Like Jack's tale, Mercy's backstory recounts crime, abandonment, and orphanhood and, like his, ironises the figure of the benefactor. After her father's death, Mercy and her mother are evicted; Mrs. Larkin imprisons the thirteen-year-old in her new hovel, and later, dresses her up and prostitutes her to an unnamed gentleman. Taken up by Buckle, her "benefactor", Mercy keeps house, soothes, and has sex with her master; although she hopes to become his wife, she is "ruined" and, ultimately, dismissed by him (Carey 1997: 78, 326). Both men sexually exploit the lower-class woman, although one gives her money and the other, a home and position as a servant. Here, Carey sutures the female version of nineteenth-century underclass British life to that of the transported criminal, and he represents Maggs and Mercy as rightfully earning their married life and happy ending.

Although Maggs, whose name puns on chatter, thievery, penny gambling, magnetism, magic, magus, and magazine, writes his obsessive letter to Phipps backwards and in invisible ink, Oates nevertheless successfully steals his secrets. As the novel embeds Maggs's repeatedly written correspondence, it interpolates an account of the author's mesmerisms of the masquerading footman and fugitive from justice, the "bolter from New South Wales" (Carey 1997: 96). A "conjurer" and "cartographer" of the "Criminal Mind", Oates justifies his burglary and plundering of Maggs's history because he may mine it for "a world as rich as London itself. What a puzzle of life exists in the dark little lane-ways of this wretch's soul, what stolen gold lies hidden in the vaults beneath his filthy streets", he chortles after his second mesmeric experiment (Carey 1997: 99). "Don't you see what I now possess?" he queries Lizzie, who favours expelling the dangerous criminal from the Oates household. "A memory I can enter and leave. [...] What a treasure house, eh, Buckle?" (Carey 1997: 96) The

Phantom that haunts Maggs's disordered memory appears through deferred action in his dreams, Oates's tales of his mesmeric sessions, and at the conclusion of Carey's novel.[6] The Phantom *is* Henry Phipps, Carey's postcolonial version of Dickens's boy with expectations, who wants, above all, not to be common and coarse and to win Estella's love. Passionately dedicated to "ensur[ing] his own comfort", Phipps appears to Maggs as the vision he has been, fragmented, throughout the novel: an "apparition", his "nightmare" in the "brutal, dreadful uniform of the 57th Foot Regiment", the British regiment that served as convict guards on transport vessels and that put down uprisings in New South Wales and captured and whipped escaped convicts in the early to mid-nineteenth century (Carey 1997: 351). Just before he tries to kill his second 'father', Phipps fantasises a man – himself? – hanging from a gallows' beam, like Miss Havisham but suspended over the new sewer-system's pit.

Burdened like Dickens with a begging father whom he dismisses privately and publicly in newspaper advertisements, Oates must write for a living, and write he does. Dispatched by the *Chronicle* to cover a Brighton gas-line explosion and killing of poor children, Oates sympathetically views the deaths as murder. Throughout the novel, Oates identifies with the mesmerised convict and mimetically hallucinates scenes from his convict's life, beginning *The Death of Maggs* several times and picturing, in Brighton, a boyish burned body as that of Jack Maggs. Here, he sees his novel's ending, as Maggs, consumed by flames, becomes a masculinised figure for Miss Havisham. Although Maggs forces Oates to burn his manuscript's and memorandum book's pages, the author again begins *The Death of Maggs*, which will crown his midlife fame, in 1859, publishing it serially in 1860 and as a "handsome volume" in 1861, the same year in which Dickens's serial publication of *Great Expectations* finished and a triple decker appeared in print (Carey 1997: 356). In Australia, Mercy collects all its editions, gifting them to a library in Sydney after having excised the dedications to Percival Buckle, an inscription first promised by Oates early in the novel.

---

[6] On mesmeric technologies and problems, see Winter 1998: 137-162; on Dickens's association with John Elliotson and his mesmeric experiments, see Kaplan 1975: 34-73, and Johnson 1952: 221, 301.

Carey's postmodern novel postulates writing as postcolonial
pastiche of a traumatic but un-cognisable British past. His magazine-
writing hack, like the young Dickens, exploits the London slums,
seeking material for his tales. Himself once a poor child (like
Dickens), deposited by an uncaring mother in an orphanage (rather
than at Warren's Blacking) when his father is jailed (as was John
Dickens), and condemned to hang for committing murder during a
street brawl, Oates re-fashions himself in the *Morning Chronicle*'s
pages. Become a "sorcerer" of metropolitan London, he "named it,
mapped it, widened its great streets, narrowed its dingy lanes, framed
its scenes with the melancholy windows of his childhood", and so
"invented a respectable life for himself" (Carey 1997: 199). Carey's
novel ends with Oates's dedication, and Oates's Chapter One, begun
en route to Gloucester, appears in Carey's Chapter Seventy-Four: "It
was a dismal January day in the year of 1818, and the yellow fog [...]
descended again like a shroud around the walls of Newgate Prison"
(Carey 1997: 298, 244).

As Carey's novel becomes an uncanny repetition of Oates's
tale, a compulsive account of its author's life and of the text's writing,
the identities of Carey's criminal and writer merge. The secret
mimesis or replication at the heart of the novel identifies writer as
criminal and criminal as writer. The Australian writer of this
postmodern, postcolonial appropriation of Dickens's fictional
autobiography writes and rights the wrongs of Britain's exploitation of
its criminalised underclass, its imperial colonial project. As the
criminal tracks down the Phantom that emerges in his mesmeric
stories, as the Thief-taker tracks down the truth about Henry Phipps,
Peter Carey tracks down the truth of colonial transportation,
exploitation, and trauma. For Carey, as for Dickens, trauma is a
symptom of the real; it is the experience you have always already
awaited, a possible future wound that will traumatically repeat past
suffering, the unrepresentable of anxiety in which the subject becomes
other, and the other becomes a metonymy for a repressed/repressive,
national, historical, imperial project. Carey's neo-Victorian rewriting
immerses us in the mesmerically recalled scene of trauma, submitting
us to the "hypnotic imitation" that reading represents, even as it
reminds us that the traumatic remembering or mimesis, into which we
readers are immersed, is a kind of fabrication or simulation, as is
hypnosis. Carey's criminal, having risen in station and fortune,

represents a disorder of memory; haunted or possessed by an intrusive traumatic recollection that refuses to be represented as past, Maggs perpetually re-experiences in a painful, dissociated, traumatic present his own haunting by the real, his 'son' Henry Phipps. Henry is a Pip without pity, a figure for Australia's history uncannily recalled as British regimentals, who punished, lashed, and whipped, leaving scars on the body politic.

Lloyd Jones's *Mister Pip* (2007) proposes a different theory of hypnotic mimesis and traumatic recollection by deferred action. Synthesising fiction with the un-cognised historical and postcolonial real, Jones retells the story of the blockade of Bougainville, an island whose citizens had protested the Panguna copper mine company's poisoning of the land, felling and burning of trees, and contaminating of river and land. Begun by Australia and Papua New Guinea in January 1990 and lasting through 1998, the blockade isolated the island from the wider world, unleashed a genocidal war against its people, and resulted in deprivation of medicines, fuel, food, and humanitarian aid (see Bougainville Freedom Movement 1996). Through his first-person narrator, the thirteen-year-old islander Matilda, Jones ventriloquises the traumatic story of genocide in a "deadpan" tone that "comes to look like a symptom of shock" as, at the novel's end, Matilda is forced to witness the bodily dismembering of her white teacher, Mr Watts, and her mother's rape, mutilation, and murder (Goldsworthy 2006). The so-called 'Redskins' precipitate Matilda's trauma, a symptom of the real, brutal experience she and the other islanders await and eventually undergo, as the malarial government soldiers attack the villagers, demanding they yield a rebel Rambo figure, whose name they imagine they see written in the sand: "PIP" (Jones 2007: 45). The unrepresentable metaphorical black hole of trauma – Matilda's possible future wound, withheld until the end – haunts the story. The novel itself represents deferred action in Matilda's a-chronological witness-bearing, undertaken from a position of safety years later in London, rather than a position of immediacy and endangerment on the island itself at the time of the atrocities. It recovers this "brutal [...] reminder of atrocities so close" to the New Zealand Jones calls home (Goldsworthy 2006), voicing its trauma by cross-dressing as an indigenous girl in a postcolonial, murderous South Seas world.

Set against this background of suffering, pillage, plunder, and murder, Matilda's traumatic story recounts an escape made possible by scenes of reading, re-reading, and re-membering Dickens's *Great Expectations*. Voiced by the teacher, Mr. Watts, whom the children call "Pop Eye", Dickens's fictional autobiography returns from cultural forgetting and repression to portray, by the structures of displacement, contemporary events as traumatic. Matilda recalls her early identification with Pip, a "new friend": "I felt like I had been spoken to by this boy Pip"; "I had come to know [him] as if he were real and I could feel his breath on my cheek" (Jones 2007: 23). Her identification is a kind of mimesis: "No one had told us kids", she says, "that you could slip inside the skin of another" or "travel to another place with marshes", where, "to our ears, the bad people spoke like pirates" (Jones 2007: 24). Matilda's imitation of Pip heralds a wider fellow feeling. "I had learned to enter the soul of another. Now I tried to do the same with Mr. Watts" (Jones 2007: 58). When Matilda tells Mr. Watts that she is "troubled" by Pip's change of character in London and by his treatment of Joe Gargery, the teacher responds: Pip "has been given the opportunity to turn himself into whomever he chooses. He is free to choose. He is even free to make bad choices" (Jones 2007: 70, 71). As the island children learn about benefactors (theirs is Mr. Watts), about what constitutes a "*gentleman*" (again, Mr. Watts), about opportunities and expectations, and about the possibility of change, they practice the skills of sympathetic re-cognition as they hypnotically imitate Dickens's character and make the nineteenth-century literary scene of trauma a symptom of the island real (Jones 2007: 53, original emphasis).

Matilda has become a fledgling critic, for she has learned not only to practice a kind of mimetic identification but to interpret fictional structure and narrative purpose as well. "We'd learned to recognize the important stuff", she says about the technology of realism Mr. Watts builds on the beach, a sandy imitation of Charles Dickens's world, itself a simulacrum of Victorian London (Jones 2007: 84). As the first reading ends, Matilda articulates "bits of story finding and connecting with each other" and discovers "pattern" in the uncanny repetition of Pip's second effort to help Magwitch escape (Jones 2007: 91-92). Mr. Watts teaches the children that fiction can confirm what they silently know, that fiction is a collection of lies as well as of opportunities for mimetic identification, that the hypnotic imitation induced by reading recalls us to trauma, a fabrication or simulation of the real. Yet when Matilda is "confused by the book's ending" – by why Pip desires Estella, why Magwitch returns – she discovers that her teacher understands the original Victorian trauma no more than does she (Jones 2007: 91).

Matilda's story embeds not only Mr. Watts's readings of Dickens's Victorian novel of trauma, but also the teacher's metropolitan reveries and the children's mothers' tales of folk ritual and religion, of Melanesian culture and heritage. As she listens to Mr. Watts's tales of his youthful visits to London, she understands that reading fiction makes us retell our own stories, learns that fiction provides escape, instruction, and pleasure. "We could escape to another place", Matilda says, to "another world to spend the night in", to "Victorian England"; we could "easily get there" (Jones 2007: 23). Matilda's mother, Delores, tells the children the native meaning of narrative purpose: "Stories have a job to do", she says; they "have to teach you something" (Jones 2007: 86). "Some stories will help you find happiness and truth", Matilda agrees, yet some stories "offer instruction" and "teach you not to make the same mistake twice" (Jones 2007: 61). Delores also instructs the class in narrative symbolism, about the ways the devil represents the Redskins in a tale of testing and conviction. From their mothers' stories, told concurrently with their hearing of *Great Expectations*, the children learn the "relevance of localized modes of belief, ritual, and understanding" (Craps and Buelens 2008: 5). Although Mr. Watts invites their participation, the children's mothers serve as figures of compelling, even compelled, witness whose testimony enforces an ethical obligation on the listener.

Imitating Dickens's characters and identifying with the author function, Matilda has begun to learn about the place and utility of literary criticism. When the Redskins return, *Great Expectations* vanishes, hidden, Matilda later learns, by her mother, Mr. Watts's rival for the native girl's love. Mr. Watts's "lie" – that *he* is Mr. Pip – thus fails to find confirmation in the book he claims will prove his fabrication real. The community's apparent refusal to identify the rebel-bearer of the name, Pip, increases their suffering, as the soldiers burn first their possessions and then their homes; the people deliver their 'payback' by burning the teacher's property. Nevertheless, he instructs the children to imagine their un-housed privacy. "Close your eyes and silently recite your name", he commands, and, doing so, Matilda learns that "the strength of one word spoken for [her] ears only" can locate her in "a room that no one else knew about", that her voice saying her name is her "special gift": that she possesses interiority or subjectivity, if not a house (Jones 2007: 124). "Now, when Mr. Dickens sat down in 1860 to write *Great Expectations*", Mr. Watts continues, "the first thing he did was clear a space for Pip's voice. That is what we did. We located that little room in ourselves where our voice is pure and alive" (Jones 2007: 125). The children then practice the critic's "special task", to "retrieve *Great Expectations*", to "dream freely", to gather and articulate story "fragments" so that Pip's story will be "as good as new" (Jones 2007: 126). The advocated process of re-membering Pip's story mimics the structure of testimony by trauma survivors, who retrospectively construct/create a coherent narrative from the fragmentary symptoms and traces of trauma that cannot be fully grasped or experienced in their entirety while initially undergone. As she treasures the book and "actively inhabit[s] that world" of Dickens/Pip/Watts, Matilda learns about her cultural "responsibility": to "make sure that Mr. Dickens's greatest book is not lost forever", to prevent members of "[f]uture generations" from accusing them all of "not looking after what we had been given to take care of" (Jones 2007: 129). Recollecting and re-membering their fragments, the children practice cultural preservation and ensure the future dissemination of Dickens's literary scene of trauma – but also their own. Hence, the ethical obligation they take upon themselves also re-members – both in the sense of recovering from forgetting and in the sense of reconstituting – the lost communal body politic of their isolated, forgotten, and traumatised island community.

The children also negotiate transcultural signification. Grasping the "gist of what is meant", they learn that the sign "*tree*" which makes one reader think of "English oak" and another of a "palm tree", enables them to "fill in the gaps with their own worlds" (Jones 2007: 131).[7] Seeking to prove to herself that she cares more

---

[7] On another reading, however, the transcultural gaps also suggest a possible untranslatability of culture-specific trauma within the same terms, problematising the application/extension of Eurocentric trauma theory – developed by and for Western culture for its (own) self-analysis – to other cultures. This dilemma has only recently

about Pip than her classmates, Matilda writes her fragments in the sand, so she may recollect, retrieve, and recount them more easily: this is her first real act of literary recovery, her hypnotic imitation of the traumatic scenario, her mimetic re-membering and recollection of a fabrication or simulation of the real. When the rebel rambos return, drunk on jungle juice and changed by the experience of guerilla warfare, and Mr. Watts says, "My name is Pip", he begins, much as did Scheherazade, to retell *his* story as Pip.[8] Matilda understands:

> Pip would be a convenient role for Mr. Watts to drop into. If he wanted, he could tell Pip's story as Mr. Dickens had written it and claim it as his own, or he could take elements from it and make it into whatever he wished, and weave something new. Mr. Watts chose the second option. (Jones 2007: 165)

As the whole village gathers nightly and listens, Mr. Watts's British metropolitan story appropriates Pip's, as he tells the children about his life with the native, now-dead Grace. One black and Bougainvillian, the other white and Australian, they create a mixed-race baby, who lives and breathes in a bicultural room filled with stories, histories, and recovered memories. As Mr. Watts's story mixes black and white, sanity and madness, Matilda appropriates Pip's trauma, but she subversively inverts the imperial boy's tale as colonial girl's witness. As Matilda "mimic[s]" and translates Pip via Watts, she identifies his tale as a "Pacific version of *Great Expectations*" that, like its original, is "serialized, parceled out over a number of nights with a deadline in mind" (Jones 2007: 175). The traumatic pun in "deadline" links story-telling, or more accurately re-imagined testimony, both to the act of individual and communal endurance and to the violent death that threatens that survival.

When the redskins emerge from the jungle for the third time, the traumatic scene evoked by the pun becomes explicitly real. Again, the soldiers demand Pip; again, Matilda refuses to betray her mother's thievery of *Great Expectations*. For the third time, she remains silent

---

begun to be investigated by trauma theorists; see, e.g., Craps and Buelens 2008: 1-12 and Rothberg 2008: 224-234.

[8] Gribble also makes this point (see Gribble 2008: 190).

as the soldiers chop Mr. Watts into pieces and feed them to the pigs. When Delores bears "witness" to her enemy's violent murder, they rape her, forcing her daughter to watch and to listen as they hack her to pieces also. This traumatic scene renders Matilda "preternaturally calm": "This is what deep, deep fear does to you", she notes in the retelling; "It turns you into a state of unfeeling"; even in "recalling these events" much later, she says, "I do not feel anything, [for] I lost the ability to feel anything that day" (Jones 2007: 202, 209). Matilda's terror rewrites Pip's overwhelming feeling of fear and dread for a Pacific island girl, reinscribes his trembled acting out and his painful re-cognition in the retelling. Whereas Pip experiences the haunting return of the repressed in this revival of childhood terror, Matilda remains dissociated from her trauma, her un-cognised memory becomes a symptom of the real she has awaited and, when that real harm happens, she bears the scars of a wound not yet worked through. Although she tries to forget her, Matilda's mother haunts her, popping up in her own world as memory, symbol, or as figure in a scene she watches. Re-presented to a disordered memory by deferred action, the mother's ghost makes Matilda re-member this unrepresentable scene of dismembering and misremembering:

> I am unexcited as I remember this; my body no longer shakes. I no longer feel physically ill. I have found I can reassemble Mr. Watts at will and whenever I like, and my account so far, I hope, is proof of that. At the time, though – well, that is a different story. I suppose I was in shock. (Jones 2007: 203)

Matilda's story, then, performs this recollecting, this re-membering of her benefactor's – and mother's – dead body as though both were the fragments of his story – and hers. As Cathy Caruth notes, the "story of psychoanalytic writing itself" recounts the bearing of witness (Caruth 1996: 8-9; see also Herman 1997). In Jones's novel, the narrator's remembering likewise bears witness, disseminating the story of trauma to the outside world.

At the story's end, Matilda becomes a literary critic, writing her dissertation on Dickens's orphans. As she "magpie[s]" through his personal papers and researches in the British Library's famed Reading Room, she learns that "Dickens, like Mr. Watts, was not quite the man

[she] thought he was" (Jones 2007: 247). She visits the Foundling Museum, where the hospital matrons changed the orphans' names, much as Herbert Pocket changed Pip's to 'Handel'. She treks to Rochester and discovers a commodified version of Dickens, deployed by entrepreneurs to sell goods and "sentimentality" (Jones 2007: 253). At the Charles Dickens Centre at Eastgate House, she discovers heritage culture: a stuffed Miss Havisham "stuck behind glass", a Dickens "mannequin" in the replica study (Jones 2007: 253-254). But she is *Great Expectations'* "new custodian":

> It taught me you can slip under the skin of another just as easily as your own, even when that skin is white and belongs to a boy alive in Dickens's England. Now, if that isn't an act of magic I don't know what is. (Jones 2007: 231)

As the novel ends, Matilda writes the first sentence of her thesis, which is also the novel's first sentence: "Everyone called him Pop Eye" (Jones 2007: 253, 1). This circularity of the narrative mimics the structure of trauma as compulsive repetition rather than the transcendence and/or closure promised by liberating narrative testimony. Not a standard literary-critical dissertation, Matilda's thesis retrospectively recollects, remembers, and finally works through the suffering from which *Great Expectations* helped her escape by representing a Victorian scene of trauma. *Mister Pip* thus re-presents its narrator's trauma by inscribing in the haunted present the wound endured in the past but repressed into the unconscious. Like her mother's bearing of witness to Mr. Watts's brutal murder, Matilda's story bears witness to her teacher's and her mother's violent dis-memberings. *Mister Pip* re-members those fragments, creating a mimetic tribute to Charles Dickens and his past, very Victorian traumas.

Kerry Goldsworthy notes that *Mister Pip* "skillful[ly] allegor[ises] colonisation." In retelling an "act of willed, group recollection", it re-presents "an image of the colonial experience, where the old-world culture is desperately but imperfectly remembered." In recounting a "recent and brutal piece of contemporary history", it has revealed those events "to a wider world" and shown that the arts may serve as a "potently redemptive force in a nightmarish situation" (Goldsworthy 2006). Similarly, Olivia Laing claims that, as a "microcosm of post-colonial literature", *Mister Pip* "hybridiz[es]" the narratives of black and white races to create a new and resonant fable" of colonial exploitation and postcolonial resistance (Laing 2007). As a postcolonial rewriting of Victorian fiction, *Mister Pip* recounts its own narrativisation, re-cognises its narratorial voice, re-members its narrative fragments, and recounts the repressed colonial wound as traumatic. It also, of course, romanticises trauma as a transcultural bridge, enabling unconditional empathy, without representing the dangers of appropriation, as does LaCapra, for instance. As neo-Victorian reconstructions of the return of the Victorian repressed, *Mister Pip* and *Jack Maggs* turn Pip's trauma of declassing into the postcolonial traumas of racial hatred and genocidal murder, of national exportation or isolation, and of the bodily wounding of a criminalised underclass.

In a genealogy of narrative trauma, Dickens's, Carey's, and Jones's novels replicate the traumatic structure of *Nachträglichkeit*. Pip Jack, and Matilda suffer from the afterwardness of trauma, whereby an event or experience only becomes understood or translated through a subsequent experience. This genealogy identifies trauma as a symptom of the narrative real, recruiting the reader, like Matilda, into the experience we await, hypnotically immersing us in the scene of trauma, acting out the anxious unrepresentability of a past wound that, presented to a disordered memory by deferred action, becomes re-presented and re-membered during the return of the repressed that recuperates a split-off fragment of the subject through mimetic identification. For Carey and Jones, then, trauma cannot be experienced across generations but must be re-experienced, must return from repression in a structure of *Nachträglichkeit*, to be identified as the trauma it was and remains. As these tales uncannily repeat, challenge, and culturally deploy Dickens's version of trauma, they invoke the mechanism of repetition compulsion to save an unrepentant world. As Cathy Caruth notes, traumatic storytelling thus invokes the "enigma of survival" (Caruth 1996: 58), which produces its incomprehensibility as well as its re-membering for a metropolitan as well as a peripheral community.

Bibliography

Bougainville Freedom Movement. 1996 'Bougainville fights for freedom', 16 May. Online at: http://www.hartford-hwp.com/archives/24/047.html (consulted 08.08.2009).

Brooke, Alan, and David Brandon. 2005. *Bound for Botany Bay: British Convict Voyages to Australia*. Richmond, UK: The National Archives.

Brown, Laura S. 1995. 'Not Outside the Range: One Feminist Perspective on Psychic Trauma', in Caruth, Cathy (ed.), *Trauma: Explorations in Memory*. Baltimore, Maryland: The Johns Hopkins University Press: 100-112.

Carey, Peter. 1997. *Jack Maggs*. New York: Vintage.

Caruth, Cathy. 1996. *Unclaimed Experience: Trauma, Narrative, and History*. Baltimore, Maryland: The Johns Hopkins University Press.

Clayton, Jay. 2003. *Charles Dickens in Cyberspace: The Afterlife of the Nineteenth-Century in Postmodern Culture*. Oxford: Oxford University Press.

Colley, Linda. 1992. *Britons: Forging the Nation 1707-1837*. New Haven: Yale University Press.

Cowie, Elizabeth. 2003. 'The Lived Nightmare: Trauma, Anxiety, and the Ethical Aesthetics of Horror', in Schneider, Steven Jay, and Daniel Shaw (eds.), *Dark Thoughts: Philosophic Reflections on Cinematic Horror*. Lanham, Maryland: Scarecrow Press: 25-46.

Craps, Stef, and Gert Buelens. 2008. 'Introduction: Postcolonial Novels', *Studies in the Novel* 40(1-2) (Spring & Summer): 1-12.

Dickens, Charles. 1996. *Great Expectations* [1860-1861] (ed. Janice Carlisle). Boston: Bedford Books of St. Martin's Press.

Forster, John. 1966. *The Life of Charles Dickens* (ed. A. J. Hoppé). London: Dent.

Frost, Alan. 1994. *Botany Bay Mirages: Illusions of Australia's Convict Beginnings*. Melbourne: Melbourne University Press.

Goldsworthy, Kerryn. 2006. 'Mister Pip', *The Sydney Morning Herald*, 2 Oct. Online at: http://www.smh.com.au/news/book-reviews/mister-pip/2006/10/02/1159641243954.html?page=fullpage (consulted 08/08/09).

Gribble, Jennifer. 2008. 'Portable Property: Postcolonial Appropriations of *Great Expectations*', in Gay, Penny, Judith Johnston, and Catherine Waters (eds.), *Victorian Turns, NeoVictorian Returns: Essays on Fiction and Culture*. Newcastle: Cambridge Scholars Publishing: 182-192.

Harrington, Ralph. 2001. 'The Railway Accident: Trains, Trauma, and Technological Crises in Nineteenth-Century Britain', in Lerner and Micale (2001): 31-56.

Herman, Judith Lewis. 1997. *Trauma and Recovery*, rev. ed. New York: Basic Books.

Hobsbawm, E.J., and George Rudé. 1975. *Captain Swing*. New York: W. W. Norton & Co.

Hughes, Robert. 1987. *The Fatal Shore: A History of the Transportation of Convicts to Australia, 1787-1868*. London: Collins Harvill.

Hutter, Albert D. 1977. 'Reconstructive Autobiography: The Experience at Warren's Blacking', *Dickens Studies Annual* 6: 1-14.

Johnson, Edgar. 1952. *Charles Dickens: His Tragedy and Triumph*. New York: Simon and Schuster.

Jones, Lloyd. 2007. *Mister Pip*. New York: Dial Press.

Joyce, Simon. 2007. *The Victorians in the Rearview Mirror*. Athens, Ohio: Ohio University Press.

Kaplan, Cora. 2007. *Victoriana: Histories, Fictions, Criticism*. New York: Columbia University Press.

Kaplan, Fred. 1975. *Dickens and Mesmerism: The Hidden Springs of Fiction*. Princeton: Princeton University Press.

Krueger, Christine (ed.). 2002. 'Introduction', in *Functions of Victorian Culture at the Present Time*. Athens, Ohio: Ohio University Press: xi-xx.

LaCapra, Dominick. 2001. *Writing History, Writing Trauma*. Baltimore, Maryland: The Johns Hopkins University Press.

Laing, Olivia. 2007. 'Pip Pip', *Guardian*, 7 July. Online at: http://www.guardian.co.uk/books/2007/jul/07/featuresreviews.guardianrevie w21 (consulted 08.08.2009).

Leavis, F.R. 1964. *The Great Tradition: George Eliot, Henry James, Joseph Conrad*. New York: New York University Press.

Lerner, Paul, and Mark S. Micale (eds.). 2001. *Traumatic Pasts: History, Psychiatry, and Trauma in the Modern Age, 1870-1930*. Cambridge: Cambridge University Press.

—— 2001. 'Trauma, Psychiatry, and History: A Conceptual and Historiographical Introduction', in Lerner and Micale (2001): 1-27.

Leys, Ruth. 2000. *Trauma: A Genealogy*. Chicago: Chicago University Press.

Mandler, Peter. 1997. *The Fall and Rise of the Stately Home*. New Haven: Yale University Press.

—— 1990. *Aristocratic Government in the Age of Reform: Whigs and Liberals, 1830-1852*. New York: Oxford University Press.

Matus, Jill L. 2003. 'Dickensian Dislocations: Trauma, Memory, and Railway Disaster', in Michie, Helena, and Ronald R. Thomas (eds.), *Nineteenth-Century Geographies: The Transformation of Space from the Victorian Age to the American Century*. New Brunswick: Rutgers University Press: 225-236.

Morgan, Gwenda, and Peter Rushton. 2004. *Eighteenth-Century Criminal Transportation: The Formation of the Criminal Atlantic*. Houndmills, Basingstoke: Palgrave Macmillan.

Rothberg, Michael. 2008. 'Decolonizing Trauma Studies', *Studies in the Novel* 40(1-2) (Spring & Summer): 224-234.

Sadoff, Dianne F. 1982. *Monsters of Affection: Dickens, Eliot, and Brontë on Fatherhood*. Baltimore, Maryland: The Johns Hopkins University Press.

——, and John Kucich. 2000. 'Introduction: Histories of the Present', in Kucich, John, and Dianne F. Sadoff (eds.), *Victorian Afterlife: Postmodern Culture Rewrites the Nineteenth Century*. Minneapolis: University of Minnesota Press: ix-xxx.

Said, Edward W. 1994. *Culture and Imperialism*. New York: Vintage Books.

Solomon, Pearl Chesler. 1975. *Dickens and Melville in Their Time*. New York: Columbia University Press.

Sweeney, Christopher. 1981. *Transported: In Place of Death: Convicts in Australia*. South Melbourne: Macmillan of Australia.

Wahrman, Dror. 1995. *Imagining the Middle Class: The Political Representation of Class in Britain, c. 1780-1840*. Cambridge: Cambridge University Press.

Winter, Alison. 1998. *Mesmerized: Powers of Mind in Victorian Britain*. Chicago: Chicago University Press.

Photography, Trauma and the Politics of War in Beryl Bainbridge's *Master Georgie*

Vanessa Guignery

Abstract:
In her neo-Victorian novel *Master Georgie* (1988), Beryl Bainbridge uses narrative plurality and the verbal description of photographs to probe epistemological issues and to approach the trauma of the Crimean War from a deliberately oblique perspective. By choosing marginal characters whose voices have not been recorded by official history, she proposes a more personal and at the same time cynical portrait of the horrors of war. The photographs alluded to in the text are often the result of manipulation and deceit meant to hide the squalid truth, and therefore raise questions as to what can be perceived of the original trauma, interrogating the import of this new medium in the Victorian period and in times of war. In the light of Cathy Caruth's contention that trauma presents a crisis of truth, this paper examines the dialogue between two heterogeneous semiotic codes (text and narrativised image) and discusses its validity as a mode of representation of personal and collective tragedies.

Keywords: Crimean War, crisis of truth, gender, images, marginal voices, narrative plurality, photography, war photographers, witnessing.

*****

> Theirs not to make reply
> Theirs not to reason why
> Theirs but to do and die
> (Lord Alfred Tennyson, 'The Charge of the Light Brigade', 1854)

Trauma theory, which has developed extensively in the last decades of the twentieth century, probes into a variety of experiences deemed traumatic, be they personal or collective, recent or ancient. War trauma in particular has been closely examined in the aftermath of the two World Wars and the horror of the Holocaust. World War I especially has inspired many poets and novelists, from Virginia Woolf's portrayal of the shell-shocked Septimus Warren Smith in *Mrs*

Dalloway (1925) and the war poetry of Siegfried Sassoon and Wilfred Owen to Pat Barker's *Regeneration* (1991, 1993, 1995) trilogy and Sebastian Faulks's *Birdsong* (1993). Much less attention has been given by contemporary writers to an earlier conflict, which took place in the mid-nineteenth century and involved several European countries: the Crimean War. More than two years elapsed between the declaration of war in March 1854 and the signing of the peace accord in April 1856; by then half a million men had died on the battlefields or in hospitals, at sea or on the steppes, by bullet and shrapnel or of cholera, disease and starvation. The Crimean War is mainly remembered nowadays in relation to two historic personages and their actions. Firstly, it is associated with the founder and originator of modern nursing, Florence Nightingale (1820-1910), who established an ordered system of hygienic hospital care in the Crimea and revolutionised the treatment of the common soldier. Secondly, it is remembered for Lord Cardigan (1797-1868)) and his legendary charge of the Light Brigade, vividly immortalised in Alfred, Lord Tennyson's famous poem of the same name and wryly described by Michael Crichton as "a spectacular feat of heroism which decimated three-quarters of [Cardigan's] forces in a successful effort to capture the wrong battery of enemy guns" (qtd. Troubetzkoy 2006: 321). It was also the first major armed conflict in history to be covered by photographers and newspaper reporters, Carol Popp de Szathmari, Roger Fenton and James Robertson being the first war photographers, and Sir William Howard Russell the first professional war correspondent, sent by the London *Times*.

In the twentieth century, comparatively few novelists have showed an interest in revisiting this horrendous battle. One of them is Garry Douglas Kilworth, author of five traditional war novels on the Crimean war, also called Sergeant 'Fancy Jack' Crossman novels after the protagonist, a shrewd and skilful sergeant with aristocratic background, member of the 88th regiment, the Connaught Rangers. The novels, *The Devil's Own* (1997), *The Valley of Death* (1998), *Soldiers in the Mist* (1999), *The Winter Soldiers* (2002) and *Attack on the Redan* (2003), all aim at glorifying the heroic acts of soldiers and defending the pride of the British army, and are very much examples of the genre or formula literature of adventure fiction. A different treatment of the theme is to be found in George MacDonald Fraser's *Flashman at the Charge* (1973), the fourth of the successful Flashman historical novels consisting of the fictional papers written by the beastly character who featured in Thomas Hughes's Victorian novel *Tom Brown's Schooldays* (1857). The vein is comic and satirical, as the supposedly heroic military man reveals himself to be a cowardly bully. Yet another perspective on the Crimean War is proposed by two female novelists, Beryl Bainbridge and Katharine McMahon, who subvert heroic and jingoistic war narratives in their neo-Victorian novels, respectively *Master Georgie* (1988) and *The Rose of Sebastopol* (2007). Using very different techniques, both novelists build up their narrative in such a way as to expose the barbarity and meaninglessness of war, intertwining personal and historical tragedies and providing two time schemes and geographical locations: the mid-1840s in England and the years 1854-1855 in the Crimea and its surroundings.[1] What the shift in time and place provides is a sense of puzzlement over the brutal move from domestic scenes and preoccupations to the absurdity and callousness of war itself. Experienced partly vicariously by characters acting as nurses, doctors or photographers, war is all the more traumatic as its causes are obscure and its developments incomprehensible. The differing versions offered by the press or by officers in *The Rose of Sebastopol* and by the various narrators and characters in *Master Georgie* raise questions as to what actually took place in the Crimea and what can be perceived of the original trauma as seen through the eyes of secondary witnesses.

In *Unclaimed Experience: Trauma, Narrative, and History*, Cathy Caruth defines trauma as "an overwhelming experience of sudden or catastrophic events in which the response to the event occurs in the often delayed, uncontrolled repetitive appearance of hallucinations and other intrusive phenomena" (Caruth 1996: 11). This delayed response, or post-traumatic stress disorder to give it its modern name, suggests that the past "has not been experienced at the time at which it occurred" (Whitehead 2005: 206), but that it returns as a form of haunting. As Ann E. Kaplan puts it, "in trauma the event has affect only" – producing emotions of terror, fear or shock – but

---

[1] Incidentally, the historian Alexis Troubetzkoy in his *Brief History of the Crimean War* (2006) also chooses to contrast these two periods, namely June 1844 when Queen Victoria entertained Tsar Nicolas I with great pomp in London and they reached a verbal agreement on the Turkish question, and the war proper which started ten years later.

"no: meaning" (Kaplan 2005: 34), and it is because the traumatic experience has not yet been given meaning, in the sense of rational thought, that the subject continues to be haunted by it. Such a temporal anachronism cannot be discerned in the case of the narrative proper of *Master Georgie* as the novel is told by three characters who give their own versions of their life stories, their different types of involvement in and reactions to the Crimean War, supposedly simultaneously with the events.[2] They therefore do not have the benefit of hindsight to reflect on their experiences, and the reader cannot evaluate the consequences that the trauma of war will have on these characters' later lives, as they have not yet had enough time to go through the "incubation period" or "latency" as Caruth calls it (Caruth 1996: 17). The reader is thus only witnessing instantaneous emotions to rather than cognitive processing of the catastrophe, even though Dr Potter in particular tries to rationalise what he is going through.

However, Beryl Bainbridge's contemporary backward glance at a 150-year old bloody European conflict is illuminating in that it comes after two traumatic world wars, the psychological effects of which on participants and witnesses have been well documented, and after the epistemological crisis which has affected historiography, questioning the possibility of ever reaching a conclusive and stable knowledge of the past. Bainbridge's historical novels,[3] though fairly conventional in terms of chronology, characterisation and narrative teleology, bear the imprint of the postmodernist suspicion towards historiography's claims to exhaustiveness, objectivity and scientific truthfulness, and instead emphasise subjectivity, incompleteness and partiality. Moreover, in *Master Georgie*, rather than telling tales of

---

[2] An example of this double temporality is, however, to be found in the episode of the amnesic soldier whose memory of his own identity and previous life (which he had forgotten after a fight at school that turned out badly) comes back to him after having his ear sliced off by the iron fragment of a shell (Bainbridge 1988: 193). Ironically, it is shell shock on the battlefront that restores memory and speech about an earlier trauma, in contrast to the usual experience of shell shock provoking aphasia, oblivion or hysteria. The soldier's elated recovery of memory is short-lived, though, as he drops dead one hour after being hit by the shell.

[3] *The Birthday Boys* (1991) deals with the failed Scott expedition to the South Pole (1910-1912), *Every Man for Himself* (1996) represents one man's account of the days preceding the sinking of the *Titanic* in April 1912, and *According to Queeney* (2001) focuses on the last years of Samuel Johnson (1765-1784).

heroism, glory and bravery, she addresses the horrors and disarray of war and does so a century and a half after the event, which may correspond to the concept of "belatedness" (Caruth 1996: 92) often referred to by trauma theorists. As Ann E. Kaplan argues, a certain period of time "must lapse before a culture or an individual finds the right time to return to trauma" (Kaplan 2005: 86).

Another interesting dimension of *Master Georgie* is its structuration around the description of photographic plates of key moments in the story, so that Bainbridge uses both narrative plurality and the medium of photography (albeit textually rather than visually rendered) to probe epistemological issues of what can be known of the conflict, approaching the trauma of war tangentially from an at the time unconventional perspective though now common framing. By choosing marginal characters, whose voices have usually failed to find an audience through official history and whose reactions to the conflict differ from public pronouncements thereon, she proposes a more personal, unstable and cynical portrait of the horrors of war. Moreover, the photographs that are described, punctuating the novel, are shown to be the result of manipulation and deceit meant to deliberately hide the squalid truth; therefore the novel questions the import and ideological application of this new medium in times of war – arguably beyond the Victorian period also. Published in 1988, *Master Georgie* may indeed be read in the light of the intensely nationalistic or partisan media coverage of conflicts that took place around the same period, for instance the 1982 Falklands War between Britain and Argentina or the Iran-Iraq War of 1980-1988. Two years later, Kuwait would fund a virtual propaganda war in the international media against the Iraqi invaders of the First Gulf War.

In the light of Cathy Caruth's contention that trauma presents a crisis of truth, one may therefore discuss the validity and reliability of both text and image as modes of representation of personal and collective tragedies in Bainbridge's novel. This chapter will also try to determine to what extent the issue of war trauma, mostly viewed from the margins, through the perspective of secondary characters in the conflict and through deceitful photographs, is approached with the benefit of the writer's and reader's hindsight on more recent conflicts and on the contemporary use of images by the media.[4]

1.   The Crimean War: "a foolish expedition"

Even though the Crimean War cost more lives than any conflict in pre-twentieth-century history, it was, to quote H.A.L. Fisher, a "contest entered without necessity, conducted without foresight", or, in the words of Frederick Engels, "a colossal comedy of errors" (qtd. Troubetzkoy 2006: xiii, xv). In *Death or Glory: The Legacy of the Crimean War*, Robert Edgerton argues that the Crimean War was "a showcase for bad generalship, bureaucratic bungling, and inept medical care" (Edgerton 1999: 3). G.M. Trevelyan famously called it "a foolish expedition", conducted "because the English people were bored by peace" (qtd. James 1981: 17). Diplomats ignored opportunities to avoid war and make peace; officers knowingly sent columns of soldiers to certain death; more men and women died from cholera, hunger and cold than in the actual fighting. What has been called "the world's most curious and unnecessary struggle" and "the only perfectly useless modern war that has been waged" (Troubetzkoy 2006: xv, 32) was marked by long periods of inertia, as well as confusion as to the actual development of the conflict. Indeed, the Crimean War apparently has the distinction of having taken longer to be declared than any other war in modern times (Troubetzkoy 2006: 118) In *Master Georgie*, Dr Potter is amazed at the contradictory information he and his companions are given:

> The military news was confusing. On our arrival we had been told of a glorious Turkish victory and assured that the danger of conflict was past, only to learn the following day that the Duke of Cambridge and Lord Raglan were at this moment on their way to Malta to make a declaration of war. (Bainbridge 1999: 84)

---

[4] Though this chapter will mainly focus on *Master Georgie* for its specific treatment of photography as a way to distort personal or collective history, parallels will be drawn where appropriate with *The Rose of Sebastopol*, so as to highlight convergences between two contemporary female novelists' approaches to deflating the mythology of British heroism.

One of the characters later refers to "the infernal muddle of the war" (Bainbridge 1999: 134), whereby the initial object of the campaign (to prevent the Russians from taking Constantinople) having been accomplished by September 1854, the allied armies nevertheless decided to advance further and lay siege to Sebastopol, a beleaguerment for which they were ill-prepared and which lasted eleven months in conditions of wretchedness and squalor. A colonel sums up the feeling of authorities: "We can hardly turn tail and go home, not after all the flag waving and drum beating" (Bainbridge 1999: 134). It is during this long siege in the autumn and winter of 1854-1855 that many soldiers died, seven-eighths of whom succumbed to cholera or to the hardships of the winter, while only one-eighth died of wounds.

In *The Rose of Sebastopol*, the characters who have remained in England read news of the front in William Howard Russell's columns published in the *Times* and notice the gradual shift of mood, from euphoric patriotic fervour and extolling of the pluck and fortitude of the British army to dispirited accounts of the appalling conditions suffered by the troops, which aroused the indignation of the British public. The change of perspective on the Crimean War and the exposure of gross mismanagement on the parts of diplomats and officers, leading to a "notoriously incompetent international butchery" in the words of E.J. Hobsbawm (qtd. Troubetzkoy 2006: 210), forbid any heroic take on the conflict. Like Bainbridge's novel, McMahon's text calls for a more subversive representation of the horrors of war as seen through the eyes of characters usually confined to the sidelines of history, above all women, who tend to function as incidental victims rather than agents or public witnesses at times of war.

2.   Oblique Perspectives

What is striking about *Master Georgie* and *The Rose of Sebastopol* is their indirect treatment of trauma, as both novelists mainly focus on characters operating in the wings of the conflict rather than on actual soldiers (though McMahon does throw light on the plight of Captain Stukeley and Lieutenant Newman). However, as Nancy K. Miller and Jason Tougaw suggest in their introduction to *Extremities: Trauma, Testimony, and Community*, "the term 'trauma' describes the experience of both victims – those who have suffered directly – and those who suffer with them, or through them, or for them" (Miller

2002: 2). The eponymous Master Georgie in Bainbridge's novel and the orphaned Henry Thewell in McMahon's book commit themselves as surgeons to the Crimea with the intention of providing medical care to wounded troops. In the course of fulfilling his duty, Thewell develops a pulmonary infection, is driven mad by the horrors of war and by his unrequited love for Rosa, his fiancée's cousin, and is shipped to Italy where he makes a slow recovery. George toils away in Scutari's Barrack Hospital because he has been deemed unsuitable to be attached to a regiment, and then in a makeshift camp hospital at Varna, where he is only tolerated because the three previous doctors died of cholera; eventually he is unexpectedly shot by a Russian soldier while carrying a wounded officer on a stretcher. Neither Henry nor George is granted a narrative voice or a passage in inner focalisation, and both are presented as ineffectual, maladjusted, with a fractured identity and defective masculinity, thus deflating the status accorded to them by their profession, social rank and gender. George, unable to express his feelings and reconcile himself to his sexual inclinations, has lived a dissolute existence in Liverpool and has come to war to get "the prop he needed" (Bainbridge 1999: 90), while Henry fails to commit to his betrothed and admit to his secret passion for her cousin, his painful experience of war transforming him into a vulnerable and inefficient person. The two novels disrupt conventional gender roles, distance themselves from Victorian models, and implicitly point to the traumatic impact of war on the masculine symbolic order, laying bare "the illusion of male mastery" (Kaplan 2005: 83).

Rather than give voice to officers, soldiers or male surgeons, the two novels choose to focus on characters who are usually ignored in traditional war narratives and whose role in the war is viewed as marginal, accessory or incongruous but which ultimately attracts the novelists' attention. These characters are often subject to what Ann E. Kaplan calls secondary or "vicarious traumatization" in that they indirectly participate in war (Kaplan 2005: 20). First among these are the female characters who tag along behind the prestigious surgeons with no obvious justification for their presence on the battlefields. It must be noted that, although nurses occupy centre or middle stage in both novels, the historical heroine Florence Nightingale remains a distant figure, thus confirming that the focus is on ordinary women and on private stories rather than on the grand historical narrative peopled with heroic figures.[5] In *Master Georgie*, Nightingale is conspicuously absent except perhaps for an oblique and throwaway hint in Myrtle's monologue: "I was thinking of a fable I'd read about a monk who every evening heard the song of a nightingale" (Bainbridge 1999: 128). In *The Rose of Sebastopol*, the famous nurse is first referred to with great admiration and respect, but is never met in the Crimea, having fallen sick herself, and she is viewed with suspicion for her very strict regulations. The legendary 'Lady with the Lamp', tending the wounded at Scutari, is thus toned down in both novels, replaced by an emphasis on ordinary figures trying to cope with the grim surroundings, toiling away in under-equipped hospitals or dying from cholera. In *Master Georgie*, the shadowy place usually reserved for women in war narratives is symbolised by the description of the blackened photograph of the orphan girl Myrtle standing by Mr Hardy's corpse, and by the unexpected and irritating blurred shape of a woman waving or beckoning in Pompey Jones's photograph of a funeral procession taking place in the camp: "It puzzled me, for we weren't encouraged to have women in the pictures" (Bainbridge 1999: 199-200). According to Ana María Sánchez-Arce, the discourse of war requires a polarised gender system, which excludes women from the public sphere altogether: "The feminine must be suppressed or idolised as weak or in need of protection for war to become a masculinised discourse" (Sánchez-Arce 2001: 97). It is precisely this essentialist and stereotypical view that Bainbridge and McMahon contest in order to propose an alternative history of the Crimean War that offers various perspectives, including those that have been silenced or repressed in the past. In the same way, trauma discourse tends to privilege the testimony of marginalised voices that have traditionally been muted.

    In 2007, Helen Rappaport devoted her book *No Place for Ladies: The Untold Story of Women in the Crimean War* to the forgotten women who made their way to the Crimea, particularly the

---

[5] In a similar way, *Master Georgie* only alludes in passing to the decimating Charge of the Light Brigade, thus deliberately avoiding the narration of a major trauma of the Crimean War, while at the same time relying on the reader's awareness of this famous event. Dr Potter remarks, "three days ago over two hundred cavalry horses of the Light Brigade stampeded into the camp, their riders having perished in a charge along the north valley" (Bainbridge 1999: 177). The heroism of the horsemen is ignored as the only fact that matters is that horses are now available.

wives of British soldiers, and lived in conditions of extreme hardship, most often dying of starvation, cholera or exhaustion. While the sacrifices and suffering of soldiers during the Crimean War are now well documented in historical accounts, the equally traumatic experiences of the wives of ordinary soldiers have remained largely untold.[6] In Bainbridge's and McMahon's novels, the wives of officers are depicted ironically for the way in which they attempt to cling to their rank and social and dress codes even in the midst of squalor, and sometimes take up a voyeuristic attitude towards war. Indeed, the Crimean War is known for the development of "war tourism", i.e. British civilians of both sexes travelled to the Crimea and scaled the hills to see the bloody battles of Alma, Balaclava and Inkermann, and enjoy the war as a spectacle.[7] Much as Marie-Luise Kohlke argues with regards to the later Indian Mutiny, "[t]rauma becomes a carnivalesque picnic" and "[s]uch voyeurism short-circuits the 'empathic unsettlement' advocated by Dominick LaCapra as the proper response to trauma and its representations" (this volume: 382). Contrary to these idle and incongruous upper-class figures, the more ordinary women are shown as taking part in everyday toil and witnessing highly distressing scenes. Instead of being relegated to the margins, female characters are granted discursive agency and set themselves free from the stereotyped gender roles that have been ascribed to them.

In *The Rose of Sebastopol*, the main character, Mariella Lingwood, expert embroideress and obedient daughter from a middle-class Victorian family, undergoes a dramatic change as she defies conventions by travelling to Italy to come to the bedside of her betrothed, only to have him ask her to go and find Rosa, her adorable cousin who left for the Crimea to offer her services as a nurse, before disappearing. Mariella and her servant travel all the way to murky Sebastopol to try and locate Rosa, are confronted by the gruesome ravages of war and cholera on their travels, and eventually become nurses themselves. In the process, Mariella overcomes some of her class prejudices and psychological fetters and finds herself face to face

---

[6] It should be noted however that Robert B. Edgerton devotes a chapter of his book to the part played by women and children in the Crimean War, entitled 'They Also Served: Women and Children' (Edgerton 1999: 137-164).

[7] A famous uninhibited Crimean spectator, photographed by Roger Fenton, was Mrs Fanny Duberly (see Kelly 2007).

with the dismal realities of war. The frantic personal quest of a character, who seems out of place in a troubled faraway country but progressively manages not to turn away in front of other people's sufferings, replaces the traditional heroic and glorious male account of the conflict.

In *Master Georgie*, one third of the book is narrated by Myrtle, an orphan girl who suffered the personal trauma of abandonment and poverty in infancy and was found at about three years old "beside the body of a woman whose throat had been nibbled by rats" (Bainbridge 1999: 3). Placed in Mr Hardy's household because of an epidemic of smallpox at the orphanage, she remains in the family and is entirely devoted to one of the sons, whom she calls Master Georgie, to the point of later secretly and willingly carrying his children to compensate for his wife's infertility. In the Crimea, the previously largely ignored Myrtle flourishes as she finds a place for herself: "it was as though Myrtle, previously lurking in mist, had now emerged into the light" (Bainbridge 1999: 105). Her voice is surprisingly cheerful, assertive, opinionated and collected in the midst of the squalor. Part of the debunking of the myth of the admirable military nurse comes from the fact that Bainbridge is not trying to portray a heroic woman tending wounded soldiers (which is partly what McMahon does in *The Rose of Sebastopol*), but chooses instead a much more complex character who has none of the devotion and compassion of the military nurses, feeling disgust towards the scrawny and ill-featured orphaned children of the camp, carelessly tripping over a moaning figure and a dead man, and taking no notice of a sick man calling out for water. She escapes all female stereotypes and puts on a more masculine appearance, cutting her hair short and wearing a man's uniform. As war wears on, however, she becomes the witness of painful scenes and one can feel her becoming more despondent and distracted until, deeply shocked and numbed by suffering, she cradles the corpse of her beloved George in her arms.

In addition to the perspective of the foundling, *Master Georgie* incorporates the points of view of an upper-class scientist, Dr Potter, and of an amoral and alert street urchin turned assistant photographer, Pompey Jones, whose blunt voice, to quote Christian Gutleben, "is particularly jarring for a reader of Victorian fiction" (Gutleben 2001: 36), as he does not abide by the rules of social decorum, acting and speaking cold-bloodedly. The multiplicity of narratives and the focus on private experience make it impossible to gather a coherent and stable picture of the war: in a typically postmodernist vein, the fragmentary and the personal prevail, denying the reader the comfort of a grand historical narrative. Just like Myrtle's, the two men's subjective accounts deconstruct conventional war narratives in that the streetwise Pompey Jones holds a very cynical and detached view of the conflict, while Dr Potter's perspective is darkened by his mental turmoil and deadly obsessions, partly provoked by the stupendous information provided by Charles Lyell's *Principles of Geology* (1830-33) about not just the extinction of the human race but "the gradual obliteration of every trace of its existence" (Bainbridge 1999: 181). This revelation makes him so pessimistic about his surroundings and his contemporaries that he often deliberately ignores them and withdraws into his own personal world. As will be made clear later, Myrtle and Potter experience trauma differently, as the girl who seems indifferent at first gradually gains awareness of the war at hand and is radically transformed by the spectacle around her, whilst the scientist's suffering is more far-reaching and has deeper roots, leading him to voluntarily distance himself from the specific conflict in which he finds himself involved.

3.   Eschewing Trauma

Part of the reason why the two novelists focus on witnesses more than on actual participants in war is that it allows them to avoid a full frontal confrontation with trauma and to approach it indirectly. Thus, instead of describing assaults and military exploits as in traditional heroic male-centred war narratives, such as those of Kilworth, the narration draws attention to what takes place in the wings and shows how characters shy away from the crude reality of what is taking place and dwell on their own private stories. Dr Potter in particular, who confesses to having been completely destabilised by the revelations of Lyell's manifesto (Bainbridge 1999: 82)[8] and is driven mad by the deaths around him, takes refuge in ancient literature, domestic details, and delusions of his own to avoid the direct confrontation with the gruesome spectacle of war: "I endeavoured to fill my head with other

---

[8] The loss of faith and certainties induced by evolutionary theories is a recurrent topic in neo-Victorian novels as Georges Letissier and Catherine Pesso-Miquel point out in this volume.

things" (Bainbridge 1999: 172). Myrtle is well aware of this process of denial and protection when she says in her monologue:

> His frequent quotations concerning death, first spouted in a dead language and then laboriously translated, become wearisome. [...] Here, in the midst of the newly dead, his references to ancient massacres merely irritate. I suppose he scuttles into the past to escape the awful present. (Bainbridge 1999: 116)

Pompey Jones draws the same conclusion when he sees Potter talking to his absent wife, as though she was there with him: "things being what they are, removing oneself from the present, by whatever ruse, seems a sensible enough way of keeping cheerful" (Bainbridge 1999: 190). The character's deliberate dwelling on ancient carnages and deaths to protect himself from present ones may echo the way neo-Victorian trauma writing also serves a purpose of escapism from violence and conflict in the readers' own time.

This defensive strategy therefore leads Potter not to react when, as he and Myrtle are looking for fruit on a plateau near Balaclava, they see a human limb lying on the ground, "a leg torn off a little above the knee, toes poking through the shreds of a cavalry boot" (Bainbridge 1999: 163). Dr Potter's immediate reaction is to tell Myrtle of his encounter with a woman who sold him a melon in Balaclava many years before and, as Myrtle is not showing any sign of interest, he finds refuge in his thoughts, meditating on the landscape around Balaclava and on a quote from Homer's *Odyssey*. As Marian Mesrobian MacCurdy remarks, "most clinicians believe that recovery from trauma depends on the ability to verbalize or narrate the traumatic image, to connect the iconic image to the cognitive process of the brain" (MacCurdy 2007: 192), hence George's concern as both friend and surgeon when Dr Potter does not say anything about the torn limb after coming back to the camp. Potter reflects, "I could have told him that I'd heard the rain drumming on the stony path and that it sounded a death rattle in my ears. I could have described the peculiar angle of the toes..."; but the scientist understands that he needs to steer clear of such horrors: "severe self-control is necessary if I am to avoid being mastered by the impressions of the moment" (Bainbridge 1999: 166, 167, original emphasis).

Dr Potter is convinced he can only cope with the terror around him by turning away from it, by refusing to let the present invade his mind. It is only when time has provided enough distance that he may be able to integrate the traumatic images into his conscious sense of the events. For the time being, when George tells him of how Balaclava looks in times of war, he admits he finds "his description of the filth on the streets, of the harbour choked with the bloated carcasses of horses, camels and the occasional human [...] disturbing", but he also adds in a cold-blooded manner: "In such circumstances, I presume death to be preferable to life" (Bainbridge 1999: 165). This sidestepping away from the realities of war testifies to a self-defence mechanism on the part of Dr Potter but also suggests that his experience of the trauma of war has had severe effects on his psyche. Even though he eschews the present horrors of war, he persists in meditating on death, which is a way of repeatedly reliving the trauma. While Potter strives to avoid dwelling on the ravages of the bloody conflict, death scenes and morbid visual images abound in the novel and interrogate not only the characters' but also the contemporary reader's reaction to them, as similar images of atrocities have become very much part of our everyday reality through the media.

4.   Images of Atrocities
A direct and often violent way of conveying trauma in either photograph or text consists in showing or describing actual scenes in gruesome detail, where the dividing line between an informative purpose and voyeurism is often blurred. In *Regarding the Pain of Others*, Susan Sontag reflects on the way in which we look at atrocious photographs and argues that "there is shame as well as shock in looking at the close-up of a real horror" (Sontag 2003: 42). She explains that faced with images of suffering, we are either voyeurs, relishing sights of degradation and pain, or cowards, unable to look; a narrative, however, triggers off a different type of reaction when it dwells on horrific scenes, because of the length of time we devote to reading a text. Before focussing on the allusion to photographs proper in *Master Georgie*, a brief examination of the novel's visual

descriptions or *ekphrasis* of atrocities will give an idea of what the text offers, for purposes of comparison with the 'visual' images.

In *Master Georgie*, Beryl Bainbridge builds up her novel to a crescendo, starting with an early and grotesque encounter with death in Victorian Liverpool – the first section is rather bombastically entitled '1846: Girl in the presence of death' – moving on to disturbing scenes involving animals dying or giving birth, and ending with appalling images of suffering and maimed bodies during the war. In 1846, the death of George's father in a brothel is depicted with bathos and irony, as his son seeks discreet ways of bringing the corpse back home and maintaining Victorian decorum. The narrative thus eschews the trauma of this untimely death to concentrate on technical details such as the position of the body slowly seized by *rigor mortis* or the means of taking Mr Hardy back home. The photograph George takes the morning after, of his father lying on the bed with Myrtle sitting next to him, deceitfully erases all traces of the circumstances of his demise during intercourse with a prostitute, providing instead a respectable image that the family and Victorian society can deal with.

The novel then draws attention to the plight of animals, undoubtedly as a strategy of displacement to circumvent the dreaded subject of human pain. Dr Potter explains that in Constantinople one evening, they were met "with two items of dreadful news": the first one, which is expatiated upon for two paragraphs and severely affects Myrtle to the point of her fainting, conveys the death of a puppy, torn to bloody shreds by dogs. The second, stated in one sentence forming a single paragraph, is England's declaration of war on Russia in March 1854 (Bainbridge 1999: 87). Five months later, reports about scenes on the front in the Crimea are replaced by the description of an excursion of two women to the hills above a lake and by the gory spectacle of a goat giving birth. War trauma is thus displaced to the margins, while what appears incidental is given central place.

However, from the second half of the book onwards, narrators start describing horrific and striking war scenes, crescendoing to the climax of the final pages. The scenes are so gruesome and vivid that sometimes they may read as a pastiche of grisly war narratives or else as one way – perhaps the only way – of effectively conveying the full scope of the horror. The trauma is often that of the powerless witnesses, who are so shocked, numbed or grown accustomed to sights of extreme suffering that they can hardly react anymore:

"There's a sameness about death that makes the emotions stiffen. [...]
Dealing with the dying, one must either blunt the senses or go mad"
(Bainbridge 1999: 128). As previously noted, Dr Potter takes refuge in
the distant past and in delusions to cope with the horrors of war.
Another type of reaction is recorded when Myrtle and Mrs Yardley
see the country boy they had met earlier seated against a tree with a
bunch of wild cherries on his lap: "only now the pink had quite gone
from his cheeks and his skin was mottled, like meat lain too long on
the slab" (Bainbridge 1999: 127-128). The incongruous simile
dehumanises the dead boy, reducing him to mere flesh, while his
companion stands in the middle of the path, his arms wrapped about
himself: "The soldier wouldn't come with us, or speak. He and the
dead boy stared at each other" (Bainbridge 1999: 128). The muteness
and petrifying gaze of the soldier can make us wonder about the
nature of his trauma. In *Unclaimed Experience*, Caruth asks whether
"the trauma [is] the encounter with death, or the ongoing experience
of having survived it", drawing attention to the oscillation between
"the story of the unbearable nature of an event and the story of the
unbearable nature of its survival"; later she adds: "the trauma consists
not only in having confronted death but *in having survived, precisely,
without knowing it*" (Caruth 1996: 7, 64, original emphasis). The
paralysed soldier as well as the shocked survivors of a Russian assault
later on in the book – "some lay down and slept, others walked about
in a trance, plucking at their faces" (Bainbridge 1999: 210) – may well
be confronted with the incomprehensibility of their own survival. Both
Myrtle and Mrs Yardley, who witness the scene of the dead boy and
the soldier, before continuing on their way, cannot help weeping at the
violent event itself or at the spectacle of the soldier's trauma – or,
perhaps, at their own survival.

   In the last section of the novel, focalised through Pompey
Jones, ghastly and unsparing descriptions and reports abound of
soldiers felled with Howitzer shells, their limbs torn off, blood
draining out of them. The fairly graphic accounts and incongruous
similes reveal Pompey's deliberate aloofness from the sheer horror of
war and may provoke shock and indignation unless one is particularly
sensible to the dark humour and potential bathos. Indeed, the narrator
refers to soldiers' "innards dangling like pale links of pork" and to a
Fusilier "sitting upright in the mud, eyes wide open and the top of his
head sliced off like he was a breakfast egg" (Bainbridge 1999: 189,

203). Ana María Sánchez-Arce interprets these images as the penetration of war by the domestic "in a clear parallel to the militarised domestic sphere" of Mrs. Hardy's household (Sánchez-Arce 2001: 98), suggesting that both the war front and the home front are places of conflict and unrestrained violence. The tropes also raise the question of "how the dead are narrated – how their bodies are glossed" (Yaeger 2002: 32). One may argue with Patricia Yaeger that the similes function to "lighten the burden of writing about the dead" by "taking a body already disfigured by violence and making a 'figure' out of it" (Yaeger 2002: 32). The critic later adds: "In troping or turning death into figures, writing is […] exposed as an act of commodification and consumption" (Yaeger 2002: 48). Bainbridge's creation is of course artistic and fictional, while Yaeger is mainly discussing academic work. Yet in both cases, the images tend to draw attention to the text as performance, to "jolt us out of pathos" (Yaeger 2002: 44), but also to confine the dead to the shadows.

The blatant dichotomy between Pompey's offhand attitude towards death and the other characters' responses to traumatic war scenes is also perceptible when a soldier bounds in with his ear blown off, speaking very agitatedly, and then suddenly drops dead. Myrtle and Potter are stunned into silence: "Myrtle took it hard. She sat with her knees splayed wide, hands held in front of her, tapping the air with invisible sticks […]. Potter curled up on his stool, hands covering his ears" (Bainbridge 1999: 193-194). Pompey Jones, on the other hand, has blunted his senses and simply attends to the practicalities of disposing of the corpse. While Potter lives in the past to escape the present, Pompey says he intends to survive, thus projecting into the future, and takes a distant view of the appalling carnage that surrounds him, plucking trophies from corpses and later cold-bloodedly joining the fight:

> After that first sickening thrust into flesh and muscle […] it became ordinary, commonplace, to pierce a man through the guts. I didn't look at faces, into fear-filled eyes, only at the width of the cloth protecting the fragile organs from the daggers of death. (Bainbridge 1999: 207-208)

The barbarity and pointlessness of the conflict is made obvious when Pompey Jones, having just jabbed a Russian boy in the throat and realising that he has become no more than a "circus animal", admits: "I dıdn't know what cause I was promoting, or why it was imperative to kill" (Bainbridge 1999: 209, 208). His precipitous and unwitting enrolment as a soldier suggests that he is not prompted by any patriotism whatsoever, the English flag being for him no more than "a tattered square of silk" (Bainbridge 1999: 209).

Pompey Jones's numbed or cynical view of events also includes his taking photographs of wounds sustained by both the living and the dead as part of his assignment for the Royal College of Surgeons, which can be seen as a form of instrumentalisation of death. In Bainbridge's novel, photographers arrange the framing and setting of their pictures in such a way as to put the trauma of war at a safe and bearable distance. The photographs are staged either to be used as objects of scientific documentation as, for example, Pompey's "study of a heap of amputated limbs" (Bainbridge 1999: 199), or to give an acceptable view of the Crimean war to people in England, craving for the visual spectacle of conflict. In both cases, the subjects are turned into objects, concepts or metaphors, and tend to disappear as subjects.

5.   Photographs: Manipulating Signs

The first photographs appeared in 1839 and were daguerreotypes: through a positive photographic process, they could produce an image but not reproduce it. The Crimean War was the first conflict to be photographed, initially by Carol Popp de Szathmari, whose photographs were unfortunately lost or destroyed, and then by James Robertson and Roger Fenton. As opposed to paintings, which were deemed to provide merely allusive information, the pictures taken by war photographers were supposed to serve as an accurate historical record of the campaign and bring "the thing itself before us" to quote *The Practical Mechanics' Journal* of January 1854 (qtd. Gernsheim 1954: 11). As Roland Barthes argues in *Camera Lucida: Reflections on Photography*, the essence or "*noeme*" of photography is indeed "That-has-been", i.e. it certifies that "*the thing has been there*" (Barthes 2000: 77, 76, original emphasis). The photograph, as a "certificate of presence", is self-authenticating, attesting that the referent "has indeed existed" (Barthes 2000: 87, 82), or, as Susan Sontag argues in *On Photography*, "there is always a presumption that something exists, or did exist, which is like what's in the picture" (Sontag 2001: 5). For Rosalind Krauss, drawing on C.S. Peirce's terminology, photography has a continuous, immediate, physical, concrete, and direct link with the referent, hence its value as index, whereas sketches and paintings, which one can draw from memory or imagination, are iconic in that they are only related to the referent through visual resemblance and imitation (Krauss 1990: 77). Barthes also points to this essential difference between photography, for which "the *necessarily* real thing [...] has been placed before the lens" – hence the certainty of its reality – and painting, which "can feign reality without having seen it" (Barthes 2000: 76). In *Master Georgie*, the photographs taken by George and Pompey Jones thus leave a trace or testimony that certify the past existence of the subjects or scenes selected, whilst Rosa's watercolours and her sketches of her cousin in *The Rose of Sebastopol* are said to "dissolve" just as Rosa herself mysteriously disappears in the Crimea (McMahon 2007: 391). However, the certificate of presence is not synonymous with accuracy or transparency, concepts which may have been called for in Victorian times but which have become highly suspect in the postmodern era.

In the mid-1850s, photographs of the Crimean War were trusted to offer "undeniably accurate representations of the realities of war and its contingent scenery, its struggles, its failures and its triumphs" (Gernsheim 1954: 11). Matthew Brady, the American photographer who insisted on the necessity for a visual record of the Civil War, described photography as the "eye of history"; Raphael Samuel notes that he was thus "invoking history in a Thucydidean sense as a commemorative act, preserving an account of deeds which would otherwise be forgotten, laying up a record for the future", for which purpose, images had to be "transparent, an objective correlative of truth" (Samuel 1994: 328). However, as Susan Sontag argues, "the photographic image [...] cannot be simply a transparency of something that happened. It is always the image that someone chose; to photograph is to frame, and to frame is to exclude" (Sontag 2003: 46). Thus, war photographers may decide to sanitise or 'throw a veil' over the trauma of war by privileging more canonical and acceptable images of heroism.

During the Crimean War, both Fenton and Robertson were taking pictures for the commercial market, thus to a certain extent profiting from trauma and making it possible for people at home to

take pleasure, albeit controversial, in the 'consumption' and
'circulation' of trauma (see Yaeger 2002: 46). Fenton produced an
opus of 360 photographs, under the patronage of Queen Victoria and
Prince Albert and financed by the Manchester publisher Thomas
Agrew & Sons, intended for sale to the general public and
commercial publication in the *Illustrated London News*. This meant
that the photographer – unlike the *Times* war reporter William Howard
Russell – avoided portraying the ravages of war in order not to offend
Victorian ideas of good taste and, indeed, subvert the aims of
nationalist propaganda. As the public would not want to buy
horrifying pictures of prostrate or maimed bodies lying in fields of
mud and as photographs of battle scenes were ruled out at that time
for technological reasons, Fenton instead photographed scenes aimed
at reassuring the public that soldiers were properly cared for after the
terrible ordeal of the first Crimean winter of 1854-1855, and at
reinforcing a sense of national pride. As Susan Sontag puts it, the
British government felt the "need to counteract the alarming printed
accounts of the unanticipated risks and privations endured by the
British soldiers" and therefore invited a well-known photographer to
"give another, more positive impression of the increasingly unpopular
war" (Sontag 2003: 48). Sontag does not hesitate to call this deceit
brought about by war photography "a disgrace" (Sontag 2003: 48).
Fenton's photographs render war "as a dignified all-male group
outing" (Sontag 2003: 50), presenting views of cheerful regimental
groups, men in sheepskin coats, a convivial party of French and
English officers, views of Balaclava and camp sites, and many
portraits of officers and men.[9] The dismal side of war is avoided
altogether in order to present a partly sanitised version of the conflict,
always away from the front lines.

　　　Some of these pictures (though by no means all of them) may
belong to what Barthes calls "*unary photographs*", which transform
reality "without doubling it, without making it vacillate" (Barthes
2000: 40, 41, original emphasis). They are "docile" photographs,
"invested by a simple *studium*", which Barthes defines as a general
field of cultural recognition marked by polite interest, and not by any

---

[9] The photograph on the back jacket of the hardback Duckworth edition of *Master
Georgie* is a picture by Fenton of his own photographic van, called 'The Artist's Van
and Servant'.

"*punctum*" (Barthes 2000: 49, 27, original emphasis), i.e. a striking detail, sting, prick, flash, burn or wound likely to capture the eye of the beholder and initiate a personal affective and/or ethical response. As Lawrence James argues, the overall impression given by Fenton's photographs is of "an army which seems well fed, entertained, comfortably housed and with a high morale", because "he was recording history for the entertainment and interest of his contemporaries upon whose money the success of his venture depended" (James 1981: 14-15). James purports that Fenton cannot be accused of complacency or deceit as he had no brief to include pictures of corpses or ruins, but his images nevertheless tell a story that only reflects what was going on in the Crimea at the time in highly selective fashion. As Ulrich Keller suggests, "the images dissolve into a series of conventions and manipulations, relativizing their purported language of absolute authenticity to the point where it constitutes just one rhetorical, story-telling genre among others" (Keller 2001: x). The supposedly transparent transmission of facts turns out to be an ideological manipulation to legitimate war on the one hand and to accommodate the English public's gusto for spectacle on the other: "war events had to be masked by their organizers to create advantageous public perceptions and to adapt them to the habits of popular consumption" (Keller 2001: x). This particular use of photography calls into question the possibility of ever having access to a valid historical knowledge of the traumas of the Crimean War through the visual record.

In *Master Georgie*, as Ana María Sánchez-Arce suggests, references to photography are "incorporated to denounce any pretence of realism" (Sánchez-Arce 2001: 94). Therefore, Pompey Jones, assistant to a war photographer sent by a British newspaper, takes pictures of the concert troupe who came to the army camp at Varna to boost the morale of soldiers dispirited by the epidemic of cholera and by the endless wait for orders to depart to the Crimea: "The results would be sent back to England, so that the public would be aware of the good times the troops were enjoying" (Bainbridge 1999: 145). The deceit, however, is exposed by Dr Potter, admittedly always beset by morbid thoughts: "Dr Potter said it was a case of securing the shadow ere the substance faded, meaning, he gloomily prophesied, that it was likely those captured by the camera would shortly be dead" (Bainbridge 1999: 145). And indeed, the next photograph taken by

Pompey Jones is one of the funeral service held for the recently deceased soldiers and officers (Bainbridge 1999: 179-180). Incidentally, this preoccupation with death relates to the project of all photography according to Barthes, which is "*flat Death*"; indeed, Barthes argues that death is the "*eidos*" of photography since, immediately after the click of the shutter, the subject is lost forever as it is transformed into an object and the photograph testifies to its absolute pastness, its death as a subject (Barthes 2000: 92, 15, original emphasis). The pictures of soldiers soon to die also point to the necessity, as Jacques Derrida argues in *Specters of Marx*, to "learn to live *with* ghosts" (Derrida 1994: xviii, original emphasis), with the spectral traces of the dead, which entails a politics of responsibility, memory and ethics when one looks at these images, "an effort to live responsibly with the loss they carry" (Rose 2007: 46). However, as Yaeger argues, the subject of photographs or texts – the ghost or spectre – often tends to disappear in the transfer from referent to object, concept or figure, so that

> we must endure – that is, become complicit in – its silence, in the attenuation of the dead within the oblivion of approximate figures (figures designed to communicate, but always encountering the emptiness of the concept, the flatness of theory, the excess of lurid projections, or the instrumentality of the body made spectacle). (Yaeger 2002: 37)

In *Master Georgie*, Dr Potter points to the limitations of photographs which cannot give any access to the actual feelings of the subjects:

> I don't know that I think much of the camera. It appears to hold reality hostage, and yet fails to snap thoughts in the head. A man can be standing there, face expressive of grief, and inside be full of either mirth or lust. The lens is powerless to catch the interior turmoil boiling within the skull. (Bainbridge 1999: 180)

As a result, the war traumas experienced by these men and the consequences on their mind-sets remain veiled, hidden beneath the flat surface of the picture. The photographs fail to give access to the subject's inner thoughts, all the more as those described in *Master Georgie* or taken by Roger Fenton entail artificial poses and therefore cannot reflect the 'essence' of the subject (a notion whose very principle, in any case, has been repeatedly challenged in the postmodern era). As Roland Barthes argues, "once I feel myself observed by the lens, everything changes: I constitute myself in the process of 'posing,' I instantaneously make another body for myself, I transform myself in advance into an image" (Barthes 2000: 10).

One of these staged pictures appears in the third section, ironically entitled "1854. Tug-of-war beside the Sweet Waters of Europe". In May 1854, just before George's wife and children go back to England, an excursion to a popular Turkish resort (the bucolic "Sweet Waters of Europe") is organised, and George insists that a photograph of the Hardy family be taken. While they all line up, "some of us rearranging ourselves in the small hope of minimising physical defects", a quarrel flares up in the background: "Behind us, a tug-of-war progressed, officers versus men, the pig-grunts of the participants punctuating the struggle" (Bainbridge 1999: 99). On the one hand, the analogical picture of the family presents a reassuring but deceptive portrait of a traditional Victorian family: the women are posing – "Beatrice, under the guise of appearing reflective, propping her chin on her finger, Annie slipping off her shoes so as to come down in height" (Bainbridge 1999: 99) – and the identity of the children's mother is enigmatic, thus pointing to the personal trauma of Annie having miscarried and become barren after falling against a wall. Indeed, George orders Dr Potter to give the elder child "to its mother, who was already clutching the younger infant to her breast", and we are later told that Myrtle murmurs to the children "as they leap like fish in her arms" (Bainbridge 1999: 99). The text thus belies what the photograph is trying to convey as Myrtle (and not Annie, George's wife) is the children's biological but unofficial mother. Moreover, George is obviously deluding himself and others by exposing to the camera the image of a devoted father and husband, while concealing his homosexuality. On the other hand, the background scene is ironic, as men are fighting in a petty "tug-of-war" instead of taking part in an actual war, thus reminding the reader of the absurdity of the Crimean

War, in which even soldiers from the same side quarrel while no military action is taking place.

Finally, the last photograph of survivors of the Crimean war is a staged and deceitful one, once again deliberately concealing the truth about war. Indeed, as Susan Sontag points out, "many of the canonical images of earlier war photography turn out to have been staged, or to have had their subjects tampered with" (Sontag 2003: 53) In the last but one page of *Master Georgie*, the photographer announces: "What we want [...] is a posed group of survivors to show the folks back home" (Bainbridge 1999: 211). As he realises that the balance is not right, he asks someone to fetch a sixth soldier and Pompey Jones brings the corpse of Master Georgie and props him between the standing soldiers: "He slumped forward and the soldier to his right supported him round the waist. 'Smile, boys, smile,' urged the photographer" (Bainbridge 1999: 212). The irony of this fictional photograph of 'survivors' and of the injunction is particularly dark as George, who never had a proper voice in the novel and died senselessly, is only "resurrected as a patriotic image designed to inspire morale" (Grubisic 2008: 159). While the photograph described by the narrator presents a cynically warped representation of reality, the text's exposure of the deception and manipulation encourages the reader to reconsider the validity of the property usually granted to photography of furnishing evidence of the real. Epistemological questions are raised as to what can be known of the Crimean War and of Victorian times in general, and what kind of 'truth' supposedly referential documents can convey about a specific historical event. This interrogation transcends the Victorian period, encouraging the reader to ask similar questions about the reliability of the coverage of contemporary traumas and conflicts by the mass media. In this particular instance, the text provides the tools that enable the reader to pierce through the deception of visual images, but the photograph on its own proposes a different "emplotment" to use Hayden White's term (White 1990: 83).

What results from *Master Georgie* is a subtle play on the two semiotic systems referred to in the novel, namely narration and photographs as mediated through text. The fictional photographs present a distorted view of domestic life and war, embellishing the truth for the sake of decorum. This warped representation of reality is in part due to the imprint of Victorian times and to the fact that war photography was in its infancy in the 1850s, but it also brings to mind enduring processes of manipulation in contemporary representations of war situations, as we saw earlier in this chapter. In *Master Georgie*, the visual images alluded to serve ideological purposes to further the myth of the stable and conventional family (Mr Hardy's visits to the brothel and George's homosexuality have to be hidden behind acceptable snapshots of the ideal family) and that of the heroic and brave English army (hence the staged photograph of survivors). However, the plurality of narratives and the cynical and debunking perspective made possible by a late twentieth-century gaze belie that epic version of personal and collective history, bluntly exposing the deceit of domestic scenes, revealing the gruesome and dismal dimensions of war, dwelling on atrocious images of maimed and agonising bodies. As Ana María Sánchez-Arce suggests, "[t]he text thus fills in what the photographs disguise, double-expose, or leave out" (Sánchez-Arce 2001: 94). The bringing together of the two media or classes of evidence shows how the truth about the Victorian past can be easily manipulated and how past traumas, instead of being acknowledged, can also be silenced and buried once more. Bainbridge, who is keenly aware of the way in which information and images can be instrumentalised and commodified, and is not bound by any jingoistic constraints, lays bare the strategies through which traumas can be deftly confined to the shadows of history, and in the process, offers a means to exhume them.

Bibliography

Bainbridge, Beryl. 1999. *Master Georgie* [1988]. London: Abacus.

Barthes, Roland. 2000. *Camera Lucida. Reflections on Photography* [1980] (tr. Richard Howard). London: Vintage Classics.

Caruth, Cathy. 1996. *Unclaimed Experience: Trauma, Narrative, and History*. Baltimore, Maryland: The Johns Hopkins University Press.

Derrida, Jacques. 1994. *Specters of Marx: The State of the Debt, the Work of Mourning, and the New International* (tr. Peggy Kamuf). London: Routledge.

Edgerton, Robert B. 1999. *Death or Glory: The Legacy of the Crimean War*. Boulder, Colorado: Westview Press.

Gernsheim, Helmut, and Alison Gernsheim. 1954. *Roger Fenton, Photographer of the Crimean War: His Photographs and his Letters From The Crimea*. London: Secker & Warburg.

Grubisic, Brett Josef. 2008. *Understanding Beryl Bainbridge*. Columbia, South Carolina: University of South Carolina Press.

Gutleben, Christian. 2001. *Nostalgic Postmodernism: The Victorian Tradition and the Contemporary British Novel*. Amsterdam & New York: Rodopi.

James, Lawrence. 1981. *1854-56 Crimea: The War with Russia from Contemporary Photographs*. Thame, Oxfordshire: Hayes Kennedy.

Kaplan, E. Ann. 2005. *Trauma Culture: The Politics of Terror and Loss in Media and Literature*. New Jersey: Rutgers University Press.

Keller, Ulrich. 2001. *The Ultimate Spectacle: A Visual History of the Crimean War*. Amsterdam: Gordon and Breach Publishers.

Kelly, Christine (ed.). 2007. *Mrs Duberly's War: Journal & Letters from the Crimea*. Oxford: Oxford University Press.

Krauss, Rosalind. 1990. *Le Photographique. Pour une théorie des écarts* (tr. Jean Kempf and Marc Bloch). Paris: Macula.

MacCurdy, Marian Mesrobian. 2007. *The Mind's Eye: Image and Memory in Writing about Trauma*. Massachusetts: University of Massachusetts Press.

McMahon, Katherine. 2007. *The Rose of Sebastopol*. London: Phoenix.

Miller, Nancy K., and Jason Tougaw (eds.). 2002. *Extremities: Trauma, Testimony, and Community*. Urbana & Chicago: University of Illinois Press.

——. 2002. 'Introduction' in Miller and Tougaw (2002): 1-21.

Rappaport, Helen. 2007. *No Place for Ladies: The Untold Story of Women in the Crimean War*. London: Aurum.

Rose Gillian. 2007. 'Spectacles and Spectres: London 7 July 2005', *New Formations* 62(1): 45-59.

Samuel, Raphael. 1994. *Theatres of Memory: Past and Present in Contemporary Culture*. London: Verso.

Sánchez-Arce, Ana María. 2001. 'The Prop they Need: Undressing and the Politics of War in Beryl Bainbridge's *Master Georgie*', in Usandizaga, Aránzazu, and Andrew Monnickendam (eds.), *Dressing Up For War: Transformations of Gender and Genre in the Discourse and Literature of War*. Amsterdam & New York: Rodopi: 93-110.

Sontag, Susan. 2001. *On Photography* [1977]. London: Picador.

——. 2003. *Regarding the Pain of Others*. New York: Picador, Farrar, Straus and Giroux.

Troubetzkoy, Alexis. 2006. *A Brief History of the Crimean War: The causes and consequences of a medieval conflict fought in a modern age*. London: Robinson.

White, Hayden. 1990. *Tropics of Discourse: Essays in Cultural Criticism*. Baltimore & London: The Johns Hopkins University Press.

Whitehead, Anne. 2005. 'Open to Suggestion: Hypnosis and History in the *Regeneration* Trilogy', Monteith, Sharon, Margaretta Jolly,, Nahem Yousaf, and Ronald Paul (eds.), *Critical Perspectives on Pat Barker*. Columbia: South Carolina Press: 203-218.

Yaeger, Patricia. 2002. 'Consuming Trauma; or, The Pleasures of Merely Circulating', in Miller and Tougaw (2002): 25-51.

The Neo-Victorian Frame of Mitchell's *Cloud Atlas*: Temporal and Traumatic Reverberations

Celia Wallhead and Marie-Luise Kohlke

Abstract:
David Mitchell's *Cloud Atlas* (2004) opens with a 39-page neo-Victorian section that suddenly ends in mid-sentence, after which the novel progresses through various temporal settings before returning to the initial narrative frame. The reader is invited to follow the clues that bind the whole together, a technique reliant on the thread of trauma that links distinct historical sufferings in interwoven virtual pasts, presents, and futures. This chapter investigates how Mitchell's starting-point, a travelogue of an American notary in the Chatham Islands in the mid-nineteenth century, informs the rest of the novel, introducing its main themes: the relations between powerful and powerless, memory and forgetting, free and slave, and how these traumatically translate into physical and mental violence. Mitchell's Darwinian-inflected vision plays with ideas of fitness and dominance, altruism and the survival of individuals and cultures, both as he looks back to Darwin's day and as he explores how these ideas continue to inform our present and a future that may or may not become our own.

Keywords: address, genocide, Holocaust, memory, David Mitchell, slavery, survival, temporal displacement, trauma, witnessing.

*****

1.   Introduction: The Temporal Entanglements of Trauma

David Mitchell begins and ends his third novel *Cloud Atlas* (2004) with a neo-Victorian section, so that we have to say, ironically, that the neo-Victorian frame is 'central' to the novel, not in the literal, physical sense of space and location, but in the figurative sense of importance, and arguably in the traumatic sense also. For the neo-Victorian section could be said to 'haunt' the rest of the novel, resurfacing continuously like the return of the repressed or an involuntary flashback to an originary traumatic scene. Though praised by Robert McFarlane for his "darkly futuristic intelligence" (qtd.

Wa_sh 2004),[1] Mitchell attributes equal and arguably *more* importance to the looking back to the Victorian age from his position of living and writing in the late twentieth, now early twenty-first century. Yet his looking back is not as straight-forward as in other emblematic neo-Victorian texts. In *The French Lieutenant's Woman* (1969), for instance, John Fowles looks back to Victorian times to overtly address such subjects as nineteenth-century sexuality and prostitution from a twentieth-century perspective, subjects which, at least in mainstream fiction, could not be explicitly rendered at the time or, indeed, prior to the controversy surrounding D.H. Lawrence's *Lady Chatterley's Lover* (1928). Similar to A.S. Byatt in *Possession* (1990), which also seeks out hidden truths, albeit on a more personal than socio-historical level, Fowles contrasts only one period with the Victorian age, namely the author's own present moment of writing. *Possession* too is limited to dual time-frames, although Byatt's Victorian intertexts also take readers back to time immemorial via mythical and classical allusiveness. In its temporality, *Cloud Atlas* proves far more complex, incorporating six or seven distinct time shifts. We say six or seven, because, although there are six recognisably different temporal settings, we have to include the 'timeless' (since invisible) frame of Mitchell's authorial hand, which orchestrates the multi-temporal collage. For the reader, the repeated temporal displacements enacted by *Cloud Atlas* could be described as mimicking postmodernity's trauma of the loss of metanarratives – such as that of historical 'Progress' – in which to ground any unified and secure subject position; historically specific subjects dissolve into substitutable textual performances or simulations without identifiable origins or, for that matter, endpoints.

The novel opens with the Victorian, though one might even say *before* the Victorian. Put differently, the Victorian is itself figured as already belated in relation to the novel genre and the particular novel being read. For the opening lines of the first section, set in the 1850s in the Chatham Islands east of New Zealand, recall Daniel Defoe's eighteenth-century *Robinson Crusoe* (1719), commonly regarded as the first novel of colonialism: "Beyond the Indian hamlet, upon a forlorn strand, I happened on a trail of recent footprints"

---

[1] McFarlane was one the judges of the 2004 Booker prize, for which Mitchell's novel was short-listed.

(Mitchell 2004a: 3).[2] Crusoe, of course, colonises and subjugates not only the island, but the native 'Other', Friday, whom Defoe figures as a willing victim of domination. Control over the Other and his/her (traumatic) story becomes a prevalent theme in Mitchell's novel.

Thereafter *Cloud Atlas* moves forward in time to 1930s Belgium, then to 1970s California, to London at the beginning of the twenty-first century, and Korea in an unspecified, genetically engineered future, before leaping ahead into a distant, indeterminate future in Hawaii, after an apocalypse has destroyed life across many parts of the planet. Then, as if it had reached an apex, the novel returns to earth, regressing in time and working its way back symmetrically through the time periods of the first half, and geographically from the Pacific to the West and back to the Pacific, until it comes full circle and ends where it started. As with any traumatic event, however, the end point is not the same as the starting-point. Much ground has been covered in between, and it is only the narrative revisitation of earlier scenes that enables the individual and collective traumas to be fully apprehended, as it were for the first time. This chapter, then, aims to work out what has been learned and felt in the interim, to trace the temporal and traumatic reverberations of the (neo-)Victorian frame in the novel as a whole, and to highlight its crucial contribution to the novel's conflicted meaning-making process.

2.   Intertextual and Intratextual Resonances

In an interview for Book World, Mitchell was asked about the inspiration for *Cloud Atlas*. His answer cites three important sources. The first is Italo Calvino's *If on a Winter's Night a Traveller* (1979, first Eng. trans. 1981), "an experimental novel in which a sequence of narratives is interrupted but never picked up again" that made him wonder "what a novel might look like if a mirror were placed at the end of a book like Calvino's so that the stories would be resolved in reverse" (Mitchell 2004b: BW03). The structure of Mitchell's novel finally turned out to be six separate novellas, which each break off in the middle but are continued and completed in the second half of the

---

[2] From *Cloud Atlas* by David Mitchell, copyright © 2004 by David Mitchell. Used by kind permission of Random House, Inc., and Curtis Brown Group Ltd, London, on behalf of David Mitchell.

text. This textual organisation mirrors the structure of trauma itself, taken to interrupt subjecthood and its telling into disjointed pre- and post-traumatic realms, which can only be reconnected through belated narration of the rupturing event. Each novella or tale in *Cloud Atlas* is composed in a different genre and is, in turn, read or witnessed by the main character of the following narrative. Byatt has commented on how the different sections work in complementarity; each ends on a "cliffhanger" and together they resemble "serialised Victorian novels" (Byatt 2004: 9). Here too we may perceive a quasi narrative mimicry of trauma theory's concerns. Serialisation evokes a kind of repetition compulsion, while the cliffhanger relies on radical uncertainty, both ontological and epistemological, that similarly characterises the open-ended traumatic event, which cannot be known or made sense of while still *in medias res*.

Mitchell's novel begins with 'The Pacific Journal of Adam Ewing', an account by a nineteenth-century American notary of his return journey from Australia to California via the Chatham Islands, which bears witness to the ongoing genocide of the indigenous Moriori people. The protagonist of the next story, Robert Frobisher, finds this diary on his patron's bookshelf. In 'Letters from Zedelghem', Frobisher, a penniless, bisexual, young English musician, provides an epistolary account of his attempts to find work as an amanuensis to a composer living in Belgium in 1931. The second and third influences Mitchell cites in the interview are clearly apparent in these two stories.

> Second, a mention of the Moriori people in Jared Diamond's multidisciplinary *Guns, Germs, and Steel* led to a trip to the Chatham Islands and an encounter with New Zealand historian Michael King's *A Land Apart*. His idea that there is nothing inevitable about civilization caught my curiosity. Knowledge can be forgotten as easily as, perhaps more easily than, it can be accrued. […]
>
> Third, a book by Frederick Delius's amanuensis, Eric Fenby, *Delius: As I Knew Him*, was worlds away from the Moriori but gave me the idea of […] the struggle between the exploited and the exploiter. (Mitchell 2004b: BW03)

Both of these sources link directly to trauma. The first raises the issue of deliberate forgetting, that is, the amnesiac response to trauma that constitutes the counterpart to testimony and witness-bearing. Furthermore, the history of the Moriori is a deeply traumatic one, the non-violent islanders having been enslaved, cannibalised, and exterminated to the point of near-extinction by warlike Maori 'settlers' brought to their shores by white colonists in 1835. Mitchell's third source also raises the spectre of slavery – a form of economic cannibalism, with one race living off another – if less directly. In 1884, at the age of twenty-two, Delius travelled from Liverpool (the one-time main port of the British slave trade) to Florida to take charge of an orange plantation, Solano Grove, as part of his father's attempt to encourage him to go into business rather than pursue a musical career. Delius's plantation workers were African-American descendants of slaves, and he appears to have drawn inspiration for his later work from listening to plantation songs, presumably former slave songs, as well as a possible affair with "a black sweetheart" (Gillespie 2000: n. p.).

The series of letters from the amanuensis Frobisher to his friend and lover, Rufus Sixsmith, is discovered by the next story's protagonist, Luisa Rey. In 'Half-Lives: The First Luisa Rey Mystery', set in Buenas Yerbas, California in 1975, the journalist Rey investigates reports of corruption at a nuclear power plant and the suspicious death of Sixsmith, by now a Nobel Prize winning scientist. (The trope of nuclear power, of course, conveniently pre-figures mankind's near extinction later in the novel, which in turn echoes the ethnic genocide perpetrated against the Moriori, this time at species level.) The eponymous hero of the following 'The Ghostly Ordeal of Timothy Cavendish' is a vanity press publisher in early twenty-first century London who, shortly after having been sent Rey's novel, has to flee the vengeful brothers of a gangster client. He is then tricked by his own brother into confinement in a nursing home in the north of England. A film dramatisation of Cavendish's story is watched by the protagonist of the subsequent narrative, 'An Orison of Sonmi–451', a genetically-engineered fabricant or clone server at Papa Song's diner (a futuristic version of MacDonalds) in a dystopian near-future in Nea So Copros, formerly Korea, from where Rey's journalist father reported on the Korean War in the 1950s. Sonmi–451 is to be executed for the crime of rebelling against the society that created and exploits her kind. In an interview by an archivist before her execution, she relates that she saw part of the movie of Cavendish's ordeal, and her final request is to be permitted to watch the film to its conclusion.

In turn, Sonmi–451's story is projected holographically in an "orison", a futuristic recording device, seen by the next section's narrator, Zachry (also spelled as Zach'ry), a tribesman living on one of the islands that make up a post-apocalyptic future Hawaii (recalling the opening Chatham Islands location), after most of humanity has been wiped out during what is referred to as "the Fall". That, of course, brings the novel full circle back to the first character, who is named Adam. In 'Sloosha's Crossin' an' Ev'rythin' After', Zachry is visited by Meronym, the aptly named member of the last remnants of a technologically advanced civilisation sinking into oblivion. Before Zachry dies, he tells his story to seemingly random strangers around a camp-fire, and this is recorded by his son, though how remains unspecified.

All the different sections thus recycle tropes of traumatic violence and victimhood, near or actual extinction (both at personal and communal/species level), and scenes of address, testimony, and witnessing. John Mullan misleadingly asserts that the reader "may notice with gratitude the 'links' to other stories that the novelist has provided, but the imaginative worlds of those other stories are, of necessity, forgotten once you have left them" (Mullan 2006: 107). Instead, reading each subsequent section (re-)produces a sense of repetition and both active and involuntary remembering, as the reader responds to perceived convergences, resonances, and interconnections between the historically distinct traumas. This *inability* to forget is guaranteed by the compulsive return to earlier stories mandated by the novel's palindrome structure. K.M. Jaszczolt argues that the different narrative strands are "connected by the hint of genetic and cultural inheritance and a near-repetition of events combined with an experience of *déjà vu* on the part of the characters" (Jaszczolt 2009: 72). Yet they are also tightly interwoven by *traumatic* legacies and re-enactments, underlined by the novel's incorporated structural echoes and reader flashbacks, which are both inaugurated by and come back to rest in the neo-Victorian frame.

The characters of subsequent sections of Mitchell's novel assume a significant witness-bearing function, already figured in Adam Ewing's role. Comparable to us, the readers, they act as secondary witnesses (re-)experiencing antecedent traumas in virtual form through text, film, and recording (or in the novel reader's case, descriptions thereof). This witnessing function enacts the situation of address, albeit at one remove, that Dori Laub posits as central to the enabling of traumatic testimony, which he suggests requires "a bonding, the intimate and total presence of an *other* – in the position of one who hears" (Laub 1992: 70, original emphasis). Judith Butler similarly argues that "the 'I' needs the other in order to survive, that the 'I' is invariably relational, that it comes into being not only through a sustaining, but through the formation of a capacity to sustain an address to another" (Butler 2009: 176). In this sense, Mitchell's traumatic subject is constructed not individually but collectively. As Richard Bradford argues, *Cloud Atlas* figures the (traumatic) past as not so much "forever beyond our comprehension" as dependent for its apprehension on "a curious dialogue as each narrator shares part of the other's story and carries it forward" (Bradford 2007: 62). John Mullan's resonant metaphor for the same structural effect is "the narrative baton handed on" (Mullan 2005b). Implicitly, each subsequent narrator-as-witness ensures the survival of the earlier story/testimony through sustaining the project/process of address. In one sense this also guarantees the 'survival' of the subject of the earlier trauma, which is resurrected *in* and *through* the other (i.e. the secondary witness) rather than being lost or dis/unremembered.

This reanimation or restoration of subjectivity in/through Otherness links directly to Mitchell's motif of the transmigration of souls. Ironically, contemplating suicide, the disillusioned Frobisher expresses his belief in reincarnation: "We do not stay dead long. Once my Luger lets me go, my birth, next time around, will be upon me in a heartbeat" (Mitchell 2004a: 471). Hence he is unlikely to permanently escape the seemingly endless cycle of human violence he deplores. Indeed, Mitchell has said of his novel that "[a]ll of the [leading] characters except one are reincarnations of the same soul" (Mitchell 2007). The birthmark shared by most of the protagonists functions as a physical sign of their interconnectedness, not just through traumas shared, relived, and witnessed, but through their possible reincarnation as one another,[3] or, put differently, it constitutes an embodied trace of inter-subjectivity. The subject is both 'Othered' through trauma, which disrupts the ability to narrate the self-as-continuity, and literally *becomes* (an) Other in the un-becoming of its singular identity, thus paradoxically regaining the continuity denied.[4] The birthmarked characters all display exceptional creativity and/or bravery, thereby enriching life on Earth rather than assisting in its destruction, contesting Jeff Turrentine's negative reading of Mitchell's reincarnation theme as focused on the endurance of evil. For Turrentine, Mitchell's novel explores "how the will to power that compels the strong to subjugate the weak is replayed perpetually in a cycle of eternal recurrence", underlining "the permanence of man's inhumanity to man" (Turrentine 2004). Yet situating the transmigration motif within the context of Mitchell's deliberate choice of island settings, for both the crucial frame and middle hinge of his novel, invites a very different reading when taking account of the apparent intertextual allusion to John Donne's 'Meditation 17' (1624):

> all mankind is of one author, and is one volume; when one man dies, one chapter is not torn out of the book, but translated into a better language; and every chapter must be so translated. [...] God's hand is in every translation, and his hand shall bind up all our scattered leaves again for the library where every book shall lie open to one another. [...] No man is an island, entire of itself; every man is a piece of the continent, a part of the main. [...] Any man's death diminishes me, because I am involved in mankind[.] (Donne 2006: 1305)

In spite of *Cloud Atlas* taking "the principles of post-modernism" to the extreme via "its smorgasbord of styles, its death-of-the-author anonymity" (Walsh 2004: 2), Mitchell actually adopts a god-like

---

[3] Louise Economides links the reincarnation theme to the "Eastern and/or Buddhist models of time structured by 'samsara' (recurring cycles of birth, suffering, death, and re-birth)" (Economides 2009: 618).

[4] The location of Rey's birthmark, for instance, coincides with that of Sonmi–451, so that the former may be reincarnated as a slave, only to be re-born free once more as Meronym, who possesses a similar mark.

authorial role more reminiscent of the traditional Victorian omniscient narrator in "translate[ing]" his neo-Victorian traumatised subject over and over again into, if not a "better", at least another language. Each section or "chapter" of *Cloud Atlas* affirmatively "translate[s]" into another/an Other. Hence, even in darkest extremity, humanity is not only lost but also always regained, as *Cloud Atlas* "bind[s] together" the "scattered leaves" of historically distinct traumas, so that the different narrative selves and traumas "lie open to one another" in a reciprocal and multi-directional temporal witnessing. To borrow Christian Gutleben and Julian Wolfrey's formulation elsewhere in this collection, *Cloud Atlas* demonstrates neo-Victorian fiction's empathic ethical "opening up to otherness" and to historical others' traumas through retrospective narrative acknowledgement (this volume: 57).

Each section refashions the previous ones, its meaning in turn transformed through subsequent (re-)mediations of earlier scenes and themes. To adapt Astrid Erll and Ann Rigney's reflections on the dynamics of cultural memory, the novel's structure "draw[s] attention to the mediatedness of memory" *per se* (Erll and Rigney 2009: 5), its ineluctable reliance on the memory work of others, and the inter-subjective dimensions of trauma. Mitchell's stories work through numerous genres: journal and epistle (both prevalent eighteenth-century genres), detective thriller, memoir, science fiction and dystopia (mostly nineteenth-, twentieth-, and twenty-first-century genres); and ending up, ironically, with the oldest and most traditional genre of all – oral narrative. This is clearly deliberate on Mitchell's part, bearing in mind that oral narrative is also the preferred medium of testimony, whether in the Fortunoff Video Archive for Holocaust Testimonies or post-conflict Truth and Reconciliation Commissions from South Africa to Chile. For all its seemingly greater immediacy and 'authenticity', however, oral testimony is no less vulnerable to expropriation. In Ewing's opening journal, for instance, Dr Goose appropriates the Other's trauma in this sense, by writing "an epic in Byronic stanzas entitled 'True History of Autua, Last Moriori'"; his lack of 'right' to voice the aborigine's trauma is underlined by the narrative's self-reflexive mocking of his attempt to find not the (ethically) right words but the right *rhyme*, when he asks Ewing what rhymes with "'streams of blood?'": "'Themes of mud?' 'Robin Hood?'" (Mitchell 2004a: 492) Here neo-Victorian literature's ethical impulse towards Otherness comes close to degenerating to the aestheticisation of violation. Mitchell seems to admit as much, when he comments on his variations on the novel's theme of predatory behaviour "in the political, economic and personal arenas" in metaphoric terms of natural selection: "Each block of narrative is subsumed by the next, like a row of ever-bigger fish eating the one in front" (Mitchell 2004b:BW03). The philosophy of Dr. Goose, the predatory Englishman in the novel's first and last sections, proves virtually identical:

> But, Adam, the world *is* wicked. Maoris prey on Moriori, Whites prey on darker-hued cousins, fleas prey on mice, cats prey on rats, Christians on infidels, first mates on cabin boys, Death on the Living. 'The weak are meat, the strong do eat.' (Mitchell 2004a: 503)

Paradoxically, Mitchell thus calls into question the very ethics of troping trauma that his novel relies on as the narrative 'glue' to hold the different sections together. In line with Turrentine's earlier cited viewpoint, historical existence becomes one long interminable trauma of inflicted and suffered violence, which can never be overcome or transcended. Trauma itself becomes a speculative consumable in (post)modern commodity culture, mercenarily feeding its own voracious narrative production.

In its negative aspect, then, trauma becomes vampiric, rather than furnishing the means of ethically engaging with the past. As much is made clear in the Belgian section, where Frobisher comes across part of Ewing's journal and writes to his friend Sixsmith, asking him to try and procure a copy of the complete work:

> Ewing puts me in mind of Melville's bumbler Cpt. Delano in *Benito Cereno*, blind to all conspirators – he hasn't spotted his trusty Dr. Henry Goose (*sic*) is a vampire, fuelling his hypochondria in order to poison him, slowly, for his money. (Mitchell 2004a: 64)

Frobisher's language echoes Goose's earlier cited articulation of an extreme version of the survival of the fittest, another (mis)appropriation of the Darwin trope Mitchell's novel shares with other, more consistently neo-Victorian fictions discussed by Georges Letissier's and Catherine Pesso-Miquel's chapters in this collection. The rest of Mitchell's novel is haunted by this self-perpetuating *ideological*, as much as temporal, neo-Victorian frame, which is insidiously recycled even as it is deconstructed. The palindrome structure of the novel means that the nineteenth-century section both feeds and *feeds off* – via intratextual cannibalism/vampiricism – the subsequent traumas. Yet why *should* a nineteenth-century cataclysm on the Chatham Islands, in terms of world history a seemingly minor event in a peripheral location far from the centres of power, be accorded such structural significance in the first place?

3.   Contesting Eurocentrism: What Counts as Trauma?

Mitchell's novel, we want to propose, attempts something quite radical vis-à-vis trauma studies. More commonly within trauma discourse, the twentieth-century "limit case" of the Holocaust (rather than any earlier or later human extremes of violence) serves as the prima facie "prime site for testing aesthetic and ethical theories about mediation and representability", about "the limits of art, of speech in the face of unspeakability" (Hirsch and Kacandes 2004: 3, 7). Yet the genocide of the Jewish people remains a curiously absent presence in Mitchell's text, never directly addressed, though repeatedly alluded to. The 'Letters from Zedelghem' section, for instance, implicitly anticipates the Holocaust in the cynical view of Morty Dhondt, who in 1931 already predicts the next conflagration:

> Another war is *always* coming, Robert. They are never properly extinguished. What sparks wars? The will to power, the backbone of human nature. The threat of violence, the fear of violence, or actual violence is the instrument of this dreadful will. […] The nation-state is merely human nature inflated to monstrous proportions. QED, nations are entities whose laws are written by violence. Thus it ever was, so ever shall it be. (Mitchell 2004a: 444)

The Nazi ideology of national and racial superiority, enacted through the eradication of 'lesser' and 'impure' beings, would assume just those prophesied "monstrous proportions" of extermination on an

industrial scale, as evolutionary pseudo-science, derived from
nineteenth-century discourses on race, evolved into xenophobic
eugenics. Similarly, in 'Half-lives: The First Luisa Rey Mystery',
Alberto Grimaldi, the CEO of Seaboard, the offending company that
profits from environmental destruction, muses on the nature of power:

> Yet how is it some men attain mastery over others
> while the vast majority live and die as minions, as
> livestock? The answer is a holy trinity. First: God-
> given gifts of charisma. Second: the discipline to
> nurture these gifts to maturity, for though humanity's
> topsoil is fertile with talent, only one seed in ten
> thousand will ever flower – for want of discipline.
> [...] Third: the will to power. This is the enigma at
> the core of the various destinies of men. What drives
> some to accrue power where the majority of their
> compatriots lose, mishandle, or eschew power? Is it
> addiction? Wealth? Survival? Natural selection? I
> propose these are all pretexts and results, not the root
> cause. The only answer can be 'There is no "Why."
> This is our nature.' 'Who' and 'What' run deeper
> than 'Why.' (Mitchell 2004a: 129, original italics)

Grimaldi's "*holy*" – or rather *unholy* – "*trinity*" not only echoes the
genocide of the Moriori but also recalls that of the Jewish peoples. It
evokes the Nazi leaders' perceived "*charisma*" heightened by clever
manipulations of the media and propaganda, as well as the regime's
ideological and military "*discipline*" and, above all, the Nietzschean
"*will to power*", linked to Nazi ideals of the Aryan superman and
Germanic super race. Indeed, Grimaldi's "*There is no 'Why'*" is an
outright quote from Primo Levi's memoir of Auschwitz, *If This Is a
Man* (1947),[5] underlining the extent to which the Nazi regime of terror
defies any compensatory meaning-making or explanation that can
encompass the atrocity.

---

[5] Newly arrived at the concentration camp, Levi, suffering of thirst, breaks off an
icicle from the window frame, only to have it snatched from his hand by a German
guard. When he queries why, he is met with the abrupt answer "*Hier ist kein warum*"
(Levi 2002: 35, original emphasis).

Mitchell's most extensive allusions to the Holocaust occur in 'An Orison of Sonmi–451'.[6] The normal nineteen-hour days worked by the clones, twelve floors underground far from the light of day, not only call to mind the worst of Victorian factories and mines, but also the murderous forced labour and slave workers of the Nazi death camps. The totalitarian regime of Nea So Copros strips its victims of any individuality, let alone humanity, viewing them as disposable and readily replaceable commodities. Fittingly, each year of clone 'service' is denoted by a star on the collar, recalling the Star of David, while the clones' appellations – production line numerals combined with their genotypes, rather than individuating given names – recall the practice of tattooing death camp prisoners with identification numbers. The fabricants' situation resembles both that of the Moriori, as they possess no sense of another world beyond their immediate surroundings, and that of death camp inmates. While the latter are desensitised by the concentrationary universe, the fabricants are fed so-called "Soap" (Mitchell 2004a: 186). On the one hand, "Soap" evokes the sinister Nazi emphasis on *Reinheit* or purity – both in the sense of purity of race (analogous to Nea So Copros non-genetically engineered "purebloods") and in the sense of cleanliness insisted upon in the camps, though practically impossible. On the other, the clone food calls to mind the literal reduction of Jewish victims' remains to raw materials, mistakenly rumoured to have included rendered body fat used in soap-making. The novel's evolutionary theme of natural selection transforms into another form of fascist 'selections'. The cannibal trope of the strong feeding on the weak, also introduced in Ewing's journal, is repeated in the regime's practice of feeding their slaves on matter recycled from other clones, which have been killed at the end of their 12-year 'cycles' or usefulness.[7]

---

[6] Most extant longer criticism on Mitchell's novel tends to focus specifically on this section, though without any comment on the prevalent Holocaust imagery (see Hayles 2009, Economides 2009). Mark Abley comments on the regime's euphemistic "distortion of language", citing the example of prostitutes being described as 'comforters' and linking this to the Japanese sexual abuse of Korean women as 'comfort women' during World War II, but again the Holocaust goes unmentioned (Abley 2008: 207).

[7] The implicit ageism in this process links back to 'The Ghastly Ordeal of Timothy Cavendish', as well as recalling the dystopian science fiction film *Logan's Run* (1976), in which people are sent to their deaths on reaching the age of thirty. A planned remake, scheduled for 2010, apparently intends to reduce the age limit from

Contrary to the clones' belief that those who have completed their service span "ascend" to be transported to so-called "Xultation" in Hawaii, a quasi clone heaven, the fabricants are, in fact, exterminated in a "slaughterhouse production line" (Mitchell 2004a: 343). Papa Song's Golden Ark, the transport vessel, is revealed as a killing machine, recalling Nazi transports of Jewish peoples to the deathcamps in cattle wagon trains or the mobile killing trucks, in which victims were gassed. Indeed, Mitchell's religiously inflected word-choices of 'ascension' and 'Xultation' themselves recall the Nazi euphemism '*Himmelweg*' or 'path to heaven' for the chimneys of the deathcamp crematoria. Meanwhile, the Archivist, chronicling Sonmi–451's story, evokes Holocaust deniers, when he refuses to believe that such "*industrialized evil*" could take place in his civilised country; Sonmi–451, however, claims that he underestimates humanity's capacity for evil:

> in a cycle as old as tribalism, ignorance of the Other engenders fear; fear engenders hatred; hatred engenders violence; violence engenders further violence until the only "rights," the only law, is whatever is willed by the most powerful. In corpocracy, this means the Juche.[8] What is willed by the Juche is the tidy xtermination of a fabricant underclass. (Mitchell 2004a: 344)

Again, the genetically engineered "underclass", to which Sonmi-451 belongs, eerily evokes the Nazi classification of Jewish people as *Untermenschen*, that is, sub-human or less-than-human.

What may initially seem like a digression into twentieth-century trauma actually has a direct bearing on Mitchell's neo-Victorian practice and his novel's focus, typical of historiographic metafiction, on "the ex-centric, the marginalized, the peripheral" individuals in and victims of history (Hutcheon 1996: 482). Of course, historically, the Jewish people have themselves been relegated to this

---

30 to 21, in line with William F. Nolan and George Clayton Johnson's original 1967 novel of the same name.

[8] Mitchell derives his term from the ideological concept of 'Juche' that forms the basis of the official state doctrine of the present-day totalitarian dictatorship of North Korea, asserting man's self-reliant mastery.

same position by dominant Christian and Islamic regimes and repeatedly excluded and persecuted as Others by the cultures to which they contributed. Yet the Holocaust, as the greatest ever threat to Jewish existence, paradoxically inscribed Jewish suffering as ineradicably *central* to the West's cultural memory of historical violence and suffering and, through the subsequent founding of the Jewish state of Israel, in Middle Eastern cultural awareness also. The Holocaust was and continues to be a particularly Eurocentric and North American centred phenomenon, both as regards the historical and geographical settings of the events themselves and their subsequent intense memorialisation in monuments and Holocaust museums. This accounts at least in part for the prominence it assumes in trauma studies, which developed in the academic institutions of the West and its liberalist soul-searching and historical conscience-raising in the postcolonial contexts of the 1990s – a period paradoxically characterised by a resurgence of Western nationalism and neo-imperialism and renewed struggles over spheres of global influence and economic dominance.

From one point of view, however, this has had the effect of 'whitening' the one-time colonial powers' 'Heart of Darkness', re-marginalising the suffering of indigenous and non-white peoples, whose agony can somehow never compare to or 'out-suffer' that of the European Jews. The often asserted uniqueness and incomparability of the Jewish Holocaust has resisted the recognition of other people's traumas as equal in historical significance or magnitude, a position somewhat difficult to sustain when comparing the duration of the suffering or the sheer number of victims of the Holocaust with those of other historical catastrophes, such as slavery. Yet even as it overshadows others traumas, the Holocaust has provided the basis of theoretical models – for the limits of representation, the ethical dilemmas arising from spectacles of suffering, the appropriate forms of commemoration and working-through – that are often unselfconsciously applied to vastly different cultural contexts. Mitchell's novel implicitly demands that we turn away from our obsessive reading of any and all traumas (then and now) through exclusively Eurocentric models of suffering that, even with the best of humanist and philanthropic intentions, privilege our own cultural denominators as indicators against which to measure what counts as 'real' human trauma worthy of remembrance.

Cloud Atlas implicitly contests the white and Eurocentric bias with in both postmodern Western trauma culture and trauma studies. In the novel, the Holocaust no longer serves as the central paradigm of extreme human suffering and barbarous inhumanity. It is demoted from its role as the essential lens or definitive frame through which to focalise and explicate both earlier and later man-made cataclysms (in so far as they *can* be explicated). Instead, Mitchell situates the nineteenth-century genocide of the Moriori islanders as the central paradigm through which we read the novel's subsequent traumas of modernity, postmodernity, and those yet to come at what might be called the end of history. The Holocaust itself is displaced to the textual unconscious. Rather than the explanatory prequel, the Holocaust appears only as the subtext and sequel of European/Western *inflicted* rather than *suffered* trauma. At the same time, as part of this problematisation of the racio-cultural focus of trauma discourse, Mitchell's novel re-enacts what it contests, by deliberately mediating the Moriori trauma through the racially prejudiced viewpoints of the colonisers (Goose and Ewing). Significantly, Mitchell chooses not to adopt a first-person indigene or part-indigene perspective, unlike other neo-Victorian writers, such as Robert Edric in *Elysium* (1995) or Matthew Kneale in *English Passengers* (2000).

The neo-Victorian frame of *Cloud Atlas* invites us to radically revise our Cartesian-based Western notions of trauma, centred on the fragmented, highly *individuated* ego and intent on finding a rational approach to working through trauma via an ordered/structured first-person narration, which will restore the subject's one-time (even if, from a postmodern point of view, always illusory) unity, autonomy, and self-sufficiency. Implicitly, this process is based on a heroic and teleological paradigm of overcoming. Dominick LaCapra vocally contests the legitimacy of such formulaic moves towards "closure in discourse" and "harmonizing or spiritually uplifting accounts of extreme events from which we attempt to derive reassurance or a benefit"; as an example of the latter, LaCapra cites the "unearned confidence about the ability of the human spirit to endure any adversity with dignity and nobility" (LaCapra 2001: 41-42). Though Mitchell's novel at times drifts close to such 'uplift' and seems to invite outright identification with his defiant protagonists, the repeated temporal and subjective shifts between sections only really permit the "virtual experience" of "empathic unsettlement", with readers prevented from fully assuming any particular victim's place (LaCapra 2001: 78). Too often, working-through can as readily serve the purpose of enabling a person (or society) to move on to another and *different* kind of story than that of keeping the traumatic story literally and experientially 'alive'. Such tendencies counteract the precarious and interdependent *holding/laying oneself open to Otherness* that Mitchell's novel advocates. Crucially, *Cloud Atlas* enables *both* a moving on to a different story and a re-living of the earlier trauma narrative/testimony through subsequent different stories.

4.   Victorian Predators and Pacifists

Cloud Atlas opens with the diary of Adam Ewing, who has business in New South Wales and finds himself having to wait a week in the Chatham Isles for his ship, the *Prophetess*, to be repaired. The opening reminds us of *Robinson Crusoe*, and Mitchell's further model, Herman Melville's part-autobiographical *Typee: A Peep at Polynesian Life* (1846), also contains a Crusoe moment. Melville's narrator and his friend Toby, who have jumped ship to explore the island, find a footpath while trying to avoid the natives, who they believe to be cannibals: "Robinson Crusoe could not have been more startled at the footprint in the sand than we were at this unwelcome discovery" (Melville 1968: 44). Mitchell's novel, however, offers an ironic postcolonial version of the scene: the cannibals are there, but the footprints are made by a white man. As Ewing notes, the British Empire has expanded to every corner of the earth, so there is no escaping the white imprint:

> Through rotting kelp, sea cocoa-nuts & bamboo, the tracks led me to their maker, a White man, his trowzers & Pea-jacket rolled up, sporting a kempt beard & an outsized Beaver, shovelling & sifting the cindery sand with a teaspoon so intently that he noticed me only after I had hailed him from ten yards away. Thus it was, I made the acquaintance of Dr Henry Goose, surgeon to the London nobility. His nationality was no surprise. If there be any eyrie so desolate, or isle so remote, that one may there resort

> unchallenged by an Englishman, 'tis not down on any
> map I ever saw. (Mitchell 2004a: 3)

The record of Ewing and Goose's first encounter in part also reworks the childhood memory of the narrator of *Heart of Darkness* (1902), Joseph Conrad's invective against the viciousness of colonialism, namely that of the beckoning blank spaces on a world map seen in a bookshop, which inspires Marlowe to become involved in the colonial enterprise. (In Mitchell's text, the 'infilling' of these spaces implicitly reconstructs the British dominated colonial world as a map of trauma.) 'Gone native', in the sense of metaphorically turning cannibal to prey on his fellow man, Goose may also be intended to evoke Conrad's Kurz.

Goose explains to Ewing that he is collecting the teeth spat out by actual cannibals, relics which, back in London, are fashioned into false teeth, fetching a good price. In the context of the indigenes, Goose brings up the subject of the 'survival of the fittest': "In days gone by this Arcadian strand was a cannibals' banqueting hall, yes, where the strong engorged themselves on the weak" (Mitchell 2004a: 3). The same pattern of evolutionary struggle pervades London society, which Goose has been forced to leave behind, supposedly on account of a prominent society member, Marchioness Grace of Mayfair, having slandered his name. Goose takes his revenge by arranging for her to purchase, unknowingly, a set of false teeth, made precisely out of such "cannibals' gnashers" (Mitchell 2004a: 4). The traces of the violent deaths of the cannibals' victims are thus literally appropriated and expunged by their transformation into another's personal profit and vengeance, as well as being aestheticised into a cosmetic asset. Trauma becomes a commodity, defined and disposed of by the more powerful. In spite of his initial suspicions of Goose – "I fancy he is a Bedlamite" (Mitchell 2004a: 4) – Ewing fails to see that Goose views even those of his own race in similar exploitative terms. Having duly established that his reputation has not reached Ewing's ears yet, Goose uses his power of speech to lull his 'innocent' new acquaintance into a false state of security. He convinces his new 'patient' that he is suffering from a dangerous disease, which requires the good doctor's treatment, while actually administering poison to the American.

Ewing's notations on the topics of conversation clearly date his account to the late 1850s, with journal references to the "'gold fever' in San Francisco", "Gibbon, Malthus & Godwin via Leeches and Locomotives" (Mitchell 2004a: 5), and Melville's South Pacific writing. The local preacher Mr D'Arnoq says that it is just fifty years since the *HMS Chatham* arrived in the Chatham Islands in 1800 – blotting out the islands' indigenous name, Rehoku, in a symbolic foreshadowing of the Moriori's fate. Oblivious of parallels with his own situation, Ewing comments, "I recall the crimes Mr. Melville imputes to Pacific missionaries in his recent account of the *Typee*" (Mitchell 2004a: 492). Ironically, Mitchell's text highlights the potential iterability and transferability of *forms of trauma* – though never, of course, their historical specifics – as well as the interchangeability of perpetrators' and victims' roles across and between different cultures and temporal contexts.

Ewing's naïve moral earnestness is typical of his time. He wants to believe that progress based on science and technology, within the framework of the Christian church, will have an inevitably beneficial effect on society. Yet he perceives no contradiction between, on the one hand, the Christian gospel of brotherhood and the liberal project of Western world improvement and, on the other, the persistence of virulent racism based on stereotyped ideas of colour, blood, and breeding, or indeed the persistence of slavery in the Chatham Islands as well as in his own country. For despite the abolition of slavery in Britain and its dominions by 1833, the American Civil War, of course, has yet to be fought over the issue at the time of Ewing's visit to the Chatham Islands. Indeed, becoming an "accidental witness" to the Moriori's fate, Ewing "at first assumes that he has encountered a natural and perhaps divinely ordained process in which an inferior race is being replaced by its [natural] superiors" (Gessert 2005: 425). Not surprisingly, Ewing is contaminated by the racism around him and fails to challenge Goose's assertion that "[i]t's one thing to throw a blackie a bone, but quite another to take him on for life! Friendships between races, Ewing, can never surpass the affection between a loyal gundog & its master" (Mitchell 2004a: 37). Instead, Ewing internalises Gosse's ideology, as evident in his journal description of a Moriori female: "She has a tinge of black blood & I fancy her mother is not far removed from the jungle breed" (Mitchell 2004a: 5-6). To the protagonist, the woman appears barely human.

Ewing is aware of the interplay of powerful and powerless on the Chathams, but oblivious of the fact that he himself is an equally powerless pawn in the hands of the powerful English imperialist Goose. In his naivety, the citizen of Britain's one-time colony resembles the "poor savages", who "[u]nsophisticated and confiding, [...] are easily led into every vice" by the "polluting examples" of – and "contaminating contact" with – "European civilizers" intent on their "ruin" (Melville 1969: 15). When Ewing witnesses a public flogging of one of the slaves,[9] the victim's fellows appear so indifferent that their observer concludes they are wholly insensitive, having evolved no innate 'civilised' sensibility: "Such inbred, bovine torpor! Pockmarked & pustular with *haki-haki*, these wretches watched the punishment, making no response but that bizarre, bee-like 'hum'" (Mitchell 2004a: 6). Yet the reader can see that the powerless are so in thrall to the powerful that they are petrified into non-resistance, just as Ewing himself does not resist Goose, albeit for other reasons:

> The whip master was a Goliath whose physique would daunt any frontier prize fighter. [...] The piteous prisoner, hoarfrosted with many harsh years, was bound naked to an A-frame. His body shuddered with each excoriating lash, his back was a vellum of bloody runes, but his insensitive face bespoke the serenity of a martyr already in the care of the Lord. (Mitchell 2004a: 6)

The indigene's body becomes the book upon which torture is both written and un-written, with Ewing's 'reading' of the victim in terms of Christian martyrdom metamorphosing abject suffering into an (implicitly uplifting) encounter with the sublime. Hence, Ewing is relieved of the need to formulate an ethical response in the face of the other's trauma, or an ethics of care/caring (since the other is – conveniently – "already in the care of the Lord"). He becomes a spectator rather than a witness, the place of the latter implicitly being left for the horrified twenty-first-century reader to assume. The whites

---

[9] In his second book, *Omoo* (1847), Melville recalls 160 floggings on the ship *United States*.

will not intervene: "Come, Adam, a wise man does not step betwixt the beast & his meat" (Mitchell 2004a: 7). Goose's words are, of course, hypocritical, since the reader will eventually realise that the Englishman is also a "beast" and Ewing his intended "meat".

Implicitly, Goose's statement also justifies the British bystander attitude to the Maori exterminations of the indigenous peaceable islanders, themselves suspected by D'Arnoq of being one-time Maori wrecked on the island but having forgotten their war-like ways. Mitchell introduces a deliberate comparison between the Moriori and the Aborigines of Tasmania, whose fate is often regarded as the first modern genocide, via Ewing's recording of the preacher's theories: "What is certain is that, after centuries or millennia of living in isolation, the Moriori lived as primitive a life as their woebegone cousins of Van Diemen's Land" (Mitchell 2004a: 11). Intertextually, Mitchell works his reading of Michael King's *A Land Apart* (1990) into D'Arnoq's explanations for the Moriori's near extinction. These include the arrival of the British settlers in 1800, followed by that of the sealers, who rapidly eliminated an important indigenous food source, and the influx of the whalers, who more indirectly accomplished the same, since their cats and accompanying rats ate the birds' eggs the Moriori relied on. The calamity was compounded by the diseases brought through contact with the white man and rounded off by the arrival of certain Maori tribes with the connivance of the British. As a result of the Maori Wars and the Treaty of Waitangi, the novel makes clear, many Maori tribes were dispossessed of their land and encouraged to seek the bounties of the Chatham Islands; nine hundred members of two clans of the Taranaki Te Ati Awa Maori were transported there by Captain Harewood on the brig *Rodney* in 1835 (Mitchell 2004a: 13). British collaboration did not end there. As D'Arnoq points out, "[t]he Maori proved themselves apt pupils of the English in 'the dark arts of colonization'"; hence "[t]he Moriori must kill or be killed" (Mitchell 2004a: 14). Obviously, the latter occurred, as the Moriori refused to change and the whites chose not to intervene and curb the atrocities of the cannibalistic Maori, who are compared to "sharks" in their blood-frenzy (Mitchell 2004a: 15). At one point D'Arnoq describes the Maori raping and pillaging the Moriori, then filleting them for their *hangi* (a barbecue cooked in the earth).

Arguably, Mitchell is also referencing other late twentieth-century trauma fictions and neo-Victorian novels, which likewise address the issue of racial extermination. The plight of the Aborigines of Tasmania is central to the Tasmanian writer Robert Drewe's identity-seeking *The Savage Crows* (1976) which incorporates the testimony of the Victorian George Robinson, who worked among – and some say betrayed – the aboriginal people and knew the last of their members. Much later, it is taken up again by Matthew Kneale in *English Passengers* (2001) and by Richard Flanagan in *Gould's Book of Fish* (2001).[10] D'Arnoq's metaphor for the fragility of the inter-tribal and inter-racial peace on the Chatham Islands is "glass" (Mitchell 2004a: 12), which also constitutes Peter Carey's framing metaphor in *Oscar and Lucinda* (1988), his novel about the settlement of the Australian outback that forcibly displaced the migratory indigenes from their ancestral lands, a process also discussed in Kate Mitchell's chapter in this collection in reference to a further neo-Victorian trauma text, Kate Grenville's *The Secret River* (2005). These neo-Victorian re-visitations of a shameful past are especially relevant considering that 'progress' has hardly eradicated genocide. Shortly before the composition of some of these novels, Hutus and Tutsis were enacting a comparable ethnic slaughter in the 1994 Rwandan Genocide, and more lately mass persecutions and killings of Kurds and Tamils have taken place. In 2008, Kevin Rudd, Prime Minister of Australia, apologised without reservation for the white settlers' treatment of Australia's indigenous inhabitants. After such an apology, one would expect there to be rectification and practical reparation (much of which, for instance with regards to land rights and ancestral title, has not been forthcoming), combined with a determination to learn from history. Yet just as the First World War turned out not to be the 'War to end all wars', Mitchell apparently has little faith in an end to ethnic cleansings.

More cynically, analogous to Goose's prospecting for cannibals' victims' teeth, *Cloud Atlas* itself could be said to mine a profitable vein. The problematisation of encounters between advanced and 'primitive' peoples will remain relevant as long as the latter persist against all odds. Protecting such peoples and their claims to ancestral lands and resources has become part of the fashionable ecological and humanitarian imperative, which is increasingly

---

[10] For a consideration of colonial trauma in these novels, see 'To Voice or not to Voice the Tasmanian Aborigines' (Wallhead 2003: 283-295).

informing neo-Victorian practice also (see Kohlke 2008: 8-9). Ironically, however, the pacifist Moriori are more truly 'Christian' than the whites who would convert, 'civilise', and – belatedly – 'protect' them. As D'Arnoq asks, "Who can deny Old Rekohu lay closer to More's Utopia than our States of Progress governed by war-hungry princelings in Versailles & Vienna, Washington & Westminster?" (Mitchell 2004a: 12)[11]

Depredation in Mitchell's novel proves all-pervasive, trans-historical, and systematic, with depredation at individual level replicated at higher levels of human organisation: "[t]he book's theme is predacity ... individuals prey on individuals, groups on groups, nations on nations" (Mitchell 2007, original ellipses), and races on other races. In the first section, two traumas coalesce, while a third is only narrowly averted. The first tragedy is large-scale, pitting one people against another. The Moriori are virtually exterminated by the Maori, within the framing context of another people, the British and the white race more generally, oppressing the native inhabitants of the South Pacific and providing the impetus and enabling conditions for the mass killings. The invasion and occupation tropes, combined with the internecine and inter-racial strife for dominance and the reference to "war-hungry princelings in [...] Washington & Westminster" cannot help but resonate uncomfortably with the West's present-day neo-imperialist endeavours to forcibly spread democracy in Iraq and Afghanistan within the context of a so-called 'War on Terror', itself an alternative form of state terror in the eyes of its opponents.

The second case is small-scale, the trauma personal, focused on the annihilation of an individual. Here, the Australian contingent, both white and mixed-race, prey upon one of their own, Rafael, who is 'Othered' by his exceptional beauty. He is sodomised with the connivance, if not outright participation, of the powerful who should protect him, especially the first mate Mr Boehaave, until Rafael can bear it no longer and takes his own life. The callous hands laugh at the

---

[11] Analogously, Melville scathingly remarked that "[t]he term 'Savage' is, I conceive, often misapplied, and indeed when I consider the vices, cruelties, and enormities of every kind that spring up in the tainted atmosphere of a feverish civilization, I am inclined to think that as far as the relative wickedness of the parties is concerned, four or five Marquesan Islanders sent to the United States as Missionaries might be quite as useful as an equal number of Americans despatched to the Islands in a similar capacity" (Melville 1968: 125–126).

situation and at Ewing's innocence: "I asked Finbar if he thought the boy was 'fitting in well.' Finbar's Delphic reply, 'Fitting *what* in well, Mr. Ewing?' left the galley cackling but myself quite in the dark" (Mitchell 2004a: 39). The rape of Rafael stands in symbolically for the imperialist 'rape' of the Chatham Islands and the literal raping of indigene women by the white and Maori colonists. Not coincidentally, the victim's name also evokes the Archangel Raphael, who in John Milton's *Paradise Lost* (1667) is appointed the task of warning Adam once more against the sin of tasting from the Tree of Knowledge.

Adam Ewing's fall from innocence constitutes the section's third trauma, though not leading to extinction in his case. Instead, Mitchell, like Melville, opts for a happy ending. The gullible American is slowly being poisoned by the vulture Goose, who is nowhere near as silly as his name suggests. Goose hopes to get his hands on the victim's money, to dispossess him as the Moriori have been dispossessed. Ewing, however, is saved by Autua, the last of the dying people, whom Ewing had earlier saved on board ship, when Autua escaped from the brutalising Maori, Kupaka, who had enslaved him. Ironically, Ewing writes in his diary: "Autua knocked on my coffin door yesterday to thank me for saving his neck. He said he was in my debt (true enough) until the day he saves *my* life (may it never dawn!)" (Mitchell 2004a: 37). Of course, the day does come, so that in one sense the life Ewing saves is quite literally his own. The optimistic turn suggests that, just as a predator will prey upon a weaker one, who in turn will prey upon someone weaker still, so the traumatic chain of exploitation may be broken by an altruist or someone simply doing a good turn, possibly initiating a very different kind of chain – of ethical response, obligation, and reciprocity. Perhaps Mitchell derived the name Autua, with the change of a letter, from Melville, who explains in a note to *Typee* that "[t]he word 'Artua,' although having some other significations, is in nearly all the Polynesian dialects used as the general designation of the gods" (Melville 1968: 175). The first section of *Cloud Atlas* thus describes the fall of man and his redemption; Autua, like Rafael, functions as a quasi messenger demanding and enacting reverence and an ethics of reciprocity and care towards the stranger and the Other.

5.   Nineteenth-Century Echoes

The neo-Victorian frame, its topics and related themes, continue to echo through the novel's subsequent narratives, so that, in a sense, the nineteenth century itself becomes a leitmotif of *Cloud Atlas* as a whole. In 'Letters from Zedelghem', Frobisher reflects on how his brother, as a soldier in World War I, would not have marched along the Belgian road that Frobisher cycles on himself, due to its having been "too deep in Hun territory" (Mitchell 2004a: 49). Yet if the Germans will soon march into Belgium once more, another time, halfway across the world, the Belgians too were empire-building – in the Congo: "The Crommelyncks did well from Congo investments, but not one male sibling survived the war, and Zedelghem's Boche 'lodgers' selectively gutted whatever was worth looting" (Mitchell 2004a: 62). The reference to the Congo Free State, in effect privately held by Leopold II from 1885 until 1908, again calls up the spectre of nineteenth-century colonialism at its most brutal and exploitative.

In 'Half-lives: The First Luisa Rey Mystery", the protagonist discovers that the suicide of Frobisher's one-time friend and lover, Rufus Sixsmith, was murder, the scientist having planned to expose the Seabord corporation's HYDRA-Zero project for its dangerous toxin levels. Pollution and environmental damage, on both a national and international scale, of course had their inception in the West's Industrial Revolution that reached its height in the nineteenth century, together with the imperialist exportation of global capitalism, with colonies providing opportunities for massive resource-stripping, as well as new markets and sites of production for Western commodities.[12] In the twentieth century, rapacious international corporations have become the new colonialists. Mitchell's novel thus links Seabord's ecological destruction back to the earlier predations against humans and the natural world on the Chatham Islands, while also foreshadowing the apocalyptic devastation to come.

---

[12] A related trend of "consciousness-raising" about the threat of imminent ecological disaster and "our environmental responsibilities, not least to future generations" is becoming increasingly significant in neo-Victorian discourse (Kohlke 2008: 9) As does neo-Victorian literature, the Rey episode frames past conflicts and dilemmas in terms of present-day concerns. The ecological strain recurs in the post-apocalyptic section, as Meronym describes how human greed precipitated the catastrophe: "*Now the Hole World is big, but it weren't big 'nuff for that hunger what made Old Uns rip out the skies an' boil up the seas an' poison soil with crazed atoms an' donkey 'bout with rotted seeds so new plagues was borned an' babbits was freak-birthed*" (Mitchell 2004: 273, original italics).

In 'The Ghastly Ordeal of Timothy Cavendish', the protagonist's loss of freedom through trickery echoes the common false imprisonment trope of nineteenth-century sensation fiction, as reproduced in numerous neo-Victorian novels such as Margaret Atwood's *Alias Grace* (1996) and Sarah Waters's *Fingersmith* (2002), which see individuals confined to asylums, usually on dubious grounds, with presumed 'madness' serving as a cover for the repression of unruly behaviour or for illegal financial gain. Earlier, Mitchell's titular "sixtysomething" protagonist is mugged by teenage girls, who manhandle him off the pavement and steal his watch, in a scene reminiscent of the child pickpockets of Charles Dickens's *Oliver Twist* (1838), though the girls hardly act from any dire necessity comparable to Fagin's gang. Cavendish's anger, however, results more from being reduced to the status of victim:

> It wasn't the watch or even the bruises or the shock that had scarred me so. It was that I was a man who had once faced down and bested a quartet of Arab ragamuffins in Aden, but in the girls' eyes I was … old, merely old. (Mitchell 2004a: 172, original ellipses)

The reference to Aden, Yemen, ceded to the British in 1838, initially controlled by the East India Company and later ruled as part of British India, evokes the golden age of British imperialism. Weak and aging, however, Cavendish can no longer 'conquer', but becomes the exploited. In a sense, he serves as a parodic image of post-imperial, diminished 'Old England' long past its glory days.[13] Unsurprisingly, though he denies being "a racialist", his reaction to a London Underground staff member as "[a] colored yeti in a clip-on uniform" proves otherwise (Mitchell 2004a: 170, 160), recalling Ewing's racist response to the Chatham indigenes. Cavendish's preparedness to classify people as Others, who can be readily denigrated and dehumanised, prefigures his own Othering by his brother's scheme to

---

[13] Not coincidentally perhaps, Zachry's people call the devil "Old Georgie" rather than 'Old Nick' (Mitchell 2004: 247–302), transforming the patron saint of England, commemorated on the flag of Empire, into the embodiment of evil.

have him institutionalised, presumably with the intention of dispossessing him, much as Goose attempted to do with Ewing.

For all its futuristic setting, 'An Orison of Sonmi–451' again raises spectres of the nineteenth century. When Sonmi–451 describes herself as a slave, the Archivist rejects her testimony outright: "slaves, *you say? Even infant consumers know, the very word* slave *is abolished throughout Nea So Copros*" (Mitchell 2004a: 189, original italics). Yet Sonmi–451 insists that "Corpocracy is built on slavery", and she appropriately resurrects nineteenth-century discourses of anti-slavery and worker's rights: "You knew that Abolitionism was as dangerous and insidious a dogma as Unionism" (Mitchell 2004a: 189, 195). Speaking of herself in the second person, the clone performs the address and subjectivity, which her society denies her as a culturally constructed, dehumanised entity; as Laub argues "when one cannot turn to a 'you' one cannot say 'thou' even to oneself" (Laub 1995: 66). She accuses the Archivist of being conscience-stricken at the thought of enslaving an individual, but not a clone, making an ethical demand on him to recognise her as a subject, rather than a mere sub-human figure to be statistically processed and 'archived'.

The only hopeful note in Sonmi–451's narrative is the reminder that all civilisations must wax and wane, including that of her oppressors. Evoking the popular nineteenth-century image of Britain as the 'Empire on which the sun never sets', Sonmi–451 warns: "All rising suns set, Archivist. Our corpocracy now smells of senility" (Mitchell 2004a: 325). Reminiscent of Victorian middle class conservatives, who sought to maintain control of the process of social change and the restive working underclass, the Archivist counsels against the dangers of violent revolution, instead advocating "*a program of incremental reforms, of cautious steps*" as "*the wisest way to proceed*" (Mitchell 2004a: 327, original italics). The hypocrisy of this strategy is confirmed by the revelation that the regime knowingly fomented Sonmi–451's rebellion and formulation of her *Declarations* against the Corpocracy, in order to make an example of her and ensure that no purebloods would ever trust or ally themselves with fabricants. Like the cannibals' victims' teeth collected by Goose and like her body after death, Sonmi–451's trauma testimony – of slavery, exploitation, murder, public condemnation and trial – will be commodified by the powerful for their own benefit.

Against all odds, however, Sonmi–451's testimony *does* survive, though presumably Nea So Copros does not. In 'Sloosha's Crossin' An' Ev'rythin'', the Prescient Meronym hands on Sonmi–451's orison as a gift to the narrator, the pacifist "Valleysman" and goatherd Zachry. His people share an island with the war-like Kona, whose predations threaten the peaceable community with extinction, its ethical stance on non-violence rendering it dangerously defenceless in a clear replication of the Maori-Moriori conflict. To Zachry's people, having lost all knowledge of technology, Sonmi–451's materialisation appears like magic, recalling the wonder with which the Victorians witnessed the birth of the projective virtual and recording technologies of photography, the phonograph, and early cinematography. Unsurprisingly, the Valleysmen elevate the clone to the status of a goddess: "Sonmi'd been birthed by a god o' Smart named Darwin, that's what we b'liefed" (Mitchell 2004a: 277). Ironically, Darwin, once the Victorian traditionalists' bogeyman, has replaced the Christian god, whom his evolutionary theory seemed to call into doubt. Yet the reductive misinterpretation of Darwin's evolutionary theory as 'survival of the fittest' is transmuted into an affirmative ethics of altruistic pacifism – the refusal to dominate and negate the Other. Elsewhere in this collection, Georges Letissier pertinently notes that Darwin theorised a "form of altruism" and "an instinct of sympathy, pushing the more evolved species to tend to the weaker and more vulnerable amongst themselves", an impulse which, just as much as any instinct for survival or domination, evolved out of the process of natural selection (this volume: 89). Zachry's tribe, which the Victorians would no doubt have deemed evidence of degeneration, embodies mankind's possible redemption, as reiterated by Adam Ewing's fate in the return to the neo-Victorian frame at the novel's close.

6.   The Ethics of Bearing After-Witness

As previously noted, *Cloud Atlas* ends with an *affirmation* of humanity's capacity for good, rather than the fall into evil inscribed in Adam Ewing's first name. [14] From Adam to Zachry, the pair form the

---

[14] Mitchell's play with names runs throughout the novel. Zachry is derived from the Biblical 'Zachariah', appropriately meaning 'the Lord *recalled*' or 'the Lord *remembered*', linking to the theme of memory, as well as warning and intercession, as in the case of Autua's symbolic connection with the angel Raphael. (Zacharias too is

A-Z of (post)modern subjectivity, the beginnings of which Mitchell's neo-Victorian frame specifically locates in the nineteenth century as the 'birth' of our own present-day trauma culture. For all the oft-proclaimed risks of desensitisation by trauma overexposure and overload, the omnipresence of trauma in our world – and the world of Mitchell's novel – constitutes a proleptic as much as retrospective call to conscience, a demand for continuous witness-bearing as a *defining*, rather than incidental, element of what it means to be human. Asked what distinguishes *Cloud Atlas* from his other novels, Mitchell answered: "It has more of a conscience. I think this is because I am now a dad. I need the world to last another century and a half, not just see me to happy old age" (Mitchell 2007). Ewing ends his journal with a comparable good resolution to create "a life worth living" and to dedicate himself to shaping "a world I *want* [my son] Jackson to inherit, not one I *fear* Jackson shall inherit"; he plans to "pledge myself to the Abolitionist cause, because I owe my life to a self-freed slave & because I must begin somewhere" (Mitchell 2004a: 508, original emphasis).

   Cloud Atlas too constitutes such a 'beginning somewhere', remembering trauma in order to imagine possible forms of resistance against the violent ideologies that engendered and continue to engender suffering. Ewing's father-in-law doubts the practicality of such idealistic sentiments, calling his son-in-law a "[n]aïve, dreaming Adam", but Ewing argues that patterns of history and the "outcomes" of society's processes of evolution are not pre-determined but produced by the chosen beliefs that inform our actions:

---

visited by an angel, announcing the miraculous pregnancy of his aged wife Elizabeth, who gives birth to John the Baptist, prophet of mankind's redemption through Christ's self-sacrifice.) Adam Ewing's surname suggests a lamb going to slaughter, while Louisa Rey's mother lives in Ewingsville, Buenas Yerbas, Los Angeles. Besides recalling Ewing and the angel trope, her residence also evokes the Chilean town involved in the bloody struggle for Chilean independence, scene of an early 1813 battle between royalist and patriot forces, in which some third of the latter perished, underlining the trans-national recurrence of historical slaughter. Zachry's brother, also named Adam, is taken into slavery by the Kona, possibly a corrupted version of 'Cain', alluding to brother-murder, implicitly Zachry's people's view of any kind of killing of humans.

> If we *believe* humanity is a ladder of tribes, a colosseum of confrontation, exploitation & bestiality, such a humanity is surely brought into being […].
>
> If we *believe* that humanity may transcend tooth & claw,[15] if we *believe* divers races & creeds can share this world […] peaceably […], if we *believe* leaders must be just, violence muzzled, power accountable & the riches of the Earth & its Oceans shared equitably, such a world will come to pass. (Mitchell 2004a: 507–508)

The closing neo-Victorian frame, the reflective epilogue on all the traumas witnessed in the course of the novel, thus constitutes an implicit call to political agency and personal responsibility towards the self and Other on the reader's part, combined with a commitment to build more equitable futures. This involves the recognition that Western nations can no longer disregard those traumas that they subjected or helped subject other peoples to in the past, as opposed to those experienced themselves. Colonial cataclysms cannot be dismissed as merely minor antecedents to the 'real', that is grand Eurocentric traumas of the twentieth century and beyond; the determining frame has been irrevocably shifted by the implicit contract between the reader and Mitchell's first and last, and thence primary I/eye-witness.

Nonetheless, Mitchell's readers might be inclined to agree with Ewing's father-in-law's scepticism, doubting humanity's sudden turn to altruism, pacifism, and ecological sustainability, instead believing such a utopian future to be indefinitely deferred and obscured by ever-threatening dark clouds on the horizon. Yet if we refuse to even imagine the possibility, such a future will never have the chance of coming into existence. As Hephzibah Anderson asks of Mitchell's novel, "if by believing the wrong story we can bring about the worst, who knows what we can achieve by believing a good story?" (Anderson 2004)

---

[15] Ewing, in the South Seas in 1850, seems to know his Tennyson, although *In Memoriam A.H.H.*, which includes the phrase "Nature, red in tooth and claw" in Canto 56, was only published that same year; however, the phrase itself was already in earlier use.

Remediated over and over again in *Cloud Atlas*, the story of trauma is simultaneously the story of the survival of story-telling itself against all odds in an information (rather than communication) age of sound-bites and ever shortening attention spans. Yet it seems worth remembering that Mitchell also highlights the precarious vulnerability and perishability of textual forms of narrative, re-emphasising the crucial role of active personal memory and creative reconstruction in sustaining witness-bearing and remembrance. Although Louisa Rey eventually gets hold of Sixsmith's damning report on Seabord, she only manages to save part of the document. The dismemberment and loss of much of the text forms part of *Could Atlas*'s meditation on the loss of historical knowledge – especially knowledge of the always disrupted/interrupted experience of trauma – which, almost inevitably, must be reconstructed from evidentiary fragments and traces, producing elisions that can only be filled in by imagination rather than documented facts. Hence the past we come to know is always in part a simulated substitute *of* and *for* the real, as Sixsmith's associate scientist, Isaac Sachs, reflects in his notebook. Employing Baudrillardean imagery, Sachs uses the example of the sinking of the Titanic to muse on how a "*simulacrum of smoke, mirrors + shadows*", that is, "*the* virtual *past*", comes to stand in for the actual event:

> *The disaster as it* actually *occurred descends into obscurity as its eyewitnesses die off, documents perish + the wreck of the ship dissolves in its Atlantic grave. Yet a* virtual *sinking of the* Titanic, *created from reworked memories, papers, hearsay, fiction – in short, belief – grows ever "truer."*[16] *The actual past is brittle, ever-dimming + ever more problematic to access + reconstruct: in contrast, the virtual past is malleable, ever-brightening + ever more difficult to circumvent/expose as fraudulent.*
>
> *The present presses the virtual past into its own service, to lend credence to its mythologies + legitimacy to the imposition of will. Power seeks + is*

---

[16] During the course of writing this article, on 31 May, 2009, the death of the last living survivor of the Titanic was reported in the media.

> *the right to "landscape" the virtual past.* (Mitchell
> 2004a: 392, original italics)

Narrations of the (traumatic) past become exercises in agency and
contestations of power in their own right, interventions into the
meaning-making of historical 'truths'.

Arguably, Sachs's deliberations also provide a metafictional
comment on the technique of writing historical and, more specifically,
neo-Victorian fiction, which recreates a simulacra that often purports
to be more 'real' than what it represents, due to its incorporation of
occluded traumas and historical injustices, as well as unpalatable and
tabooed subjects, not openly addressed in the earlier period or
deliberately excised from the record. The simulacra or re-imagined
virtual past thus assumes greater 'authenticity' – and, paradoxically,
greater historical 'objectivity' – with writers engaging in "what might
be called a *new(meta)realism*" in spite of the evidently fabricated
nature of the product (Kohlke 2004: 156).[17] Ironically, Sachs's
possible implication in the blowing up of the Seabord executive jet
renders his musings doubly virtual; they literally disintegrate in the
explosion, alongside the CEO and himself:

> The jet's metals, plastics, circuitry, its passengers,
> their bones, clothes, notebooks, and brains all lose
> definition in flames exceeding 1200 degrees C. The
> uncreated and the dead exist solely in our actual and
> virtual pasts. (Mitchell 2004a: 393)

Hence, both Rey's and Mitchell's readers are invited to reconstruct the
traumatic past from *spectral* or *no-longer existing* traces of history's
forgotten victims, "[t]he uncreated and the dead".[18]

---

[17] The novel's later post-apocalyptic section at times seems to contradict the ideology
of the simulacra, as when, in response to a question from Zachry, Meronym confirms
that usually *"the true true is diff'rent to the seemin' true"*, constituting the reason
"why true true is presher'n'rarer 'n diamonds" (Mitchell 2004: 274, original italics).
In the case of trauma, however, there *is* no "true true", only the simulacra of trauma
reproduced in its traces and after-effects.
[18] Indeed, even this ambiguous trace in Rey's novel is likely lost, when her
manuscript, sent to the publisher Cavendish, apparently remains unpublished, due to
the letter's false imprisonment in a 'secure' old people's home.

Mitchell refuses 'uncreation', staging alternative forms of bearing after-witness, even when texts are lost. Seemingly, Zachry's people possess neither reading nor writing (Mullan 2005a), only the remnants of a "school'ry" room and a few books (Mitchell 2004a: 247–248), which are destroyed in an attack by the Kona. Hence, unlike the literate narrator of Russell Hoban's *Riddley Walker* (1980), arguably a model for this section,[19] neither Zachry nor his son can record their "yarnin" (Mitchell 2004a: 309), a word with overtones of 'embroidering the truth', but also perhaps of the human 'yearning' to be heard and remembered. The fact that Zachry's community has no means of storing primary witnesses' literal voices in audio or written archive to testify to the fact of historical suffering does not render their suffering any less real. Instead, a communal, performative, and what might be called '*virtual witnessing*' determines its 'truth' and preserves it within collective memory, since ephemeral oral testimony depends for its survival on the participatory repetition and retelling by those who come after – reproducing not only the testimony but also *the act of testifying*. In one sense, testimony here functions like a Victorian spiritualist séance: the dead are enabled to speak their suffering through their narrators as quasi mediums, thus preventing their own and their traumas' unbecoming.[20] As in Ewing's movement from passive, reluctant and wilfully blind to active witness as described in the novel's neo-Victorian frame, *Cloud Atlas* as a whole draws its readers into an analogous ethical and communal act of bearing after-witness to the otherwise 'uncreated' of history, in the process opening ourselves up to Otherness as part of being human.

---

[19] Mullan also draws a parallel between Meronym and Zachry's relationship and that of the literate Robinson Crusoe and the illiterate Friday, linking the post-apocalyptic and opening colonial sections of the text. The other resonant intertextuality he perceives is with Mark Twain's *Huckleberry Finn* (1884), with its similarly illiterate and colloquial, albeit teenage narrator (Mullan 2005a: 23).

[20] Sonmi-451's appearance in Meronym's orison partakes of a similar spiritualist virtuality, even more so as Zachry's people cannot comprehend or interpret her enigmatic speech, so that their secondary witnessing is all the more imaginative. For a discussion of the prominence of the spectral trope in neo-Victorian literature, see Arias and Pulham 2010.

Acknowledgements

The authors gratefully acknowledge the kind permission of Random House, Inc., and Curtis Brown Group Ltd, London, on behalf of David Mitchell, to quote from *Cloud Atlas* (copyright © David Mitchell 2004).

Bibliography

Abley, Mark. 2008. *The Prodigal Tongue: Dispatches from the Future of English.* New York: Houghton Mifflin. [GOOGLE Books, consulted 31.01.2010]

Anderson, Hephzibah. 2004. 'Time and Emotion Study', Review of *Cloud Atlas. The Observer,* 29 February. Online at: http://www.guardian.co.uk/books/2004/feb/29/fiction.davidmitchell (consulted 01.07.2009).

Arias, Rosario, and Patricia Pulham (eds.). 2010. *Haunting and Spectrality in Neo-Victorian Fiction: Possessing the Past.* Houndmills, Basingstoke and New York: Palgrave Macmillan.

Bradford, Richard. 2007. *The Novel Now: Contemporary British Fiction.* Oxford: Blackwell. [GOOGLE Books, consulted 31.01.2010]

Butler, Judith. 2009. *Frames of War: When Is Life Grievable?* London & New York: Verso.

Byatt, A.S. 1990. *Possession: A Romance.* London: Chatto & Windus.

——. 2004. 'Overlapping Lives' [Review of *Cloud Atlas*], *The Guardian*, Review section, 6 March: 9.

Donne, John. 2006. 'Meditation 17' from *Devotions upon Emergent Occasions* [1624], in Greenblatt, Stephen, and M.H. Abrams (eds.), *The Norton Anthology of English Literature*, 8th Edn., Vol. 1. New York & London: W.W. Norton & Company: 1305-1306.

Drewe, Robert. 1976. *The Savage Crows.* Harmondsworth: Penguin.

Economides, Louise. 2009. 'Recycled Creatures and Rogue Genomes: Biotechnology in Mary Shelley's *Frankenstein* and David Mitchell's *Cloud Atlas*', *Literature Compass* 6(3) (May): 615-631.

Edric, Robert. 1995. *Elysium.* London: Duckworth.

Erll, Astrid, and Ann Rigney (eds.), in collaboration with Laura Basu and Paulus Bijl. 2009. 'Introduction: Cultural Memory and its Dynamics', in *Mediation, Remediation, and the Dynamics of Cultural Memory.* Berlin & New York: Walter de Gruyter, 2009: 1-11.

Flanagan, Richard. 2001. *Gould's Book of Fish.* Sydney & London: Macmillan.

Fowles, John. 1969. *The French Lieutenant's Woman.* London: Jonathan Cape.

Gessert, George. 2005. 'Cloud Atlas [Review]', *Leonardo* 38(5): 425-426.

Gillespie, Don. 2000. 'Frederick Delius's "Zwei Braune Augen"', in Newsom, Jon, and Alfred Mann (eds.), *The Rosaleen Moldenhauer Memorial. Music History from Primary Sources: A Guide to the Moldenhauer Archives* [electronic version], Washington D.C.: Library of Congress, n. p. Online at: http://rs6.loc.gov/ammem/collections/moldenhauer/2428126.pdf (consulted 14.10.2009).

Hayles, N. Katherine. 2009. 'RFID: Human Agency and Meaning in Information-Intensive Environments', *Theory, Culture & Society* 26(2-3) (Mar.-May): 47-72.

Hirsch, Marianne, and Irene Kacandes. 2004. 'Introduction', in *Teaching the Representation of the Holocaust*. New York: The Modern Language Association of America: 1-33.

Hutcheon, Linda. 2005. '"The Pastime of Past Time": Fiction, History, Historiographic Metafiction', in Hoffman, Michael J., and Patrick D. Murphy (eds.), *Essentials of the Theory of Fiction*. London: Leicester University Press: 473-495.

Jaszczolt, K[atarzyna] M. 2009. *Representing Time: An Essay on Temporality as Modality*. Oxford: Oxford University Press. [GOOGLE Books, consulted 31/01/2010]

Kneale, Matthew. 2001. *English Passengers* [2000]. Harmondsworth: Penguin.

King, Michael. 1990. *A Land Apart: The Chatham Island of New Zealand*. London: Random Century.

Kohlke, Marie-Luise. 2004. 'Into History through the Back Door: The "Past Historic" in *Nights at the Circus* and *Affinity*', *Women: A Cultural Review* 15(2) (July): 153-166.

——. 2008. 'Introduction: Speculations in and on the Neo-Victorian Encounter,' *Neo-Victorian Studies* 1(1) (Autumn): 1-18.

LaCapra, Dominick. 2001. *Writing History, Writing Trauma*. Baltimore & London: The Johns Hopkins University Press.

Laub, Dori. 1992. 'Bearing Witness or the Vicissitudes of Listening', in Shoshana Felman and Dori Laub, *Testimony: Crises of Witnessing in Literature, Psychoanalysis and History*. New York & London: Routledge: 57-75.

——. 1995. 'Truth and Testimony: The Process and the Struggle', in Cathy Caruth (ed.), *Trauma; Explorations in Memory*. Baltimore and London: The Johns Hopkins University Press: 61-75.

Levi, Primo. 2002. *If This Is a Man* and *The Truce* (tr. Stuart Woolf) [1987]. London: Abacus.

Melville, Herman. 1968. *Typee. A Peep at Polynesian Life,* (*The Writings of Herman Melville*, vol. 1) [1846]. Evanston & Chicago: Northwestern University Press & The Newberry Library.

Mitchell, David. 2004a. *Cloud Atlas.* London: Sceptre.

——. 2004b. 'Q&A: Book World Talks With David Mitchell', *The Washington Post,* August 22, BW03. Online at: http://www.washingtonpost.com/wp-dyn/articles/A17231-2004Aug19.html (consulted 30.09.2007).

——. 2007. Interview on Bookclub, BBC Radio 4, June. Online at: http://www.bbc.co.uk/radio4/arts/bookclub/ram/bookclub_20070603.ram (consulted 30.09.2007).

Mullan, John. 2005a. 'Words o' knowin: John Mullan analyses Cloud Atlas by David Mitchell'. Week one: oral narrative. *The Guardian*, review section: Culture/Books, 19 March. Online at: www.guardian.co.uk/books/2005/mar/19/fiction.davidmitchell (consulted 01.04.2009).

——. 2005b. '*Cloud Atlas*: Savagery upon a forlorn strand: John Mullan analyses Cloud Atlas by David Mitchell'. Week three: antique prose. *The Guardian*, review section: Culture/Books, 2 April. Online at: www.guardian.co.uk/books/2005/apr/02/fiction.davidmitchell (consulted 01.04.2009).

252 Celia Wallhead and Marie-Luise Kohlke

——. 2006. *How Novels Work*. Oxford: Oxford University Press. [GOOGLE Books, consulted 31/01/2010]

Turrentine, Jeff. 2004. 'Fantastic Voyage' [Review]. *The Washington Post*, 22 August. Online at: http://www.washingtonpost.com/ac2/wp-dyn/A17232-2004Aug19?language=printer (consulted 01.04.2009).

Wallhead, Celia. 2003. 'To Voice or not to Voice the Tasmanian Aborigines: Novels by Matthew Kneale and Richard Flanagan', *Revista Alicantina de Estudios Ingleses* 16: 283-295.

Walsh, John. 2004. 'David Mitchell: Fantastic voyage', *Independent*, 5 Oct. Online at: http://www.independent.co.uk/arts-entertainment/books/features/david-mitchell-fantastic-voyage-550888.html (consulted 12.12.2009).

Australia's 'Other' History Wars:
Trauma and the Work of Cultural Memory
in Kate Grenville's *The Secret River*

Kate Mitchell

Abstract:

Kate Grenville's *The Secret River* (2005) enacts a narrative return to the violent trauma of Aboriginal dispossession and destruction upon which Australia is founded, situating its reader complexly, as both witness to and complicit in the events it retells. Her use of fiction to represent this trauma made Grenville the focus of heated public debate about the role of fiction in representing the past, a debate that repeatedly cast her project as historically dubious. However, rather than approaching the novel as a corrupted form of history's reconstruction of past events, it seems more useful to situate this text as an act of memory in the present, which shapes both past and future. Even as it represents the past, Grenville's novel addresses a present both deeply divided and in danger of forgetting its history. It uses the affective power of fiction to reinscribe and reactivate Aboriginal Australian history in the contemporary historical imaginary.

Keywords: cultural memory, Kate Grenville, historical fiction, historiographic metafiction, history, history wars, memory, national trauma, *The Secret River*.

*****

In an interview for Radio National, Australia, Kate Grenville was asked where she would position her novel *The Secret River* (2005) in relation to Australia's 'history wars', a series of heated and protracted debates among public intellectuals over the details, effects, and meanings of the country's colonial history and, more specifically, its frontier conflicts between the British 'settlers' and the indigenous population. Grenville suggested that she saw her novel "up on a ladder, looking down on the history wars, outside the fray" (Grenville 2005b). These and other comments made by Grenville incensed historians, because they seemed to elevate fiction as a mode of historical understanding; the ensuing debates about the relative merits of fiction and history for representing historical truth most authentically proved so prolonged, public, and energetic that this issue was dubbed the "new front of [Australia's] history wars" (Sullivan, 2006). *The Secret River* is not alone in its revisiting of Australia's traumatic history. Indeed, in recent decades, both novelists and historians have returned obsessively to the story of the European 'settlement' of Australia, revisiting nineteenth-century scenes of frontier violence with an insistence that suggests its location (or construction) as *the* originary trauma in the Australian imaginary. The extensive interviews and talks given by Grenville, combined with the publication of her writing memoir, *Searching for the Secret River* (2006), in which she describes her method of research and writing in detail, have made the novel, as much as Grenville herself, a persistent focus of these debates.

Literary critics and historians alike have been much more concerned with discussing Grenville's claims about her novel's use of history than with analysing the novel itself. Rather than interrogate its success or failure as a historical representation, this chapter focuses on the ways in which Grenville's neo-Victorian narrative shapes Australia's present relationship to – and in terms of – a traumatic past. While *The Secret River* returns to frontier conflict in the nineteenth century as a violent trauma that indelibly shaped Australia, I want to propose that it *does* so primarily in order to confront a contemporary trauma that stems from the stalling of the nation's reconciliation process. The novel dramatises not only frontier conflict, but also the attempt to forget this past and white Australians' complicity in its ongoing, structural effects. Positioning the novel as a counterforce to this forgetting, as a 'technology of memory', or a 'memory text', enables me to shift focus away from Grenville's much debated historiographical 'failures' to discuss her use of the past to address a still deeply divided present. *The Secret River* is less concerned with revealing a secret history than with performing memory; it writes Australia's traumatic history into contemporary cultural memory, eschewing objectivity in favour of constructing an affective approach to a shameful traumatic past and its ongoing, discriminatory effects.

1.   History, Fiction, Historical Fiction

Given her subject matter, Grenville could hardly escape being asked where she would position her novel in relation to the history wars. In contrast to the "polarised" positions of historians, she suggested, the novelist can approach the past in "a different way, which is the way of empathising [with] and [exercising] imaginative understanding of those difficult events" (Grenville 2005b). Perhaps understandably, Inga Clendinnen (2006), along with other historians such as Mark McKenna (2005) and John Hirst (2006), have objected to an image that functionally places Grenville and her novel in a superior position to squabbling historians. However, the outraged and defensive tone of Clendinnen's critique in particular, and the personal tone of its attacks on Grenville, shifted the focus of the history wars to literature.[1] Clendinnen claims that historians and novelists "used to jog along their adjacent paths reasonably companionably", before Australian novelists forgot their place and attempted to 'colonise' history, "doing their best to bump historians off the track. It seems that they have decided it is for them to write the history of this country, and to admonish and nurture its soul" (Clendinnen 2006: 16). Clendinnen and Grenville thus mark out two very different roles for fiction in historical knowledge; where Grenville asserts the power of imaginative empathy, Clendinnen asserts that it is for the historian, and the historian alone, to write the past.

The terms of this debate are hardly new. Historical fiction has always occupied an uneasy place on the contested border of history and fiction. Indeed, usually described as a hybrid (Ferris 1991: 33; Wesseling 1991: 46; Wallace 2005: 3), the genre enacts the problematic nature of this border in its very form. For Diana Wallace, the genre is not only an admixture, but also "a kind of oxymoron, joining 'history' (what is 'true'/'fact') with 'fiction' (what is 'untrue'/'invented', but may aim at a different kind of truth)" (Wallace, 2005: x). Her use of bracketing and quotation marks here produces history and fiction, and their respective relationships to truth,

---

[1] In *After the Celebration: Australian Fiction 1989-2007*, Ken Gelder and Paul Salzman offer a similar argument, positioning Grenville's novels among a number of Australian historical novels, beginning with David Malouf's *Remembering Babylon* (1993), whose themes and concerns collided with debates about history and the historian's role in representing Australia's past (Gelder and Salzmann 2009: 64-94).

as problematic, emphasising the way in which history and fiction often seek to define themselves in opposition to each other.

The difference between history and fiction appears "commonsensical": history claims to be true, while fiction does not (Mink 1978: 129). And yet, since at least the nineteenth century, when history began to define and separate itself from other forms of rhetoric, including literature, forming its own professional discipline, the boundary between them has been fiercely contested, drawn and redrawn. Hayden White observes that for historians in the eighteenth century,

> the crucial opposition was between "truth" and "error," rather than between "fact" and "fancy," with it being understood that many kinds of truth, even history, could only be presented to the reader by means of fictional techniques of representation. (White 1978: 123)

It was accepted that historians were rhetoricians, that historical narratives were 'fictive', that is, 'constructed', and employed the same literary devices that comprised literature. Historians saw their task as discovering the meaning of past events, and this meaning might best surface through a combination of what actually happened – what is generally considered 'fact' – and what *could have* happened – details lost to the historical record but which do not obviously contradict it. History's meaning was deeply embedded in rhetoric. Its objective was to offer the past for reflection and judgement, but not, primarily, to create an empirically proven representation of the past via the use of critical methodologies. Its purpose was firmly philosophical, functioning to enlighten and instruct the present. As White argues, whereas historians in the eighteenth and early nineteenth centuries saw imagination as integral to their representations of the past, the nineteenth-century professionalisation of history aligned the discipline to science, and fiction came to be seen as "a hindrance to the understanding of reality rather than as a way of apprehending it" (White, 1978: 123); imagination was excised from history (White 1937: 66). It is to this traditional notion of history that Clendinnen appeals when she excoriates Grenville, arguing that "[h]istorians are the permanent spoilsports of imaginative games played with the past"

(Clendinnen 2006: 20). Clendinnen describes herself "flinch[ing] from what looked like opportunistic transpositions and elisions" in Grenville's use of the archives, and even more from Grenville's appeal to "empathetic" understanding; for Clendinnen, the novelist's empathy is "untutored" and blocks historical knowledge (Clendinnen 2006: 16, 22). It fails to recognise the alterity of the past, the absolute difference between self and historical other.

Clendinnen's critique of the novelist's use of imaginative empathy perhaps goes to the heart of the debates about the role of fiction in the production of historical knowledge. Within debates about the novel since its very origins, history has often been credited with the role of the stable context against which fiction's portrayal of the past can be judged as true, faithful, and authentic, or, in contrast, as false, bogus, and inauthentic. However, because of its specific attributes, fiction is sometimes credited with being best suited to telling a particular kind of truth about the past. This has been the case especially in the critical reception of historical fiction where the subject matter has included the personal, the private, and the individual (Wesseling 1991: 48; Ferris 1991: 197) or – as pertinent to Grenville's novel – where the historical record is insufficient. Fiction provides a more diverting, affective account of the past than 'dry' objective history. While the border between history and fiction has required repeated reiteration and qualification, and their respective merits as methods of historical recollection have been debated since the nineteenth century, underlying these disputes was a confidence that the past could in fact be known.

However, challenges to the historian's role as custodian of the past had been mounting throughout the twentieth century in debates about the very possibility of knowing the past, sometimes initiated by historians themselves. In the late nineteenth and early twentieth century, for example, the perspectivism of Benedetto Croce and R. G. Collingwood challenged the neutrality of the historian, suggesting that he or she was inescapably influenced by his or her own circumstances, perceptions and prejudices. In the latter half of the twentieth century, the position of history as the authoritative element in the dyad, as the 'real' that fiction must truthfully reflect, was more thoroughly challenged by postmodernism's problematisation of conventional historiography. By emphasising their shared origins in language and narrative, and by critiquing history's claim to the transparent representation of historical reality, postmodernism has once again brought history and fiction into close proximity as verbal constructions of reality. The postmodern challenge to traditional history turns upon the issue of reference in history and fiction, and particularly upon the distinction between the events of the past and the meaning attributed to them in both history and fiction (White 1999: 70) Or, as Linda Hutcheon observes, one effect of postmodernism's problematisation of history is "a new self-consciousness about the distinction between the brute events of the past and the historical *facts* we construct out of them. Facts are events to which we have given meaning" (Hutcheon 1989: 54). Here, history is no longer a stable entity, the assurance of an extra-textual reality or context against which literature can be understood. Nor is it a stable context against which historical fiction can be judged as true or false. As the sheer number of historical novels published in the last three decades attests, novelists have indeed been exploring their role in producing historical knowledge afresh. For Mark McKenna, the history wars exacerbated this challenge and may indeed have been more influential in eroding history's authority. In his own critique of Grenville's novel, he suggests that one unfortunate effect "of seeing historians at war" was the erosion of public belief in historians' ability to tell the truth, casting them instead "in this partisan image of federal politics, cultural warriors peddling rival versions of the truth" (McKenna 2005).

Grenville clearly positions her novel as an imaginative supplement to the historical record, an exercise in sketching in the blanks of both personal and collective histories. She loosely based her novel on the life of her ancestor, Solomon Wiseman. The family story Grenville inherited from her mother incorporates a number of enduring Australian archetypes, including the exiled convict, whose sentence appears harsh compared to his crime, and the courageous pioneer turned self-made man:[2]

> My mother had told me stories about the first of our
> family to come to Australia – my great-great-great
> grandfather was a lighterman on the Thames, pinched

---

[2] In her review of the novel, Eleanor Collins pertinently identifies "three powerful Australian myths" playing against each other in the novel: the worthy convict, the toiling pioneer, and, disrupting each of the others, the "fraught but insistent story of first contact" (Collins 2005: 40).

a load of timber and was transported there for the term of his natural life. Within six years of arriving here, he'd become a free man and 'taken up land' on the banks of the Hawkesbury River. He went on to make buckets of money, built a fine stone house, and called himself "the King of the River". (Grenville 2006b: 149)

This is an easily recognisable plot, and one that supports Australia's orthodox national narrative of the 'settlement' of Australia and heroicised versions of early pioneer life in the colony. Grenville retains this archetypal structure for her fictional William Thornhill who, like Wiseman, is transported from grinding poverty as a Thames lighterman and finds himself in an utterly foreign land whose landscape he cannot 'read'.[3] Nonetheless, he manages to re-create himself as a lighterman on the Hawkesbury River, servicing the outlying areas of the Sydney Cove settlement. While his wife, Sal, dreams of returning to England, Thornhill becomes increasingly attuned to the possibilities available to him in the new colony. The novel closes upon Thornhill as a wealthy landowner and businessman, an important figure in the colony. However, into this familiar structure, Grenville inserts another story which, albeit briefly, radically disrupts and subverts its course. This is the suppressed story of Aboriginal dispossession and destruction, upon which the 'settlement' of Australia and the narrative of self-made success stories like Thornhill's are predicated.

---

[3] Grenville's novel begins by telling the traumatic story of the transported convict which, elsewhere in this volume, Dianne F. Sadoff argues is suppressed by Victorian fiction and largely elided in trauma studies but taken up in a number of neo-Victorian narratives. Grenville's entanglement of the convict's trauma with the trauma s/he then, in some cases, inflicted upon Aboriginal Australians suggests a complex relationship between the two, most notable, perhaps when Thornhill, freshly evicted from his home country, attempts to similarly expel the Aboriginal man he encounters on his first night in Australia: "*Damn your eyes be* off, he shouted. *Go to the Devil!* After so long as a felon, hunched under the threat of the lash, he felt himself expanding back into his full size" (Grenville 2005: 5). This suggestion, here and elsewhere in the novel, that Thornhill's traumatic experience as a transported convict informs his behaviour toward the Aboriginal population is troubled by the implication that this exonerates his role in the destruction of Australian Aborigines or at least explains it. However, as I suggest in what follows, the novel does not, ultimately, exonerate Thornhill.

In *Searching for the Secret River,* Grenville describes looking at a watercolour of her ancestor's villa on the Hawkesbury and noticing that there were no Aboriginal people in it. Grenville makes this moment central to defining her project: "I had to move the eyeline along, re-frame the scene. I had to put them back into the picture" (Grenville 2006a: 97). This is a very neat image for Australia's own ongoing need to write indigenous Australians into every aspect of the country's history, filling in missing details.[4] In response to this need, Grenville had intended to write a factual work, believing that "this was a tale that drew its power from the fact that it was real" and that "this subject matter had to be handled in the authoritative voice of non-fiction" (Grenville 2006a 146, 165). Yet as she explains, she was thwarted by the paucity of the historical record. Months spent in the archives did not yield any information about her ancestor's 'encounters' with the indigenous population: "In the hundreds of pages of documents by and about Wiseman, there was absolute silence on the matter of the original inhabitants" (Grenville 2006a: 95).

2.   "The Great Australian Silence"
Grenville links this encounter with silence to the silences within the narrative about Wiseman that she had inherited from her family. She then links both archival and familial silence to "The Great Australian Silence" that the anthropologist W.H. Stanner identified in 1968, namely the omission of Aboriginal people from the narratives of the nation that kept concealed a "secret river of blood in Australian history" (qtd. Macintyre and Clark 2003: 43). Grenville has acknowledged the influence of Stanner, both in her title and in remarks made in interviews (see Grenville 2005b).

Her novel dramatises the way in which Australian Aboriginal history has been passed down as a series of silences and omissions. Thornhill's relationship with his wife Sal functions as an image of white Australia's negotiation of memory and forgetting in relation to its violent past: "the thing about having things unspoken between two

---

[4] Stuart Macintyre and Anna Clark argue that Aboriginal people were a "prominent feature" of the history written during the colonial period and that it was only with federation and the establishment of the nation-state at the end of the nineteenth century that they were written out of Australia's history (Macintyre and Clark 2003: 43). Macintyre and Clark's *The History Wars* (2003) provides a useful overview of the debates surrounding Australia's conflicted racial history, then and now.

people, he was beginning to see, was that when you had set your foot along that path it was easier to go on than to go back" (Grenville 2005a: 155). Sal is Thornhill's childhood sweetheart, to whose father Thornhill was apprenticed at age fourteen as a lighterman. When Thornhill is caught stealing lumber in order to stave off his family's starvation, Sal works to have his sentence commuted from death to transportation. And when the judge declares she may accompany him, she goes with him to New South Wales, though other women "declined accepting that indulgence" (Grenville 2005a: 71). She gives birth to their second son during the long voyage. Throughout the novel she stoically endures the hardships of Sydney Town and, later, the more pronounced hardships and dangers on the Hawkesbury River. However, her mind remains firmly fixed on returning to England.

When he discovers the novel's first massacre, the poison in the flour, Thornhill resolutely refuses to remember it: "He did not look back to see the place where the birds circled over Darkey Creek" (Grenville 2005a: 278). Having made a brief, ineffectual attempt to assist a young boy still dying, Thornhill returns to his boat and sails away up the Hawkesbury as usual, reflecting that he would never tell what he had seen to the other white men on the river, some of whom, he acknowledges, were most likely responsible for the deaths. It is in relation to Sal that he most clearly recognises his desire to keep silent: "He knew he would never share with Sal the picture of this boy. That was another thing he was going to lock away in the closed room in his memory, where he could pretend it did not exist" (Grenville 2005a: 278). He categorically refuses to assume the ethical role of witness, which the present-day reader is implicitly called upon to assume in the protagonist's stead. In a sense, this (re)produces (in reverse) a double consciousness that mimics Thornhill's own: of knowing but deliberately repressing knowledge of the trauma of the racial 'Other'. The reader, in contrast, participates in Thornhill's repression but assumes belated ownership of the shameful knowledge of white inflicted genocide.

Indeed as Collins observes "[w]hen terrible violence is described, the role of the reader, or witness, becomes disturbingly ambiguous" (Collins 2006: 44). While Smasher refers to the *Gazette* as evidence for the truth of the novel's final, culminating massacre, readers are able to compare the journalistic account of the horrific events at Blackwood's with Thornhill's own experience of it. They adopt the role of the witness:

> The *Gazette* had run a piece about the day up at
> Blackwood's. […] Sal told Thornhill what it said. The
> natives had been guilty of depredations and outrages.
> There had been an affray and the settlers had
> dispersed them. (Grenville 2005a: 322-323)

Thornhill reflects that this both tells what happened and does not: "It was not exactly false. Nor was it quite the way Thornhill remembered" (Grenville 2005a: 323). Here the novel dramatises the way official accounts also record a silence at exactly the moment when they appear to speak: "The *Gazette* did not mention the woman Thornhill could not forget, baring her teeth at him in the gloom, the blood so bright on her skin. Or the boy, arching like a fish against the goox in Sagitty's damper" (Grenville 2005a: 322).

At the end of the novel, the landscape itself will stand silent witness to the atrocity committed by the white settlers against the original owners of the land:

> He would glance over at where river-oaks circled a
> patch of bare yellow earth beside the lagoon, marking
> where the bonfire had burned into the night.
> Something had happened to the dirt in that spot so
> that not as much as a blade of grass had grown there
> ever since. Nothing was written on the ground. Nor
> was it written on any page. But the blankness itself
> might tell the story to anyone who had eyes to see.
> (Grenville 2005a: 325)

This gestures forward, into the future, inviting Grenville's reader to also 'read' the blankness, bearing witness to the events it both speaks and conceals.

Yet the reader's role as witness is complicated by the narrative perspective, which is almost entirely Thornhill's. This strategy fosters the readers' partial identification with Thornhill. Grenville's depiction of him thus accounts for some of the specific cultural reasons that might make him active in both seizing land and violently driving away the traditional owners. The effect is to invite the readers' understanding of these events as the acts of ordinary people, as acts they might have committed themselves. Grenville suggests that

> The pressures that might push a[n ordinary] person towards one response or another was the heart of the story I wanted to tell. Fear, compassion, government policy, peer pressure, miscommunication, self-interest – all these went into the mix. (Grenville 2006b: 151)

Through their part-identification, readers are implicated in Thornhill's complicity with the worst abuses of the colonising power, including his inaction and silence in the face of 'settler' atrocities, as well as his actual participation in the final massacre. When he fails to assist the aboriginal woman enslaved, chained, and sexually abused by Smasher, Thornhill connects words to guilt, telling himself that describing what he had seen to Sal would "make him the same as Smasher, as if Smasher's mind had got into his when he saw the woman in the hut and felt that instant of temptation. He had done nothing to help her. Now the evil was part of him" (Grenville 2005a: 253). The short paragraph in which Thornhill imagines that telling Sal would force him to confront his own complicity is separated from the text surrounding it. It stands alone as a stark depiction of Thornhill's guilt due to inaction. It is a disjunction, a moment of pause, between the moment with the woman at Smasher's place itself and a description of Thornhill's trading success along the Hawkesbury. The narrative then skips forward two weeks, describing how in the interim Thornhill had avoided Smasher, had "tried to put the picture of the woman and the red jewels of blood on her skin away in some part of his memory where he did not have to see it" (Grenville 2005a: 255). The effect is an assertion of the ordinary – a description of the river at night, of the coming harvest – as a counterpoint to the memory not only of the woman herself, but of Thornhill's sense of his own shame. The endorsement of the banal everyday is an attempt to cover over the memory of both. Moreover, this sequence, which shifts from Thornhill's guilt to his trading success, establishes a clear link between the two, making the point that the success of the colony was built upon silences such as Thornhill's.

By writing the novel from Thornhill's point of view, Grenville places her reader in the position of perpetrator, inviting white Australians to identify with and hence become shamefully complicit in the dispossession and destruction of Aboriginal Australians and in the subsequent silencing of this story, the national cult of forgetting.[5] When Thornhill returns from the massacre, his exchange with Sal dramatises the national resistance to knowledge of frontier violence. Here, the unacknowledged event becomes "part of the new thing that had taken up residence with them [...] a space of silence between husband and wife. It made a little shadow, the thing not spoken of" (Grenville 2005a: 324). Although she had no prior knowledge of or role to play in the massacre itself, Sal's silence, and her resistance to any acknowledgment of what Thornhill has done in order to ensure her safety, render her complicit: "I hope you ain't done nothing, she said at last. On account of me pushing at you. [...] Here Will, give your hands a wash, she said. Her voice was ordinary enough, but she would not look into his face" (Grenville 2005a: 323).

In addition to mirroring white Australians' complicity in frontier conflict, their relationship also depicts the incorporation of this violence into the lives of ordinary families. As Fiona Probyn-Rapsey points out, the relationship between Thornhill and Sal "draws an image of how complicity with historical injustice lies at the heart of the domestic, the familial and the everyday" (Probyn-Rapsey 2007: 72). The reader is asked to recognise his or her complicity but is prevented from identifying fully with Thornhill, because of his lack of empathy and his refusal to act as an ethical witness, a role that the twenty-first century reader expects of him/herself. The effect is that the novel thus combines affect with critical awareness, so that rather than collapse the difference between (contemporary white Australian) self and (nineteenth-century British colonial) other, the novel inhabits the space between the two. If Grenville courts the reader's empathy, it

---

[5] This is strikingly similar to Toni Morrison's observation of a "national amnesia" in America, regarding slavery. In an interview with Bonnie Angelo, she says of *Beloved* (1987): "I thought this has got to be the least read of all the books I'd written because it is about something that the characters don't want to remember, I don't want to remember, black people don't want to remember, white people don't want to remember. I mean, it's national amnesia" (Morrison 1989). Jill Matus writes about *Beloved* in terms of "Morrison's concern to bear witness to the forgotten or erased past of African Americans" (Matus 1998: 103).

is empathy of the "unsettling" kind identified by Dominick LaCapra, asking us to "recognize the unsettling possibility of such behavior and experience in him- or herself" (LaCapra 2001: 41). By representing not only the traumatic events themselves but also the process by which they are repeatedly forgotten, the novel thus functions as what James Young calls "received history", that is, "the combined study of both what happened *and how it is passed down to us*" (Young 1997: 41, emphasis added). It records a version of frontier conflict as well as imagining the way in which that conflict was written out of Australia's cultural memory.

3.   Renewed Forgetting: Contemporary Australia

In fact, it seems fair to say that by 2005, some thirty-five years after Stanner coined the phrase, this silence, this secret regarding Australia's secret river of blood, was no longer kept. In histories, anthropologies, courts of law, newspapers, magazines and elsewhere, Australia's violent origins had become a matter for public discussion. Moreover, these origins had become linked to more recent and ongoing crimes against Aboriginal Australians. In the 1980s the publication of the *The Stolen Generation* (1980), a report detailing the practice of forcibly removing Aboriginal children from their parents and raising them in white families (a practice that occurred until the 1970s), together with preparations for the bicentennial celebrations of the European 'settlement' of Australia in 1988, functioned not only to disclose the 'secret', but to link it to the ongoing discrimination against Aboriginal Australians. The shameful realities of frontier violence and the Stolen Generations were forced upon the national consciousness. By 2005, when *The Secret River* was published, the challenge for contemporary Australia in relation to its Aboriginal history had shifted from the need to disclose an untold story to the need to remember and commemorate it effectively. The ongoing challenge has become how to acknowledge this haunting presence and incorporate it into our national identity, and, just as importantly, how to formulate an ethical response to its continuing overt as well as insidious effects. The issue at stake is not historical knowledge but rather a politics of remembering.

Stanner himself links the great Australian silence not to history but to memory, describing the omission of indigenous Australians in the country's history as "a cult of forgetfulness practised on a national scale" (qtd. Macintyre and Clark 2003: 44). Similarly, Kay Schaffer and Sidonie Smith describe the counter-celebration of the 1988 bicentennial, organised by Aboriginal activists, as a "counter-*remembrance* of settlement-as-invasion [which] contested what other Australians celebrated in their patriotic tribute to the unified fictions that sustained their belonging as citizens of Australia" (Schaffer and Smith 2004: 86, emphasis added). They deliberately contrast these two separate events: "the formal, orderly, structured, and commemorative official celebration of Australia as a white settler nation" with "the informal, unscripted, and disruptive protest of an alter-nation" (Schaffer and Smith 2004: 86). The former, official celebrations, provided for with a budget of $200 million Australian dollars, focused on celebrating the anniversary of European settlement in Australia and two hundred years of nation building. The latter took the form of a protest march, beginning on the morning of 26 January (Australia Day) with a mourning corroboree, that is, a traditional Aboriginal gathering involving singing and dancing. White Australians were invited to join the last half of the march, as well as the culminating rally. This protest mourned the invasion of Australia and the subsequent destruction of its indigenous population. It also celebrated the survival of Aboriginal history and culture. Once more, the issue was not one of historical knowledge as such, but of how to commemorate specific events *appropriately* and *from whose perspective*, namely that of the colonisers or the colonised.

Australian public debate in the last two decades since the bicentennial celebrations has been characterised by deep division over what form a response should take: the acknowledgement of shame and/or guilt, an apology, or various forms of reparation and compensation, including the possibility of restoring native land titles to the dispossessed. The historian Robert Manne and the philosopher Raymond Gaita assert that the usurpation of indigenous rights requires "an appropriate acknowledgement": "guilt", they argue, would constitute an incongruous reaction, since "no individual could bear responsibility for the crimes of others"; instead they advocate "shame" as the proper, implicitly ethical response, "because Australians were implicated in their country's past and shared a legacy of historical shame" (qtd. MacIntyre and Clark 2003: 145). In effect, they are asking white Australians to empathise with the victims of colonial violence, while identifying themselves with the perpetrators, enacting a double consciousness that mimics Schaffer and Smith's previously cited split between "nation" and "alter-nation". That consciousness also partakes of a doubled temporality,[6] which interweaves postcolonial present and colonial past in the ethical act of shameful recognition/acceptance of the traumatic *continuity* rather than dissociation from and rupture with the past *as* past, as implied by the prefix 'post-'.

Acknowledgements of guilt and/or shame produce a current of societal anxiety, relating to the possible effects on 'traditional' Australian history and national identity, as well as the material effects of reparation. Especially divisive was the report generated by the Human Rights and Equal Opportunity Commission's inquiry into the removal of Aboriginal children entitled *Bringing Them Home* (1997). The authors found that the systematic and forcible removal of Aboriginal children from their families in a strategy to 'breed out' the Aboriginal people amounted to genocide, as it is defined by the United Nations Convention on the Prevention and Punishment of the Crime of Genocide (1948). The Leader of the Opposition, Kim Beazley, wept as he tabled the report in Parliament, and afterward various groups, including state parliaments, churches, trade unions and schools, offered formal apologies to the Aboriginal community. Prime Minister John Howard issued a personal apology but would not allow an apology on behalf of the Commonwealth Parliament. One effect of the Australian Government's refusal to make an apology, and the attempt to focus on a more 'celebratory' narrative of Australian history, was a significant stalling of the reconciliation process.[7] Conservative voices sought to re-centre more triumphant narratives, accounts that effectively sought to write indigenous Australians back out of the nation's history, heralding a new form of willed forgetting. As Meaghan Morris argues:

> Since the election of John Howard's government, disavowal and sheer ignorance about Australian

---

[6] This dual temporality mirrors that commonly found in neo-Victorian fiction, much of which plays with the modern-day consciousness of the reader invited to identify with nineteenth-century characters and their – from the reader's point of view – often regressive and racist worldviews.

[7] The incumbent Prime Minister Kevin Rudd apologised to the Aboriginal people of Australia on behalf of the government on 13 February 2008.

> culture and history ha[ve] acquired a respectability
> unthinkable three years ago; there is renewed fervour
> for 'roping off' the past and pulling 'rowdy
> Aborigines' into line; there is, once again, white
> debate about assimilating Aborigines, and a growing
> disinclination to hear stories about mothers and the
> children parted or thrown together by policy in the
> past. We are being asked to forget about the past few
> years of remembering. (Morris 2006: 120)

It is this desire to rope off the past, to relegate it *to the past*, that Grenville resists. When Grenville situates her reader as complicit in settler-colonial relations, she points not only to the past but to the continuing existence of the frontier in Australia today.[8] Probyn-Rapsey argues that as Australia continues to take faltering steps toward reconciliation, the focus of debates should be on recognising complicity rather than on guilt and shame. A focus on guilt, she suggests, sometimes indicates an assertion of non-Aboriginal legitimacy predicated on "expiation, a washing away, a clean slate, a critical distance between then and now". This fantasy of a clean slate fails to account for "*present* injustice, continuing injustice" (Probyn Rapsey 2007: 67). In contrast, she uses the term complicity to describe "a structural relationship that cannot be expiated fully because it exists in multiple, networked forms." This, she argues, is the network in which Australians are still located: "the settler colonial state" (Probyn Rapsey 2007: 68). Recognition of the complicity this entails is an ethical confrontation with responsibility. Since our complicity in colonisation is structural, not simply individual, there can be no resolution. Complicity implies that our stories are entangled and enmeshed, and in this sense complicity belies critical distance; there is no outside.'

4.   The Historical Novel as an Act of Memory

It is in the context, of a renewed effort to foreclose reconciliation and to forget the violence of invasion and the trauma of the systematic eradication of Aborigines that we need to understand Grenville's

---

[8] For an interesting discussion of Grenville's participation in this frontier, see Gall 2003.

novel, namely as an effort to perform memory in order to actively counteract renewed forgetting. Meaghan Morris relates the *ethical* struggle over the responsibilities of communal memory to the transformation of repressed knowledge about the much more recent and ongoing trauma of the Stolen Generations into active public remembrance. She observes that

> we cannot not know now that the extermination of Aboriginality – culture, identity, kinship – was the aim of assimilation. [...] [W]e cannot not know now that the policy's application in Australia to Aboriginal people had a systematically racist, deliberately ethnocidal purpose; and that the 'taking' of Aboriginal children was practiced on a horrifically large scale. [...] Only now, however, is some notion of the scale of the trauma and disruption that this policy created beginning to filter through to the *white* Australians in whose idealised name it was practised. Or, rather than speaking of an 'idea' filtering through, I should say that only recently have we begun to develop a collective capacity to comprehend, to empathise, to imagine that trauma and disruption. This is also a matter of a politics of remembering. (Morris 2006: 106-107)

Morris distinguishes between knowing what has happened ("we did") and *understanding* that knowledge. Understanding, here is more than cognitive knowledge. The politics of remembering traumatic and shameful events, whose effects are still ongoing, demands an *affective*, as well as a rational, response. This requires that we develop an historical consciousness that might be informed by history, but which carves a productive role for a range of media, including novels, in producing memory and keeping it active. Novels are not simply "corrupted history" (Rigney, 2007: 154). Their capacity to produce an affective, empathetic response can perform important functions. Dominick LaCapra's notion of "empathetic unsettlement" accounts for the ways in which objectivity is insufficient for understanding the past, particularly the traumatic past. He argues that empathetic unsettlement "poses a barrier to closure in discourse", by resisting objectification and "attending to, even trying in limited ways, to recapture the possibly split-off, affective dimension of the experience of others" (LaCapra 2001: 42), which might give added weight and 'authenticity' to different and contesting versions of the past. Indeed, LaCapra defines "affectivity as a crucial aspect of understanding in the historian or other observer or analyst" (LaCapra 2001: 40), an indispensable facilitator of, rather than obstruction to, historical knowledge of traumatic events. This applies equally where the "analyst" is a literary practitioner:

> narratives in fiction may also involve truth claims [...] by providing insight into phenomena such as slavery or the Holocaust, by offering a reading of a process or period, or by giving at least a plausible "feel" for experience and emotion which may be difficult to arrive at through restricted documentary methods. (LaCapra 2001: 13)

In this way, LaCapra formulates a strategic and positive role for fiction in the process of historical recollection.

Grenville emphasises the experiential aspects of her project. She describes her realisation that "I didn't have to approach the past in a forensic frame of mind. I could experience the past – as if it were happening here and now" (Grenville 2006a: 47). In a sense, this shift is one from historical analysis to imaginative empathy. And it is this imagined experience that she seeks to recreate for the reader. By attempting to provide "an experience for a reader in which they could understand what that moment of our past was really like" (Grenville 2006b: 152-153), through creating an effect of immediacy of events and places, she rewrites Sydney Harbour and the Hawkesbury River as sites of traumatic memory. At the same time, she also offers her own novel as a site of memory and 'revisitation', creating associational images that provoke remembrance of the Aboriginal people of Australia who lived there two centuries ago.

It is in a similar sense that Toni Morrison calls her novel *Beloved* a "memorial" to lives lost to slavery. Her magical realist novel self-consciously eschews historical representation in favour of memory, or in the novel's lexicon, 'rememory', as a means to honour the past, to understand its reverberations in the present, and to find a way to move forward:

> There is no place here where I can go, or where you can go, and think about, or not think about, or summon the presences of, or recollect the absences of – slaves … Something that reminds us of the ones who made the journey, and those who did not make it. There is no suitable memorial – or plaque, or wreath, or wall, or park, or skyscraper lobby. There's no three hundred foot tower … And because such a place does not exist that I know of, the book had to. (Morrison, qtd. Rody 1995: 98, original ellipses)

By suggesting that her novel serves as a substitute for non-existent national memorials to slavery, Morrison implicitly positions historical fictions among other modes of historical recollection outside of academic history. Positioning historical fictions as memory texts, alongside museums, monuments, and public commemorations, foregrounds the ways that historical novels seek to establish connections between past and present identities, to interpret the past in and for the specific needs of the present, and to witness to traumatic events long silenced and suppressed.

Aleida Assmann argues that "[h]istory turns into memory when it is transformed into forms of shared knowledge and collective identification and participation" (Assmann 2006: 216). This formulation suggests engagement with the past, participation on the part of both the author and the reader. Historical novels, I suggest, form part of the ways in which cultural memory is organised, mediated and constructed and are a significant means through which we engage with the past today. They are examples of what Marita Sturken calls "technologies of memory, not vessels of memory in which memory passively resides so much as objects through which memories are shared, produced, and given meaning' (Sturken 1997: 9). Rather than romanticise memory as an unmediated form of historical recollection, Marianne Hirsch and Valerie Smith, too, develop a notion of memory that incorporates its own contestation via the technologies of memory transmission, which invariably mediate and shape its content: "Acts of memory […] are thus acts of performance, representation, and interpretation" (Hirsch and Smith 2002: 5).

In *Searching for the Secret River* Grenville locates her decision to write about frontier conflict during the Reconciliation Walk across the Sydney Harbour Bridge in May of 2000. In this passage, while thoroughly enjoying the day and the symbolism of what she is doing, Grenville is confronted by the sight of a group of aboriginal men and women who are not walking, but watching. She catches the eye of one woman, feels a "pulse of connectedness" and then feels her "warm inner glow" extinguished by the realisation that the truth behind this "connectedness" might be that Grenville's ancestor and the woman's own had met, two hundred years earlier. Grenville's never quite articulated fear is that this imagined meeting could well have had violent consequences:

> This woman's ancestors had been in Australia for a long time. Sixty thousand years was the current figure. Her ancestors might have been living on the shores of Sydney Harbour when the First Fleet sailed in.
> The blade I was feeling was the knowledge that my ancestor had been here too. Solomon Wiseman hadn't arrived on that first convoy, but he'd arrived within twenty years of it. His ship would have anchored in this bay. He'd have come ashore right underneath where an Aboriginal woman and I were exchanging smiles. (Grenville 2006a: 12)

For the historian there are, perhaps, several problems with this passage as an act of historical recollection: Grenville's assumption that she knows the meaning of the aboriginal woman's gaze; the assumption of aboriginal homogeneity implicit in her linking of this woman's ancestry to the spot on which they were walking, when the woman could have come from any one of Australia's indigene nations; the compression of time, so that it matters little whether Wiseman arrived on the First Fleet or twenty years later, after two decades of contact between the British colonials and the indigenous population.

Yet the real interest of Grenville's articulation of this moment – and act – of memory lies in the impact it has on her sense of herself in the present, her affective engagement with a knowledge she has previously only recognised cognitively and in a distanced way: "In that instant of putting my own ancestor together with this woman's ancestor, everything swivelled: the country, the place, my sense of myself in it" (Grenville 2006a: 13). It seems to me that, as detailed in this encounter with a woman on a bridge, Grenville's primary purpose is not to know what actually happened in the past and to accurately represent it, but to rewrite her family story in a way that repositions Grenville herself, taking account of her "swivelled" sense of identity. It is in these terms that film director Neil Armfield described the novel at the NSW Premier's Awards presentation. He suggests that having read the book, "[y]ou can never see Sydney without feeling the memory that laps at the harbour's shores. Your sense of what connects the great mass of Australia to the past and to the world is profoundly, unforgettably enriched" (qtd. Sullivan 2006). Although Armfield does not communicate much of a sense of what that memory might consist of, he captures the sense of Grenville's novel as a memory text, both offering itself as a technology of memory and redirecting our understanding of Australia's landscape as unmarked sites of mourning. Grenville's novel performs the work of creating a shared space, in which Grenville and her readers can meaningfully consider, remember, and acknowledge a present relationship to a difficult past, not once but repeatedly and continuously. It writes the past into our present cultural memory, always tempted by forgetfulness, as *not*-past and *never*-past. Thus, Grenville's novel remains inextricably bound to the very fabric of the present. Gabrielle Spiegel writes that

> [t]o the extent that memory 'reincarnates,' 'resurrects,' 're-cycles,' and makes the past 'reappear' and live again in the present, it cannot perform historically since it refuses to keep the past in the past, to draw the line as it were, that is constitutive of the modern enterprise of historiography. (Spiegel 2002: 162)

This 'keeping alive' Australian Indigenes' historical trauma, rather than 'drawing a line' under it, constitutes an apt description of Grenville's project. Grenville's novel, I am proposing, constitutes such an active 'technology' rather than a passive 'vessel' of Australian memories of trauma. By situating the novel in relation to memory, as outlined above, we can understand better the way in which this novel addresses itself not just to the past, but to the past, present, *and* future. Indeed, for Mieke Bal, this temporal positioning is what constitutes the act of memory *per se*, as "an activity occurring in the present, in which the past is continuously modified and redescribed even as it continues to shape the future" (Bal 1999: vii). Grenville's dedication, "to the Aboriginal people of Australia, past, present and future" (Grenville 2005a), is structured in precisely this way.

Grenville's most startling gesture toward the future comes at the end of the novel in a material representation of white Australia's continuing complicity. Collins points out that the ending of this novel belies its conventional form, since in "the classic novel", all "the uncertainties, errors and miscommunications that create the plot" are eventually "cleared up at its resolution, so that all the important characters, the narrator and the reader are in alignment" (Collins 2006: 40). In contrast, *The Secret River* ends with "an image of profound separation and difference" (Collins 2006: 40), as Jack, the only Aboriginal man left since the massacre, refuses Sal's guilty helpless charity. Probyn-Rapsey links these ineffectual gestures to structural, and therefore unfinished, complicity that looks ahead to Australia's continuing inequities: "The novel suggests that white complicity manifests in a kind of caring-and-sharing humanitarianism that is also a pointed reminder of ongoing complicity" (Probyn-Rapsey 2007: 77). She notes that Sal's "penance" or expiation significantly "does not include a recognition of Jack's claims to the land" (Probyn-Rapsey 2007: 77). In fact, urged by Sal, Thornhill attempts to "set aside a patch of ground for him, fenced it nicely", capturing in miniature "the reserve that the Governor had set aside at Sackville" where "[s]uch others as there might have been had retreated [...] and lived on what the Governor was pleased to provide" (Grenville 2005a: 327). The narrator's comments about the reserve itself provide the clearest signpost to contemporary Australia. On the one hand, this perhaps signals the resistance to defeat that Grenville sought to depict, since despite

> [l]earned gentlemen [who] announced that the blackness would be bred out in a few generations [...] [t]he place was full of children running and calling

everywhere, and even if some of them had lighter skins than others, there was no mistaking that they were part of the tribe. In spite of everything, it seemed that the blacks were not going to disappear. (Grenville 2005a: 327)

Yet while this does sound a happier note in some respects, and gesture toward the celebration of the survival of Aboriginal culture, to the twenty-first century reader it also looks ahead to the increasingly persistent – and increasingly violent – attempts to eradicate "the blackness" throughout the twentieth century.

Importantly for our understanding of novels as memory objects, John Frow developed the logic of textuality as a figure of memory. The logic of textuality defies the ownership of the past by one body or another, whether historian or novelist, and suggests, moreover, that there is no one final truth: "rather than having a meaning and a truth determined once and for all by its status as event, its meaning and its truth are constituted retroactively and repeatedly" (Frow 1997: 154). Understood this way, memory connects with the problematisation of history and fiction, and its emphasis on the "multiplicity and dispersion of truth(s)" (Hutcheon 1988: 108). In this sense, Grenville's novel refuses to see Australia's past and its abuses as definitively determined, instead participating in the on-going constitution of its multiple 'truths' *in* and *for* the present. Frow's "non-existence of the past" thus produces the past's continuous (re)production in such a way as to resist conservative voices' implicit appeals to a new kind of forgetfulness. Memory is not *retrieved*, for "the time of textuality is not the linear, before-and-after, cause-and-effect time embedded in the logic of the archive but the time of a continuous analeptic and proleptic shaping" (Frow 1997: 154). Memory is a creative act, a construction of the past "under conditions and constraints determined by the present" (Frow 1997: 119).

Thus, throughout *The Secret River*, we witness this continual process of shaping and reshaping memory to fit the needs of the present. Although this is clearly not a work of metafiction, the novel dramatises the way that stories are constructed and circulated, told and retold, changing with each telling. For instance, when Saggity, the white man who poisoned the flour at 'Darkey Creek', is found speared on his property, and his house and crops burnt, his dog's throat cut,

Smasher '[takes] the story over. Anyone would have thought he had been there himself" (Grenville 2005a: 290). With each re-telling Smasher adds details that suggest that this was an act of blood-lust, rather than revenge, on the part of the Aborigines. His goal is to whip the settlers into a frenzy of fear and hatred, so that they will commit a massacre. Similarly, at the end of the novel, when he finds himself a wealthy landowner, Thornhill himself rewrites his own history to excise his low status in London and make his crime into the more exciting tale of espionage. He uses a story that another ex-convict has relinquished in favour of a new one:

> In this place, where everyone had started fresh-born on the day of their arrival, stories were like those shells down on the beach. A crab might live in one for a while, until he grew too big for it, and then he would scuttle around to another, the next size up. (Grenville 2005a: 321)

Elsewhere, more malicious stories also circulate as truth, endorsed by the colony's newspaper, and propagated by the 'settlers' with various motivations, ranging from a desire to share their fear to the desire to incite war against the Aborigines. Smasher, particularly, delights in telling and retelling stories of "outrage and depredations": "[h]e had not seen that for himself [...] but swore with a hand on his red flannel heart that it was in the *Gazette*, so it must be true" (Grenville 2005a: 157). Here private rumour and gossip intermingle with the public account given in the colony's newspaper, circulating tales of atrocity and strife.

In the novel's economy, various forms of storytelling compete in the attempt to gain ownership: of land, of people, of stories. As Collins observes, throughout the novel "[t]he always unequal conflict over whose 'illiterate' markings will be recognised, who will possess the land, raises a wider question about marking and the bringing into being of meaning" (Collins 2006: 42). A few weeks into their time on the Hawkesbury, Thornhill attempts to climb the ridge that overlooks 'his' property: "It would be another way to possess the place, to look down and think *everything I see, I own*". However, he finds that he is unable to climb the ridge after all, that "a man set against that was no more than an ant toiling up and down until he was swallowed".

Defeated by the sheer scale of the place, he settles instead for "the platform of flat rock that ran around the base of the ridge like a step" and begins to survey the view of 'his' land (Grenville 2005a: 153). However, it is here, as he seeks "another way to possess the place", that he is confronted with prior occupation; he sees some rock art, depicting a fish, which he recognises as a bream, so that "he had to recognise a human hand at work" (Grenville 2005a: 154). Gradually he realises that he is looking at a picture of his own arrival, that his own boat, the *Hope*, is also pictured there. "He hears himself exclaim, a high blurt of indignation. It was the same tone he had heard from a gentleman in Fish Street Hill when William Warner had lifted the watch out of his pocket" (Grenville 2005a: 154). He feels as though something had been stolen from him and attempts to hide this evidence of prior occupation by scuffing it with his foot, but the picture is etched too deep into the stone to permit erasure.

The Secret River essentially ends with the orthodox narrative of Australia's 'settlement' by Europeans, figured in Thornhill himself, who has constructed a new identity for himself with various props, including a villa, a portrait, a telescope, silk slippers for his wife, and a new story to explain his own origins. In fact, we are uncomfortably aware that Thornhill suffers no apparent ill-effects from his role in the bloody massacre. His land has swelled to three hundred acres, he has built his big stone house on the hill, and he and Willie run a successful river trade with the *Hope* and the *Sarah*: "William Thornhill was something of a king" (Grenville 2005a: 314). Yet, rather than feel triumphant, he is depicted as forever ill at ease. His house, which he and Sal name Cobham Hall for the large country estate in England in which her mother was once in service, has walls half a yard thick, while the staircase could be "hinged up after the manner of a drawbridge" and the area surrounding the house has been stripped of every bush: "there was nothing that a man might hide behind" (Grenville 2005a: 315). Even more troubling is the image of Thornhill himself, vigilantly watching with his telescope: "Every day he sat here, watching, waiting, while dusk gathered in the valley, scanning the trees and the silent rocks. Until it was fully dark he could not make himself put the glass down and turn away" (Grenville 2005a: 334). Despite his thick walls and vigilant pose, it seems that Thornhill is hoping, as much as dreading, to see an Aboriginal man or woman on the cliff top. Each time "he had to recognise that it was no human, just

ano her tree, the size and posture of a man", he registers "a new
emptiness" (Grenville 2005a: 333). It is more difficult to discern the
meaning of his sense of being "*Too late, too late*", as he relinquishes
the telescope in the dark with a "hollow feeling" (Grenville 2005a:
334, original emphasis). His sense that he has worked for, and should
feel triumph in, all that he now owns is undercut by a sense of
belatedness and loss. As Lyn McCredden describes, at the end of the
novel, Thornhill's psychic state is "complexly rendered", seemingly
"much more volatile and driven than mere nostalgia or regret"
(McCredden 2007: 23).

Revealingly, the image of Thornhill's house, built resolutely
over the rock with the fish carved upon it, shielding his children and
his children's children from the secret, is actually a reworking from a
more organic image. Grenville admits that she

> didn't want the book to end with defeat for the
> Aboriginal people. I had in mind a short scene at the
> end in which something about the land itself would
> demonstrate that the Aboriginal people hadn't been
> destroyed. (Grenville 2006: 163)

The planned image was of "a tree by the river that had grown over a
rock [... so that] you could see the tree would eventually cover the
entire rock like an octopus flowing over its prey" (Grenville 2006:
163). Of her decision not to use this image, Grenville comments only
that it was too "heavy-handed [...] a parallel that was much too neat"
(Grenville 2006: 163), but the shift from tree to stone building in the
novel as published also has the advantage of being less organic, since
the building is, after all, a contrivance. The image of a house erected
over the stone with its carving of a fish conveys a sense of purpose, of
deliberately concealment; it gestures toward the 'cult of forgetting'
upon which white Australia was founded.

This image, together with the volatility of Thornhill's psyche,
leaves us with a sense of white Australian identity as "riven",
"unsettled", even "haunted" (McCredden 2007: 13). We are far from
what Adam Gall has described as the reader's positioning as the "good
settler", when he argues that "[p]art of being the good settler in this
liberal imaginary is the rehearsal of an unflinching examination, and
re-evaluation of aspects of the national past" (Gall 2008: 101). Ken

Gelder and Paul Salzman argue similarly that the novel constructs "a complacent, post-settler reading position" (Gelder and Salzman 2009: 88), a position strikingly similar to the dissociation described by Marie-Luise Kohlke elsewhere in this collection, whereby white readers of neo-Victorian Mutiny fiction "dis-identify with *who they are no longer*" (this volume: 377). Kohlke links this reading position to an acknowledgment of guilt and shame which attempts to expiate and transcend the past. This is certainly a risk in Grenville's novel. However, as I have suggested, the complex network of complicity enacted by the novel, and the shifts between empathetic engagement and critical distance from Thornhill himself, are designed specifically to trouble contemporary complacency. Nonetheless, this project is polemical and not without its problems and pitfalls. One such is that in addressing itself to white readers, and representing events only through a white consciousness, it potentially sidelines, even silences, Aboriginal voices once again.

Indeed, in terms of its politics, Grenville's novel has not yet settled into its own particular place in Australian cultural memory. Variously received as a white-washing, black armband, or balanced account of our settler-colonial past, it has, nonetheless, performed cultural memory in important ways by writing back into our cultural imagination a story we were in danger of forgetting afresh. It directly confronts a cultural climate in which it has become possible for white Australians to resist owning our traumatic past by claiming their temporal distance from the events. Grenville's novel uses a range of strategies to efface this distance, not to suggest we are the 'same' now as the British colonials were then, but to sketch in the lines of complicity that inveterately tie us to our colonial forebears. Moreover, the novel stands as a site of memory and of mourning, re-mapping the places that bear mute, unmarked witness to traumatic events. James Bradley, in a response to Clendinnen's castigation of Grenville, conceptualises the relationship between historians and novelists as "symbiotic", suggesting that in recent decades historians and novelists have, in slightly different ways, been engaged in complementary tasks:

> one a mapping of the real, of what was, the other a mapping of the subconscious, of the way we understand the real, and of the way we understand

ourselves. [... K]nowing the facts is one thing [...]
incorporating them into our sense of ourselves is
altogether another. (Bradley 2006: 74)

Taking the much-debated facts of frontier conflict and incorporating
them into our cultural memory, Grenville retells a painful past that
demands to be told and retold against the possibility of forgetting.

Bibliography

Assman, Aleida. 2006. 'Memory, Individual and Collective', in Goodin, Robert E.,
    and Charles Tilly (eds.), *The Oxford Handbook of Contextual Political
    Analysis*. Oxford: Oxford University Press: 210-224.
Bal, Meike. 1999. 'Introduction', in Bal, Mieke, Jonathan Crew and Leo Spitzer
    (eds.), *Acts of Memory: cultural recall in the present.* Hanover: University
    Press of New England: vii-xvii.
Bradley, James. 2006. Correspondence, in Davidson, Robyn, 'No Fixed Address:
    Nomads and the Fate of the Planet', *Quarterly Essay* 24: 72-76.
Collins, Eleanor. 2006. 'Poison in the Flour', *Meanjin* 65(1): 38-47.
Clendinnen, Inga. 2006. 'The History Question: Who Owns the Past?', *Quarterly
    Essay* 23: 1-72.
Ferris, Ina. 1991. *The Achievement of Literary Authority: Gender, History and the
    Waverley Novels.* Ithaca: Cornell University Press.
Frow, John. 1997. *Time and Commodity Culture: Essays in Cultural Theory and
    Postmodernity.* Oxford: Clarendon Press.
Gall, Adam. 2008. 'Taking/Taking Up: Recognition and the Frontier in Grenville's
    The Secret River', *JASAL*, Special Issue: *The Colonial Present*: 94-104.
Gelder, Ken, and Paul Salzman. 2009. *After the Celebration: Australian Fiction 1989-
    2007.* Melbourne: Melbourne University Press.
Grenville, Kate. 2005a. *The Secret River*. Melbourne: Text.
——   2005b. 'Interview with Ramona Koval', Books and Writing, Radio
    National, 17 July. Online at:
http://www.abc.net.au/rn/arts/bwriting/stories/s1414510.htm (consulted 31.10.2009)
——   2006a. *Searching for the Secret River*. Melbourne: Text.
——   2006b. 'Secret River - Secret History', *The Sydney Papers* (Summer): 148-
    153.
Hirsch, Marianne, and Valerie Smith. 2002. 'Feminism and Cultural Memory: An
    Introduction', *Signs* 28(1), Special Issue: *Gender and Cultural Memory*: 1-
    19.
Hirst, John. 2006. *Sense and Nonsense in Australian History*. Melbourne: Black Inc.
    Agenda.
Hutcheon, Linda. 1988. *A Poetics of Postmodernism: History, Theory, Fiction*. New
    York & London: Routledge.
Hutton, Patrick. 1993. *History as an Art of Memory*. Hanover & London: University
    Press of New England.

——.   1989. *The Politics of Postmodernism*. London & New York: Routledge.

LaCapra, Dominick. 2001. *Writing History, Writing Trauma*. Baltimore & London: The Johns Hopkins University Press.

Macintyre, Stuart, and Anna. Clark. 2003. *The History Wars*. Melbourne: Melbourne University Press.

Matus, Jill. 1998. *Toni Morrison*. Manchester: Manchester University Press.

McCredden, Lyn. 2007. 'Haunted Identities and the Possible Futures of "Aust. Lit."', *JASAL* Special Issue: *Spectres, Screens, Shadows, Mirrors*: 12-24.

McKenna, Mark. 2005. 'Writing the Past: History, Literature and the Public Sphere in Australia', *Humanities Writing Project Lecture Transcripts*. Online at: http://www.humanitieswritingproject.net.au/McKenna.pdf   (consulted 01.10.2009).

Mink, Louis O. 1978. 'Narrative Form as a Cognitive Instrument', in Canary, Robert H., and Henry Kozicki (eds.), *The Writing of History: Literary Form and Historical Understanding*. Madison, Wisconsin: University of Wisconsin Press: 129-150.

Morris, Meaghan. 2006. *Identity Anecdotes: Translation and Media Culture*. London: Sage.

Morrison, Toni. 1989. 'The Pain of Being Black', Interview with Bonnie Angelo, *Time*. May 22. Online at: http://www.time.com/time/community/pulitzerinterview.html   (consulted 01.10.2009).

Probyn-Rapsey, Fiona. 2007. 'Complicity, Critique, Methodology', *ARIEL: A Review of International English Literature*, 38(2): 65-82.

Rigney, Ann. 2004. 'Portable Monuments: Literature, Cultural Memory, and the Case of Jeanie Deans', *Poetics Today*, 25(2): 361-396.

——.   2007. 'Being an improper historian', in Jenkins, Keith, Sue Morgan and Alun Munslow (eds.), *Manifestos for History*. London & New York: Routledge: 149-159.

Rody, Caroline. 1995. 'Toni Morrison's *Beloved*: History, "Rememory," and a "Clamor for a Kiss"', *American Literary History* 7(1): 92-119.

Schaffer, Kay, and Sidonie Smith. 2004. *Human Rights and Narrated Lives: The Ethics of Recognition*. Basingstoke: Palgrave.

Spiegal, Gabrielle M. 2002. 'Memory and History: Liturgical Time and Historical Time', *History and Theory*, 41(2): 149-162.

Sturken, Marita. 1997. *Tangled Memories: The Vietnam War, the Aids Epidemic, and the Politics of Remembering*. Berkeley, Los Angeles & London: University of California Press.

Sullivan, Jane. 2006. 'Making a Fiction of History', Review of Kate Grenville's *The Secret River*, *The Age*, 21 October. Online at: http://www.theage.com.au/news/books/making-a-fiction-of-history/2006/10/19/1160851069362.html (consulted 01.10.2009)

Wallace, Diana. 2005. *The Woman's Historical Novel: British Women Writers, 1900-2000*. New York: Palgrave Macmillan.

Wesseling, Elisabeth. 1991. *Writing History as a Prophet: Postmodernist Innovations of the Historical Novel*. Amsterdam & Philadelphia: John Benjamin's Publishing Company.

White, Hayden. 1978. 'The Fictions of Factual Representation', in *Tropics of Discourse: Essays in Cultural Criticism*. Baltimore & London: The Johns Hopkins University Press: 121-134.

——. 1987. 'The Politics of Historical Interpretation: Discipline and De-Sublimation', in *The Content of the Form*. Baltimore & London: The Johns Hopkins University Press: 58-82.

——. 1999. *Figural Realism: Studies in the Mimesis Effect*. Baltimore & London: The Johns Hopkins University Press.

Young, James E. 1997. 'Toward a Received History of the Holocaust', *History and Theory* 36(4): 21-43.

Part III

Contesting Colonialism:

Crises of Nationhood, Empire and Afterimages

Famine, Femininity, Family:
Rememory and Reconciliation
in Nuala O'Faolain's *My Dream of You*

Ann Heilmann

Abstract:
Traumatic experience is often related to a sense of belatedness, only graspable through geographical and temporal distance, as in the case of the self-exiled Irish narrator of Nuala O'Faolain's *My Dream of You* (2001), who returns to her native country to research a nineteenth-century House of Lords divorce case for a planned novel. In her mourning for her closest friend, the protagonist Kathleen's investigations become an attempted working-through of her own traumas as well as of her cultural heritage: the final years of the Great Hunger, the setting of the affair which led to the historical 1856 Talbot case for 'criminal conversation' brought by an Anglo-Irish landlord against his wife and their Irish coachman. Confronting character and readers alike with the unwieldiness and instability of legal and documentary evidence, the novel problematises conceptualisations of authenticity, appropriation, textuality, and genre (autobiography, historiography, neo-Victorianism, the postmodern text), dramatising the conjunction of eros and thanatos, femininity and famishment.

Keywords: famine, family, narrative, neo-Victorian, Nuala O'Faolain, postmodern, reconciliation, romantic escapism, Talbot divorce case, trauma tourism.

*****

In his discussion of 'Irish Studies and Traumaculture', Conor Carville draws attention to the recent turn to what he provocatively calls "pathography" in Irish literature and culture (Carville 2008: 47). With reference to the concept of "wound culture" (Seltzer 1997), he asserts that, in the wake of the 150th commemoration of the Irish Famine, literary as well as government-sponsored discourses have come to define contemporary Irish identity through collective trauma narrative (Carville 2008: 47-53). To illustrate this point Carville cites a range of memoirs published since the 1990s, which construct "parallels between personal histories bedevilled by the secrets and violence of childhood and the history of the nation as a whole" (Carville 2008: 47). Examples include among others Roddy Doyle's *Paddy Clark Ha Ha Ha* (1993), Frank McCourt's *Angela's Ashes* (1996), and Hugo Hamilton's *The Speckled People* (2003). In its attention to sexual politics in the aetiology of trauma and the formation of the gendered Irish subject, journalist, autobiographer, and novelist Nuala O'Faolain's *Are You Somebody?* (1996) represents a "feminist countertradition" (Dougherty 2007: 55). O'Faolain's first novel, *My Dream of You* (2001), places this feminist agenda firmly in the historical context of the Great Hunger of 1845-52: the potato blight which, exacerbated by English laissez-faire politics, the landlord system, and food exportation even in the starvation years, erased an eighth of Ireland's 8.1 million population and drove another eighth into exile (Lloyd 2005: 153). This essay argues that in its focus on the close correlation between personal and national catastrophe, and the paradigmatic collaterality established between the forces of family, femininity, and famine, O'Faolain uses the framework of the neo-Victorian novel to reconstitute contemporary Irish trauma narrative in a specifically female configuration. It establishes, as Miriam O'Kane Mara has noted, "the interconnectedness of history and the history of the Famine with women's experience in postcolonial Ireland" (O'Kane Mara 2007: 198). At the same time *My Dream of You* politicises the neo-Victorian motif of the family anti-romance, which serves as a metaphor for the contemporary's conflictual relationship with the past.[1]

Traumatic experience, Cathy Caruth contends, is often related to a sense of belatedness that expresses itself through geographical and temporal dislocation: "since the traumatic event is not experienced as it occurs, it is fully evident only in connection with another place, and in another time" (Caruth 1996b: 8). To the exiled Irish narrator of *My Dream of You* this "other" place and time is an Anglo-Irish manor house during the latter part of the Famine. Set in the final year of the closing decade of the twentieth century, O'Faolain's novel enacts a psychological journey of reconciliation

---

[1] For a discussion of neo-Victorianism's engagement with trauma and mourning through the device of the fictional family memoir see Heilmann and Llewellyn 2010, chapter 1.

with the past through personal and collectivised "rememory". Toni Morrison prominently conceptualised rememory as the memory traces and scars that remain imprinted on the collective consciousness long after the originary traumatic event has disappeared from view: "If a house burns down, it's gone, but the place – the picture of it – stays, and not just in my rememory, but out there, in the world" (Morrison 1987: 36).[2] In its feminist postcolonial project of examining contemporary Anglo-Irish gender politics in the light of a factual mid-Victorian sexual scandal, the novel connects processes of (re)memory and mourning with the theme of traumatic inheritance through the fictionalised interpolation of actual historic events. In doing so, O'Faolain's female protagonist, like Caruth's trauma survivor, "bear[s] witness to a past that was never fully experienced as it occurred. Trauma [...] does not simply serve as record of the past but precisely registers the force of an experience that is not yet fully owned" (Caruth 1996c: 151). Like the postcolonial texts discussed by Dianne Sadoff and Elodie Rousselot elsewhere in this collection, *My Dream of You* also engages with the Freudian concept of *Nachträglichkeit*,[3] but instead of being concerned with mapping the emergence of a 'new world' identity forged from the experience of colonisation the novel revolves around the continuity of trauma born from the convergence of colonial and indigenous, internal(ised) oppression.

This is illustrated in the way in which O'Faolain's contemporary protagonist, forty-nine-year-old Kathleen (Caitlín) de Burca, conceptualises her troubled private life through the lens of nineteenth-century marital breakdown. Devastated by the sudden death of her best friend, colleague, and substitute 'mother'/partner Jimmy, and in recognition of his advice that "You have to go back [...] before you can go on" (O'Faolain 2001: 176), she retires from her post as travel writer for a London newspaper to return to her native Ireland, for the first time in thirty years, with the aim of

---

[2] That the Victorians drew analogies between the African American experience of slavery and the Irish Famine is illustrated in the titles of novels like W.C. Upton's *Uncle Pat's Cabin* (1882) and, notoriously, in Thomas Carlyle's 1849 essay 'The Nigger Question' and its dismissal of the emancipated West Indies as "Negro Ireland" (Carlyle 1899: 353).

[3] *Nachträglichkeit* is defined as a delayed response to an earlier incident, the traumatic nature of which is comprehended only after the event (see Freud 1895: 352-356 and Bronfen 1998: 255-256).

investigating an 1856 House of Lords divorce case, Talbot versus Talbot, for a novel she plans to write.[4] In a life rooted in exile and marked by perpetual flight (her job involving her in almost continuous peripatetic overseas travel), Jimmy, a gay American, and Alex, the paternal if monkish editor-in-chief, have come to stand in for the family from which Kathleen severed herself in her flight from Ireland, a personal exodus whose traumatic import is associated with that of the Famine survivors a century and a half earlier: "I was driven out of the country by pain […] I left headlong, cursing this rotten Ireland, dying to get out. How many of them were exactly the same?" (O'Faolain 2001: 176) Recalling the moment the boat pulled out of the harbour, she invokes Ford Madox Brown's haunting painting of (English) emigration, *The Last of England* (1855): "There was no reaction to the last of Ireland" (O'Faolain 2001: 426). Like Brown's stony-faced couple staring ahead rather than back, her Irish fellow-passengers displayed no emotion: a detachment which in Kathleen's case signals a profound and lasting sense of alienation. London, which she initially embraced as a refuge from a home and country oppressive of women, reconstituted itself as a second place of exile after the collapse of a passionate love affair in her early twenties. Since then she has lived "in a state of suspended animation" in a shabby basement flat, an "ideal mausoleum" for her buried dreams and also symptomatic of her continuing status, after three decades, as an outsider and alien to English society (O'Faolain 2001: 18, 278). As an Irish woman she is persistently cast, and as a result of her emotional numbness and long-term depression acquiesces, in the role of colonial sexual object. In the course of her "journey home" through both her immediate personal and her nation's collective past, she begins to open herself up to repressed memories and, "with everything inside [her] trembling from shocks of remembrance", tackles her personal

---

[4] This factual case coincided with parliamentary debates (1854, 1856-57) about the introduction of a divorce bill. Prior to the Matrimonial Causes Act of 1857, which established divorce through the law courts, divorce could only be obtained through a Private Act of Parliament, which had to be preceded by a decree of divorce "a mensa et thoro" from the ecclesiastical courts and by a successful civil prosecution for "criminal conversation" against the wife's alleged lover (Shanley 1989: 36-44). For a different example of neo-Victorianism's engagement with a factual Victorian marriage scandal and prominent divorce case (Codrington versus Codrington), which involved the founder of the feminist Victoria Press, Emily Faithfull, see Emma Donoghue's *The Sealed Letter* (2008).

grievances and grief in the process of imaginatively reconstructing legal and national history (O'Faolain 2001: 181).

The ghosts Kathleen must lay to rest are all fractured love stories, played out against the apocalyptic backdrop of the Famine and its later twentieth-century psychical-emotional reverberations. The 1856 "criminal conversations" case brought by Richard (factually John) Talbot (originally Crosbie) against his wife Marianne (Mary Anne or Mary Ann, née McCausland) and their groom William Mullan (Mullane),[5] which resulted in Marianne's loss of her daughter and mental collapse, provide a dramatic context for Kathleen's own dysfunctional family experience (the withdrawn mother who could not love nor care for her children; the neglectful, violent, or absentee father). Even more pointedly, it affords analogies with her shattered relationship with her one-time lover Hugo, the upper-class English journalism and law student who presented her with a copy of the 1856 House of Lords *Judgment* and, after discovering her infidelity with a flatmate, evicted her with as much ruthless determination as John Talbot did his wife. The first impulse towards tackling the shadow these ruptures have cast over her life comes when Kathleen recalls a poem memorised at school, Walter de la Mare's 'The Listeners' (1912), with its haunting refrain "Is there anybody there?":

> A picture formed at the back of my mind, of silent ghosts waiting and listening, and me, the Traveller, riding up and calling to them. Whether these were the ghosts of Marianne Talbot and William Mullan [...] or of my father and mother [...] I didn't bother to decide. [...] It was [...] me outside somewhere, calling, and tragic ghosts listening to me and waiting for me to free them [.] (O'Faolain 2001: 19)

---

[5] John Crosbie and his wife assumed the name of Talbot after he inherited Mount Talbot from an uncle (House of Lords 1856: 4). Mrs Talbot's first name is variously rendered as Marianne in the House of Lords *Judgment* (1856: 4); as Mary Anne in (her defence counsel) William Keogh's *Speech* (1855: 1) and the High Court of Delegates' 'Judgment' (appended to Paget 1856: 91); and as Mary Ann in the *Times* report of 'Talbot's Divorce' (23 May 1856). Likewise Mullan is referred to as such in the House of Lords *Judgment* (1856: 7), but as Mullane in Keogh (1855: 3) and Paget (1856: 4); and Mullen in Mr Whiteside's speech in the 'Case of "Talbot v. Talbot"', *Hansard* (1856).

The image of the traveller (so emblematic of Kathleen, the travel writer) knocking on the door of a cottage inhabited only by the dead is a powerful metaphor for the Famine (and also, rather uncannily, of the neo-Victorian author's act of resurrecting the dead).[6] As David Lloyd has detailed, images of spectrality and haunting are "indissociable" from Irish history and typically serve to invoke either the need for retribution,[7] or else a "future possibility" in the form of conciliation (Lloyd 2005: 156). The long-term aftermath of the Famine becomes manifest to Kathleen on her car journey through Ireland, when she is struck by the lack of picturesque historic villages, a sight common enough in Britain: "Ruins of medieval abbeys and castles. Then nothing. Then the buildings from my grandparents' time" (O'Faolain 2001: 45).[8] The erasure of entire villages, the devastation caused to the family life of generations, she reflects, must have left as lasting a mark on the collective psyche. She considers the impact of this national cataclysm on her own family and identity: "The trauma must be deep in the genetic material of which I was made. – I cannot forget it [...] yet I have no memory of it. It is not mine; but who else can own it?" (O'Faolain 2001: 65) Only later generations descended from survivors are able to reclaim and rememorise an "unimaginable catastrophe", whose profound repercussions are still stamped onto the landscape and the common unconscious of the nation (O'Faolain 2001: 64). "It wasn't 'sorrow'", she angrily retorts, when her English TravelWrite editor cautions her against producing yet another book on the Irish Famine, "It was our Holocaust. [...] The British government was glad that we were being exterminated by accident" (O'Faolain 2001: 74).

---

[6] For a discussion of the neo-Victorian metaphor of haunting see Rousselot's and Sadoff's essays in this book; see also Arias and Pulham 2010.

[7] This is suggested in Richard D'Alton Williams's 1883 *Poems*, in particular 'Song of the Irish-American Regiments', in which a "ghastly spectre throng" enjoins the living to "fight their [ancestors'] wrong" (qtd. Corporaal 2009: 145).

[8] O'Faolain here echoes Victorian witness accounts such as that by Harriet Martineau in *Letters from Ireland* (1852): "groups of ruins [...] staring fragments of old castles, and churches, and monasteries; and worse than these, a very large number of unroofed cottages. For miles together [...] there is scarcely a token of human presence but the useless gables and the empty doorways and window-spaces of pairs or rows of deserted cottages. [...] Yet, while substantial stone walls are thus staring in the traveller's face, what cabins – actual dwellings of families – are here and there distinguishable in the midst of the bog! Styles of mud, bulging and tottering, grass-grown, half-swamped with bog water, and the soil around all poached with the tread of bare feet" (Martineau 2001: 71).

Kathleen's response here signals her over-identification with the historical victims (her use of "we" collapsing the collective past with the individual present), a position that the historian and trauma theorist Dominick LaCapra specifically cautions against. While uncritical identification involves a process of transference which, in its "total fusion of self and other", effectuates a sense of "surrogate victimage", it is only through "empathetic unsettlement", the act of "put[ting] oneself in the other's position while recognizing the difference of that position and hence not taking the other's place", that it becomes possible to "counteract[t] victimization, including self-victimization" (LaCapra 2001: 36, 38, 40, 78). This is a lesson Kathleen has to learn painfully in the course of her inner journey. At its outset, she seeks to trace the psychological and emotional impact of the Famine on the survivors and subsequent generations, leading up to the present time. Passed on from generation to generation, with the memory fading yet the wound, never healed, remaining imprinted on the national and individual psyche, how did this traumatic event continue to affect relations between husband and wife and parents and children? Was this the root cause, she ponders, for her own unloving family environment?

> I put the two things together, home and the Famine, and I used to wonder whether something that had happened more than a hundred years ago, and that was almost forgotten, could have been so terrible that it knocked all the happiness out of people. (O'Faolain 2001: 5)

As Nan Leech, the retired Ballygall librarian whom Kathleen consults about the Talbot case, points out, however, the psychological after-effects of survival must have been complicated by feelings of guilt. In drawing attention to the dilemma of how people could have safeguarded their own lives without becoming complicit with the ruin of others, the novel engages with Lawrence Langer's notion of "choiceless choice": the suspension or meaninglessness of any concept of moral responsibility in the extreme absence of choice for the victims of genocide, who are faced with a situation in which saving one life comes at the cost of another's death, and where survival adds an additional layer of victimisation, that of presumed culpability (Langer 1988: 120, 126). For one way of ensuring survival during the Famine, Nan reminds Kathleen, was to guard the landlords' fields, thus warding off starvation by turning away the starving:

> you can be sure that our ancestors weren't out among the cabins of the dying any more than the gentry were. If you and I are sitting here in a warm room having a nice talk, we have to ask ourselves how our own people survived. What did our people do at the time, that you and I came to be born? (O'Faolain 2001: 67)

This may explain why, even a century and a half on, there is an impetus towards silence and denial: when Kathleen talks to a local octogenarian, Mr Flannery, he refutes the idea that the region was affected by the Famine. "They often deny there was a famine, the old people", her landlord Bertie explains, "They don't want it talked about. It's better to stay silent about misfortune" (O'Faolain 2001: 408). Yet the root cause of all emotional fallout in the post-Famine generations, the novel suggests, is exactly this refusal to confront and work through the past.

Collusion and complicity with the destruction of others are important facets of the Talbot case. The story of Marianne Talbot and William Mullan is also the story of betrayal from within, on the part of the servants who testified against the couple. (Kathleen's novel draft epitomises this in the torture of Mullan's dog by the two men who expose the couple to Richard Talbot, one of whom then attempts to rape Marianne.[9]) Having read Marianne's brother-in-law Thomas Paget's petition, *A Statement of Facts* (1855), Kathleen notes that a central plank of the plea for her innocence was the English colonialist belief that "Richard Talbot was able to get away with framing Marianne *because* they were in Ireland – *because* Irish witnesses were such liars that they could be got to say anything" (O'Faolain 2001: 293). In the historical case both Paget and the defence counsel, William Keogh, took pains to highlight the discreditable nature of the staff witnesses called by Mr Talbot, providing evidence of their

---

[9] The attempted rape of Mrs Talbot by the butler Halloran features in the actual case; he was dismissed as a credible witness by the High Court of Delegates and the House of Lords.

bribery and intimidation. Interestingly, since much of the evidence relied on clerics (relatives or close acquaintances of John and/or Marianne), Keogh also intimated corruption at higher places: "clergymen pervade the whole of this case [...] They had a finger in every part of it" (Keogh 1855: 17-18). The House of Lords, having dismissed some of the previous witnesses, arrived at its *Judgment* largely on the basis of the testimonies provided by five Anglican ministers and two upper-class witnesses (female relatives of John Talbot's who had not come forward previously). With the exception of the Reverend William McClelland, O'Faolain does not exploit this aspect of the case, even though an emphasis on an ecclesiastical conspiracy would have provided a parallel with Kathleen's personal family trauma. (The reason for her exodus from Ireland was the agony to which the Catholic Church condemned her dying mother when it prohibited pain killers, because her cancerous body harboured a child, who died with her.) Religion ultimately cannot be the anchor of the story, because Kathleen – as she is to learn, to her detriment – becomes wholly absorbed with another determinant: passion.

What initially proves so irresistible to Kathleen about the case is the idea of a grand passion overcoming all obstacles; desires of such intensity that they prevailed over the near-invincible barriers of class, race and ethnicity, even language, in an extreme situation of crisis:

> there could hardly have been two people less likely to be drawn to each other than an Anglo-Irish landlord's wife and an Irish servant. Each of them came from a powerful culture which had at its very core the defining of the other as alien. [...] They didn't even have a native language in common [...] It seemed to me that William Mullan and Mrs Talbot had been builders – had made love in the literal sense of "made" – had manufactured love. (O'Faolain 2001: 57)

The enormity of the social gulf between the purported lovers was invoked by both the defence – as evidence of the absurdity of the charge – and the High Court and House of Lords – as an intimation of Mrs Talbot's irreparable disgrace, a degradation sanitised only in insanity.[10] For Kathleen, by contrast, it serves as proof of the authenticity and strength of feeling that brought the couple together. To explore this instance of passion overruling all other considerations becomes a matter of great personal importance for her, given that her own dreams of fulfilment came to nothing, a failure surpassed only by that of her mother, who persisted in clinging to the romantic ideal even as it condemned her to a death-in-life existence. That the affair between Marianne and Mullan should have occurred in the final years of the Famine (1849-52) constitutes its "most interesting" aspect for Kathleen (O'Faolain 2001: 23). Was it, she wonders, born from sheer despair, a kind of dance of death? Or, alternatively, did it represent an ardent reassertion of life and vitality in the face of general devastation?

In the first two chapters of her novel-in-progress, "The Talbot Book", Kathleen provides a graphic account of the starvation that Marianne, sheltered though she was in the big house with plenty of supplies, could not have been able to ignore. Her aversion to the "turf ash" smell of the bed curtains and soft furnishings within can be interpreted as a displaced response to what is happening without (O'Faolain 2001: 160). After catching sight of corpses on outings, Marianne has become housebound; her synaesthesia reflects her shocked awareness of the situation, but is also a corollary of claustrophobia, and in this sense is reminiscent of Charlotte Perkins Gilman's turn-of-the-century story of depression induced by domestic imprisonment, 'The Yellow Wallpaper' (1892), in which the heroine complains about the "yellow" smell of the wallpaper of the room that confines her (Gilman 1981: 28). Unlike the factual Mrs Talbot, however, who according to witness statements suffered from material

---

[10] See Lord Brougham's summing up, House of Lords *Judgment*: "I abstain from any other remark except one; namely, the improbability of any gentlewoman having fallen into such a course of misconduct, and of that course of misconduct having led to such grossly imprudent and thoughtless unreflecting methods of gratifying the passion which appeared to prevail over her mind. Unhappily, the evidence which is in the case with respect to her nervous state, her irritability, her excitable state after the discovery, seems to reflect some little light backwards upon what very possibly might have been the cause of her acting with less prudence, less common discretion, less thought, and less foresight than almost any one in such circumstances would have done. She appears to have been a woman not of strong mind; and in persons not of strong mind you will not seldom find the strength of passion that exceeds reason" (House of Lords 1856: 60).

deprivation at the hands of her husband, Kathleen's fictional Marianne does not have to go without luxuries. In contrast, two of the actual Mrs Talbot's maids testified to her being reduced to borrowing from her servants for lack of an allowance, and to her being able to repay them only slowly in instalments, by drawing on stamps and her daughter's pocket money (qtd. Paget 1855: 34-36). Even more significantly, Mrs Talbot was denied "proper nourishment"; as her maid Margaret Hall deposed, "I have seen and known her lunch for several days to consist of nothing more than a cut off a dry round of beef, and no drink but beer, not good enough for a decent servant to drink" (qtd. Paget 1855: 41). Here, then, direct analogies emerge between the Famine and female dispossession and malnourishment in marriage. Yet while Kathleen reverses the ethnic power dynamics by making Marianne an Englishwoman expelled from her home by an Anglo-Irish landlord,[11] she does not turn her into a destitute, famished wife, for a victim could not occupy the role of subversive heroine; nor would Marianne be able to lavish any gifts on her lover. That Mrs Talbot took special care to ensure that Mullan was fed, clothed, and housed well, according to servants testifying for her husband (see House of Lords 1856: 12-13, 95), is crucial to Kathleen's agenda: it surely was "affection" and not "just a physical affair" (O'Faolain 2001: 43). Indeed, her protagonist demonstratively engaged in revolutionary domestic politics when she invited her groom to take her husband's place in the drawing room, where the lovers were seen holding hands or, like an established married couple, peacefully sitting at either side of the fire (see House of Lords 1856: 19). The social and sexual threat posed to established hegemonies by 'gentlemen' becoming exchangeable with their low-born servants – an attitude more customary for upper-class men towards their wives and mistresses – is likely to have contributed to the unanimous verdict of the House of Lords.

Coinciding as it does with an affair of her own, with Shay, a man who is entirely unsuitable in any sense other than that of offering temporary sexual-cum-parental attention, Kathleen's romantic impulse turns, to adapt Elodie Rousselot's words elsewhere in this collection, "historical commemoration" into "a means of sexual [and, crucially,

---

[11] The historical Mrs Talbot came from an Anglo-Irish family resident in Derry (Keogh 1855: 2).

emotional] gratification" (this volume: 356).[12] Her endeavour imaginatively to relive Marianne's passion is coupled with the desire to breathe life back into the people named in the documents, to recreate them as individuals, to unearth the 'human' story beneath the legal case. A photograph of Mount Talbot reinforces her sense of a missing story when she compares it with a rare family snapshot: "one photo, all people and no house: one, all house and no people" (O'Faolain 2001: 85). She decides that she will "put the people back into the picture", and after her first "Talbot Book" chapter notes with satisfaction that she has "given Marianne and William Mullan fragments of a past, though the Judgment did not" (O'Faolain 2001: 85, 171). Indeed, not only did the *Judgment* withhold the personal history of the main personalities, it even ignored the reality of the Famine that surrounded them. When in her early twenties she first read the document, Kathleen was outraged at a reference to the Talbots, like "most families", having an "Irish car[riage]" (House of Lords 1856: 9): "I like that bit about most families, I remember saying. 1849, you said? 'Most families' were either dead in the Famine or getting the hell out of Ireland" (O'Faolain 2001: 3).

In her fictionalised version Kathleen simplifies the more complex sequence of events. She has the Talbots take up residency at Mount Talbot in 1847-48 at the height of the Famine, whereas in documented legal history they only arrived there three years later, in 1851, having previously lived at two other estates. Witness accounts from both these sites would later incriminate Marianne Talbot and William Mullan.[13] The actual case revolved around whether an affair could have taken place in the earlier locations due to Mullan's treatment for gonorrhoea in 1849 (House of Lords 1856: 39-41, Keogh 1855: 53-54). Mullan's body was thus constructed as a site of multiple contagion: Irish, low-born, and diseased, he was an impossible, unpardonable choice for a lady, who, in the words of Lord St Leonards, "degraded herself at once to his condition" (House of

---

[12] In his fantasies of Laura Secord, the character David McDougal in Jane Urquart's *The Whirlpool*, discussed by Rousselot, bears some resemblance with O'Faolain's Kathleen.

[13] From 1848-50, the Talbots lived at Summer Hill or Summerhill, near Mallow, County Cork, followed by Eden Hill in the same locality until May-June 1851; see Paget 1856: 2; see also the *Times* account of the 'Talbot's Divorce' proceedings (13 March and 5 May 1856), and House of Lords 1856: 4-6.

Lords 1856: 88). Perhaps unsurprisingly, Kathleen's novel draft omits all references to Mullan's venereal disease (an indication of his contact with prostitutes) and, rather, depicts him as a man fastidious, even chaste, in his private life. Here, Mullan's profound sense of place and undisputed leadership position among the locals in his capacity as the last representative of a long-established family serve to provide a contrast between the 'real' and the 'upstart' gentry, the Talbots having lived in mud huts not so long ago. This also, of course, diminishes the disparity between the lovers. Mullan's strong attachment to his deceased mother, who taught him tenderness for women and animals, is contrasted with Marianne's psychological vulnerability and troubled father-relationship (the death of her mother when she was three was left unexplained, and after twenty years of endeavouring to please her father, she is still unable to do so, having failed to produce a male heir). Again, the couple are moved into closer proximity, reducing the shock factor of a relationship between them, while Marianne's dysphoric family history simultaneously enables Kathleen to address her own.

Kathleen also takes care to contextualise Richard Talbot's psychology of the emotionally fragile adult, who has never entirely recovered from his childhood experience of being bullied as a 'Paddy' in his English boarding school. There would be nothing worse than to be placed on a par with the Irish, hence perhaps the ruthlessness of his proceedings against his wife and his groom once they have been discovered.[14] What holds husband and wife together in the early period is the child, Mab (Marianne Jane, not named in the legal documents), who introduces life and laughter to Mount Talbot, but whom a four-month illness (symbolic of the calamity outside) leaves greatly subdued in spirit; what brings the lovers together is, again, the child, whose bilingualism builds a bridge between the two cultures.

Kathleen's *mise-en-scène* of the Talbot case performs a precarious balancing act between Seamus Heaney's notion of the "poetic dig" (Heaney 1980: 41), romance literature, and literary tourism. In 'Feeling into Words', from *Preoccupations*, Heaney refers to poetry's power to act "as revelation of the self to the self, as restoration of the culture to itself", as a marker of "continuity, with the

---

[14] Talbot was awarded £2000 damages against Mullan, who evaded a prison sentence for non-payment by emigrating to the United States (Paget 1856: 15).

aura and authenticity of archaeological finds" (Heaney 1980: 41). It is
this intensity of words and images "as bearers of history" that
Kathleen wishes to achieve with her novel (Heaney 1980: 45), but her
all too sentimental desire to locate, take mental possession of, and thus
recapture the 'authentic' setting of the Talbot story has an adverse
effect on her project of conceptual and visionary recovery. Just as, on
first arrival in Ireland, she involuntarily assumed travel writer mode,
jotting down her impressions of the 'locals' (partly in order to
maintain emotional distance), so now she cannot resist the allure of
exploring the sites featured in the case in order to retrace the steps of
the lovers. Thus she stays in the Talbot Arms hotel, formerly the
vicarage, from which the stern and unforgiving Reverend McClelland
conducted Marianne to Dublin, where he extracted a confession of
guilt from a woman so distressed and terrified that she hid underneath
furniture and searched for her child behind curtains (Paget 1855: 14,
50; Paget 1856: 23, 29-30, 35). Kathleen's excitement grows when
she reads Paget's *Statement of Facts* (1855) in Ballygall library, the
very building where Talbot acted as a magistrate. On visiting the
ruined Mount Talbot estate, her exhilaration reaches a point of excess,
when she compares the seven places where the lovers were seen by
witnesses with the seven Stations of the Cross. Miss Leech, on her last
outing before departing for a cancer hospice, brings Kathleen back to
reality by debunking her romantic interest in Coby Castle, which
could not possibly have featured in the Talbot case, given that it was
not built until the 1880s. Like Margaret Atwood's historian of war in
The Robber Bride (1993), Tony Fremont, who collects memorabilia
(leaves, plants, sand) from historical battlefields in order to address
her childhood trauma of family collapse, Kathleen seeks to rebuild her
fractured relationship with her past and her parents by means of
connecting with another family trauma. In doing so, however, she
indulges in a form of 'trauma tourism', that is, the visitation of sites
connected with suffering not to further empathy and historical
understanding, but rather to pursue self-indulgent emotional
excitement and gratification.

      This desire for romantic hyperbole is consistently demystified
by the radical amateur historian Nan Leech. As Kim McMullen notes,
Nan prompts a "critical unmasking of the [romance] genre" and its
political conservatism of reaffirming the *status quo* (McMullen 2004:
143): "the Talbot story is just the kind of thing an English audience

would be interested in. History without the economics, history without the politics, history without the mess" (O'Faolain 2001: 97). Nan's reaffirmation of Henry James's verdict against historical fiction as "humbug" will ultimately persuade Kathleen to abandon her plans for publication,[15] but for the time being Kathleen finds it impossible to turn her back on Marianne and Mullan: "if I gathered the bits and pieces of the Talbot story into a tale, just for my own satisfaction, I wouldn't be trying to humbug anyone, would I?" (O'Faolain 2001: 282, 139). The fragmented nature of her "tale", inserted as its "bits and pieces" are between memories of Kathleen's own past and her affair with Shay, indicates the entirely self-reflective purpose it is meant to serve. Indeed, Kathleen's quest for the grand tragic Irish love story is not so dissimilar from the escapist fantasies of the London millionaire daughter with distant Irish roots, who flies in her wedding party to get married barefoot and with flowers in her hair. Not surprisingly, given her romantic investment, Kathleen feels deflated when she learns about Marianne's descent into insanity. In the historical case, the defence relied on a number of physicians, most notably John Connolly (a highly ambiguous figure),[16] in attributing

---

[15] Nan argues that "Historical fiction is condemned to be second-rate. You may multiply the little facts that can be got from pictures and documents, relics and prints, as much as you like, the historical novel is almost impossible to do [...] You have to think with your modern apparatus [...] you have to simplify back by an amazing tour de force – and even then it's all humbug" (O'Faolain 2001:139). James's actual statement, in a letter to Miss Jewett of 5 October 1901, reads as follows: "The 'historic' novel is, for me, condemned [...] to a fatal *cheapness*, for the simple reason that the difficulty of the job is inordinate & that a mere *escamotage*, in the interest of ease, & of the abysmal public *naiveté*, becomes inevitable. You may multiply the little facts that can be got from pictures & documents, relics & prints, as much as you like – *the* real thing is almost impossible to do [...] You have to *think* with your modern apparatus a man, a woman [...] whose own thinking was intensely-otherwise conditioned, you have to simplify back by an amazing tour de force – & even then it's all humbug." (qtd. Horne 2000: 360).

[16] As director of Hanwell Asylum Connolly had been a prominent voice for reform in the treatment of the insane (see Showalter 1987: 42-50), but from the late 1830s he developed an over-eagerness in certifying mental disorders and 'moral insanity' in large numbers of individuals. He was shortly to be involved in another notorious case, this time acting for the husband: in 1858 he declared Edward Bulwer-Lytton's estranged wife Rosina "demented" (Rosina later exposed her husband and his mad-doctors in *A Blighted Life* [1880]). In the same year the spectre of Connolly exerted a threatening influence on Catherine Dickens, hastening her agreement to separate from her novelist husband (Sutherland 1995: 73-80).

Marianne's confession to Reverend McClelland and others to madness induced by cruel treatment and intense emotional and mental intimidation (Paget 1855: 50-65, Paget 1856: 82).[17] To Kathleen, however, the idea of her heroine having succumbed to mental illness is intolerable:

> That she was, in historical fact, mad – frail and mad – only seven months after Richard Talbot and the Reverend McClelland put her away, changed my picture of her. [...] I'd liked to think of her as strong and plump – juicy with health, like Kate Winslet in *Titanic*. I'd thought of her as being brought from England to a remote and desolate spot in Ireland over which the suffering of the Famine hung like a miasma, and being sufficiently young and vital to insist, even in that place, on a sensual life. [...] I thought of her as having shy eyes and a modest manner, but naturally red lips and a body that wanted to burst the hooks and buttons of the rich clothes that contained it. [...] But how did my blooming, lusty Marianne go mad? (O'Faolain 2001: 286-287)

Insane, Marianne is reduced to passive victimhood rather than heroic trauma survival: she is no longer – perhaps never was – the agent of subversive acts, whom Kathleen had invoked in her fantasies.

---

[17] After being found in Mullan's room, in the company of her daughter, Mrs Talbot was publicly accused of adultery by her husband. Exposed to sexual harassment by the butler, she was taken to Dublin by the Reverend McClelland, where she was seen by two further clergymen, one of whom moved her to Windsor. Her brother-in-law, having discovered where she was held, gained access only after threatening legal action. During her confinement her signature was obtained for a proxy solicitor (see Keogh 1855: 26-30, 34-36). In his *Letter to His Excellency* Paget includes a "Memorandum of a Conversation with Mary Anne, in presence of my Wife [her sister]", in which Mrs Talbot describes the pressure exerted on her to extract a confession and the subterfuge with which she was made to give her consent to a proxy: "Mrs. Tennant [the guard] said I was wicked, and none of my friends would have me [...] I remember signing a paper [...] Mrs. Tennant told me it came from my father, and I must sign it [...] she told me the words I was to write – she told me to write [...] *what she called a confession* [...] she said if I did not write what she told me I should be locked up and starved till I did [...] she said I was to live with her always [...] for my relations would never have me" (qtd. Paget 1856: 82).

Kathleen feels confounded by the complexity of a story that changes at every turn, becoming more unwieldy with each new document unearthed. Her discovery of another deposition by Thomas Paget, *A Letter to His Excellency* (1856), and a newspaper story (which O'Faolain purloined from the *Times* account of the divorce proceedings) raise a new set of questions. Did Marianne indeed go mad (as Paget affirms)? Or might she have pretended madness in order to save herself, after being rescued from confinement and offered a refuge with the Paget family, in effect employing madness as a proto-feminist survival strategy to evade the infliction of further trauma?[18] To what extent was Marianne 'guilty', then? Kathleen begins to concede that there might never have been an affair with Mullan at all, as well as considering the possibility of her heroine having 'used' Mullan, the way her own best female friend's titled father used Kathleen "to feel himself" (O'Faolain 2001: 224). Could Marianne really have entertained a simultaneous affair with another man, one from her own class, as the Reverend Sargent (Sergent) claimed?[19] Might Marianne even, Kathleen wonders, have taken monstrous advantage of Mullan by having "an affair with someone of her own kind and a completely innocent Mullan been made the scapegoat?" (O'Faolain 2001: 397) Who was the man on the floor? "It couldn't have been *McClelland* [...] could it?", she ponders; "his

---

[18] The real Mrs Talbot's acquiescence with the diagnosis, in the eyes of one of the House of Lord judges, implied her sense of guilt. After freely admitting her adultery to a number of witnesses, when she was returned to a part of her family convinced of her innocence and determined to prove it, what could she do but fall in line with their expectations (see House of Lords 1856: 74-75)? Paget's *A Letter to His Excellency* includes a statement drawn up after a conversation between Marianne and her sister, Katherine Geraldine Paget, in which Marianne avows to feeling "as if I had been mad, and now as if I could begin to think again" (qtd. Paget 1856: 85).

[19] The Reverend Abraham Sergent's (Sargent in the House of Lords *Judgment*) testimony about an incident he witnessed in Summer Hill is reported in the *Times* account of the 'Talbot's Divorce' (5 May 1856): "Upon one occasion he had called upon the Talbots when Mr. Talbot was out. He saw a bloodhound running towards him, and he ran into the house without knocking at the door. He opened a door leading into the drawing-room, and saw Mrs. Talbot lying on the floor with her clothes raised. There was a man kneeling on the ground by her." That this witness statement did much in sealing Mrs Talbot's fate is indicated in Lord St Leonards's refusal to countenance the idea that the man in question could have been anybody other than Mullan. The thought of yet another man being indulged by an upper-class wife and mother in degrading physical circumstances was clearly unpalatable (House of Lords 1856: 82-83).

behaviour was so excessively punitive that it suggested that he desired her" (O'Faolain 2001: 397-398).

A casualty of nineteenth-century patriarchy, Marianne might have been the innocent victim of a cruel and scheming husband, an internally colonised subject systematically deprived of her money and even the very necessities of food. And when, probably due to under-nourishment, she failed to produce an heir – her barrenness an emblem of a feminised, colonised, infertile, starving Ireland (O'Kane Mara 2007: 202) – that same 'coloniser' concocted a wild accusation of adultery with the help of a pair of notorious ruffians in order to get rid of her and find himself a new, more fertile wife. Talbot required an heir to secure his rights to Mount Talbot (Keogh 1855: 2-3). Did he deliberately drive her mad? But why, then, if there was no affair, did Mullan attempt to see Marianne, when she was held in a Dublin house by McClelland, purportedly to ask her to accompany him to America, and why should McClelland have destroyed Mullan's note, given that it would have provided further incriminating evidence? Kathleen becomes ever more uncertain in her capacity as author: "What was the right ending to the Marianne Talbot story?" (O'Faolain 2001: 396) She admits to herself that her endeavour to get at the heart of the story and create a credible version from it, one that would belie James's condemnation of historical fiction, is doomed to failure: "I couldn't see any way of writing about Marianne Talbot that wouldn't be like bad costume drama" (O'Faolain 2001: 399).

To Nan Leech, by contrast, the twists and turns in the inherently unstable set of legal and periodical press accounts and depositions appear like the Victorian equivalent of a postmodern narrative:

> I'm amused […] of the story being so modern in the end. Because this story does exactly what a lot of the highbrow fiction coming into the library these days does – it keeps changing as you look at it. You don't know what to believe. Our readers hate that, of course. (O'Faolain 2001: 381)

The reference to conventional readerly tastes delicately hints at Kathleen's own unpreparedness for giving the story its due as a writer – and is also a metafictional aside to the postmodernist reader of this novel about the pleasures of engaging in the neo-Victorian game with historical sources.[20] In addition, the extreme instability of the "story" challenges our conceptual definition and differentiation of fiction and history: "By using an actual historic event and continually retelling that event, O'Faolain indicates the importance of history to fiction, but also the importance of fiction to history", highlighting "the ways history *is* fiction" (O'Kane Mara 2007: 199, emphasis added). This should make it easier for Kathleen to mould the material for her own purposes, but her writerly impulse of developing her fictional version is being inhibited by her naïve belief in the truthfulness of the historical documents and her persistent self-referentiality, her tendency to over-read the texts and the conflicting stories they tell by always relating them back to her own experience; in LaCapra's terms, she has not moved beyond "unmediated identification" (LaCapra 2001: 99). Whereas Nan is sceptical about Marianne's double infidelity – "why did the Reverend Sargent call at Mount Talbot when he knew Richard would be out? And since when do hostile dogs [...] chase a man *into* a house instead of keep him away from it?" (O'Faolain 2001: 381, original emphasis) – Kathleen has little doubt about its veracity, because it recalls her own reckless behaviour in her relationship with Hugo. That Marianne might have mistaken sexual abandon for passion is crucial to her own story and even more so that of her mother, the woman who never left her bedroom for long enough to attain a sense of self.[21] Marianne at least must have got something out of it to vindicate two lives sacrificed to the grand illusion of an all-consuming passion. In this sense, Kathleen's trauma fiction can be read not just as an attempted belated working-through of Victorian victims' suffering of literal and emotional famishment, or even of her own personal and familial traumas, but as compulsive repetition and unconscious re-enactment. Marianne's story once again leaves Kathleen 'famished' for passion.

Nonetheless this autobiographical approach proves therapeutic to Kathleen's own trajectory in helping her address painful memories

---

[20] In her *New York Times* review, Catherine Lockerbie duly noted the novel's "knowingness" about its "fictional enterprise" (Lockerbie 2001: 14).

[21] Kathleen's mother spends most of her time in her bedroom reading novels and waiting for her husband's return at weekends; the couple's otherwise dysfunctional marriage is kept alive through sexual passion. These few hours constitute the mother's life; both parents are indifferent to their children.

and ultimately change direction, by turning down Shay's offer of a life
suspended in waiting, punctuated by fleeting moments of fulfilment.
Yet it proves counterproductive to her literary project; her novel does
not progress beyond the first two chapters. This is not for lack of
inspiration. Indeed, further ideas for how to develop the story are
proposed by Bertie, who tells her of the local legends about the
'afterlife' of Mount Talbot. The estate, already in a dilapidating
condition, was inherited by a female recluse with the iron
determination to maintain her station in life in the face of financial
ruin. With nobody but herself in the deserted house, she still employed
a butler, insisting that he conduct his duties in the most traditional of
ways. In her eagerness to return to Britain, she awaited the Anglo-
Irish treaty with impatience and set off the very night of its
implementation, only to die, en route, in the Shelbourne Hotel in
Dublin. Here is a script for a different, if still tragic, Anglo-Irish story.
    Another local Mount Talbot story invokes the Gothic, as when
the baby of the maid forced to testify against Marianne, having cried
every single night of her mother's absence, breathed its last on the day
of her return:

> They knew at the time that a curse had been brought
> on the place [… T]he night Mrs Talbot was put out,
> the old nurse that lived in the house that was a bit of a
> witch said, The crows will fly through the rooms of
> this house yet! And there you are – He pointed up at
> the slope. […] The crows do fly through it.
> (O'Faolain 2001: 408)

Kathleen herself contemplates the Gothic mode when she discovers
that "McClelland died very soon after the Talbot scandal. I wandered
into imagining the where and how of his death" (O'Faolain 2001:
404). Yet the opportunity for an aesthetic experimentation with genre
and style, which would enable her to exercise her writerly capacity to
create alternative versions of the story (a strategy adopted in other
neo-Victorian novels, as discussed by Celia Wallhead and Marie-
Luise Kohlke in their contribution to this collection) is circumvented.
Kathleen decides to discontinue her novel and – for her own sake –
write the romantic dénouement she desires, now that in her own life
she has ended her relationship with Shay:

> I didn't *know* the truth of what happened at Mount
> Talbot and I would never know it. There were too
> many contexts missing. […] I could *choose* what to
> believe about the Talbot scandal. I *would* choose what
> to believe. (O'Faolain 2001: 435)

While in LaCapra's terms Kathleen here might be considered
to seek the "facile uplift, harmonization, or closure" that "empathetic
unsettlement" eschews, her narrative nevertheless fulfils the condition
he sees as essential, that is a movement towards "both acting out and
working through" the trauma in question (LaCapra 2001: 78). Thus
she brings the story she has carried with her all her life to a conclusion
with a vision of Mullan's imaginary reunion with Marianne in death,
at a time when, through Shay, she has gained a sense of closure in
remembering Hugo. Accordingly, she can finally let go – of the story,
the past, and her desire of a grand romantic-because-destructive
passion – and is able to reconstitute herself in the process: "It didn't
matter that there wouldn't be a book. […] I was perfectly free […]
Newborn, even" (O'Faolain 2001: 442).[22] Here, then, a narrative
fantasy ending provides emotional consolation to personal trauma,
even as it fails to address the historical trauma.

The recuperative energies set free in Kathleen's "resurrection
from the past" enable her also, finally, to reach some sort of tentative
accommodation with her childhood and the memory of her parents
(O'Faolain 2003: 160). If at the start of her project of self-regeneration
she bewailed her condition – "I am motherless in every direction, I
mourned" (O'Faolain 2001: 316) – her journey to the past releases not
only painful but also positive memories. She recalls her father asking
her to take charge of Uncle Ned's farm, thus for once signalling an
awareness of her as an individual, and of the subsequent mushrooming
expedition during which he burst into song. Similarly, she remembers
her one shopping spree with her mother after she had won the school
poetry prize, when her mother, herself a reject from her own family,
expressed a pride in her daughter that had never been bestowed on her
by her own mother. And she recollects the day of her departure for

---

[22] Just as Kathleen gains a sense of renewal through writing (which then enables her
to abandon her novel project), so O'Faolain noted in her second autobiography *Almost
There* that *My Dream of You* "brought me up from underground. I've been my own
Orpheus" (O'Faolain 2003: 168).

Dublin and university life, when her family regrouped itself as a unit for the first and only time and she had her last 'real' conversation with her mother and her youngest brother, who later died from illness caused by neglect. From grieving for herself she progresses to mourning the lost opportunities, shattered desires, and pointlessly failed lives of her parents:

> Without expecting to, I started to cry. I cried and cried, soaking the pillow and the sheet under my neck. Tears poured from me, like blood from an artery. […] I was so sorry for my poor mother […] Even my father, I was sorry for. (O'Faolain 2001: 334)

At this point, then, Kathleen finally moves from her initial position of over-identification to LaCapra's "empathetic unsettlement". She garners enough strength to confront her most traumatic memory, repressed ever since her desperate flight from Ireland three decades earlier, of witnessing her mother's agony in a Catholic hospital, whose authorities refused to give her any medication or pain relief for uterine cancer because she was pregnant. Like Marianne Talbot a century before, her mother was sacrificed to the patriarchal imperative of child-bearing even unto death. As in Lloyd Jones's *Mister Pip*, examined by Dianne Sadoff in this collection, the 're-membering' of the mother's dying body ultimately exorcises the spectre that haunts the text (this volume: 186).

In approaching a sense of reconciliation with the past, Kathleen visits her brother Danny and his family, sharing an embrace "like [that among] survivors" (O'Faolain 2001: 182). Though the impact of childhood neglect and emotional trauma has left permanent marks on Danny too, who battles with a drink problem, she leaves the farm he took on from their uncle with a sense that, whatever mess her parents and her own generation have made of life, the family will continue: the farm "was always the Burkes' place. Before the Famine even, it was in our family" (O'Faolain 2001: 187). She stops blaming others and for the first time in her life embraces the legacy of maturity, age, and insight, impressing on her sister Nora, another escapee from home: "We're middle-aged women now and we have to forgive the past – for our own sakes […] And the way to do that is to see the parents – and to see ourselves – as *precious*. Just for having existed!" (O'Faolain 2001: 445) The novel ends with Kathleen's return journey to England: "Like Marianne. No home, like Marianne. No child, like Marianne. No lover. No occupation" (O'Faolain 2001: 446). Nor does she possess a completed neo-Victorian novel either. James's strictures on historical fiction, which always overshadowed her writing project, are now replaced by his affirmation of the centrality of a life shared with a community of others: "that was what Henry James said: we need never fear not to be good enough, if we are only social enough [James 1983: 124]. See, if I *tried* I would not end up in a basement again" (O'Faolain 2001: 444). This is why she rejects the idea of confining herself to a clandestine relationship with Shay: "We would never be out in the world together [...] any more than my mother and father had been. [...] We would have made our own Windsor, our own Shore Road" (O'Faolain 2001: 453).[23] In a first step towards building her new life out of the social basement, she will take charge of her former editor, Alex, who is mourning the death of his mother, his only companion in life, returning the care he had previously bestowed on her. Kathleen has come full circle from estrangement to personal engagement.

This developmental journey from rememory to reconciliation is possible only because Kathleen learns to reject her romanticising impulse and especially her inclination for trauma tourism. If, as Caruth argues, the "ability to recover the past is, in trauma, closely and paradoxically tied up [...] with the inability to have access to it" (Caruth 1996c: 152), O'Faolain's novel illustrates the complexities of the neo-Victorian endeavour to appropriate and possess the past through imaginative engagement with documentary materials, which themselves are narrative versions of a reality that must remain forever inaccessible. By making Kathleen confront her escapist desire and overcome it, O'Faolain problematises the "morbid cult of sentimentality and victimhood" that Carville defines as contemporary trauma culture's greatest challenge (Carville 2008: 56). In that she has

---

[23] Mrs Talbot was confined in Windsor before being released into the care of the Pagets; Shore Road is the street in which Kathleen's parents lived. As O'Faolain recorded in *Almost There*, she initially planned to conclude the novel with Kathleen accepting Shay's proposition, just as she herself has acquiesced in a similar situation with her lover Joseph, but "I discovered that under my own hands, Kathleen was changing"; "Kathleen's sheer busyness [...] made her incompatible with the passivity of the role I had planned for her" (2003: 147, 148).

her embrace a new and differently constituted affective relationship as a means of addressing the past, she also resists what David Lloyd calls the 'inward-turning decathexis or separation from that which has been lost' in today's communal historical mourning (Lloyd 2000: 221).

Acknowledgements

I am grateful to Evelyn Flanagan, Special Collections, and Ann Woulfe, both of University College Dublin, for their assistance with procuring a copy of the House of Lords *Judgment*; to Tony Ward, University of Hull, for advice on law sources; and to Scot Brewster, University of Salford, for drawing my attention to Seamus Heaney's "poetic dig". Special thanks go to Marie-Luise Kohlke for invaluable advice on trauma literature.

Bibliography

Arias, Rosario and Patricia Pulham (eds.). 2010 *Haunting and Spectrality in Neo-Victorian Fiction: Possessing the Past*. Basingstoke: Palgrave Macmillan.

Atwood, Margaret. 1994. *The Robber Bride*. London: Virago.

Brorfen, Elisabeth. 1998. *The Knotted Subject: Hysteria and Its Discontents*. Princeton, New Jersey: Princeton University Press.

Bulwer Lytton, Rosina. 1994. *A Blighted Life: A True Story* [1880]. Bristol: Thoemmes.

Carlyle, Thomas. 1899. 'The Nigger Question' [1849], in *Critical and Miscellaneous Essays*, 5 vols. London: Chapman and Hall, IV: 348-383.

Caruth, Cathy (ed.). 1996a. *Trauma: Explorations in Memory*. Baltimore: Johns Hopkins University Press.

——. 1996b. 'Introduction' to Part I, 'Trauma and Experience', in Caruth (1996a): 3-12.

——. 1996c. 'Introduction' to Part II, 'Recapturing the Past', in Caruth (1996a): 151-157.

Carville, Conor. 2008. '"Keeping That Wound Green": Irish Studies and Traumaculture', in Alcobia-Murphy, Shane (ed.), *What Rough Beasts? Irish and Scottish Studies in the New Millennium*. Newcastle: Cambridge Scholars Publishing: 45-71.

'Case of "Talbot v. Talbot"', *Hansard*, 28 February 1856, 140 cc1544-1563. Online at: http://hansard.millbanksystems.com/commons/1856/feb/28/case-of-talbot-v-talbot (consulted 28.11.2008).

Corporaal, Marguérite. 2009. 'Memories of the Great Famine and Ethnic Identity in Novels by Victorian Irish Women Writers', *English Studies*, 90(2) (April): 142-156.

De La Mare, Walter. 1912. *The Listeners and Other Poems*. London: Faber and Faber.

Donoghue, Emma. 2008. *The Sealed Letter*. Boston: Mariner Books, Houghton Mifflin Harcourt.

Dougherty, Jane Elizabeth. 2007. 'Nuala O'Faolain and the Unwritten Irish Girlhood', *New Hibernian Review/Iris Éireannach Nua*, 11(2) (Summer): 50-65.

Doyle, Roddy. 1993. *Paddy Clarke Ha Ha Ha*. London: Vintage.

Freud, Sigmund. 1966. *Project for a Scientific Psychology* [1895], vol.1 of *The Standard Edition of the Complete Psychological Works of Sigmund Freud* [1950] (tr. and ed. James Strachey, in collaboration with Anna Freud, assisted by Alix Stratchey and Alan Tyson). London: Hogarth Press.

Gilman, Charlotte Perkins. 1981. *The Yellow Wallpaper* [1892]. London: Virago.

Hamilton, Hugo. 2003. *The Speckled People*. London: Fourth Estate.

Heaney, Seamus. 1980. *Preoccupations: Selected Prose 1968-78*. London: Faber and Faber.

Heilmann, Ann, and Mark Llewellyn. 2010. *Neo-Victorianism: The Victorians in the Twenty-First Century, 1999-2009*. Basingstoke: Palgrave Macmillan.

High Court of Delegates. [1855.] 'Judgment Talbot v. Talbot', repr. from the Report appended to a Letter to the Honorable Justice Torrens, by John Padget, in Paget, Thomas Tertius. 1856. *A Letter to His Excellency the Lord Lieutenant of Ireland, on The Judgment of the High Court of Delegates in the Case of Talbot v. Talbot*. London: Ridgway, Blenkarn: 91-107.

Horne, Philip (ed.). 2000. *Henry James: A Life in Letters*. London: Penguin.

House of Lords. 1856. *Talbot v. Talbot, Judgment of the Lord Chancellor, Lord Brougham, and Lord St.Leonards, on the second reading of Talbot's Divorce Bill, May 22, 1856*. Dublin: UCD Library.

James, Henry. 1983. *Autobiography: A Small Boy and Others* (ed. Frederick W. Dupee). Princeton, New Jersey: Princeton University Press.

Keogh, W[illia]m. 1855. *Talbot v. Talbot: A Report of the Speech of Wm. Keogh, Esq., M.P., Solicitor General for Ireland, on Behalf of the Appellant, before the High Court of Delegates, January 8, 1855*. London: Thomas Blenkarn.

LaCapra, Dominick. 2001. *Writing History, Writing Trauma*. Baltimore: The Johns Hopkins University Press.

Langer, Lawrence L. 1988. 'The Dilemma of Choice in the Death Camps', in Rosenberg, Alan, and Gerald E. Myers (eds.), *Echoes from the Holocaust: Philosophical Reflections on a Dark Time*. Philadelphia: Temple University Press: 118-27.

Lloyd, David. 2000. 'Colonial Trauma / Postcolonial Recovery?', *Interventions* 2(2): 212-228.

——. 2005. 'The Indigent Sublime: Specters of Irish Hunger', *Representations* 92 (Fall): 152-185.

Lockerbie, Catherine. 2001. 'Woman on the Verge', *New York Times*, 4 March: 14.

Martineau, Harriet. 2001. *Letters from Ireland* [1852]. Dublin: Irish Academic Press.

McCourt, Frank. 1996. *Angela's Ashes*. London: Harper Perennial.

McMullen, Kim. 2004. 'New Ireland / Hidden Ireland: Reading Recent Irish Fiction', *Kenyon Review* 26(2) (Spring): 126-148.

Morrison, Toni. 1987. *Beloved*. London: Picador.

O'Faolain, Nuala. 1996. *Are You Somebody?: The Accidental Memoir of a Dublin Woman*. New York: Hendry Holt and Co.

——. 2001. *My Dream of You*. London: Penguin.

——. 2003. *Almost There*. New York: Riverhead Books.

O'Kane Mara, Miriam. 2007. '(Re)producing Identity and Creating Famine in Nuala O'Faolain's *My Dream of You*', *Studies in Contemporary Fiction* 48(2): 197-216.

Paget, Thomas Tertius. 1855. *Talbot v. Talbot: A Statement of Facts*. London: Thomas Blenkarn.

——. 1856. *A Letter to His Excellency the Lord Lieutenant of Ireland, on The Judgment of the High Court of Delegates in the Case of Talbot v. Talbot*. London: Ridgway, Blenkarn.

Seltzer, Mark. 1997. 'Wound Culture: Trauma in the Pathological Public Sphere', *October* **80**: 3-26.

Shanley, Mary Lyndon. 1989. *Feminism, Marriage, and the Law in Victorian England*. Princeton, New Jersey: Princeton University Press.

Showalter, Elaine. 1987. *The Female Malady: Women, Madness and English Culture, 1830-1980*. London: Virago.

Sutherland, John. 1995. *Victorian Fiction: Writers, Publishers, Readers*. Basingstoke: Palgrave.

'Talbot v. Talbot', *Times*, 1 March 1856, 9, issue 22304, col. E; 3 March, 11, issue 22305, col. F; 6 March, 11, issue 22308, col. E;

'Talbot's Divorce', *Times*, 13 March, 10, issue 22314, col. D; 15 March, 5, issue 22316, col. D; 5 May, 10, issue 22359, col. B; 23 May, 5, issue 22375, col. A.

Upton, W.C. 1882. *Uncle Pat's Cabin: Life Among the Agricultural Labourers of Ireland*. Dublin: Gill & Son.

Unmanning Exoticism: The Breakdown
of Christian Manliness in *The Book of the Heathen*

Elisabeth Wesseling

Abstract:
This chapter interprets Robert Edric's *The Book of the Heathen* (2000) as a
contemporary historical novel that criticises orientalism, or, rather, exoticism, by
focusing on the ideals of masculinity that bolster up the exoticist project. Edric's
novel registers the breakdown of the moral ideal of Christian manliness within the
brutal colonial conditions of the late nineteenth-century Congo. Colonialism and
Christian manliness are shown to be fundamentally at odds with each other, contrary
to the Victorian inclination to view them as mutually enhancing forces. The
disillusionment of its leading characters unfolds a specific perspective on colonial
trauma as profound moral disorientation. Although the novel evokes a world that
existed more than a hundred years ago, subverting a moral ideal that may seem quaint
to contemporary readers at first sight, this is, in fact, an urgent and topical work that
exemplifies our profound complicity within the (post-)colonial order. This novel pre-
empts illusions of self-righteousness and moral superiority vis-à-vis the colonial past,
as well as nostalgic escapes into bygone periods.

Keywords: anthropology/ethnography,   cannibalism,   Christian   manliness,
colonialism, Congo, Robert Edric, exoticism, imperial romance, neo-Victorianism,
post-colonialism, trauma.

*****

Robert Edric's *The Book of the Heathen* (2000), a historical novel
about Anglo-Belgian rivalry in the Congo around 1897, has been
plotted as a suspense story, winding its way back slowly through a
puzzling series of events, until it finally climaxes in a horrifying
dénouement. Its graphic description of a lengthy torture scene situates
this work squarely within the genre of the "neo-Victorian trauma
novel" (Kohlke 2009: 25). Narratives in this vein outdo each other in
detailed representations of atrocity, up to the point at which ethical
questions concerning the purpose and admissibility of representing the

physical pain of others become unavoidable. What is the point of locating violent conflict in the colonial past, considering the fact that our own day and time certainly are not short of brutalities either? Why dwell on the details of physical mutilation at such length, exposing both author and audience to the charge of taking voyeuristic pleasure in watching the pain of others? Similar issues may be raised with regard to the obsession with sexual perversion in neo-Victorian fiction. Why credit the Victorians, of all people, with sustained indulgence in prostitution, an adventurous inclination to gay escapades beyond the pale of the contemporary sexual imagination (as in Sarah Waters's writing, for example), and an overall predilection for sado-masochistic excess? In short, why are neo-Victorian representations of sex and violence so often 'over the top'? Recent scholarship on neo-Victorian literature provides us with the beginning of an answer to these questions.

1.   Emotional Anemia and the Exoticist Cure

According to Marie-Luise Kohlke, the neo-Victorian preoccupation with sexual perversion and imperial violence may be regarded as a form of neo-Orientalism. Orientalist fantasies, which used to be projected upon the remote, little known places on the globe that were not yet tainted by the blight of industrial modernity, are now displaced along a temporal axis (Kohlke 2008: 351-354). It has often been argued that the homogenising regime of modernity transforms citizens into producers and consumers of commodities at the expense of suppressing their spontaneous, pre-reflexive drives and inclinations.[1] Modernisation is thought to go hand in hand with a deterioration of our capacity for intense feeling and emotion and a flattening out of authenticity and individuality. Ongoing civilisation demands its toll in the eclipse of passion, or so the argument goes. In compensation,

---

[1] This critique of modernity reverberates all throughout twentieth-century Theory. Beginning with Sigmund Freud's *Das Unbehagen in der Kultur* (1930) *(Civilization and its Discontents)*, and followed up by Norbert Elias, *Ueber den Prozess der Zivilisation* (1939) *(The Civilizing Process)*, it became a central theme in the work of the Frankfurt Schule, most notably in Theodor Adorno and Max Horkheimer's *Dialektik der Aufklärung* (1947) *(Dialectic of Enlightenment)*. From that point onwards, it was further developed by advocates of the counterculture of the sixties, especially Herbert Marcuse, *One-Dimensional Man* (1964). Lastly, it continued to impact on postmodern thinkers such as Fredric Jameson, *Postmodernism, or the Cultural Logic of Late Capitalism* (1991).

modern man grows obsessed with the 'primitive' regions of this world, where he might still catch a glimpse of the primal energies he was forced to relinquish for the sake of progress. The Orient is constructed as a place where *eros* and *thanatos* still reign supreme. In this exotic locale, the uncivilised heathens are thought to indulge their sexual and aggressive impulses free from qualms or inhibitions (Said 1978). Now that the world has been mapped, colonised and modernised on a global scale, however, it has become increasingly difficult to project exoticising fantasies on specific geopolitical regions. In keeping with the dictum that "the past is a foreign country",[2] we now turn to previous epochs in order seek momentary relief from the discontents of civilisation. Judging from the popularity of neo-Victorian fiction, the Victorian epoch seems to have substituted exotic locales as an imaginary realm that is to compensate us for our supposed loss of heart-felt experience. In other words, the contemporary fascination with the Victorian age is a form of nostalgic regret over what we thought we have lost. Following this line of argumentation, the preoccupation with excessive sexual perversion and violence in neo-Victorian trauma novels may then be regarded as rather extreme measures for making the audience feel at least *something*, whether good or bad. Having said as much, the exact nature of this nostalgia begs further analysis, for, contrary to what is commonly thought, nostalgia is not necessarily a simplistic, reactionary or escapist emotion (see Gutleben 2001: 185-217), but comes in many different modalities. The purpose of this chapter, then, is to problematise the nostalgic quality of *The Book of the Heathen* and to probe the exact nature of the orientalist, or more accurately "exoticist",[3] imagination in this novel.

Exoticism was paramount in nineteenth-century adventure fiction and travel writing ("imperial romance" in short).[4] These genres

---

[2] In all likelihood, this saying derives from the opening sentence of Leslie Poles Hartley's novel *The Go-Between* (1953): "The past is a foreign country: they do things differently there."

[3] I prefer Chris Bongie's concept of "exoticism" to Said's "orientalism", because the latter concept is, however vaguely, still attached to the so-called Middle Eastern and Maghreb regions of the globe, while Edric's novel is set in central Africa. Exoticism is not specifically associated with the Orient, but may be applied to any non-Western region and therefore is the more comprehensive term.

[4] This widely used term, introduced by Patrick Brantlinger (1990), is useful in that it emphasises that both adventure fiction and travel writing articulate the same narrative

revolve around heroic attempts to escape from the standardisation of modern mass society through a quest for "authentic experience" and "sovereign individuality" (Bongie 1991: 5). A traveller-explorer may either seek to transcend stultifying modernity by re-asserting his individuality in a confrontation with the wilderness, a contest that is usually concluded by a return to civilisation. Or he may struggle to cast off the shackles of modern society altogether because he is erotically attracted to the other, seeking a more permanent assimilation to what he believes the other to be. Chris Bongie terms these related but different tendencies as "imperial exoticism" and "exoticizing exoticism" (Bongie 1991). Needless to say, both fantasy structures are oriented towards the psychic and social needs of modern man, rather than the subjectivity of foreign peoples and are, in that sense, equally imperialistic.

Although Bongie does not pay much attention to the matter, exoticism not only feeds on racial and ethnic difference, but also on differences in gender and class. Exoticism demands a story of conquest or seduction, focused on a feminised object (the Orient is a metaphorical woman) while featuring a hero who personifies masculine values. If this hero does not already have a high social status from the very start, he is bound to earn his social ascendancy in the course of the story through his exploits of bravery.

I would like to contend that *The Book of the Heathen* unravels exoticism by de-naturalising the gender dimension of this narrative scheme. This mode of subversion chimes in with the ethics of the epoch in which this novel is set. Gender concepts were imbued with strong moral connotations during the Victorian age. In fact, Victorian public morality was premised on idealised images of masculinity. Accordingly, Edric's neo-Victorian critique of the exoticist project disrupts the typically Victorian intertwinement of morality and manliness by exposing moral debasement within the male-dominated world of European colonialism. Since this is a historical novel, however, we first need to investigate the productive tension between fact and fiction that defines the genre, before broaching its ethical problematic.

---

fantasy structures, in spite of the fact that the second body of literature purports to have been produced in the documentary mode, while the first counts as fiction.

2.   Historical Background

The story of *The Book of the Heathen* is focalised from beginning to end by a representative of the British upper class, the privileged aristocrat James Russell Frasier. In the opening scenes, Russell presents himself as a disoriented, traumatised man, while the subsequent story gradually works towards the revelation of the horrors that caused this state of mind. The story is rendered in a terse, impassioned style, divulging scattered clues to the reader without much comment or explication. In effect, the text could be said to replicate the way that trauma ruptures narrative and the witness' faculty of making sense of his overwhelming experience. Consequently, we have to piece these clues together ourselves by reading between the lines, in order to reconstruct this novel's highly convoluted plot, like an analyst deciphering the traces of trauma.

As is customary in historical novels, Edric explicitly situates his story in real historical place and time: "Concessionary Station, Ukassa Falls, 1897". The Ukassa Falls are located in East Congo, in the heart of the wilderness, far away from the Atlantic Coast. Around 1897,[5] the infamous rubber trade was gathering momentum, while atrocity stories about the ruthless exploitation of native labourers had begun to filter out of the colony, casting serious doubt upon the professed humanitarian intentions of King Leopold II (1835-1909) of civilising the Congo and liberating the natives from 'Arab' slave traders.[6] In 1895, the legitimacy of the Congo Free State was put to the test when the colonial regime executed a British merchant, Charles Henry Stokes. Stokes was hanged after a summary trial that charged him with collaboration with slave traders. Public outcry over this event in the international press has gone down into history as the so-called "Stokes affair" (see Louis 1965: 572-584). The charges levelled against Stokes were patently sham, in the sense that the Congo Free State itself was guilty of a duplicitous attitude towards the slave merchants, sometimes competing and at other times collaborating with them in the common project of exploiting the territory's precious

---

[5] In 1891, Dunlop invented the inflatable tyre, while Henry Ford introduced the mass production of automobiles in 1896. These technological innovations generated a soaring demand for rubber and, for a while, Leopold's colony was the only area in the world that could supply this precious commodity.

[6] These so-called 'Arabs' were really Africans, mostly from Zanzibar, or 'Swahili', as they would be referred to nowadays.

resources of ivory, rubber and human labour. Although King Leopold II had committed himself to the suppression of the Congo slave trade during the Berlin Conference over the partition of Africa in 1885, this did not keep him from appointing the fabulously wealthy and politically influential Zanzibari slave trader Hamed bin Mohammed bin Juma bin Rajab el Murjebi, alias Tippu Tip, to the post of governor of East Congo from 1887 to 1892. While the slave trade was indeed suppressed in West Congo, it was condoned in the East, both during and after Tippu Tip's rule (see H. Wesseling 2005). When the demand for labour became truly pressing around 1900, the Congo Free State even bought slaves from Swahili traders in order to keep up with the international demand for rubber. Just as importantly, the system of forced labour that the Congolese were subjected to by the colonial regime was an equally vile, if not worse, form of slavery in itself.[7] Clearly, then, Stokes's execution was a show trial that was meant to demonstrate to the powerful British empire who was in charge of this particular part of the world. The Stokes affair was probably the first major incident to drive the message home that the Congo Free State, which Britain condoned as a buffer state against French colonial power, had developed a political and economic dynamic that could not be readily controlled.

This is the historical background against which the plot of *The Book of the Heathen* unfolds. Strikingly, the novel hardly breathes a word about what most authors focus on when writing about this time and place, namely the gruesome terror of the 'red rubber' period. The Concessionary Station at Ukassa Falls belongs to a British Concession

---

[7] In order to meet the ever increasing demand for rubber, King Leopold and his Concession companies resorted to extreme measures. The natives were forced to venture into the jungle in search of productive rubber vines. As the exploitation of rubber became ever more intense, they had to penetrate deeper and deeper into the woods, sometimes marching for several weeks before they could finally tap a vine. The woods were often swampy, and the men could not easily find food there. So as to make sure that the villagers would return with an ample supply of rubber, their wives were taken hostage by the so-called *Force Publique*, King Leopold's private army, consisting of armed native conscripts commanded by European officers. The *Force Publique* placed 'sentries' in almost every village, who terrorised the native population by floggings, mutilations, rapes, hostage-takings and executions. Soon enough, the Congo became one of the greatest economic successes and one of the gravest humanitarian disasters in the history of European colonisation.

company that exploits a stone quarry. There is only a brief reference to a Belgian company across the river, which is much more profitable than its British counterpart (undoubtedly because it exploits rubber), but no mention whatsoever is made of rubber vines, hostage huts, chain gangs, death groves, mutilations or shootings. Edric has chosen to pass over the economic dimension of colonial exploitation in order to focus on its scientific and religious underpinnings. The major characters in this novel are scientists, missionaries and administrators.

Both Frasier and his friend Nicholas Frere, who has been confined to a Belgian jail as he awaits trial for his alleged murder of a native girl, are successful, well-published scientists. Frasier is a cartographer, while Frere is a naturalist with a burgeoning interest in ethnography. Both having been beguiled into embarking on a career in the tropics by the exoticist fantasies propagated by Victorian travel writing and adventure fiction,[8] Frasier and Frere dream of going where no (Western) man has gone before, in order to make their name as heroic discoverers of unknown regions and cultures. In short, they dream of becoming a second Sir Henry Morton Stanley (1841-1904) or David Livingstone (1813-1873), as did so many other Victorian males swayed by the lure of Africa's 'Heart of Darkness', seeking the confrontation with the unknown in order to finally subdue and control it, out of a thirst for truly fulfilling experience and a desire to distinguish themselves from the common herd.

As soon as Frasier and Frere have entered into The Company's service, however, they begin to realise the extent of their delusion: "He [Frere] had expected a wilderness in which to wander, but instead he found only a place already long since sacrificed to the gods of profit and loss" (Edric 2001: 118). Rather than sallying forth into "the Great Unknown" (Edric 2001: 63), they are only allowed to tread the paths staked out for them by The Company. Clearly, modernity has managed to reproduce itself in the colonies, with the result that modern *ennui* also comes to dominate life in the Congo. Feelings of emptiness and meaninglessness begin to dog the two friends, but they are not yet willing to give up on their heroic dreams.

---

[8] I am referring to the Victorian writings by David Livingstone, Henry Morton Stanley, Charles Kingsley, George Alfred Henty, R.M. Ballantyne, as well as to later imperial romances that became quite popular during the closing decades of the nineteenth century, such as the works of Robert Louis Stevenson, Rudyard Kipling and H. Rider Haggard (see Daly 2007).

Soon enough Frere, who is definitely the more adventurous of the two,[9] begins to resort to extreme measures in order to alleviate his debilitating sense of boredom and disappointment. He picks up the habit of sneaking out on furtive expeditions to reputed cannibal infested regions, occasionally dragging Frasier along. Like many other ethnographers of his time, Frere grows obsessed with cannibalism. Cannibalism functioned as the ultimate signifier of otherness, as well as the justification of the civilising mission *par excellence* within the imperialist imaginary, and colonial regimes relied on science to produce irrefutable proof of it in the regions they wanted to exploit.[10] Indeed, this was the fundamental rationale of nineteenth-century anthropology and ethnography (Goldman 1999).

However, the scientific legitimation for Frere's scopophilic urges cannot fully account for its obsessive intensity, compelling him to engage in risky behaviour. The scientific thirst for knowledge is obviously enhanced in Frere's case by an a-rational, erotic attraction to ultimate otherness, highlighted by his self-confessed willingness to even participate in cannibalistic rituals if necessary. In the overall absence of eligible female partners in general and of his fiancée in particular, Frere's sexual impulses seem to have taken a strange turn. One could say that his exoticism evolves from 'imperial' to 'exoticising' in the course of the story. As The Company does not really challenge him to prove his mettle, his allegiances shift from an identification with 'civilisation' to an overriding desire to literally assimilate himself to savagery. Because Frasier does not really share Frere's penchant for cannibalism, Frere finally decides to enter the lion's den alone. He stays away for fifty-one days at a stretch, until he is brought back to the Concessionary Station by a local authority called Hammad, a character obviously modelled on Tippu Tip.[11] Frere

---

[9] Frere's greater spunk and ambition have everything to do with his lower, middle class social status. Contrary to Frasier, who has it all (the name, the titles, the history, the land, the property), Frere has to 'earn' a high social status through his achievements.

[10] The problem was that the evidence produced was nearly always refutable (see Arens 1979), as is also the case in Edric's novel.

[11] As a fictional counterpart to Tippu Tip, Hammad constitutes a bit of an anachronism here, as Tippu Tip withdrew himself from the East Congo around 1890. As a symbol for the un-abating presence of similar slave traders in the region, however, Hammad's presence here is perfectly appropriate.

is handed over to the Belgian authorities, who appear to have good reasons for treating him as a criminal.

Frere and Frasier are balanced by another couple whose lives have also become closely intertwined, namely the Belgian Cornelius van Klees, quartermaster of the Concessionary Station at Ukassa Falls, and his compatriot Father Klein, both from Ypres. The Jesuit priest embodies another widely shared feature of neo-Victorian fiction, namely sexual depravity. Klein terrorises his congregation of (mostly) female converts, maintaining downright sado-masochistic relationships with these former female slaves, most of whom, once freed, are reduced to making their living by prostitution, re-enacting the sexual abuses of slavery. Klein is pathologically obsessed with the sexual promiscuity of others, regarding it his duty to castigate the sinners in highly theatrical ways, until the demons of lasciviousness have been publicly exorcised. He feels he has the right to intervene in Cornelius' affair with a native woman who lived at his mission post, selling her on to Hammad's Zanzibari brothels, while baptising the fruit of this relationship 'Magdalene'. The child's name indicates that the sins of the fathers will be visited upon the children as long as Klein can help it, in a version of deliberately induced transgenerational trauma. Perversely, Klein is a close associate of Hammad the slave merchant; he sells enslaved women to Hammad like cattle and disposes of their lives as he sees fit. This has a profoundly traumatic impact on the life of Cornelius, who not only looses the woman he loves, but also his child, who supposedly died of a fever. At least, that is what Klein told him, though there is nothing to prove the truth of his assertion, since Klein decided to bury the illicit offspring of this *métissage*, or miscegenation, in an unmarked grave. The two men are united by a deeply felt hatred for each other, Klein envying Cornelius' love life, while Cornelius blames Klein for the loss of the woman whom, in defiance of prevailing racial ideologies, he intended to marry.

Klein is severely disgruntled over the fact that his mission post has been cut off from the Concessionary Station at Ukassa Falls, leaving him to fend for himself and to look for other sources of protection and financial support. It does not take much imagination to realise that this must have been the work of the quartermaster Cornelius, so as to revenge the loss of the woman he loved. Klein, the text implies, eventually strikes back at Cornelius by also depriving him of his daughter, a murder for which Frere may be held to account. Arguably, Klein's crime and its traumatic after-effects 'haunt' Edric's novel as much as does Frere's unspecified offence. For the latter's actual 'crime' is only revealed in the final pages of the novel, when Frere 'testifies' to Frasier, just before he is sent off to be judged by a Belgian court residing in Stanleyville. Within the context of Anglo-Belgian competition over dominance in the Congo region, the fact that a representative of the mighty British Empire is subjected to the jurisdiction of the lesser colonial power Belgium is particularly humiliating.

Edric's decision to focus on cannibalism, rather than the inequities of the rubber trade, is significant. While the red rubber period was specific to the history of the Congo, cannibalism belongs to the staple of colonial discourse *per se*. There are few, if no colonised peoples who have not been accused of some form of cannibalism or another in the history of their encounters with European colonisers. No matter whether dealing with the natives of South America, the Caribbean, India, New Zealand, Australia or Africa, the ultimate truth about indigenous peoples was always sought in the exposure of their reputed cannibalism. Cannibalism did not just mark the absolute difference between Western citizens and primitive savages, but it also underlined the need to erase the otherness of the other. It serves as the most solid proof of the depravity of the heathen one could wish for, and colonial regimes relied on science to produce this proof (Goldmann 1999: 1-27). Cultures that cultivated cannibalism could not be condoned and needed to be eradicated as thoroughly as possible by missionary projects of conversion and/or forcible administrative and judicial suppression. Translated into the terms of Edric's novel, one could say that it is the ethnographer Frere's task to produce the rationale for the missionary labours of Klein.[12] In the tangled web of *The Book of the Heathen*, Frere's

---

[12] Frere's Francophone name means both 'brother' and 'friar'. Both connotations are to the point. He is a brother to Frasier in more ways than one, as he is betrothed to Frasier's sister Caroline and therefore about to become his brother-in-law. Furthermore, he figures as Frasier's alter ego, as is also indicated by the close alliteration between their two names. Lastly, one could also interpret the name in a Baudelairean sense, as a reference to the reader (see the closing line of 'Au lecteur' from *Les fleurs du mal* (1857): "Hypocrite lecteur – mon semblable – mon frère!" The whole poem, which argues that *ennui* is a worse monster than the very devil himself or whatever evil we may conjure up, directly bears on the problematic of this

ethnographical field trips do indeed contribute to Klein's schemes in the end, but in a highly twisted way. Deliberately seeking out the haunts of tribes with a reputation of cannibalism, Frere eventually finds what he was looking for, and much more than that, for one also gets the disconcerting impression that the 'cannibals' were equally intent on finding him.

Frere confides to Frasier that he fell seriously ill during his solo expedition and was barely conscious for several days at a stretch, until he finally woke up to set his eyes on three 'Aruwimi', a tribe renowned for its cannibalism, according to Frere. Strangely enough, they seem to mean him no harm. On the contrary, they revive him of their own accord with food and drink. Frere guesses that they have their mind set on something else, which eventually arrives in a canoe steered by one of Hammad's men. This "feather-gatherer" brings the three men a young girl, a seven-year old, according to Frere's estimations, "considerably paler than any of the men, another tribe completely" (Edric 2001: 312, 313). Frere is then made to witness how the girl is mauled and mutilated, until he feels compelled to put her out of her misery with his last bullet, after which he lapses back into unconsciousness. He next wakes to find himself being taken into custody on the charge of having murdered the feather-gatherer's 'daughter'. In the concluding scene of the novel, Frere is transported to Stanleyville by steamer, where a show trial awaits him that bears a close resemblance to the Stokes affair. As was the case with Stokes, Frere's trial obviously does not aim to dispense justice, but to show who is in charge of this region, namely the unholy alliance between Belgian colonials and Zanzibari slave traders, who mean to monopolise the profitable trade in the Congo 'Free' State as much as they possibly can, a trade they view Frere as having interfered with by risking its exposure.

The details of this drama suggest that Klein and Hammad must have had a hand in its enactment. The mangled child has the same age as the age at which van Klees' daughter supposedly died, and she is of light skin, hence in all likelihood a child of mixed blood.

novel. Baudelaire suggests that the 'hypocritical reader' is closely familiar with *ennui* and that he is drawn to the moral depravity of *Les fleurs du mal* to escape from its clutches. Frere's name reminds us of the fact we are implicated in his moral debasement as well. The third meaning of 'friar' links Frere to Klein and is indicative of the plot in which Klein involves Frere.

Klein, then, did not just sell the mother, but also the daughter to Hammad, who uses the child to consolidate his political position in conspiracy with the Belgian colonials, who are keen on diminishing British influence.[13] On his diverse trips and excursions, Frere manifested his obsession with cannibalism in ways that could not have escaped the notice of those in control over the region. The possibility presents itself that Frere may have been framed in a political plot. In this case, Frere did not witness an authentic cannibalistic ritual, but a show that was put on especially for him. One might stipulate that Hammad and his men took advantage of his long spell of unconsciousness to transport him to the spot where the 'cannibal feast' is eventually staged.

In any case, one is bound to observe that Frere did not actually watch a cannibalistic act (the girl was not eaten), but rather a torture scene, which he *assumed* to be part of an elaborate cannibalistic ritual. It is quite likely that Hammad's men made a concerted effort to live up to the ethnographer's expectations of what cannibalism must be like: a cruel, horrifying, merciless and elaborate ritual, in short pure savagery. Rather than being the passive and innocent witness of cannibalism, Frere seems to become its inadvertent producer, through what Patricia Yaeger would describe as his eagerness to 'consume' the sufferings of others – in this case victims' cannibalistic consumption – in an invidious self-perpetuating (inter)cultural 'circulation' of trauma. In some sense, Frere's brutal colonial world resembles the postmodern "academic world" of trauma studies, with its writers and readers busily engaged in "consuming trauma – eating, swallowing, perusing, consuming, exchanging, circulating, creating professional connections – through its stories about the dead" (Yaeger 2002: 29). Too often, Yaeger suggests, participants in these processes fail to reflect on the ethical implications of their practice and ask the crucial question: "How are we allowed to taste the dead's bodies, to put their lives in our mouths?" (Yaeger 2002: 29)

---

[13] One could also argue the other way round in order to warrant the plausibility of the plot, in which Frere seems to have been entrapped. How did the feather-gatherer get hold of Cornelius' daughter? He must have received her from Hammad. How did Hammad come to have the girl in his possession? He must have bought her from Klein. As both the feather-gatherer and the Aruwimi are too poor and insignificant to be in a position to buy slaves and dispose of them as they see fit, they must have received orders from Hammad as to how to deal with the girl.

Once in jail, Frere comes to realise that his supposedly innocuous scientific desire to observe and discover (to the extent of engaging in an act of participatory observation if necessary) has never been innocent in the first place. Rather than exploring the subjectivity of the native habitants of foreign regions, all Western ethnography seems to do is to project its own obsessions, fears and desires onto the exoticised other, which is an act of violence *per se*, even if no blood is shed. How violent these fantasies actually are is literally 'fleshed out' by the Aruwimi tribesmen, who stage the worst nightmares of the colonisers. The (likely) frame-up of the indigenous people is a curious variation on Homi Bhabha's concept of "colonial mimicry", that is, "the desire for a reformed, recognizable Other, *as a subject of a difference that is almost the same, but not quite"* (Bhabha 1994: 85, original emphasis). In other words, colonialism exerts pressure on native populations to conform to the colonials, but not fully, for that would undermine the hierarchy between coloniser and colonised. Here, something else happens: the Aruwimi conform not to what the colonials want them to be, but to what they fear them be, with equally destabilising effects. Once Frere has made the crucial move of giving in to his perverse scopophilia, there is no turning back to morally responsible behaviour anymore. All he is left with is the "choiceless choice" (Langer 1982: 67-131) of either killing the victimised girl himself or watching her being killed slowly by tribesmen. This might go some way to explaining why Frere makes no effort whatsoever to exculpate himself, knowing himself to be guilty, no matter what the charges may be.

The final upshot of this intricate plot is an overall loss of moral integrity, at least where the male characters are concerned. Klein has defiled the cloth by affiliating himself to the slave trade; Cornelius comes to realise that he should never have abandoned his mistress and child at the mission post in the first place; Frere has become an agent in the death of the child, while the servants of the law conspire with a slave trader, giving precedence to profit over justice. To top it all off, Frasier proves to be utterly incapable of protecting his friend against the fate that awaits him, in spite of his high social rank and considerable scientific achievements. He too becomes a trauma victim by proxy, implicated in the barbarity of colonial power that (re)produces itself through what it claims to disavow. The men, then, all soil their hands in one way or another, while the women (who in Edric's novel are all indigenous women) are victimised. The reading public, finally, is severely compromised as well. Frere's voyeuristic urge to witness a cannibal scene manoeuvres the readers of Edric's novel into the position of "trauma tourists" or "tourists of history" (Sturken 2007). Trauma tourists seek diversion from a relatively peaceful (and possibly boring) present by visiting spectacular sites of violent historical conflict and atrocity, such as Civil War, WWI and WWII battlefields, the Auschwitz concentration camp, or Ground Zero, for far more dubious purposes than the ethical ones motivating the 'ideal' visitor. The latter visits such sites to self-consciously participate in personal or collective acts of mourning and commemoration, which counteract the wilful forgetting of past offences and suffering, while also struggling for some sort of historical knowledge and understanding of the associated events. In contrast, trauma tourists are, in effect, thrill seekers, who view such sites in terms of historical drama and spectacle, in which they seek to inject themselves vicariously, exploiting the pain of others as a mere pastime. Edric's novel positions the reader precariously between these two locations and subjectivities, inviting us to reflect on the complex reader motivations and responses engaged in neo-Victorian traumatic re-enactments. Again, we are led to ask: what purpose does the overall disgrace in the novel serve?

3.   Manliness at Stake
The corruption of the colonisers in *The Book of the Heathen*, I want to propose, can be interpreted as a neo-Victorian critique of exoticism that undermines the ideals of masculinity on which it was based, more specifically, the moral ideal of Christian manliness. This ethical framework, also called "manly Christianity", "manly morality," or "muscular Christianity", is central to both the Victorian age and Edric's historical novel, which does not really represent the shaping events, but rather the manners, morals and mindset of *fin-de-siècle* imperialism.[14] First propagated by Charles Kingsley, this ideal attempted to construct a counter-image to the disreputable association

---

[14] The first three terms are basically synonyms and were used interchangeably by the advocates of Christian manliness. The term "muscular Christianity", however, is a derogatory expression that was used by Kingsley's detractors, such as Leslie Stephen.

of Christianity with docility, submission, effeminacy and weakness.[15] These effeminate connotations of Christianity were conducive to its increasing marginalisation in public life and its relegation to the 'feminine' private sphere. Kingsley and his detractors struggled to reclaim Christianity as a powerful public force of social reform by endowing it with an outspokenly masculine image.

Kingsley combined anthropology with theology by taking God's incarnation in a male body as the cornerstone of his ethics. If God chose the male body as his earthly abode, then, he reasoned, there must be a redemptive dimension to man's embodiment, including his physical drives and needs, that is, man's aggressive and sexual impulses. It was a sin to block the flow of manly *thumos*, Kingsley felt, considering the fact that God had created man that way. Masculine physical energy was a force that could be mobilised for useful social purposes, such as combating the evils of slavery or the capitalist exploitation of the working class. Christian manliness was an activist ideal, in that it propagated the belief that the world could be shaped and controlled through men who combined physical vigour with moral strength. The manly Christian naturally aspired to go out into the world in order to change it for the better. Accordingly, the ideal took root within the contexts of social reform movements, such as the missionary movement, Christian Socialism, and Boy Scouts organisations, all promoting qualities such as moral resolution, stamina, boldness, authority, stoic patience and aggressive energy. From Kingley and his supporters' perspective, these virtues could be useful to the reformation of society if channelled in the right direction.

Kingsley and kindred souls, such as Thomas Hughes, constructed a repertoire of manly virtues by eclectically amalgamating bits and pieces drawn from diverse cultural sources. Initially, they sought for guidance in the Bible itself, stressing the more vigorous aspects of Christ, who drove merchants and traders out of the temple by the strength of his arm. They also cherished a strong predilection for the writings of St. Paul, who frequently employed military and

---

[15] Although Kingsley was extremely influential, this does not mean that the propagation of Christian manliness was, so to speak, a one-man show. On the contrary, the close association between manliness and morality was widespread and deeply felt on both sides of the Atlantic. See Mangan and Walvin 1987 for a highly informative overview of the widespread dissemination of manly Christianity; so too Hall 1994.

athletic metaphors in order to describe the Christian life. Secondly, Christian manliness drew inspiration from Classical antiquity, that is, from the ideal of a sound mind in a sound body (or *kaloskagathos*), which endowed sports and games with great dignity and importance. Thirdly, moral manliness tinkered with medieval notions of chivalry and honour, structured around militarism, feudalism and rigid gender roles. The honour ethic extolled strength and courage on the battlefield, as well as care for and protection of the weak: women, children, the aged and disabled Lastly, Christian manliness identified itself with aristocratic martial virtues that were also embraced by the upwardly mobile middle class. As Norman Vance sums up the heterogeneous concept:

> For the purposes of the present discussion 'manliness' can be summarized as physical manliness, ideas of chivalry and gentlemanliness, and moral manliness, all of which tend to incorporate something of the patriotic and military qualities which 'manliness' may also connote. (Vance 1985: 10)

Christian manliness also had its enemies, of course. According to Vance, manly morality was formulated in opposition to effeminacy, rather than womanliness (Vance 1985: 113-120). Kingsley was a staunch opponent of Roman Catholic celibacy, cherishing an almost mystical belief in the sanctification of married love, including sexuality, as a road to God. Moreover, he adhered to the well-established Victorian notion that manliness needed the corrective or civilising influence of womanliness in order to prevent it from degenerating into mere brutal force. Kingsley associated effeminacy not so much with women, but with metropolitan modernity. The industrial, capitalist world undercut the athletic, robust manliness that was the stuff of true goodness in Kingsley's view. His support of empire must be seen in the light of his critique of modern mass society. In the colonies, one could still gain access to the primitive wilderness where a man could prove his mettle. Degeneration and modernisation went hand in hand from the perspective of muscular Christianity, and therefore it was imperative that British men were provided with the opportunity to recover their primal energy in imperial frontier territories (see Wee 1994).

Significantly, the two men to which he dedicated his historical novel *Westward Ho!* (1855) were an aggressive imperialistic conqueror and a missionary, who did not shun the use of violence if needs be, namely Sir James Brooke, the Rajah of Sarawak (1803-1868), and George Augustus Selwyn, Bishop of New Zealand and Lichfield (1809-1878). Kingsley credited these worthies with the display of a specific type of "English virtue, at once manful and godly, practical and enthusiastic, prudent and self-sacrificing" (Kingsley 1989: epigraph), which in his view, they had inherited from the Elizabethans.

In other words, Christian manliness fed into "imperial exoticism" and vice versa, through a shared critique of modernity and a joint valorisation of male heroism, constructing a rich cultural repertoire for fleshing out the heroes of colonial exploration and conquest. As such, Christian manliness exerted a strong impact on imperial romance, most notably on juvenile adventure fiction written by authors such as George Henty and R.M. Ballantyne, including the numerous missionary tales that showcased the heroic exploits of missionaries abroad, sporting titles such as *Missionary Heroes, Missionary Martyrs*, and so forth.[16] Such stories were expressly produced for the purpose of inspiring new generations of young men to take up the civilising mission, providing them with edifying exempla of Christian heroes (see Kearney 1983). Christian manliness, then, could be embodied by a large array of social roles and professions, such as the family man, the school teacher, the soldier, the traveller-explorer and the missionary. Kingsley also considered the practice of science as a manly and morally uplifting occupation. Science implied the cultivation of moral and intellectual courage, Kingsley felt: "And therefore we may say that what knowledge of Nature we have – and we have very little – we owe to the courage of those men – and they have been very few – who have been inspired to face Nature boldly [...]" (Kingsley 1880: 249, original parentheses). In fact, Kingsley himself was a devoted naturalist.

Edric revokes Christian manliness through the distinctive features of Frasier and Frere, who seem expressly cut out so as to embody this 'moral' ideal. Frasier obviously belongs to the best that England could have bred, coming from an ancient aristocratic family

---

[16] Most of these works were published by George Alfred Seeley in London around the end of the nineteenth century.

of baronets, bishops, and Members of Parliament and having been educated at Rugby, Trinity, and Sandhurst. He has already proven his prowess on the battlefield in India and Afghanistan, and also with General Sir Henry Brackenbury (1837-1914) in Egypt, where he was wounded several times. His military exploits were rewarded with the honorific epithet "Served with Honour and Distinction" (Edric 2001: 21). Frere, although decidedly less privileged than Frasier, seems to have been predestined for heroic martyrdom. His family name carries the connotation of 'friar', while his third name, Stephen, was given to him in honour of the martyr Stephen, who was stoned to death, a remarkable omen for a man who is to be employed by a company that exploits a stone quarry. Frere is energetic and gifted; he is a 'manly' scientist, fully determined to face boldly any fact about cannibalism that he may uncover. He is also an avid Bible reader, as we may infer from the second epigraph to the novel.[17] Frere is the type of young man who believes that the world needs him. Both Frere and Frasier are highly ambitious and determined to gain control over the uncharted regions of this world through cartography and ethnography, in order to make the wilderness safe for civilisation, so to speak.

As the plot unfolds, however, Edric's novel details the demise rather than attainment of the cherished moral ideal. Why of all people do Frere and Frasier fail to live up to the role they have been tailored for? In brief, their failure may be attributed to the blinding effect of the exoticist imagination, which renders them incapable of truly facing up to the alien world of the colony. Frere and Frasier fail to identify the innocents and enemies, whom one should respectively protect and combat. The essential materials for exercising the manly virtues do not seem to be at hand, or at least not in a way that is easily recognisable for European males in the grips of exoticism. By the time some male protagonists finally manage to identify the 'real' enemies and victims, it is already far too late.

The exoticist imagination is so hung up on cherished images of male white supremacy that it tends to be oblivious to the fact that

---

[17] This epigraph reads as follows: "... thou knowest the people,/ that they are set upon mischief./ For they said unto me/ 'Make us gods, which shall/ go before us ...'/ Exodus, 32, 22-23/ Marked in the personal Bible of/ N.E.S. Frere (1864-1897)/ The Pitt-Rivers Museum, Oxford" (Edric 2001: epigraph, original ellipses). Undoubtedly, we are to interpret the false gods from the biblical passage as references to the "modern gods of profit and loss" worshiped by The Company.

(Christian) manliness depends quite strongly on the context of familial relations. However, colonialism and family life prove to be warring forces in Edric's novel and, it could be argued, outside fiction also. Concessionary stations and mission posts were male dominated worlds, and it is precisely in such homo-social settings that ideals of masculinity cease to make sense. In the initial stages of settlement, colonisers tended to leave their wives and loved ones at home for reasons of expediency, a form of segregation for which British colonial administrators were prepared by public school from the age of seven onwards. Families, then, were not only torn apart in the homeland but also in the colonies. Furthermore, once abroad, colonisers disrupted indigenous family life likewise, by taking native women – often forcibly – as concubines and creating no end of trouble for the children resulting from such *métissage*. In addition, they targeted native children as easily malleable converts for missionary projects, 'innocent lost souls' whom one might legitimately remove from their biological parents in the name of civilisation.

The Book of the Heathen tries to convey a sense of such a spouse-less, anti-family world. The only women in and around Ukassa Falls are native women, and the colonisers are hard put to establish non-exploitative relationships with them, as is borne out by the alienating names they have bestowed upon them. Klein's converts 'Felicity' and 'Perpetua' have been called after the first female martyrs, indicating his preparedness to sacrifice them to the good cause, while Cornelius' child 'Magdalene' has been burdened with the name of Christ's follower, a reformed prostitute. Even Cornelius participates in the curious fashion of re-christening native women, although the new name of his mistress, 'Evangeline', differs from the others in that it carries positive connotations ('bearer of good tidings'). This abuse of indigenous women conflicts with the chivalric and gentlemanly aspects of manly Christianity and exerts a degrading effect on all involved, with the possible exception of Cornelius van Klees, who stands out from the rest in several ways. He is the only character in the novel who is referred to by his first name, indicating that he has managed to retain something of his humanity and individuality after decades of life in the colony, contrary to the other 'old soldiers', who seem to have become mere figures or functions.[18] Furthermore, he is the only man to establish a relationship with a native woman that comes close to love and affection, up to the point of seriously considering marriage to her. He is also the only white man who finally comes to understand that Felicity and Perpetua deserve his pity and protection, although his resolve comes too late to benefit them. Taken all together, Cornelius comes across as the only half-way decent man in long-standing service of The Company. In the overall dearth of objects of affection as well as clearly identifiable enemies, the men turn against each other in a *bellum omnium contra omnes* (the war of all against all), which, according to Thomas Hobbes, defines the primitive state of society before the onset of civilisation. Consequently, honourable men are hard to find in the colonial society of the Congo. Rather than engaging in a joint effort to convert the heathen, the energy of the colonisers is wasted on internal competition and strife over the division of the loot, including the human spoils.

The exoticism of the colonials pre-empts any true understanding of native women and men alike. Unfortunately for them, the male inhabitants of the Congo cannot be conveniently lumped together as wholly alien or wholly other, as they differ immensely amongst each other in terms of social status and power. Particularly the character of Hammad unsettles all distinctions between primitivism and civilisation, considering his wealth and influence, his scheming and plotting, and his cunning political manoeuvres, outdoing the power play in any modern metropolis in terms of sophistication and corruption. Certainly, Hammad is not the type of man one could fight with the strength of one's arm in order to recuperate a primal manly energy. Collaboration seems to be the only way of dealing with him, which is exactly what the Belgians do, in a way that comes uncomfortably close to the "rotten compromises" of modern politics.[19] At this point, one cannot fail to notice that the

---

[18] One is hard put to remember characters such as 'Abbot', 'Bone' or 'Fletcher', mere guards at the Concessionary Station, mere cogs in the machinery of The Company.
[19] The term derives from Avishai Margalit's *On Compromise and Rotten Compromises* (2009), which explores the moral limits to acceptable political compromise. Briefly put, rotten compromises are agreements that consolidate and expand the power of dictatorial regimes; the Munich Pact (1938) that permitted the

highly ambivalent position of Hammad/Tippu Tip, at times the enemy, at other times the ally of the Belgian colonial regime, closely resembles more contemporary dealings with unruly and evasive potentates and agitators such as Saddam Hussein or Osama Bin Laden. Like Hammad, they were the beneficiaries of Western munificence (read: 'weapons') at times, while providing the major excuse for intervening in the affairs of the Middle East at others. On the rare occasion that the Congo natives do seem to behave like 'proper' natives, that is, during the 'cannibal' feast, they are most likely only impersonating a role rather than exposing their true selves, while Frere's 'protective' behaviour towards the native girl is but a grim parody or perversion of the chivalric paternalism that characterises heroic manliness.

In keeping with the gender dichotomy inherent in the ethics of honour, the failure to live up to the standards of manly Christianity is felt most keenly vis-à-vis the women who are to inspire chivalric behaviour in their loved ones. Thus Frere confesses to Granville Beaufoy Montague Nash, a Company bureaucrat who arrives to inquire into Frere's case, that the most traumatic part of his disgrace is picturing himself in the eyes of his betrothed, Frasier's sister Caroline:

> He [Frere] said that he loved her, that he had never loved anyone before her, and that the hardest part of what he now had to endure was the knowledge that he had brought shame on her, that he had disgraced himself and that she would now feel only disgust and contempt for him as long as she lived. (Edric 2001: 287)

Apparently, this gruelling shame is not felt when picturing oneself in the eyes of indigenous women, who are not credited with the civilising influence attributed to white women.

In *The Book of the Heathen*, both colonisers and natives end up worshipping the same false gods, namely the modern gods of profit and loss, who are adverse to any sort of heroism in their followers, only demanding cowardly compromise, deception and conformism.

Nazis to annex Czechoslovakia's Sudentenland figuring as a particularly disconcerting example.

Contrary to the conventional image of the heathen as illiterate and ignorant, these heathens have books – the books of the Bible, the books of science, the books of the law – but this fact does not seem to make much difference. Apparently, the accumulated knowledge of the West cannot function as an infallible guide to truth and wisdom in the unfamiliar surroundings of the tropics, for Father Klein's Bible has not kept him from terrorising his congregation, nor did it prevent Frere from enmeshing himself in a hopeless moral quandary. The books of science, namely Frasier's maps and Frere's ethnographic inquiries, at best only provide an illusion of control, for the objects of their inquiries continue to elude them, frustrating "imperial exoticism". Moreover, the products of their research are appropriated by higher commercial and political forces. Strikingly, Frasier's maps and Frere's diaries are taken away from them by Hammad and the Belgian authorities. The books of the law, finally, do not keep Nash from becoming an accomplice in an unjust show trial. Although Nash understands very well that Frere cannot be properly accused of having 'murdered' the native girl, he nevertheless decides to hand him over to the Belgian court that will undoubtedly execute him. Sadly, the founding institutions of Western civilisation – science, religion and the law – break down in the hopeless muddle of the colony. Its moral bankruptcy is epitomised by the shoot-out at the end of the novel, when the two men from Ypres,[20] Cornelius and Klein, take the law into their own hands and kill each other.

.   Although the hardships of living at the outskirts of empire were thought to inspire and enhance manly morality at the time, *The Book of the Heathen* suggests that colonialism and Christian manliness were in fact fundamentally at odds with one another. This discrepancy generates a traumatic crisis of values or moral aporia, quite similar to the type of trauma discussed in Catherine Pesso-Miquel's contribution to this volume on the traumatic crisis or loss of faith. The intense mental pain of loosing one's moral bearings is figured forth in the concluding scene of *The Book of the Heathen* in

---

[20] As is widely known, Ypres was the site of the major battles of World War I. According to Norman Vance, the ideal of manly Christianity died in the trenches of the First World War, as registered in the works of the war poets (Vance 1985: 201-206). It is tempting to interpret the Congo episode as a prelude to the process of the gradual demise of Western supremacy begun in the colonies, including the breakdown of Christian manliness.

the image of an all-encompassing and unredeemed darkness that calls its famous predecessor Joseph Conrad's *Heart of Darkness* (1899) to mind.

4.   Exoticism against Itself

What could be the rationale of writing yet another novel about the trials and tribulations of the Congo, half a century after decolonisation, a century after Conrad, and a century-and-a-half after Kingsley? In answer to these questions, I find it helpful to categorise *The Book of the Heathen* not just as a neo-Victorian, but also as a postcolonial novel, in the sense of Catherine Nash's definition of the postcolonial as "neither a celebration of the end of colonialism nor the simple reproduction of the colonial in the present, but the mutated, impure and unsettling legacies of colonialism" (Nash 2002: 225). The adjective "impure" is particularly important here. Postcolonialism is about a loss of innocence, about a growing awareness of complicity with the inequities of the globalising world order as it has emerged in the wake of Europe's and America's colonial pasts. This awareness cannot be instilled in us without the necessary efforts. Those who might consider Christian manliness a rather quaint and outmoded ideal, of which we need not be reminded any longer, might be surprised to read the following lines, written by Robert Kagan, a prominent member of PNAC (Project for a New American Century),[21] in response to Europe's persistent criticism of the aggressive ways in which the United States conducted its so-called War on Terror:

> It is time to stop pretending that Europeans and Americans share a common view of the world, or even that they occupy the same world. On the all-important question of power – the efficacy of power, the morality of power, the desirability of power – American and European perspectives are diverging. Europe is turning away from power, or to put it a little differently, it is moving beyond power into a self-contained world of laws and rules and transnational negotiation and cooperation. It is entering a post-

---

[21] PNAC, a neo-conservative thinktank, was a major advisor of the George W. Bush administration.

> historical paradise of peace and relative prosperity, the realization of Kant's "Perpetual Peace." The United States, meanwhile, remains mired in history, exercising power in the anarchic Hobbesian world where international laws and rules are unreliable and where true security and the defense and promotion of a liberal order still depend on the possession and use of military might. That is why on major strategic and international questions today, Americans are from Mars and Europeans are from Venus: They agree on little and understand one another less and less. (Kagan 2002)

Throughout his article 'Power and Weakness', Kagan associates Europe with femininity ("Venus"), weakness and irresponsible naïvety, which it can only afford because the United States are masculine ("Mars"),[22] powerful and courageous enough to assume full moral responsibility for the (armed) protection of Western democracies, including those of Europe. Kagan's article makes it painfully clear that the paternalist association of masculinity and morality is re-installed whenever neo-imperialist interventions are at stake. Therefore, it will do us no harm to have Edric remind us of the fact that colonialism destroyed, rather than consolidated, moral masculinity.[23]

Obviously, we not only inherited the flawed association of masculinity with moral rightness from the Victorians, but also the whole exoticist project within which these values were embedded. This returns us to the question that opened this chapter: why is the neo-Victorian trauma novel given to such excessive portrayals of sexual perversion and physical violence? According to Kohlke, the "neo-Victorian sexsation" appeals to us because we furtively credit ourselves with a sense of superiority, by attributing illicit desires and deviances to the Victorians that were utterly taboo to them:

---

[22] The astronomical metaphors obviously allude to the title of John Gray's well known book on gender difference, *Men are from Mars, Women are from Venus* (1992).

[23] Analogously, the neo-colonial strain of late twentieth-century Western politics (the Gulf War, the Iraq War, the War on Terror) may well have enhanced the postmodern crisis in masculinity, identified by the emergent field of masculinity studies (see, e.g., Connell 1995, Faludi 1999 and 2007).

> We enjoy neo-Victorian fiction in part to feel debased
> or outraged, to revel in degradation, *reading for
> defilement*. By projecting illicit and unmentionable
> desires onto the past, we conveniently reassert our
> own supposedly enlightened stance towards sexuality
> and social progress. (Kohlke 2008: 346)

Literary trauma tourism is subject to similar charges. By dwelling on
the violent conflicts of the past, we tacitly cherish the assumption that
our age is the more civilised and enlightened one. Nevertheless, I want
to argue that *The Book of the Heathen* produces a different effect, in
that it simultaneously *blocks* a sense of moral superiority on the
reader's part. Rather than elevating the present above the past, we are
deeply implicated in the novel's moral quandary. How is this effect
achieved?

Interestingly, *The Book of the Heathen* is not only a
manifestation of contemporary exoticism, riding the wave of the neo-
Victorian craze, but it also turns exoticism into a topic for critical
reflection. If we grant that neo-Victorianism exchanges the exoticism
of place for the neo-exoticism of time, then we have to conclude that
this trade-off is frustrated in Edric's novel. Turning to the Victorian
age in order to flee from the contemporary atrophy of experience, we
are confronted with a story about fictional characters who vainly
attempt to escape from the mindlessness of their daily routines
through the exoticism of place that we have already given up on.
Frere's obsession with the spectacularly perverse and illicit practices
that he attributes to the geographical other mirrors our own interest in
the supposedly prurient, criminal and violent aspects of the temporal
other. Frere and Frasier soon discover to their dismay that even the
Congo, a part of Africa barely mapped in their own time, had already
fallen prey to the disenchantment of modernity. As participants in "the
scramble for Africa" (Pakenham 1991), they belong to the first
witnesses of the rise of global modernity, a process that began in the
late nineteenth century and has come to define the world order of the
twenty-first century. Thus, the exoticism of *The Book of the Heathen*
resembles a snake that bites its own tail.

Because Frere's predicament is so similar to ours, the
misfiring of his quest also strikes back at us. When he finally finds the
thing he was looking for, he is forced to admit that this was not what

he was looking for at all. Frere's case is a particularly strong illustration of the fact that desire cannot meet its object, for if it does, the object destroys desire. Ironically, the exoticist cure for the impoverishment of affect replaces emotional anaemia by the total numbing of trauma. As Frere's exoticist project fails, so does ours. This is probably not really the type of defilement we were looking for. Certainly, Frere's debasement blocks the nostalgic desire to return to and identify with the past, but throws us back on ourselves, forcing us to look *at*, rather than *through*, our own nostalgic exoticism and the temptations of trauma tourism. Thus, the conventional link between nostalgia and escapism is severed. *The Book of the Heathen* moves beyond the sensationalism that turns trauma into a topic for voyeuristic pleasure through its promotion of the type of "empathic unsettlement" that "requires self-consciousness of one's own subject position as an ethically addressed, secondary witness, rather than co-sufferer or mere avid spectator" (Kohlke, this volume: 382). Edric's characters mirror, rather than compensate for, our plight, as the exoticising impulse is turned back upon itself, enabling us to recognise it for what it has been all along: an unsettling and unmitigated self-reflection.

Bibliography

Arens, William Edward. 1979. *The Man-Eating Myth: Anthropology & Anthropophagy*. Oxford: Oxford University Press.

Bhabha, Homi. 1994. *The Location of Culture*. London: Routledge.

Bongie, Chris. 1991. *Exotic Memories: Literature, Colonialism and the Fin de Siècle*. Stanford: Stanford University Press.

Brantlinger, Patrick. 1990. *Rule of Darkness: British Literature and Imperialism* [1988]. Ithaca: Cornell University Press.

Connell, Robert William. 1995. *Masculinities*. Berkeley: University of California Press.

Daly, Nicholas. 2007. 'Colonialism and Popular Literature at the Fin de Siècle', in Begam, Richard, and Michael Valdez Moses (eds.), *Modernism and Colonialism: British and Irish Literature, 1899-1939*. Durham & London: Duke University Press: 19-43.

Edric, Robert. 2001. *The Book of the Heathen* [2000]. London: Black Swan.

Faludi, Susan. 1999. *Stifled: The Betrayal of the American Man*. London: Chatto & Windus.

——. 2007. *The Terror Dream: Myth and Misogyny in Insecure America*. New York: Metropolitan Books.

Goldman, Laurence R. (ed.). 1999. *The Anthropology of Cannibalism*. Westport, Connecticut: Greenwood.

Gutleben, Christian. 2001. *Nostalgic Postmodernism: The Victorian Tradition and the Contemporary British Novel*. Amsterdam: Rodopi.

Hall, Donald E. (ed.). 1994. *Muscular Christianity: Embodying the Victorian Age*. Cambridge: Cambridge University Press.

Kagan, Robert. 2002. 'Power and Weakness: Why the United States and Europe see the world differently', *Policy Review* (June/July). Online at: http://www.hoover.org/publications/policyreview/3413481.html (consulted 07.01.2008).

Kearney, Anthony. 1983. 'The Missionary Hero in Children's Literature', *Children's Literature in Education* 14: 104-112.

Kingsley, Charles. 1880. *Scientific Lectures and Essays*. London: Macmillan.

Kohlke, Marie-Luise. 2008. 'The Neo-Victorian Sexsation: Literary Excursions into the Nineteenth Century Erotic', in Kohlke, Marie-Luise, and Luisa Orza (eds.), *Probing the Problematics: Sex and Sexuality* [e-Book]. Oxford: Inter-Disciplinary Press: 345-356. Online at: http://www.inter-disciplinary.net/publishing/id-press/ebooks/probing-the-problematics-sex-and-sexuality/ (consulted 07.10.2009).

——. 2009. 'Nostalgic Violence? Neo-Victorian (Re-)Visions of Historical Conflict', in Guggisberg, Marika, and David Weir (eds.), *Understanding Violence: Contexts and Portrayals* [e-Book]. Oxford: Interdisciplinary Press: 25-39. Online at: http://www.inter-disciplinary.net/publishing/id-press/ebooks/understanding-violence-contexts-and-portrayals/ (consulted 05.12.2009).

Langer, Lawrence. 1982. *Versions of Survival: The Holocaust and the Human Spirit*. Albany: State University of New York Press.

Louis, William Roger. 1965. 'The Stokes Affair and the Origins of the Anti-Congo Campaign, 1895-6', *Revue Belge de philologie et d'histoire* 4: 572-584.

Mangan, James Anthony; and James Walvin (eds.). 1987. *Manliness and Morality: Middle-Class Masculinity in Britain and America, 1800-1940*. Manchester: Manchester University Press.

Margalit, Avishai. 2009. *On Compromise and Rotten Compromises*. Princeton: Princeton University Press.

Nash, Catherine. 2002. 'Cultural Geography: Postcolonial Cultural Geographies', *Progress in Human Geography* 26(2): 219-230.

Pakenham, Thomas. 1991. *The Scramble for Africa: White Man's Conquest of the Dark Continent 1876-1912*. London: Weidenfeld and Nicolson.

Said, Edward W. 1978. *Orientalism*. London: Routledge and Kegan Paul.

Sturken, Marita. 2007. *Tourists of History: Memory, Kitsch, and Consumerism from Oklahoma City to Ground Zero*. Durham, North Carolina: Duke University Press.

Vance, Norman. 1985. *The Sinews of the Spirit: The Ideal of Christian Manliness in Victorian Literature and Religious Thought*. Cambridge: Cambridge University Press.

Wee, C.J. Wan-Ling. 1994. 'Christian Manliness and National Identity: The Problematic Construction of a Racially "Pure" Nation', in Hall (1994): 66-88.

Wesseling, Hendrik Lodewijk. 2005. *Verdeel en heers: De deling van Afrika 1880-1914* [1999]. Amsterdam: Bakker.

Yeager, Patricia. 2002. 'Consuming Trauma; or, The Pleasures of Merely Circulating', in Miller, Nancy K., and Jason Tougaw (eds.), *Extremities: Trauma, Testimony, and Community*. Urbana & Chicago: University of Illinois Press: 2002: 25-51.

Turmoil, Trauma and Mourning
in Jane Urquhart's *The Whirlpool*

Elodie Rousselot

Abstract:
Recent scholarship on British neo-Victorian fiction has presented contemporary authors' returns to the nineteenth century as an expression of nostalgia for this period and for the work of their Victorian literary predecessors. In the context of non-British texts however, those returns to bygone times of Victorian 'literary greatness' may be used to different effect: that of re-appropriating and challenging, rather than confirming, these typical nostalgic drives. This is the case in Jane Urquhart's novel *The Whirlpool* (1986), set in the wilderness of Niagara Falls, Canada, but framed by a narrative sequence focused on Robert Browning's death in 1889 Venice. The use of irony and the presence of 'postmodern gaps' in the novel's quotational process serve to highlight and undermine the lingering effects of the Victorian canon on new poetic voices. The novel's focus on issues of death and decay in the old world of Europe also emphasises the renewal potential present in the Canadian wild. By presenting the act of mourning as a specifically Victorian cultural expression and ideological by-product of the British Empire, the novel successfully challenges the political and historical legacy of colonisation in Canada. In this context, mourning is used as a commemorative process to inscribe otherwise silenced histories, and thus contributes to the establishment of a Canadian historical consciousness.

Keywords: Canada, history, melancholia, mourning, postcolonial, postmodernism, satire, Jane Urquhart.

*****

In his study on British neo-Victorian fiction, Christian Gutleben has successfully demonstrated how contemporary authors' return to the nineteenth century is in part motivated by a nostalgic drive for the work of their Victorian literary predecessors (Gutleben 2001). The cultural preoccupation with re-imagining the nineteenth century in its aesthetic and socio-historical contexts from a contemporary perspective has also been likened to an attempt at reviving this era,

including some of its traditionalist values, as denoted in the term
"retro-Victorian" (Shuttleworth 1998). In this respect, the neo-
Victorian may be seen to be participating in the postmodern
questioning of the epistemological and ideological basis of history, or
more generally, in an expression of discontent with the present,
compounded by an "acknowledgement of the unsurpassed quality" of
the Victorian literary canon (Gutleben 2001: 19). In the context of
non-British fiction however, those returns to Victorian cultural values
and literary aesthetics may be used to different effect. The Canadian
writer Margaret Atwood's *Alias Grace* (1996) draws extensively from
a large body of Victorian canonical references in its re-telling of a
murder case in 1840s Upper Canada. Yet the purpose of such wide
referencing is not to celebrate the latter, but rather to illustrate the
process of cultural colonisation in nineteenth-century Canada and
highlight the political discrimination underpinning the treatment of
minorities in the colony. Similarly, the Australian writer Peter Carey's
True History of the Kelly Gang (2000) returns to the politics of
Empire in nineteenth-century New South Wales to reveal the part
played by British colonial discourses in the persecution of Irish
settlers.

       This essay focuses on an earlier instance of the Canadian neo-
Victorian novel, Jane Urquhart's *The Whirlpool* (1986), which also
uses a framework of Victorian cultural references to re-consider
moments of unrest in Canada's past. On the outset, the novels cited all
seem to belong to a wider project, that of using the neo-Victorian as a
means of commemorating historical and cultural trauma, rather than
celebrating past excellence. This seems to be compounded by their
deliberate attempt to contest the "grand narratives" of Empire and
shed a sense of history still informed by Eurocentric nineteenth-
century discourses, now perceived as detrimental to the development
of a postcolonial Canadian or Australian historical consciousness.
Jean-François Lyotard has defined postmodernism precisely as this
"incredulity toward metanarratives", explaining that such "grand
narratives" can no longer be used to legitimate knowledge (Lyotard
1984: xxiv). Equally, Lyotard recognised that "little narratives" (or
"micronarratives") remained "the quintessential form of imaginative
invention" (Lyotard 1984: 60), particularly in their challenging of
traditional understandings of the concept of 'historical truth'. I will
show how *The Whirlpool* returns to Canada's past to enact the

liberation of such silenced, micro-histories, as well as contest oppressive Victorian cultural and political legacies, in the present time.

Ato Quayson polemically suggested that "postmodernism can never fully explain the state of the contemporary world without first becoming postcolonial and vice versa" (Quayson 2000: 106). Even though postcolonialism and postmodernism do not always overlap, particularly in terms of political commitment, Theo D'haen's notion of "counter-postmodernism", to describe the practices of postcolonial and feminist writers drawing from postmodernist ideas in their work to respond to prevalent imperial and patriarchal discourses, could offer a means of bridging both theoretical movements (D'haen 1994, qtd. Steenman-Marcusse 2001: 38). Linda Hutcheon has noted indeed that postcolonialism and postmodernism shared a similar thematic concern with notions of centre and margins (Hutcheon 1990: 168), while Conny Steenman-Marcusse, writing about Canadian culture, observed that "Canada's diversity of languages, races and ethnicities [was] an ideal breeding ground for postmodernist ideas of relativism, subjective truth and scepticism about unity" (Steenman-Marcusse 2001: 19). In the context of our discussion, the neo-Victorian will be used as one such bridge, a postmodern prism through which the novel's postcolonial project may be considered.

In turn, this will enable us to assess the way in which the novel's use of Victorian literary and historical discourses contributes to the construction of a distinct Canadian national and cultural identity in the present, an identity which seems inextricably bound up with the re-writing of Canada's past. Indeed, Urquhart's novel belongs to the late twentieth-century trend which has seen many Canadian writers return to their nation's past in their work. Possible explanations for this phenomenon include "the overthrow of a colonial mentality in which Canadian history was dismissed as negligible", "an increasing desire to interrogate and challenge a narrowly defined national past", as well as "an anxiety about distinguishing Canadian culture and identity from that of the United States in an era of increasing economic, cultural, and political integration" (Wyile 2007: 6). These factors all play a part in Urquhart's work, therefore inscribing it firmly within wider national concerns about the development of a distinct Canadian cultural identity. These factors will also allow us to examine the extent to which the Canadian context transforms the use of Victorian themes and references in the novel.

In its contestation of the mis-appropriations of Canada's colonial past, *The Whirlpool* returns specifically to moments of trauma in the colonisation process. These traumatic events, it will be argued, are depicted as necessary in the text in allowing the separation between mother country and colony, and the establishment of the latter's own historical narrative, distinct from that of Empire. The novel's thematic fascination with issues of death and mourning will be presented as partaking of a specifically Victorian cultural expression, and therefore shown to be an ideological by-product of the British Empire in the colonies. In successfully subverting such cultural influence, however, the novel reveals and challenges the Victorian political and historical tradition in Canada. In this respect, the description of intellectual and physical decay in the old world of Europe will be used to emphasise the renewal potential present in the young Canadian nation. I will also examine the ways in which mourning, as a form of revision and as a means of liberation, constitutes both a thematic focus and a narrative strategy in the text. In this context, mourning will be distinguished from nostalgia and shown to be part of a commemorative process used to inscribe otherwise silenced histories, therefore contributing to the establishment of a Canadian historical consciousness.

1.   Death, Decay and Neo-Victorian Derision
The Whirlpool's return to Victorian culture is made explicit in its narrative structure, which is set in 1889 in the wilderness of Niagara Falls, Canada, but framed by a narrative sequence focused on the death of the Victorian poet Robert Browning, the same year in Venice. This narrative sequence acts as a cultural framework of references and quotations through which the action set in the Canadian setting needs to be apprehended. It also works to establish death and mourning as important thematic concerns in the text. Francis O'Gorman has noted that "mourning might easily be said to constitute one of the defining features of Victorian literature *as* Victorian", whereby "some of the most celebrated contemplations of loss in the Western canon are to be found in the Victorian period" (O'Gorman 2007: 155). The Venetian sequence seems self-consciously aware of this and uses the quintessential Victorian concern with death and mourning as means of

satirising some of the cultural tropes of the period, as well as some of its great literary figures. We find Browning, for instance, contemplating his impending death and "imagining the reactions of his friends, what his future biographers would have to say" about the event (Urquhart 1986: 4). Browning's preoccupation with the lasting impression his work will make is further conveyed in the narrative by his satisfaction that "he had prudently written his death poem at Asolo in direct response to having received a copy of Tennyson's 'Crossing the Bar'. [...] How he detested that poem!" (Urquhart 1986: 4) In having Browning confess that he has avoided such obvious sentimentality as exhibited in Tennyson's "death poem", but that he nonetheless hopes to have provided something "for the weeping maidens" (Urquhart 1986: 4), the novel seeks to satirise the self-engrossed aspect of writing one's own commemoration poem.

This process can also be seen as representative of excess in Victorian mourning practices: if for Tennyson and others, "poetry might, however uncertainly, carry a man's *legacy* beyond the grave", and "survive after the poet as an echo of life" (O'Gorman 2007: 160; original emphasis), then timing, above and over artistic gift, is key for the process to achieve its desired effect. Indeed, O'Gorman has noted that "Tennyson's most sustained contemplation on posterity, aside from *In Memoriam AHH*, is to be found in what he had believed would be his final volume, *Tiresias and Other Poems* (1885)" (O'Gorman 2007: 173). This was not the case, however, as the Poet Laureate went on to publish two further volumes of poems and several isolated works before his death in 1892. The anxiety about control over one's poetic legacy, one's "echo of life" from death, is therefore presented as a cultural and artistic process symbolic of the Victorian period, one that is turned to ridicule in the novel, as will be discussed later. The satirical stance towards the writing of one's own elegiac poem, as well as other forms of Victorian mourning rituals, is part of a wider project in the novel that aims to subvert the influence of Victorian cultural discourses in the Canadian colonies.

This is visible in the narrative sequence set in Niagara Falls, where the fictional character of Maud Grady, the local undertaker, insists on strictly observing the prescribed two-year mourning period after the death of her husband. Marlene Goldman has noticed that "Maud continue[s] to subscribe to a European protocol", in which "she dutifully follow[s] the cultural codes and transform[s] herself from a proper wife to an equally proper widow" (Goldman 1996: 28-29). If Maud's mourning practice illustrates the upholding of Victorian social customs in the colonies (visible, for instance, in the description of the funeral brooch she makes out of a lock of her husband's hair, and in her wearing mourning garb for two full years), then that same practice is also undermined in the novel, as evident in the focus on black crape, the uncomfortable fabric imported from England that codified mourning rituals in the nineteenth century. We learn that "[i]n ten years, enough crape had been produced [in England] to completely cover the province of Quebec. In twenty, the whole empire could have been wrapped; a depressing parcel with a black sheen" (Urquhart 1986: 15). The idea of excess in terms of Victorian mourning rituals is suggested here again through the image of the British Empire as a "depressing parcel with a black sheen": the oppressive hold of Victorian cultural values over the colonies seems to be symbolised by this metaphor of colonial landscape dressed in black.

Maud's personal mourning ritual, particularly the wearing of crape, "hadn't been at all pleasant" for her:

> Apart from the physical discomfort, there was the accompanying fear of weather; of heat and of precipitation. The smallest bit of moisture, fog, or even minor amounts of perspiration would cause the colour of the fabric to bleed through to her skin. (Urquhart 1986: 16)

This results in black marks on her body, not dissimilar to bruises caused by physical violence. On a literal level, these stains seem intended to illustrate the forceful imprint of Victorian cultural codes in the colonies, while figuratively they could also be read as marks of imperial violence on the colonial body. Such marks indicate that the upholding of imported British social and cultural traditions stifles personal and creative expression in the colony, as will be explored in the next section. Suffice to say that these descriptions of the bodily consequences of wearing crape, with the mention of perspiration and staining, undercut the solemn occasion that the wearing of the fabric is supposed to mark. This focus on Maud's bodily functions, rather than on her spiritual state of mind, turns the commemoration of her husband's death into a grotesque event, highlighting how inappropriate these mourning traditions from the mother country are to the hot, wild and humid setting of Niagara Falls. In fact, despite her adherence to these rituals, Maud can "no longer bring his face clearly into her mind" and finds "it more and more difficult to believe that she had ever been married at all" (Urquhart 1986: 23). Maud's clinging on to these mourning customs and protocol becomes an end in itself, distinct from the event and the object supposedly commemorated.

In this respect, the novel's thematic concern with issues of death and mourning may be productively considered in conjunction with Freud's essay on 'Mourning and Melancholia' (1917). Freud recognises the similarities between the symptoms of mourning and those of melancholia. According to Freud, mourning is a necessary and healthy response to trauma, a process which ultimately leads to the subject achieving detachment and liberation from the lost object, or from the memory of the traumatic event. In cases of melancholia, however, the object of loss is unclear or unknown to the subject; as a result, the latter internalises the sense of loss and is unable to accomplish the necessary detachment from the traumatic event. This process may also in turn lead to a loss of ego or diminution of self-regard in the melancholic (Freud 1987: 253-254). This distinction between mourning and melancholia offers a useful framework within which the topics of death and trauma in Urquhart's text may be examined. The novel seems to present Victorian mourning and elegiac practices as akin to Freud's definition of melancholia: in Maud's case, the object of loss has become unclear and the mourning process itself replaces it, whereby mourning, and not her husband, is being commemorated. With Browning and the writing of *Asolando* (1889) earlier, his own poem of mourning, melancholia stems from the fact that the (anticipated) object of loss is the self of the poet, and that this object becomes internalised in a process which cannot lead to a successful separation between the mourner and his 'loss'.

In the Venetian sequence, Browning's anxiety over his literary posterity also assumes melancholic proportions, as evident in the poet's visitation by apparitions of Percy Bysshe Shelley (1792-1822), his literary predecessor and the idol of his young literary days. As he approaches the time of his own death, Browning becomes increasingly obsessed with the presence of Shelley's drowned corpse in his rooms: "Limp and drifting, the drowned man looked as supple

as a mermaid" (Urquhart 1986: 230). These apparitions seem to
denote a distinctively Bloomian anxiety of influence in Browning's
concern with his own literary legacy, as well as evoke the spectral
trope common to much neo-Victorian fiction, both as a signal of
unresolved or forgotten cultural traumas, and as a sign of the past's
often baleful influence over the present. Browning's perceived sense
of (artistic) inferiority is exacerbated in the novel by his relatively
uneventful ending, compared to Shelley's tragic death: "[t]he absolute
grace" of Shelley's death makes Browning wish "for the drama and
the luxury of a death by water. [...] All that cool white marble in
exchange for the shifting sands of Lerici" (Urquhart 1986: 231). This
process of literary 'haunting' is overlaid in the novel with fragmented
quotations from Browning's early poem *Pauline* (1832), in which he
writes about Shelley as the "suntreader" figure of his early poetic
days:

> He now knew that he had said too much. [...] All this
> chatter filling up the space of Shelley's more
> important silence. [...] *Suntreader*. And now
> Browning understood. It was Shelley's absence he
> had carried with him all these years [...] *Suntreader,
> soft star*. The formless form he never possessed and
> was never possessed by. (Urquhart 1986: 229-230)

Pauline is heavily autobiographical in parts and testifies to the poet
coming to terms with Shelley's influence upon his life and early work.
It describes that influence as now diminished, and the speaker sets out
to try and understand the course of his own development; yet the
poem ends on an ambiguous note where the allegiance to the spirit of
his former poetic mentor seems reaffirmed. The novel thus stages the
literary 'haunting' that Urquhart herself enacts via the resurrection of
Browning and his poetry. Simultaneously, however, the trope parallels
the ghostly possession of the colony by the spirit of Empire, situating
the issue of cultural inheritance – and hence of the neo-Victorian itself
as a form of homage thereto – as inherently traumatic.

This literary 'haunting', conveyed through material and/or
textual traces – Shelley's dead body and the quotes from Browning's
early work – is also described as a kind of "absence", the "formless
form" Browning claims to have never possessed or been possessed by.

The contradictory nature of this overlay of presence with absence, poetic echoes with silence, can again be read in terms of Freud's definition of melancholia. In Browning's case, the object of loss is internalised in the form of an absence, a silence. Consequently, Browning cannot achieve detachment from the vision of Shelley's dead body and its accompanying sense of anxiety over artistic status; in fact, the memory of Shelley's death seems to heighten Browning's awareness of "[h]ow inadequate his words seemed now compared to Shelley's experience, how silly this monotonous bedridden death" (Urquhart 1986: 229). The aesthetic and cultural readings that Browning makes of Shelley's tragic ending become a source of creative and intellectual paralysis for the poet. His commemoration practice and concern with death as *the* cultural signifier prevent him from adopting more successful forms of mourning. In fact, in parallel to the anxiety experienced by Browning over his literary legacy, the depiction of his "monotonous bedridden death", together with the grotesque vision of Shelley's corpse as a "supple mermaid", ironically undermine the solemnity of both poets' deaths for a modern audience. As a result, both men's cultural status and legacy are turned to derision, as conveyed symbolically through the image of the "limp and drifting" poetic body.

Hilary M. Schor recognises a similar commemorative practice and concern with death in the neo-Victorian novel's return to the literary tradition of the nineteenth century:

> To the extent that the realist novel is a collection of material things, [...] it must bring things to life, keep them in life, arrest their decay. But it also studies decay: the novel is primarily an animist fantasy, of making the dead live, of making "mere" forms "matter." (Schor 2000: 244)

According to Schor, the neo-Victorian novel partakes of this process, a process which she compares to melancholia, the inability to mourn the past successfully. For Andrew Williamson however, those neo-Victorian returns to past literary traditions may be essential in opening these traditions up to renewal and diversity. Indeed, Williamson sees the neo-Victorian process of "reading" (and "writing") literary history as a means of, simultaneously, mourning and "resurrecting" the latter:

> A singular reading [...] is no different from a singular
> mourning. One reading of a text must be open to other
> readings; indeed, only through this hospitality can
> literary history be refreshed with new readings, new
> understandings. (Williamson 2008: 129).

Williamson adds that, in this respect, neo-Victorian fiction "establishes further the relation between mourning literary history and the potential this mourning has to keep it alive and relaunch it" (Williamson 2008: 123). Equally, in his discussion of the "aesthetics of nostalgia" developed by the neo-Victorian novel, both as a thematic concern and as a narrative strategy, Gutleben focuses on the genre's "revival of a bygone tradition" (Gutleben 2001: 193). Concurrent to this revival, Gutleben notices that the neo-Victorian text tends to demystify the great literary figures of the past, a process which "is also, at least partially, an appropriation of the myth's prestige" (Gutleben 2001: 92). The paradoxical nature of this subversion/celebration process, however, lies in the fact that, for neo-Victorian authors, the Victorian literary figure may be seen as a "mythic ancestor", so that their relationship to such figures may be described as "one of identification and rejection, of allegiance and distancing" (Gutleben 2001: 185-186). Hence, *The Whirlpool*'s derisive stance towards nineteenth-century canonical figures and aesthetic discourses may in fact confirm, even as it undermines, the "prestige" of such figures and discourses.

The conflicted relationship to literary ancestors and literary history is explored thematically in Urquhart's text through the description of Browning's Shelleyan anxiety of influence. We find Browning not only haunted by visions of Shelley's dead body, but also by lines from his predecessor's work, lines which seem to prevent the flow of his own creative expression: "With a kind of slow horror, Browning realized that he was seeing his beloved city [Venice] through Shelley's eyes and immediately his inner voice began again" to recite Shelley's work (Urquhart 1986: 10). Shelley and Browning's poetic visions seem to be in competition with one another, as both wrote on the same Italian landscape. Perhaps this is akin to the novelistic position of the neo-Victorian author, who returns to tropes and locales already written about by his/her literary predecessor? In any case, the intrusion occasioned by Shelley in Browning's perception of his Venetian setting can be likened to the effect of British canonical voices on the aesthetic rendering of Canada's landscape in the next section. In the Venetian sequence, Browning confesses that city features which "two weeks earlier would have delighted him [...] now seemed used and lifeless" (Urquhart 1986: 9), while he becomes "peculiarly aware of the smells which he had previously ignored [...] a putrid odour which spoke less of blossom than decay" (Urquhart 1986: 10). Shelley's 'Lines Written Among the Euganean Hills' (1818) is the cause for this vision of the city rotting and turning to decay, a poem which "had been one of his [Browning's] favourites in his youth and, as a result, his mind was now capable of reciting it to him, word for word" (Urquhart 1986: 10). Shelley's poem was written in direct response to the death of one of his children, but its dark subject matter is presented rather as a source of annoyance and disruption in the novel, thereby subverting its original mourning purpose.

Linda Hutcheon's definition of irony as "a doubled or split discourse which has the potential to subvert from within" is useful in this context, particularly as "a popular rhetorical strategy for working within existing discourses and contesting them at the same time" (Hutcheon 1991: 73). This form of irony, which closely corresponds to Hutcheon's definition of postmodernism, helps us understand the paradoxical endorsement/rejection process typically found in neo-Victorian fiction: the canonical voices quoted in the novel seem to be celebrated *within* by its fictional characters, but are in fact subverted *without* by the text. The novel's quotational process therefore both relies on, and undermines, the reader's knowledge of Shelley's poem, a knowledge not put in the service of celebration but in that of contestation. The partial and fragmentary citational technique employed in the text further complicates this process by preventing a complete awareness of the details of the original source (as with *Pauline* earlier), yet requiring an understanding of its implications to appreciate the set of thematic references being evoked. Irony can thus be a powerfully subversive tool for neo-Victorian and postcolonial authors attempting to re-think the cultural legacy of the nineteenth century. This is visible for instance with Shelley's poem 'Ozymandias' (1818), which

> repeated itself four times in his [Browning's] mind
> except that, to his great annoyance, he found that he
> could not remember the last three lines and kept
> ending with *Look on my works, ye Mighty, and
> despair.* (Urquhart 1986: 8)

The last three lines which escape Browning in fact moderate the
imperious injunction of King Ramses II:

> Nothing beside remains: round the decay
> Of that colossal wreck, boundless and bare,
> The lone and level sands stretch far away. (l. 12-14)

The poem's warning against human hubris is lost in Browning's
version, which on the contrary emphasises the assumed superiority
and sustained hold of the (literary) predecessor over posterity ("Look
on my works, ye Mighty, and despair"). The interrupted poem thus
works to reinforce Browning's anxiety over his future legacy, and
possibly suggests that Shelley himself is calling upon Browning for
submission and admiration, the same imperatives supposedly
encountered by the author of neo-Victorian fiction. However, the
description of a slightly ludicrous Browning fighting off Shelley's
verse, as well as the readers' knowledge of the missing lines, here
again ironically undermine such tendency to celebrate the literary
voices of the past. These are symbolically recalled in the form of the
decaying "colossal wreck" that the text points towards but fails to
mention, an association of ideas which both relies on the readers'
awareness of the poem's original meaning, and subverts the latter. The
perceived status of the great voices from the literary past and their
cultural legacy is implicitly suggested in the idea of physical, but also
intellectual, "decay", symbolically embodied in the novel by the city
of Venice, and contrasted with the renewal potential of the Niagara
Falls setting.

     The use of irony and the presence of 'postmodern gaps' in the
novel's quotational process therefore serve to highlight and undermine
the lingering effects of the Victorian canon on new poetic voices, as
will be explored in the next section. The paradoxical mode of the
postmodern also recalls the very nature of nostalgia, a discourse which
"both resists and requires the obliteration of the past" (Colley 1998:

209, qtd. Gutleben 2001: 193). In this perspective, the neo-Victorian novel seems engaged in endless repetitions of the past, trapped in a traumatic cycle of melancholic returns to what is longed for, but must no longer be (or no longer allowed to be), for the elegiac mode to function. Indeed, the latter requires the very sense of loss which its discourse attempts to remedy, the elegiac motif therefore re-instating the very absence it seeks to answer. *The Whirlpool*'s nostalgic drive however, rather resembles the discursive strategy of mourning, whereby the return to the literary figures of the past and their canonical work becomes a means of achieving detachment from the cultural hegemony of the mother country, and addressing the sense of loss experienced from the lack of a distinct Canadian cultural identity. *The Whirlpool*, I want to propose, deliberately breaks from the British past and its Eurocentric visions of literary excellence to allow the emergence of a Canadian cultural consciousness.

2.   Trauma, Mourning and Renewal in the Colony

The neo-Victorian straddling of two distinct cultures (the nineteenth century and the present) is made yet more complex in *The Whirlpool* by its dual setting (Venice and the town of Niagara Falls): the purpose of this narrative structure is to contrast these various locales and historical moments, to prompt a re-examination of their cultural and aesthetic discourses. This contrast is not performed along the lines of 'old versus new', however, but rather along those of 'new *within* old', which further conveys the paradoxical nature of the neo-Victorian. In this respect, the choice of Venice as the setting for part of the action may be significant in terms of the city's political history: Venice, of course, was an important maritime power and centre of commerce up until the end of the seventeenth century; by 1866 however, when it finally joined the newly created Kingdom of Italy as part of the Risorgimento process, it had lost most of its former power. This decline is suggested in the novel through the descriptions of the city's decay. Alison Chapman has outlined the Brownings' involvement in Italian politics and their fervent support of the Risorgimento process, the latter connoting, in Italian, "resurgence, renaissance and the resurrection of the [state] body" (Chapman 2003: 72). The development of the 'new' country of Italy could therefore offer a parallel with the emergent Canadian nation in the New World. In this context, the body politic of Canada, mentioned earlier in terms of the 'marked' colonial body, needs to be 'resurrected' from prevalent nineteenth-century Eurocentric values. The image of the colonies wrapped in mourning precisely conveys this idea of 'new within old': this description of the British Empire and its association with black crape highlight the stifling and deadening effects of Old World cultural practices on the New World of the colonies, while also suggesting that new visions/codes are to be found beneath such old discourses. The setting of Venice reinforces this concept: the decayed vision of the city within the new country of Italy may therefore be likened to the decay of Europe in the New World of Canada, whereby both Italy and Canada have to leave a past linked to former European supremacy behind to forge new cultural and political identities.

This transition is visible in the character of David McDougal, a military historian who seeks to break from discourses of Empire by inscribing Canada's own historical and political narrative. For that purpose, he sets out to write a book of Canadian history, explicitly guided by the need to "think Canadian":

> 'this country needs thinkers; thinkers that think Canadian. [...] Do they think Canadian at the University of Toronto?', he asks, 'No, they don't. They think Britain... the Empire and all that nonsense.' (Urquhart 1986: 66-67; original ellipses)

McDougal's project focuses on a traumatic event in Canadian history, the Battle of Lundy's Lane, of which he wants to produce an 'authoritative' account to prove that it was won by Canadians, not Americans. The battle was fought in 1814, in present-day Niagara Falls, and opposed British troops (composed of British and Canadian soldiers) to American forces. It is one of the deadliest battles ever fought on Canadian soil, causing upwards of 1,600 deaths and casualties, but the exact nature of its outcome remains to this day uncertain, historical debate still raging as to which side won.[1] By presenting this episode as an important moment in Canada's past, but failing to give any details as to the circumstances surrounding it, Urquhart seems to be relying on a knowledge which can be expected

---

[1] For a more detailed account of the events, see Donald E. Graves's *Where Right and Glory Lead! The Battle of Lundy's Lane 1814* (1997).

of a Canadian audience, but probably not of a foreign one. As with the novel's fragmentary quotational process earlier, we have here again an instance of 'postmodern gaps'.

Brian McHale has explained how such fragmentation is part of "a postmodernist poetics exploring and problematizing the ontologies of worlds and texts", a fragmentation which takes place at "the levels of language, narrative structure, and the material medium (the printed book)" to suggest the disintegration of a continuous, united sense of self (McHale 1992: 254). In Urquhart's text, these gaps represent the ruptures in knowledge and, indeed, knowability, produced by trauma in the individual and collective cultural consciousness. They also indicate an attempt to position as central a traumatic episode which would otherwise be considered secondary/peripheral. The novel's wider project of returning to moments of past trauma to release silenced histories and contest mis-appropriations in Canada's past adopts this paradoxical mode of inscribing such traumatic moments by refusing to narrate them in traditional forms. Their significance is consequently felt more palpably in the text through this deliberate absence of expression, which links to the trope of unrepresentability common in trauma discourse.

This absence also confronts the flawed nature of historical representation, as noticeable in the discursive bias of McDougal's endeavour. Through its emphasis on "thinking Canadian" and its concern with which side won, his work ends up reiterating the same kind of representational problematic that would be encountered in military narratives of the British Empire. In an interview with Herb Wyile, Urquhart explained that she did "believe in 'thinking Canadian'", but that she didn't think it was "as easy as David McDougal thought it was, to pin down exactly what Canadian is":

> I don't think it's necessarily the fact of winning the war of 1812 or not winning it, or winning the Battle of Lundy's Lane. [... T]here's more to history than the battles. Also I'm made nervous by this business of Canada having to have a moment of definition, and it seems that it's either when we won the Battle of Lundy's Lane or it's the Battle of Vimy Ridge [...] I

don't think nationhood can be that easily defined.
(Urquhart 2007: 85)

McDougal's approach therefore illustrates just those kinds of
unilateral, simplistic visions of what constitutes national identity,
which Urquhart calls into question. Additionally, his understanding of
the process of historical commemoration closely follows the
conventions established by European military history and,
paradoxically, makes little allowance for a Canadian specificity. This
is explicit in the description he gives of his "pure" museum:

> David desperately wanted a pure museum… one
> where he could place the relics of the thin history of
> the country where he lived. […] In his museum there
> would be no natural history [but rather] bullets and
> buttons and cannon-balls. The cannons themselves if
> he could find them. […] Maps, autographs,
> commissions signed by famous generals […] copies
> of great speeches given by men approaching battle.
> (Urquhart 1986: 166-167, unbracketed ellipses in the
> original)

McDougal's "pure museum" embodies the kind of attitude criticised
by Urquhart above: she did confess that she "was being very ironic"
with his character (Urquhart 2007: 85). This use of irony allows
Urquhart to respond to the pervasive hold of old, traditional historical
methods in the recording of Canada's past, as visible in McDougal's
selection process. The latter confirms hegemonic visions which favour
the grand political deeds over local realities, as indicated by the
removal of Canada's "natural history".

   Urquhart further illustrates how McDougal's explicit focus on
narrative details and factual evidence causes him to neglect the
affective dimension of the conflict, in favour of its political and
strategic outcomes. This becomes apparent in the novel when his
"pure" museum is contrasted to the "historical room" of Niagara Falls,
where "masses of objects [are] crammed into a closed space"
(Urquhart 1986: 166). There McDougal stumbles across a "small
appliquéd quilt" meant to represent a cemetery, framed by "a border
of coffins, each with a name" and dated 1813 (Urquhart 1986: 166-

167). The morbid subject matter of the quilt becomes clearer when McDougal notices "evidence of missing stitches in the spot [on the border of the quilt] where the coffins had been removed, had been taken into the velvet graveyard" in the centre of the quilt (Urquhart 1986: 167). The "calculated" nature of the quilt horrifies McDougal: he feels that the unknown seamstress is in some way responsible for the deaths she merely recorded in the form of the fabric coffins 'buried' in her tapestry, forgetting in the process that these deaths were caused by the war (Urquhart 1986: 167). His horror at this anonymous artefact suggests that he has lost sight of the atrocities his authoritative account was supposed to commemorate. The novel's refusal to adopt conventional narrative forms in its evocation of past trauma is visible in this instance: the quilt succeeds in releasing silenced histories from Canada's past, something which the "commissions signed by famous generals" and the "copies of great speeches given by men approaching battle" fail to accomplish.

In fact, McDougal's obsession with preserving Canada's "thin history" through his work and his museum project leads him to overlook the actual experiencing of past trauma. His commemoration process, more concerned with the "relics" of Canada's past than with its emotional implications, becomes an end in itself and is indicative of the same kind of excess in Victorian mourning practices already discussed in relation to Browning's death poem and Maud's mourning rituals. Ultimately, such a process prevents the healthy separation between past trauma and present reality, and may be likened to a form of melancholia, as defined earlier. In this respect, McDougal's museum becomes one such locus of melancholic return, excessively preoccupied as it is with the memory of loss and the conservation of death (as in "relics"). In fact, despite McDougal's comment that "[t]his country buries its history so fast people with memories are considered insane" (Urquhart 1986: 77), the novel facilitates a reading of McDougal's own obsession with remembering as a form of neurosis. In his 'First Lecture on Psycho-analysis', Freud links the idea of reminiscence (for instance in the shape of mnemic symbols such as monuments and memorials) to the recalling of traumatic events/experiences in the remote past. However, in cases where the patient emotionally clings to the memory of the traumatic event, from which they cannot be freed and for which they neglect what is most immediate, such reminiscences can lead to a form of hysterical neurosis (Freud 1957: 16-17). In this perspective, McDougal's "relics" serve not as memorials, but as fetishised objects of loss, while his attitude towards the events he is trying to record may be symbolically compared to this neurotic state.

This is visible in the novel through his fascination with Laura Secord, the Canadian heroine who showed extreme endurance during the war of 1812 in braving a thirty kilometer walk through the wilderness to warn the British Lieutenant James Fitzgibbon of an impending American attack. This crucial warning enabled the British and Canadians to make necessary preparations and to win the ensuing battle against the American forces, but Laura Secord never received any recognition for this military victory in her lifetime. McDougal's interest in Laura Secord's story is not motivated by a wish to contest this elision in the record; rather, he develops historical fantasies of an erotic nature about his wife Fleda, fancying that she is the nineteenth-century Canadian heroine: "My wife is very much like Laura Secord. I think that may be one of the reasons I married her" (Urquhart 1986: 80). These fantasies lead him to impose role-play games on his wife as part of their love-making, and to pretend that she is "the young, slim woman alone, walking through the enemy-infested, beast-ridden woods", imagining that "Fitzgibbon would be strangely moved by her appearance [...] that Fitzgibbon would dismiss his colleagues so that he could speak to Laura alone" (Urquhart 1986: 79, 47). McDougal's obsessive reminiscence of Laura Secord's ordeal therefore causes him to neglect what is real and immediate – his wife – and to emotionally cling to a traumatic memory from the distant past.

In this respect, Laura Secord's traumatic experience is re-appropriated and re-read in erotic terms by the male historian, who seems to use historical commemoration as a means of sexual gratification. McDougal's historical obsession is further exemplified by his insistence that his wife wear the dress that allegedly belonged to Laura Secord. This object, as with his other collected "relics" of Canada's past, is not used to reveal silenced or overlooked histories, but rather to 'enshrine' prevalent (male) historical versions of the past. Patricia Yaeger has commented on the appropriation process inherent in academic writing about past trauma, as part of "a ritual of nationalizing identity" (Yaeger 2002: 47). She notes that "[i]n troping or turning death into figures, writing is once more exposed as an act of commodification and consumption: a space where death is converted into pleasure" (Yaeger 2002: 48). McDougal's attitude is also reminiscent of the kind of 'trauma tourism' described by Ann Heilmann as "the visitation of sites connected with suffering, not to further empathy and historical understanding, but rather to pursue self-indulgent emotional excitement and gratification" (this volume: 298). The novel therefore illustrates the detrimental effect conventional narrative forms can have on the inscription of past trauma; in this case, the female subject, even when heroic, is reduced to an object of male sexual fantasy by old, traditional historical discourses.

However, such old forms of historical recording may be successfully replaced by new visions that take into consideration the affect of trauma and its Canadian specificity. Maud, for instance, uses mourning as a source of individual expression and shows how historical commemoration can become a means of liberation from the colonial past. Peter Widdowson has noted that such returns to hegemonic historical records and practices usually indicate a feminist and/or postcolonial drive in contemporary "re-visionary" fiction, as well as a demand that

> past texts' complicity in oppression [...] be revised and re-visioned as part of the process of restoring a voice, a history and an identity to those hitherto exploited, marginalized and silenced by dominant interests and ideologies. (Widdowson 2006: 505-506)

Maud's commemorative efforts seem to partake of a similar cultural and political thrust: as part of her profession, it is her responsibility to keep a record of the anonymous bodies – suicides or foolhardy swimmers – found in the Niagara River and its deadly whirlpool. This administrative task leads to a more private form of remembering, however, as is visible in Maud's gathering of the personal objects found on the unclaimed bodies:

> Who was this man, this D.N.? She would more than likely never know. Who was the keeper of his memories? [...] Earlier in the morning she had taken all these sad relics into the long hall cupboard where she kept the possessions of the nameless floaters. [...] This cupboard was Maud's own personal reliquary.

> She wanted to enclose and protect the fragmented
> evidence of these smothered lives, to hold memories
> of their memories. This was her museum. (Urquhart
> 1986: 89-90)

Maud's "reliquary" is contrasted to McDougal's "pure museum"
earlier: the "sad relics" she collects do not recall heroic deeds by
famous figures, but rather attempt to capture the memories of
individual, anonymous lives. Her inscription process focuses precisely
on remembering the pain of these "smothered lives", on naming the
"nameless", and consequently on acknowledging the silenced, micro-
histories of Canada's past. Through her efforts, the untold narratives
of these mysterious deaths can be, if not recovered, at least witnessed.
Her self-appointment as the "keeper of [their] memories" also
indicates the personal nature of her recording process: unlike
McDougal's official research on the site of the Battle of Lundy's
Lane, where Maud's undertaker's establishment stands, her
remembrance of these nameless victims remains private. This is
visible in the document where she keeps these records: "like almost
everything described inside it, the book itself was unidentified. [...] A
smaller document than the battleground that Grady and Son stood
upon, its history was not finished. The book was not yet full"
(Urquhart 1986: 42). The implied hierarchy between the battle site and
Maud's unidentified document echoes that between the old values of
Europe and the new Canadian vision. In this respect, official forms of
historical commemoration (suggested by "the battleground") seem to
be rejected in favour of Maud's personal, "unfinished" micronarrative.

Maud's two-year mourning period for the death of her
husband has already been shown to illustrate how the upholding of
Victorian social customs in the colonies can become stifling and,
ultimately, meaningless. Conversely, her commemoration of the
drowned bodies seems to yield more of an insight into the significance
of their deaths than conventional Victorian mourning rituals. In this
respect, Maud successfully subverts prevalent Victorian cultural
aesthetics of death and mourning by elaborating new ways of
inscribing and mourning trauma. This is also ironically suggested by
her name, through its association with the tragic Tennysonian heroine:
unlike the titular Maud of the poem (1855), the novel's character is
left in charge of the family funeral home after her husband's death,

and turns death and the dying into a source of individual expression, as well as a money-making enterprise. Although this may be read as yet another form of trauma appropriation, Laura Hancu agrees that Maud constitutes "an alternative subject who breaks the frame of the passive object of love in Tennyson's famous poem. The Maud of this novel is […] a creative woman who manages to pick herself up and run a thriving business" (Hancu 1995: 63, note 5). Maud therefore illustrates how breaking from the stifling values of the mother country and its cultural legacy can lead to renewal in the colony.

Maud's record keeping also documents a specifically Canadian phenomenon: the ceaseless appeal of the Niagara whirlpool to suicides and intrepid swimmers attempting to brave its currents. One of the dead bodies found by Maud bridges both descriptions, namely that of the young Ontario poet Patrick who is ultimately vanquished by his fascination with the landscape features he cannot conjure in his work. Patrick's inability to understand the surrounding wilderness causes him to think that swimming through its whirlpool is the only way he can emotionally, as well as physically, experience it, and therefore be able to write about it. Patrick seems to be replicating prevalent nineteenth-century European landscape aesthetics in his attempt to engage with the wilderness on a personal level; his interest in such aesthetics is made visible by his estranged wife's comment that "night after night he disappear[s] into the old-world landscape with Wordsworth, Coleridge, or Browning", and that he is "never going to find Wordsworth's daffodils here" (Urquhart 1986: 63). Patrick's drowning in the Niagara River therefore suggests his failure to adapt his aesthetic sensibilities to those of the New World, thus leading him to commit a form of artistic suicide.

The pervasive hold of British literary and cultural legacies in the colony, as symbolically suggested by Patrick's death, is also noticeable in Fleda McDougal's interaction with her surroundings:

> She had secretly, all the while, been imagining poems filled with the smell of cedars carried on the breath of a northern wind. Scotch pines, white pines. […] Wondering how Wordsworth or Browning would interpret landscape such as this or events such as these [intrepid swimmers braving the whirlpool], she turned away. (Urquhart 1986: 114)

Fleda's attitude illustrates how the persisting influence of the canonical voices from the mother country can cause the act of aesthetic interpretation to remain firmly in the grasp of these voices, leaving the New World setting untranslated, and possibly untranslatable, in those kinds of Eurocentric cultural terms. However, by promoting a symbolic parallel between the minority status of nineteenth-century Canadian writing, represented by Patrick, and the British literary canon, suggested by Shelley and Browning, the novel seems to be questioning the sustained hold of these landscape aesthetics. This is confirmed by the reversal of the expected hierarchy of voices enacted in the text: the European setting and its canonical figures are kept in the margins of the narrative, while the main focus of the novel is on the Canadian locale. In this respect, Patrick's death mirrors and re-writes Shelley's by drawing from the similar trope of the drowned poet, already mentioned as a source of poetic envy and anxiety for Browning. The cultural significance of Shelley's death, grotesquely conveyed through his "limp and drifting" body in the neo-Victorian text, is further undermined by Patrick's tragic and anonymous drowning: the latter succeeds in inscribing a poetic voice which would have otherwise remained silent, and is part of the novel's wider project of contesting the presence of these Victorian literary and cultural legacies in the colony. This is further achieved by some of the intertextual echoes found in the Niagara Falls setting: *Adonais* (1821), for instance, becomes one of the small toy boats Fleda sends out on the whirlpool, thus ironically undermining the revered status of Shelley's elegiac poem for his fellow Romantic Keats. Laura Hancu has commented on the novel's protest "against the Romantic image of the dying poet regenerated through his verse" by reducing *Adonais* to "an emblematic toy boat confined to the whirlpool" (Hancu 1995: 63, note 2). This may also be linked to the paradoxical nature of the elegiac mode, requiring and re-instating the very sense of loss its discourse attempts to contest. This seems compounded by the fact that the toy boat is caught in an endless cycle of circular journeys, following the currents of the whirlpool and unable to disengage itself from its stream. This visual metaphor adequately conveys the effects of the elegiac motif in the text, endlessly returning to the object of loss, endlessly repeating its absence.

In fact, the whirlpool itself offers a fitting metaphor for the novel's complex series of returns to the past: "In one sense the whirlpool was like memory; like obsession connected to memory, like history that stayed in one spot, moving nowhere and endlessly repeating itself" (Urquhart 1986: 43). Like the whirlpool, the neo-Victorian novel seems confined to a cycle of traumatic repeats and returns to the past, apparently driven by an obsessive need to re-visit its predecessors' culture as a means of expressing its own struggle to find an 'authentic' voice with which to speak of the past, paralleling the postcolonial struggle of self-differentiation from the imperial centre. This idea of repetition constitutes both a narrative strategy and a thematic concern in Urquhart's text: Browning is haunted by Shelley, McDougal is obsessed with Laura Secord, and Maud compulsively follows all Victorian mourning codes. The negative effects of these attitudes are addressed in the novel, likening the inability to move on artistically or to mourn historically to a form of melancholia, an internalisation of loss which ultimately prevents detachment from the latter and the establishment of a separate sense of self. If the whirlpool acts as a metaphor for the detrimental effects of memory and history, *The Whirlpool*, however, shows how returning to the past may be crucial in achieving a successful release from its cultural and political hegemony. This seems especially true in relation to 'minor' or disregarded instances of past trauma, such as Laura Secord's ordeal, the drowned bodies in the Niagara River, or Patrick's death. The inscription of these events is presented as necessary in the text to allow the separation between mother country and colony, between the deceased and the living, so that the mourning process can take place and lead to renewal.

David Lloyd has explained that the haunting trope in postcolonial cultural expressions was key in establishing a relation to the past "structured around the notion of survival or living on rather than recovery", so as to "ground a different mode of historicization" in contemporary discourses about past trauma (Lloyd 2000: 219-220). Commenting on the "irrecoverable" loss occasioned by such past trauma, Judith Butler also recognises

> a melancholic agency who cannot know its history as the past, cannot capture its history through chronology, and does not know who it is except as the survival, the persistence of a certain unavowability that haunts the present. (Butler 2003: 468)

In the Canadian neo-Victorian context however, mourning, that "certain unavowability" haunting the present, is re-appropriated and used as a valid discursive strategy in the establishment of a distinct cultural and historical consciousness for the nation. Indeed, despite the paradoxical nature of mourning, where "loss must be marked" while "it cannot be represented", where "loss fractures representation itself" as well as "precipitat[ing] its own modes of expression", Butler notes that such "[l]oss becomes condition and necessity for a certain sense of community", whereby "belonging now takes place in and through a common sense of loss" (Butler 2003: 467, 468).

Cathy Caruth's definition of trauma as "the confrontation with an event that, in its unexpectedness or horror, cannot be placed within the schemes of prior knowledge", an event that "continually returns, in its exactness, at a later time" is also useful in this context (Caruth 1995: 153). Caruth observes that "[n]ot having been fully integrated as it occurred", that event cannot be "integrated into a completed story of the past" (Caruth 1995: 153). Such conception of trauma as an irresolvable residue (visible for instance in Shelley's death, or in the Battle of Lundy's Lane) is overturned and undermined in the text through the novel's contestation of the flawed nature of traditional methods of historical representation. In this respect, Canadian neo-Victorianism presents mourning and the commemoration of trauma as means of revision and liberation from Victorian cultural and historical discourses in Canada. This is achieved all the more effectively through the neo-Victorian novel's derisive stance towards such discourses: its return to canonical texts, figures and events of the past is not motivated by a wish to re-establish their cultural superiority, but rather to work against their grain. Urquhart's novel thus evinces a clear postmodern turn, enacting what Hutcheon has described as postmodernism's "contradictory cultural enterprise", one that "uses and abuses the very structures and values it takes to task", in this case, those of Victorian culture (Hutcheon 1988: 106).

The same ambivalence is visible in the novel's ambiguous ending: Fleda leaves her husband and mysteriously vanishes into the surrounding wilderness. Her eventual assimilation into the landscape which has resisted her – and Patrick's – aesthetic interpretation seems to be the only way Fleda can escape from the Eurocentric literary discourses discussed earlier. Her vanishing also reflects the novel's rejection of conventional methods of historical representation, and its paradoxical mode of inscribing trauma by refusing to narrate it in traditional forms. The last words Fleda enters in her diary indicate as much by recalling Laura Secord's long walk across the wilderness: "Nobody understood. It wasn't the message that was important. It was the walk. The journey. Setting forth" (Urquhart 1986: 214). Unlike the static spot at the centre of the whirlpool, going nowhere and endlessly repeating itself, Fleda attempts to break from the detrimental effects of conventional historical commemoration by "setting forth" on a journey, re-inscribing Laura Secord's earlier trail in the process. The latter's purpose, namely the warning of an impending American attack, is read as playing into the set of traditional historical and cultural values Fleda seeks to flee. For that purpose, and as a symbolic response to her husband's earlier objectification of both herself and the nineteenth-century heroine, Fleda "followed Laura Secord's route but she carried with her no deep messages" (Urquhart 1986: 228). Fleda's disappearance therefore symbolically counteracts Canada's sustained haunting by canonical figures from the mother country, while her departure also works to defeat the pervasive influence of such cultural and political legacies and establish a (renewed) Canadian historical consciousness. She leaves behind her copies of Browning and other Victorian works, and takes with her no message, no narrative.

Bibliography

Butler, Judith. 2003. 'Afterword: After Loss, What Then?' in Eng, David L., and David Kazanjian (eds.), *Loss: The Politics of Mourning*. Berkeley: University of California Press: 467-473.

Caruth, Cathy. 1995. 'Recapturing the Past: Introduction' in Caruth, Cathy (ed.), *Trauma: Explorations in Memory*. Baltimore, Maryland: The Johns Hopkins University Press: 151-157.

Chapman, Alison. 2003. 'Risorgimenti: Spiritualism, Politics and Elizabeth Barrett Browning' in Chapman, Alison, and Jane Stabler (eds.), *Unfolding the South: Nineteenth-Century British Women Writers and Artists in Italy*. Manchester: Manchester University Press: 70-89.

Colley, Ann C. 1998. *Nostalgia and Recollection in Victorian Culture*. London: Macmillan.

D'haen, Theo. 1994. 'Countering Postmodernism', *REAL: Research in English and American Literature* 10: 49-64.

Freud, Sigmund. 1957. 'Five Lectures on Psycho-Analysis' [1909] in *The Standard Edition of the Complete Psychological Works of Sigmund Freud*, vol. 11 (tr.

and ed. James Strachey, in collaboration with Anna Freud, assisted by Alix Stratchey and Alan Tyson). London: Hogarth Press: 7-56.

——. 1987. 'Mourning and Melancholia' [1917] in *On Metapsychology: The Theory of Psychoanalysis,* Pelican Freud Library, vol. 11 (tr. and ed. James Strachey, and ed. Angela Richards). Harmondsworth: Penguin Books: 245-268.

Goldman, Marlene. 1996. 'Translating the Sublime: Jane Urquhart's *The Whirlpool*', *Canadian Literature* 150: 23-42.

Gutleben, Christian. 2001. *Nostalgic Postmodernism: The Victorian Tradition and the Contemporary British Novel.* Amsterdam: Rodopi.

Hancu, Laura. 1995. 'Escaping the Frame: Circumscribing the Narrative in *The Whirlpool*', *Studies in Canadian Literature/Études en littérature canadienne* 20(1): 45-64.

Hutcheon, Linda. 1988. *A Poetics of Postmodernism: History, Theory, Fiction.* London: Routledge.

——. 1990. 'Circling the Downspout of Empire', in Adam, Ian, and Helen Tiffin (eds.), *Past the Last Post: Theorizing Post-Colonialism and Post-Modernism.* Calgary: University of Calgary Press: 167-191.

——. 1991. *Splitting Images: Contemporary Canadian Ironies.* Don Mills, Ontario: Oxford University Press.

Lloyd, David. 2000. 'Colonial Trauma/Postcolonial Recovery?', *Interventions* 2(2) (July): 212-228.

Lyotard, Jean-François. 1984. *The Postmodern Condition: A Report on Knowledge* (tr. Geoff Bennington and Brian Massumi). Minneapolis: University of Minnesota Press.

McHale, Brian. 1992. *Constructing Postmodernism.* London: Routledge.

O'Gorman, Francis. 2007. 'Browning, Grief, and the Strangeness of Dramatic Verse', *The Cambridge Quarterly* 36(2): 155-173.

Quayson, Ato. 2000. 'Postcolonialism and Postmodernism' in Schwarz, Henry, and Sangeeta Ray (eds.), *A Companion to Postcolonial Studies.* Oxford: Blackwell: 87-111.

Schor, Hilary M. 2000. 'Sorting, Morphing, and Mourning: A.S. Byatt Ghostwrites Victorian Fiction' in Kucich, John, and Dianne F. Sadoff (eds.), *Victorian Afterlife: Postmodern Culture Rewrites the Nineteenth Century.* Minneapolis: University of Minnesota Press: 234-251.

Shuttleworth, Sally. 1998. 'Natural History: The Retro-Victorian Novel' in Shaffer, Elinor (ed.), *The Third Culture: Literature and Science.* New York: Walter de Gruyter: 253-268.

Steenman-Marcusse, Conny. 2001. *Re-Writing Pioneer Women in Anglo-Canadian Literature.* Amsterdam: Rodopi.

Urquhart, Jane. 1986. *The Whirlpool.* Toronto: McClelland & Stewart.

——. 2007. 'Confessions of a Historical Geographer' in Wyile, Herb (ed.), *Speaking in the Past Tense: Canadian Novelists on Writing Historical Fiction.* Waterloo, Ontario: Wilfrid Laurier University Press: 79-103.

Widdowson, Peter. 2006. '"Writing Back": Contemporary Re-Visionary Fiction', *Textual Practice* 20(3): 491-507.

Williamson, Andrew. 2008. '"The Dead Man Touch'd Me From the Past": Reading as Mourning, Mourning as Reading in A.S. Byatt's "The Conjugial Angel"', *Neo-Victorian Studies* (Autumn) 1(1): 110-137.

Wyile, Herb. 2007. 'Introduction' in Wyile, Herb (ed.), *Speaking in the Past Tense: Canadian Novelists on Writing Historical Fiction*. Waterloo, Ontario: Wilfrid Laurier University Press: 1-24.

Yaeger, Patricia. 2002. 'Consuming Trauma; or, The Pleasures of Merely Circulating' in Miller, Nancy K., and Jason Tougaw (eds.), *Extremities: Trauma, Testimony, and Community*. Chicago: University of Illinois Press: 25-51.

Tipoo's Tiger on the Loose:
Neo-Victorian Witness-Bearing
and the Trauma of the Indian Mutiny

Marie-Luise Kohlke

Abstract:
The wake of the Indian Mutiny of 1857-58, or India's First War of Independence, produced a flood of contemporary writings commemorating one of the great nineteenth-century traumas. The Mutiny remains as much a trope of fascination for neo-Victorian writers, who interrogate the Uprising as a defining act of imperial violence, which simultaneously foreshadowed the empire's eventual demise. An apex of barbarity on both sides, the Mutiny's conjunction of racial, religious, and nationalist causes and geopolitical interests could be said to uncannily presage today's 'clash of cultures' and global terror. This chapter explores the neo-Victorian politicisation of trauma with regards to the Mutiny, the different strategies employed to figure the conflict's unspeakable horrors, and their ethical dilemmas with regards to commemoration, exoneration, and symbolic redress.

Keywords: *The Devil's Wind: Nana Saheb's Story,* imperialism, Indian Mutiny, *The Mutiny*, neo-Victorian novel, *Nightrunners of Bengal*, *The Siege of Krishnapur*, trauma, unrepresentability, violence.

*****

1. The Indian Tiger: Hear It Roar

In the English writer Julian Rathbone's novel *The Mutiny* (2007), published to coincide with the 150th anniversary of the Revolt of 1857-58,[1] Azimullah Khan, agent and advisor to the soon-to-be rebel leader Dhondu Pant, Nana Saheb of Bithur, dispossessed of his

---

[1] The terms 'Mutiny', 'Revolt', 'Uprising', etc. remain contentious, suggesting as they do illegitimate resistance against a legitimate government, rather than justified opposition against unlawful rule. Hence the use of such terms, as well as 'rebels', 'Eastern', 'Western', etc., should be read within implied inverted commas.

hereditary rights by the British, visits the East India House in London to plead his master's case.[2] While being kept waiting, Azimullah peruses a collection of Indian artefacts, among them "a large lacquered tiger crouching full length over a prostrate redcoat, mauling the poor soldier's throat. Tipoo's Tiger. An automaton taken from the rebel Tipoo Sahib's palace some sixty years earlier" (Rathbone 2007: 63). The trophy represents very different things for Azimullah and its new owners.[3] The Indian evidently delights in the symbolic celebration of the one-time might of Tipu Sultan, also known as the Tiger of Mysore, a powerful indigenous ruler and French ally who obstructed the expansion of British rule in India for nearly two decades. Implicitly, Tipoo's Tiger also prefigures the Uprising and the slaughter of the British to come, inverting the Victorians' assumed superiority over their colonial subjects. Yet the artefact further allows another reading, whereby Tipoo's Tiger serves as testament to an ineradicable barbarism and cruelty underlying Indian 'nature', requiring ever vigilant control by the British rule of law and order. Its exhibition as a trophy of British military conquest and a harmless exotic spectacle of fun vanquishes the primitive Indian threat.

From the nineteenth-century British perspective, the Mutiny reinforced convictions in Indian lawless barbarism, which Edward Thompson suggests contributed to the ruthlessness of British reprisals: "the men who served in India during these years often felt that they were exterminating vermin" (Thompson 1925: 137). Tipoo's Tiger was on the loose once more. Thus Cardinal Nicholas Wiseman condemned "these hordes of savage mutineers" who "have not merely resumed the barbarity of their ancient condition, but borrowed the ferocity of the tiger in his jungle, to torture, to mutilate, to agonise, and to destroy" (qtd. Herbert 2008: 31). The tiger motif functions as an example of the interplay between what Astrid Erll terms "premediation" and "remediation", that is, the "pre-form[ing] and re-

---

[2] Though recognised by the British administration as rightful heir to the personal fortune of Baji Rao II, his adopted father, in line with Dalhousie's Doctrine of Lapse Nana Saheb was stripped of his rights to the former Peshwa's title, pension, and special privileges (such as exemption from the jurisdiction of the courts).

[3] There appears to be no discussion about Britain's rights to retain Indian spoils comparable to that regarding the Elgin Marbles. Tipoo's Tiger is still on view in London today, as part of the collections of the Victoria and Albert Museum.; see http://footguards00.tripod.com/09GALLERY/Art/09_cornw-tipu.htm.

shap[ing]" of cultural memory (Erll 2009: 111, 131). On the one hand, it serves as a 'cue' that triggers culture-specific images, narratives, and associations that are already part of each observer's "semantic memory", providing pre-existing "schemata for new experience and its representation" (Erll 2009: 111). On the other, the motif's repeated recyclings appear to authenticate and amplify the 'reality' of the events of 1857-58 that they actually help to produce, by contributing to a growing "canon of existent medial constructions" (Erll 2009: 111), which facilitate, stabilise, and modify cultural memory. In *Nightrunners of Bengal* (1951) by the expatriate English writer John Masters, himself a former officer in the British Indian army, Sumitra Lakshmi, the promiscuous Rani of Kishanpur – unfairly modelled on the real-life rebel leader Lakshmibai, the Rani of Jhansi – is compared to a "tigress with wings" (Masters 1988: 53). Symbolically apt, the rebels plot Mutiny under cover of a tiger-hunt, during which the protagonist officer Rodney Savage saves Sumitra from a wounded tigress, in other words 'saving her from herself' as the British liked to think of themselves as saving India from the Indians (see Greenberger 1969: 22). Rodney slays the beast and, during his later love-making with Sumitra, fondly thinks of her as his "sweet tigress with her claws gone" (Masters 1988: 84). In *The Siege of Krishnapur* (1973) the British-Irish writer J.G. Farrell has the beleaguered colonisers employ Hari, the Westernised son of the local Maharaja, as a human shield to protect the hospital of the British compound, confining him to the adjacent stable that once housed a former Resident's pair of tigers: "Now, where once the tigers had lived, Hari strode endlessly back and forth behind the bars" (Farrell 1999: 175). In *The Devil's Wind: Nana Saheb's Story* (1972), by the Indian English-language author Manohar Malgonkar,[4] however, the titular protagonist employs the tiger trope

---

[4] The term 'neo-Victorian' could be seen as problematic applied to Indian, especially post-Independence fiction, seemingly seeking to claim it for an anglicised or Western dominated genre. Repeatedly, however, the neo-Victorian constructs itself as a self-consciously *postcolonial* form of writing back *against* the centres of power, often from the perspective of the externally and internally colonised. Hence the textual politics of neo-Victorian texts by British authors and those of former colonies (not only India, but also Australia, Canada, etc.) often display more convergence than outright differences. Accordingly, this essay employs 'neo-Victorian' in its broadest sense, as a thematic umbrella term for historical fiction re-creating the nineteenth century and its ideological concerns from latter-day perspectives, irrespective of writers' nationalities or texts' particular geographical settings.

more subversively as an emblem of the desire for liberty and self-determination. He describes his generation as one "that had known only British rule; we were like animals born in a zoo, never knowing what it was to be in the jungles, roaming, free" (Malgonkar 1988: 24).

The Indian Mutiny, re-titled India's First War of Independence by Indian nationalist and postcolonial historians, constituted one of nineteenth-century Britain's greatest crises. Christopher Herbert goes so far as to describe it "as the supreme trauma of the age" (Herbert 2008: 2). It struck at the heart of the Victorians' self-confidence in their destined mission as beneficent rulers of other races, replacing barbarism with the *Pax Britannica* and spreading enlightened civilisation to grateful coloured peoples around the globe. In Farrell's novel, George Fleury, arriving in India shortly before the outbreak of hostilities, enquires nonplussed of a Company official, "Why, if the Indian people are happier under our rule [...] do they not emigrate from those native states like Hyderabad which are so dreadfully misgoverned and come and live in British India?" (Farrell 1999: 37) Farrell's ironic evocation of geopolitics resonates uncannily with their continued dominance in globalised world economies and international relations of the present day, as well as the resulting flow of economic migrants and political and conflict refugees. The Mutiny's excessive violence and conjunction of racial, religious, and nationalist causes could also be read as eerily presaging today's 'clash of cultures' and the age of global terror, exacerbated by Western nations' neo-imperialist engagements in the Middle East and Asian subcontinent. Gautam Chakravarty scathingly remarks on how the Victorians' "vast, thriving military-industrial machinery, which policed the global beat" anticipated today's capitalist neo-colonialism:

> the civilising mission created jobs and funnelled wealth home along with ornamental freebies like Indian diamonds and the Elgin marbles, while State Department platitudes on democracy fuel the squadrons that bomb ancient civilisations for oil and gas. (Chakravarty 2005: 2)

Similarly, the re-enactment of the lures of professed Victorian world-improvements, in novels such as *Nightrunners of Bengal*, "anticipates, in several ways, the postcolonial modalities of charities and NGOs in the third world" (Kerr 2008: 158). The Mutiny trope thus provides a nexus linking past and present traumas and ways of dealing with their long-term after-effects. Such trans-historical correlations no doubt contribute to the subject's abiding appeal.

More than any of the other bloody conflicts during Queen Victoria's reign, the Mutiny threw into doubt not only the temporal limits of Britannia's power, but also her people's very identity as a chosen race and nation, the standard-bearers of civilisation. The potential loss of the 'Jewel in the Crown' threatened to leave Britain unrecognisably diminished, the British cultural imaginary of heroic nationhood by now inextricably entwined with her colonial 'Other': "India was so integral to the British national self-image that the idea of a Britain without India was almost inconceivable" (Booker 2000: 19). The Mutiny, I want to suggest, serves not only as the symbolic 'birth' of empire, by catalysing the colony's transfer to the direct control of the Crown by the Government of India Act in 1858 and the subsequent proclamation of Queen Victoria as Empress of India in 1876. It also functions as an imaginary point of origin for the twentieth-century British identity crisis and 'trauma' of the loss of empire, of having to cede its place as dominant world power to the US, the Soviet Union, and later China and seeing its remaining prestige assimilated into the collective of the European Union. As at the time of the 1982 Falklands War under the premiership of Margaret Thatcher (the advocate, famously, of 'Victorian values'), resurgences in British nationalist sentiments have tended to precipitate a concomitant proliferation in artistic recreations of the Raj. Commenting on this phenomenon, Salman Rushdie employs a metaphor charged with traumatic connotations:

> The recrudescence of imperialist ideology and the popularity of Raj fictions put one in mind of the phantom twitchings of an amputated limb. [...] Britain is in danger of entering a condition of cultural psychosis, in which it begins once again to strut and posture like a great power while, in fact, its power diminishes every year. (Rushdie 1992: 132)

What I will call 'neo-Victorian Mutiny fiction', then, might be described as a symptom of Posttraumatic Stress Disorder – at the level of the collective and cultural rather than individual psyche.[5] In a kind of traumatic displacement, the cultural imaginary seeks recourse to a time before imperial decline, but paradoxically relives that trauma through the moment of foundational violence that both creates the empire and pre-figures its eventual demise.

2.   Mutiny Fiction and Trauma Discourse

The extent of the traumatic impact of 1857-58 is evident from the veritable flood of British writings commemorating the events, which began to appear almost immediately. These ranged from official investigative post-counterinsurgency reports and the emotive personal memoirs of East India Company officials, military personnel, and British civilians caught up in the violence, to later romance and sensation fiction about the period, as well as campaign histories and military biographies. What most such writings shared was a focus on British suffering and heroism, while "the actions and initiative of the [indigenous] people are, needless to say, substantially lost" (Roy 1994: 3). So too is their suffering. Darshan Perusek notes that "[t]he entire corpus of primary material" includes only a single contemporary account by an Indian witness (Perusek 1992: 290).

Literary outpourings of Victorian national grief and rage persisted with little abatement into the next century, almost as if the British nation were engaged in a simultaneous obsessive repetition and frantic working-through of its collective trauma. Curiously, however, trauma theorists have neglected the Mutiny as a useful case study for analysing processes of national mourning, commemoration and forgetting of extraordinary violence and suffering. Only recently and very tentatively has scholarship on the Uprising begun to relate the events of 1857-58 to wider cultural discourses of trauma.[6] In

---

[5] The term, usually abbreviated as PTSD, was officially coined in 1980 in the American Psychiatric Association's diagnostic manual, in large part in response to the conditions and treatment of U.S. veterans of the Vietnam War (1959-75). The anxiety disorder results from a threat to subjects' physical or psychological integrity during traumatic events. Significantly, this need not involve outright harm to the self, but can equally result from witnessing others' trauma, especially that of persons closely connected to and identified with by the self, e.g. in terms of race or nationality.

[6] See, e.g., Herbert's *War of No Pity: The Indian Mutiny and Victorian Trauma* (2008). Herbert's use of trauma theory, however, is restricted to a handful of quotations (recycled several times) from Cathy Caruth's *Unclaimed Experience:*

contrast, colonialism and other major nineteenth-century traumas, such as slavery and the Great Irish Famine of 1845-52, have already received important analysis in this regard (see Lloyd 2000 and 2005; Vickroy 2002; Whitehead 2004; Craps and Buelens 2008; Rothberg 2008). Most significantly, such recent work has begun to problematise trauma theory's universalising Eurocentric bias, and its conceptual limits when applied to colonised cultures and non-Western contexts. As Michael Rothberg notes, these may obstruct, rather than promote, trauma studies' "aspirations for cross-cultural understanding", as they risk "reproducing the terms and frameworks that we set out to disable" (Rothberg 2008: 226). That same problematic reproduction also haunts neo-Victorian re-imaginings of the Mutiny.

With its re-enactment of inter-societal conflict and clashing belief and value systems, neo-Victorian Mutiny fiction highlights the cultural politics of trauma, including perspectival bias, processes of 'Othering', and the significance accorded traumatic memory within constructions of nationhood. Yet in spite of predating the emergence of trauma theory as such, Victorian Mutiny literature already anticipated some of its concepts, especially the final 'unimaginability' of the catastrophe that overwhelms rationalising and signifying faculties. As summed up by John Mowitt, "trauma has, through its study, come to designate an expressive limit – the unspeakable event" (Mowitt 2000: 272). Herbert identifies an analogous limit at work in Victorian writing on the Mutiny:

> Far from seeming a quarry of materials readily and unproblematically translatable [...] the great Indian upheaval seemed to many to define itself first and foremost by virtue of its unnerving recalcitrance to representation. It was a story that in many ways, so contemporaries never tired of stating, *could not be written*. (Herbert 2009: 20, original emphasis)

Herbert cites numerous examples, among them Henry Mead's reference, as early as 1857, to British victims' "horrible tortures", of which "we dare not trust ourselves to speak", and Seton Merriman's

---

Trauma, Narrative, and History (1996), a crucial weakness of his thought-provoking study.

novel *Flotsam* (1892), whose narrator describes 1857 as "a year truly of […] unspeakable horror" (qtd. Herbert 2008: 20-21). The "topos of unspeakability", then, is far more than "the curious rhetorical device" Erll takes it to be (Erll 2009: 113). Implicitly, Victorian writers constructed traumatic knowledge much as do latter-day theorists, as paradoxically resistant to its envisioned object and its transmission. Geoffrey H. Hartman situates traumatic knowledge as "a contradiction in terms" – "as close to nescience as to knowledge", always on the verge of transforming phantasmagorically into "unconscious or not-knowing knowledge" (Hartman 1995: 536; 544). Trauma 'others' knowledge and its would-be subjects, severing consciousness from the event itself. What narrative captures is only ever the trace and wake of trauma, its symptoms, reverberations and after-images, leaving an unassimilable and irreducible residue – or excess – of the unrepresentable. To adapt Cathy Caruth's terms, trauma narratives can only "speak about and speak through" trauma, but never speak the trauma itself, defying witness even as they demand it (Caruth 1996: 4-5). Some eighty years before the "powerful black hole" of Shoah became *the* paradigmatic border-event of historical trauma (Seligmann-Silva 2003: 144), the Mutiny functioned as an analogous limit-case of unrepresentability, a limit contested but also reinscribed by neo-Victorian writing on the subject.

Unlike their neo-Victorian counterparts, most nineteenth-century Mutiny narratives are not overtly concerned with ethical debates around the aestheticisations of pain and exploitative spectacle or with the democratisation of trauma in terms of identity politics. They focus mainly on British suffering, with indigenous pain and death often treated cavalierly. Nor is the traumatic event, as common in present-day fiction, held to bypass the subject altogether, whose conceptual grasp and signifying abilities are confounded by the truncated experience (or more accurately 'non-experience' in the first instance), which is suspended until the crisis can be belatedly relived and comprehended by being given narrative form. Strictly speaking, then, neo-Victorian literature projects "the traumatized subject" anachronistically backwards in time, since this form of subjectivity only emerges as "a new kind of contemporary identity" within the later context of twentieth/twenty-first century trauma culture (Bennett and Kennedy 2003: 4).

Likewise, Victorian Mutiny fictions display little interest in problematising the ideological, sometimes pathological, biases that underpin practices of national mourning and commemoration, which become a major focal point in neo-Victorian novels. Malgonkar's Nana Saheb, for instance, notes how "there was the keenest rivalry among the [British] column commanders to possess [his] skull as a table ornament, as an inkstand or an ash tray" (Malgonkar 1988: 255). Later, he describes the Bibighar, site of the massacre of British women and children hostages at Kanpur (or Cawnpore), as "a shrine that could not fail to make you burn with hatred for the other race", as "a memorial as much to British atrocities as to our own", the British violence having preceded and, according to Nana, precipitated the hostage killings, as well as avenging them with still greater ferocity (Malgonkar 1988: 302). In a sense, violence itself serves as a perverted form of communal commemoration.[7] Another case in point is the Memorial Garden at Kanpur, a "veritable vortex of symbolic investment", to borrow Ann Rigney's reformulation of Pierre Nora's concept of communal *lieux de mémoire* or 'sites of memory' (qtd. Erll 2009: 110). This garden is dominated by Carlo Marochetti's mourning angel, which the city's indigenous inhabitants were forced to pay for, though themselves banned from the grounds. Returning secretly to the city after his defeat, Nana Saheb reflects:

> The memorial was for the British dead, the garden for the British living. The Indian dead had no memorial, nor the living Indians a garden; in fact, they were forbidden entry into the Memorial Garden, even though, of course, the gardeners and other menials were Indian. (Malgonkar 1988: 297)

Yet Indian commemorative practice displays a comparable formative relativity. Following independence, Marochetti's angel was replaced by a statue of Nana Saheb's general and close friend Tantya Topi, on many accounts himself implicated in the Bibighar killings, so that, in a further act of symbolical violence, the executioners triumphed once

---

[7] See also Malgonkar's later discussion and footnote on the death of Dafedar Zaffar Ali, a 'loyal' sepoy driven out of the Kanpur encampment and executed after the city's fall. Dafedar left an injunction for his son to avenge him by killing Colonel Neill's son in turn, who was duly shot by Mahzar Ali in 1887 (Malgonkar 1988: 304).

more over the slain. Rathbone's *The Mutiny* also refers to the banyan tree, from which presumed perpetrators were later hung by British victors: "A century later this [tree] was revered as a memorial to the Martyrs of Cawnpore, that is the murderers" (Rathbone 2007: 317). In each case, national memory deliberately seeks to limit or exclude the racial other's participative claim to victimhood. In the wake of the Uprising, Ramesh Rawat notes, "[e]ach side remembered the savagery and brutalities of the other" (Rawat 1998: 103), while selectively sidelining those that would occasion self-blame. Anne Whitehead pertinently stresses how "[c]ollective memory is imbricated in political structures and produces narratives which are used to support group interests and mobilise loyalties" in ways that potentially distort the traumatic communal pasts it helps to create (Whitehead 2004: 43).

    Much as do memory sites, Victorian Mutiny narratives show little concern for the silencing of alternative, that is, Indian rememberings of suffering. As late as 1992, Ralph J. Crane asserted, with reference to Malgonkar's novel, that "there has only been a single Mutiny novel written from an Indian viewpoint" (Crane 1992: 15).[8] Neo-Victorian Mutiny fictions, especially those from the latter parts of the twentieth century and beyond, responding to the emergence of postcolonial theory and 'history from below', often focus on just such distortions, elisions, and deliberate ideological blind spots. In this they resemble subaltern historians' work on the Mutiny, which Perusek argues evince two main objectives:

> the dismantling of elitist historiography by decoding biases and value judgements in records, testimonies, and narratives of the ruling-classes; [and] the restoration to subaltern groups of their 'agency,' their role in history as 'subjects,' with an ideology and political agenda of their own. (Perusek 1992: 295)

Much the same case can be made for the neo-Victorian novel, which "honours the dead and silenced", by textualising "concerns with

---

[8] Crane disregards several earlier antecedents written in or translated into English (see note 12), including Shoshee Chunder Dutt's novel *Shunkar* (1877-78). R. Veena further notes that "the National Archives, Delhi, have a handful of novels [on the Uprising] written by Indians in vernacular languages, before Independence, all of which are listed under Proscribed Publications" (Veena 1999: 1).

(mis)representations of the past, often revisiting and revising the position allocated to those who have been underrepresented, marginalised or dismissed by the dominant culture" (Arias Doblas 2005: 87), so as to accord them a belated hearing as subjects in their own right. This trend towards fictive restitution is further amplified by neo-Victorian novels dealing specifically with historical trauma. Like trauma texts more generally, they function as "a kind of testimonial literary history", giving oppressed groups an otherwise unavailable "access to public discourse" (Vickroy 2002: 172).

Ironically, as regards present-day Mutiny fictions written from a centralised and privileged white subject position by descendants of imperialists, such "identitarian trauma politics" (Luckhurst 2008: 88) often intersect with an *anti*-identitarian desire to differentiate writers/readers from a now politically incorrect national/racial identity constituted through violent subjugations of peoples of other cultures. Such narratives tend to widen the focus so as to recover and include the trauma of the colonised alongside, or instead of, the trauma of the imperialists, or else parody the latter's claim to the Indian Mutiny as first and foremost a *British* rather than Indian trauma. Though seemingly aimed at producing more inclusive and self-conscious "communit[ies] of remembering" (Erll 2006: 169), these strategies raise new problems. White post-imperialist readers may be invited to identify with *who they are not*, so as to opportunely dis-identify with *who they are no longer*, potentially serving the evasion of historical accountability. Through the literary confession of shame and contrition, Gomathi Narayanan suggests, writers engage in an attempted "re-identification through expiation" of the one-time imperial power into a modern postcolonial nation: "the British novelist, by his candour in revealing the perversions and repressions of the Empire is purging himself [and his readers] of the taint of colonialism" (Narayanan 1986: 29; 5). In effect, s/he becomes (or appropriates the place of) the *postcolonial* subject. Yet such retrospective 'house-cleaning' tends to obscure the operations of hegemony in privileging the present trauma of British post-imperialist guilt over the past trauma of the colonised Indians.

Narayanan's discussion of the "scapegoating" function, by which characters "concentrate in themselves all the guilt for which their society seeks atonement", is a case in point, not so much in the sense of villains whose deaths expel guilt from the community, but

rather in the sense of heroicised martyr figures, whose sacrifice serves
to restore society's claim to moral goodness (Narayanan 1986: 5-6).
Suffering 'with' and 'for' India in *Nightrunners of Bengal*, Rodney's
torments and afflictions certainly serve this function, redeeming both
him and the imperial enterprise in what Peter Morey dismissively
refers to as "Master's usual exculpatory fricassee of self-fulfilment,
duty and service" (Morey 2000: 100). Hence Rodney's descent into
temporary madness eventually enables a "retrenchment of his ethnic
and imperial identity" (Kerr 2008: 156). It serves not as punishment
but self-confirmation. *The Mutiny* too employs scapegoating, when the
lawyer Tom Harding, overcome with guilt at having to arbitrarily
execute and hang villagers who earlier saved his life, commits suicide
by hanging himself in turn, and again in the ending of the novel that
describes the future of his lost son Stephen. In a questionable gesture
of symbolic atonement, both instances produce what Narayanan calls
"a complete identification with the injured party" (Narayanan 1986:
86). Saved by his *ayah* Lavanya from the Cawnpore massacre,
adopted by her and her newfound husband Gulam in a rural idyll far
from the conflict, the young Stephen turns into "an Indian lad [...] and
soon forgot that he had ever been anything else" (Rathbone 2007:
436). The imperialist becomes wholly indigenised and subsequently
offers further reparation for the crimes of his one-time countrymen by
assuming a role of public responsibility. He becomes a lawyer and
eventually a high court judge, dying in 1935, perhaps having
supported the nationalist movement that would lead to India's
independence, though the latter is not made explicit.[9]

  Where, one might ask, is the Indian trauma in all this, in line
with the neo-Victorian's granting of belated recognition to
imperialism's victims and their subaltern suffering? It seems to
dissipate into *ressentiment*, or what Mowitt terms "trauma envy" –
"that which authorizes the specifically moral condemnation of others"
(Mowitt 2000: 280), as when Rodney rages at Indian degeneracy: "Let
these animals drown in the ordure they wallowed in – plot,
counterplot, treason, treachery, vice, procurement, murder, dope,
sadism" (Masters 1988: 150). Trauma narrative's capacity for cultural

---

[9] Indeed, the 'sacrifice' of his racial identity once again confirms the British people's
'natural' superiority, for rather than following in his adopted peasant father's
footsteps, the indigenised Stephen replicates his biological lawyer-father's career.

critique becomes compromised by its envious desire for a (counter) claim to suffering, comparable to that of the Other, levelling demands to traumatic subjectivity and collapsing traumatic particularity into sameness. As Mowitt explains,

> trauma has come to be invested with such authority and legitimacy that it elicits a concomitant desire to have suffered it, or if not the unspeakable event itself, then the testimonial agency it is said to produce. (Mowitt 2000: 283)

Here the sting in the tail of 'unrepresentability' makes itself felt. As Mowitt argues, trauma studies – and arguably trauma narratives also – deliberately install and maintain "a profound difference between 'the unspeakable' and the 'as yet unspoken'" so as to establish their "specialist knowledge" and role as arbitrators of cultural meaning and memory (Mowitt 2000: 272). Mowitt interprets this as a displacement of "the political with the ethical", as the 'unspeakable' actually constitutes an *effect* of trauma studies rather than its discovered object; the unrepresentable becomes a "gesture of consolation" afforded the less powerless – those not deemed capable of speaking/representing their trauma – by those empowered through their superior/specialist knowledge to do so (Mowitt 2000: 273).[10] There is no equal access to trauma or its voicing. It seems no coincidence that trauma studies remains a discipline firmly based within Western academia, spearheaded by predominantly Western 'experts', capable of 'reading' trauma and rendering it 'readable' for others across different times and cultures. In a process of cultural reproduction, supremacy is rendered "synonymous with the logic of signification" (Mowitt 2000: 274) or, for that matter, of continued *non-signification*, justified as an instance of the unrepresentable. As Gutleben and Wolfreys suggest, "the unspeakableness of trauma is paradoxically what arouses and encourages speech in the fictional restitutions of the topic" (this volume: 68), validating literary and critical production.

---

[10] Unsurprisingly, many postcolonial writers evince a "deliberate eschewal of the Western discourse of unspeakability, recourse to which is seen as politically debilitating" (Craps and Buelens 2008: 5).

The remainder of this chapter, then, will focus on modes of strategic representation and non-representation, exploring how these undermine the neo-Victorian's political engagement and capacity for cultural critique by once again policing what is and can be said (and *by* and *of* whom). Yet the constraints of this chapter only permit consideration of a small selection of texts from a prolific genre. A full overview would need to consider novels, plays, and films produced since 1901, both before and after Indian Independence in 1947, by both Anglo-Indian and Indo-Anglian authors, not just texts set during the actual Uprising, but also ones that evoke the traumatic memory of the Mutiny for following generations or re-enact the events in later historical contexts.[11] Neo-Victorian Mutiny fiction includes fictionalised biographies of major iconic figures from the Indian side of the conflict, such as the Rani of Jhansi, Nana Saheb, or Mangal Pandey, as well as numerous novels sometimes unfairly dismissed as minor or undistinguished examples of historical romance and adventure fiction.[12] The early to mid-seventies in particular evinced a resurgence of Mutiny fiction, perhaps in response to the violence of the Indo-Pakistan War of 1971, which led to the founding of the independent state of Bangladesh, and the internal unrest of the later Indian Emergency from 1975-1977. It seems likely that both crises recalled India' own struggle for nationhood, as well as the country's ethnic and religious divisions that contributed to the Uprising. Not surprisingly, the years leading up to the 150th anniversary of the Uprising in 2007 produced another literary surge. Contrary to Chakravarty's view that later Mutiny fiction is "vestigal to a project that came to an end in 1947" (Chakravarty 2005: 8), neo-Victorian

---

[11] Examples of the latter include Maud Diver's *Captain Desmond V.C.* (1908), Andrew Ward's *Blood-Seed* (1985), Barbara Cleverly's *The Last Kashmiri Rose* (2001), and Elisabeth McNeill's *The Lady of Cawnpore* (2004).

[12] For biographical novels, see, e.g., Vrindavan Lal Varma's *Lakshmi Bai: The Rani of Jhansi* (1946, first English trans. 2001), G.D. Khosla's *The Last Mughal* (1969), Ketan Mehta's film *The Rising: The Ballad of Mangal Pandey* (2005), and Jaishree Misra's *Rani* (2007), as well as Malgonkar's novel. Most Mutiny fiction could arguably be classed as at least in part historical romance and/or adventure fiction. The better known examples include Patricia Wentworth's *The Devil's Wind* (1912), Talbot Mundy's *Rung Ho! A Novel of India* (1914), C. Lestock Reid's *Masque of the Mutiny* (1947), M. M. Kaye's *Shadow of the Moon* (1957, rev. 1979), Norman Partington's *Flow Red the Ganges* (1972), and George MacDonald Fraser's *Flashman in the Great Game* (1975).

Mutiny fiction continues to thrive, crucially reflecting on the interconnections between colonial pasts and postcolonial presents.

3.   Unequal Suffering

In *The Siege of Krishnapur*, a fictive version of the siege of Lucknow, the omniscient comic mode resists any participative reader immersion in a middle voice, facilitating only the superficial (and pleasurable) shudder of horror. The novel holds its readers at an ironic but also *too* safe distance from events, with even the bloodiest scenes presented in hallucinatory slapstick mode. After the first wave of attack on the British compound,

> [t]he veranda was littered with dead pensioners, or what looked like bits of pensioners, it was hard to be sure in the gloom. The two Sikhs lolled against each other, stone dead, with what could have been blood but was probably only *pan* juice trickling from their mouths. (Farrell 1999: 136)

The laconic tone recalls the observation made by the journalist William Russell, accompanying the British relief forces to Lucknow, that "blood does not show so much on the dark skin as on the white" (qtd. Perusek 1992: 288). Repeatedly, terrific violence is transmuted into staged farce, as in the fantastic Mad Hatter moment when the Collector, suffering a bout of fever-induced derangement, cries, "Let us have tea on the lawn again!" while people die in droves beneath his window (Farrell 1999: 214).[13] So too in the depiction of the final assault when, running out of ammunition, the British employ anything to hand to load their cannon, with absurdly horrific results:

> A sepoy here was trying to remove a silver fork from one of his lungs, another had received a piece of lightning-conductor in his kidneys. A sepoy with a green turban had had his spine shattered by [the statue] *The Spirit of Science*; others had been struck

---

[13] For further connections between Lewis Carroll's *Alice in Wonderland* (1865) and what Ronald Binns calls Farrell's "absurdist vision of Victorian imperialism", see Binns 1986: 76-79.

down by teaspoons, by fish-knives, by marbles; an
unfortunate *subadar* had been plucked from this
world by the silver sugar-tongs embedded in his
brain. (Farrell 1999: 289)

Such massacre can hardly be taken seriously, no more than Fleury's
idiotic 'heroic' pose as Robin Hood "just come from Sherwood
Forest" in his new suit of green, cut from the billiard table baize
(Farrell 1999: 192), which collapses the iconic defender of the
oppressed with the colonial oppressor.[14] Although Farrell's madcap
descriptions of death and dying counter traditionally heroic versions
of the siege,[15] they do so at the cost of excising any ethical demands
on the reader's conscience or sensibility.

Farrell's narrative strategy sensationalises trauma, turning it
into spectacle, as death is put on display for pleasurable consumption.
This places the reader in an analogous position to the "vast crowd" of
Indian onlookers who, during the early parts of the siege, assemble on
a daily basis on the hill above the Residency to watch the slaughter,
coming "as to a fair or festival" complete with refreshments, "music
and dancing" (Farrell 1999: 174). Such voyeurism short-circuits the
"empathic unsettlement" advocated by Dominick LaCapra as the
proper response to trauma and its representations, a form of virtual
experience that specifically resists a transferential and appropriating
over-identification that would instrumentalise or claim another's
trauma as one's own, or else universalise that trauma's historical
particularity (LaCapra 2001: 41-42, 78-79, 102-104). For empathic
unsettlement requires self-consciousness of one's own subject position
as an ethically addressed, secondary witness, rather than co-sufferer or
mere avid spectator. Farrell's dark humour, however, renders the
recognition of such address all but impossible. Trauma becomes a
carnivalesque picnic; pain serves as the delicacies on which we dine,
disabling rather than facilitating empathy. To borrow Patricia
Yaeger's trenchant terminology, Farrell's trauma scenes "jar the act of

---

[14] For an alternative reading of this scene and Fleury's masquerade as "a mark of
personal and national identity", contrasting the social disintegration around him, see
Boccardi 2009: 172.
[15] Erll interprets Farrell's "demythologising mode" as part of a deliberate
"deconstruction of the British 'stock-figured' memory of 1857 with its larger-than-life
heroes and villains" (Erll 2006: 175, 176).

compassion" and "deflect an audience's rapport even as they summon us" to bear witness to suffering (Yaeger 2006: 402, 405).

For all its subversive black humour, Farrell's representation proves resistant, at times even antithetical, to trauma writing's function as a compensatory surrogate witness-bearing. When speaking of the dead, Yaeger suggests, an ethical responsibility arises on the part of writers and readers, who must ask themselves: "What weight should they have in our texts?" (Yaeger 2002: 27) Something similar is suggested by Judith Butler's notion of "precariousness", the admission of reciprocal vulnerability and of "the fact that one's life is always in some sense in the hands of the other", nowhere more so than at the ending of lives in violence and the way such endings are ideologically framed, constructed, and co-opted as 'grievable' or not (Butler 2009: 14). In the scenes cited above, the dead are accorded no "proper weight, substance, dignity" and are granted "too little care" (Yaeger 2002: 28, 32). Like Tipoo's Tiger, they are turned into innocuous figures of fun, their suffering evacuated, or, in Butler's terms, rendered unrecognisable *as* human suffering in the first place. Though the responses of the British are rendered as comically incongruous, the facetious descriptions of the dead seem reserved especially for non-British actors. Furthermore, Indian characters, like Hari or the sepoy pensioners helping to defend the Residency, are left undeveloped, so that the indigenes remain an anonymous and undifferentiated crowd, in line with common Orientalist motifs of the East as a monstrously teeming multitude and riotous mob (see Kerr 2008: 53-60). Hence, to some extent at least, Farrell remains "a crypto-racialist" (Goonetilleke 2004: 422). If, as Butler proposes, recognition of reciprocal precarity "imposes an obligation upon us" (Butler 2009: 2), that obligation is deliberately evaded by Farrell's novel, where radically precarious lives are readily disposed of for comic effect.

A comparable partisan representation of violence becomes apparent in *Nightrunners of Bengal*, though from the novel's inscription – "To/ The Sepoy of India/ 1695-1947" – the reader might expect a revisionist account of the Mutiny that seeks to seriously address the indigenes' neglected trauma. Yet in spite of balancing Indian with British acts of barbarity, Masters's approach is hardly as democratic as some critics suggest. Neither are the outrages of both sides depicted as "equally gory" (Crane 1992:16), nor is Masters

genuinely objective as regards "his horror of the cruelty of his
compatriots", though he does at least emphasise "the humanity of
many Indians who protected the British" even at great risk to their
own lives (Islam 1979: 101). The death throes of the British at
Bhowani are narrated in graphic detail, one after the other, in a litany
of Indian barbarism. This is further heightened by Masters's dubious
resort to the motif of white women's rape by Indian assailants, so
prevalent in nineteenth-century newspaper reports contemporary to
the Uprising, as well as later Mutiny fictions. Yet even the post-
Mutiny British administration, after extensive official investigations,
concluded this offence had no real basis in fact. Masters not only
recycles one of the most vicious racist stereotypes, but exacerbates the
horror by repeatedly shifting into the victim's mind, as Lady Isobel
Hatton-Dunn tries to protect her friend Dotty, who is about to give
birth hiding under the bed:

> *She screamed continuously, but not too loudly.* [...]
> Almighty and most merciful God, give me strength
> and mercy. [...] *If she, Isobel, could make noise they
> wouldn't hear Dotty's groans. She kept up her
> screams, not feeling the man who grasped her and
> sweated to his climax.* Scream again, carefully, just
> right. Let another sepoy replace the first – no, the
> fourth, that was. [...] Scream [...] so that they will
> keep on, and not kill me and drown my cries.
> (Masters 1988: 198, original emphases)

Of course, her efforts prove in vain; Dotty is discovered and though
the men's violence momentarily abates, as they move instinctively to
assist in the birth, another sepoy kicks Dotty's Indian helper aside,
shoots the mother, and appears to stamp on the newborn, before
dispatching the witnessing Isabel also. In contrast, rapes of Indian
women by British men are indicated but not dwelt on or individuated;
arriving in Gondwara, Rodney sees the corpses of Indian civilians in
the street – "the women's sexual parts were torn and bared to the
flies" (Masters 1988: 288) – and is told that, in spite of their best
efforts, the authorities have been unable to identify the perpetrators.

   Similarly, Rodney's own acts of murder, of his one-time
friend Prithvi Chand and a young villager of Chalisgon where he and

his party find sanctuary – doubly horrific because committed against people assisting rather than threatening him – are dealt with in summary fashion. The first killing with a stone strike to the head seems intended to evoke Cain's primal brother-murder, but such a reading fits uneasily with Rodney's appellation of Prithvi as "you nigger devil" (Masters 1988: 238). The later surreptitious murder is not depicted outright, but only recalled laconically in passing: "the young fellow was dead, bayoneted to death and buried under leaves in a bear's grave up the valley" (Masters 1988: 247). Significantly, both murders are mitigated by Rodney's evident paranoid and dissociative state, which resembles what is now termed Posttraumatic Stress Disorder, resulting from the horror of witnessing the slaughter of his compatriots, including his wife. The murders are thus figured as a temporary aberration, not subject to his conscious will and moral agency, exculpating Rodney – and by extension the British – from historical accountability for his and his nation's violent actions. As David Rubin notes, "it is the crimes of the Indians that preoccupy" Masters and his protagonist (Rubin 1986: 33), in contrast to the *sufferings* of the British. The sufferings of the Indians meanwhile disappear into the abyss of the unimaginable.

Furthermore, since *Nightrunners of Bengal* ends while the Mutiny is still on-going, British retaliatory violence barely features. Booker's comment on *The Siege of Krishnapur*, the Indian section of which concludes at a similar point, applies equally to Masters's novel: "It therefore omits the spectacular violence wrought upon Indians by the British once the tide in the Mutiny had turned" (Booker 2000: 112). Only two such acts are detailed by Masters, the blowing from the guns of the identified 'traitor' Girdhari Lall and the later torturing to death of a sepoy from Rodney's former regiment. Singular targeted British atrocities are juxtaposed against indiscriminate mass murders by the Indians, eliding British mass executions, collective punishments of whole communities, and arbitrary slaughters of civilians in the brutal suppression of the Revolt. Indian suffering is also never shown from the indigenous victims' perspectives. Of the tortured sepoy, Rodney notes: "His eyeballs were rolled up and out of sight, and he did not know what they were doing to him" (Masters 1988: 318). Even during the execution, the focus swerves from the condemned man's death to the British reactions and Rodney's trauma at discerning a taste for 'Indian' barbarism in his fellow Englishmen:

> He had a new memory to set beside the others – the
> corpses in so many rooms and streets and gardens –
> and live with. The memory would not be of Girdhari
> Lall, but of the faces of the English gunners. It was
> right for them to execute a mutineer; but they had
> liked doing it. They would behave like animals, and
> kill every Indian who crossed their path, and burn the
> land from end to end, and do it joyfully. (Masters
> 1988: 302)

In spite of Masters's political correctness in apportioning the capacity
for inhumanity among Britons and Indians alike, *Nightrunners of
Bengal*, much like Farrell's novel, finally leaves the trauma of the
Indians ungrievable.

This is hardly surprising since Masters's indigenous
characters, again like Farrell's, are only sketched in, often
melodramatically; not even Sumitra and the loyal Thug Piroo are
realised as rounded human beings. Masters seems unable "to see,
rather than simply look at (or through or past) Indians" (Rubin 1986:
44). The native population throughout the novel is depicted in
stereotypical fashion as either vicious and treacherous, inclined to
mob rule like the murderous sepoys, or childlike and easily (mis)led.
Colonel Bulstrode, for instance, is described as loving the natives "as
a father loves a pack of half-witted sons" (Masters 1988: 26). Piroo
rescues the protagonist out of naive admiration for Rodney's father
(the very man who helped eradicate the practice of thuggee!), while
the Silver Guru, an Irishman gone native, finds it a simple matter to
manipulate the Indians for his own subversive purposes, namely a
displaced vengeance for the imperialist exploitation of his own
homeland. Implicitly, such characterisation calls into question the
colonised's capability to rule themselves, even four years after India's
independence and Partition, supporting critics' condemnation of the
novel as a "neo-imperialistic fantasy" (Narayanan 1986: 28) and an
attempted "imaginative recolonization" of post-Independence India
(Morey 2000: 93). Even when Rodney breaks down in tears during the
final battle, watching the same men who once served loyally under his
command "devoured" by the "ravenous guns" (Masters 1988: 315), he
does not mourn their lost lives, so much as the betrayed dream of the
British-Indian paternalistic covenant. It is exactly this covenant that

Rodney attempts to resurrect by promising to raise the rebel Rani's son alongside his own, when he allows her to escape at the novel's close.

Like Masters, Rathbone attempts a more even-handed acknowledgement of British and Indian violence, constructing deliberate parallels between atrocities committed by both sides (see Kohlke 2009: 31-33). Yet overall the trauma of the British is still depicted in greater detail than that of the Indian population. The violent death of the pregnant Charlotte Chambers at the hands of a Meerut butcher, who first slits her throat and then disembowels her, is described almost avidly. The passage incorporates melodramatic and highly emotive imagery that (albeit anachronistically) seems intended to evoke Jack the Ripper, as when "using almost surgical skill, [he] dissected out from her womb the still living foetus of a tiny girl, cut the umbilical chord and placed the baby on its dead mother's breast" (Rathbone 2007: 153). In contrast, the elderly peasant, attacking the British survey team that orders the destruction of his village temples to make way for the railway, is summarily dispatched in three brief sentences. While Charlotte is sacralised as a ritualistic sacrifice and subversive pietà figure, the Indian is abjected: "Writhing, jerking, choking on his own blood, the old man expires" (Rathbone 2007: 43). Similarly, the Satichaura Ghat massacre of the survivors of the Cawnpore siege and the later Bibighar killings are lingered over. The sensationalist language and horrifying immediacy of the latter scene is amplified by the use of present participles:

> The amount of blood was appalling, spouting, gushing, pouring over everybody, everything. The noise too was hellish: screams of pain, grunts of rage, terrible anguish cut off with gasping, bubbling sobs, the clang of metal when a blade hit a doorway or pillar. What made it yet more awful was the density of the crowd – one hundred and ninety-seven victims, of whom one hundred and twenty-four were children or babies, crushed into less than five hundred square feet. (Rathbone 2007: 315)

Note the particular appeal to reader empathy and outrage by the emphasis on the high proportion of child victims. Yet the vicious and humiliating punishment of the presumed perpetrators is rendered with emotional detachment, counteracting reader empathy, pity, and guilt:

> Those who were deemed to have played leading roles were forced to eat pork and beef before being hanged. The Bibigarh murderers were made to lick up at least a square foot each of blood on the floor of the building before they too were hanged on a large banyan tree nearby. (Rathbone 2007: 317)

Any ethical investment in the scene is further frustrated by Rathbone's next sentence, the earlier cited condemnation of the tree's subsequent function as a memory site commemorating the Indian 'martyrs'.

While Rathbone never condones British violence, he situates it, at least in part, as understandable in terms of retaliatory outrage at the Cawnpore massacres. It is supposedly only after news of the killings reached England that "the suppression of the mutiny [...] became a crusade in which no cruelty could be condemned" (Rathbone 2007: 318). While Rathbone emphasises how Nana Saheb orders the 2nd cavalry into Cawnpore's new town "to plunder the shops and businesses of Native Christians", some of whom "were burnt alive in their homes" (Rathbone 2007: 262), the repeated wholesale burning of communities by British forces is glossed over. The description of the army's wounded, reserves, and camp followers taking "time out to trash and burn the towns and villages they passed through" (Rathbone 2007: 304) evokes a strangely bodiless crime, circumventing the full horror of the offence. In contrast, Malgonkar situates the Bibigarh killings as a reprisal for the prior sacking of Fattepur, its women raped before the village is set alight:

> Those who tried to escape, even women and children, were thrown back into the fire or shot while escaping. Even as they were retreating, our sepoys looked back in horror and swore vengeance. If that was what the white man did to his victims, it was up to them to wreak a similar vengeance. (Malgonkar 1988: 214)[16]

---

[16] Like Masters, Malgonkar later deploys the rape topos in its more traditional form, albeit subversively, when Nana rescues Colonel Wheeler's mixed-race daughter Eliza,

Hence the subalterns' violence at Cawnpore could be viewed as a traumatic *repetition and replication* of British colonial power, rather than the *precedent* precipitating barbaric reprisals. Likewise, Rathbone's stereotypical representation of Nana as the vainglorious cowardly arch-villain, directly implicated in the atrocities, obscures what Rudrangshu Mukherjee describes as the "collective" dimension of the Satichaura Ghat affair as "an expression of an entire society's hatred and rejection of an alien order", staged as a public execution (Mukherjee 1990: 110). Further ideological compromising on Rathbone's part relates to the extreme punishment of blowing prisoners from cannon mouths. In *The Mutiny*, instead of the British, it is the rebel commander Tatya Tope who threatens to apply the penalty,[17] should the Bibighar guards refuse to kill the hostages: "He was referring to a form of execution *common* under the Mughals, and *occasionally* used by the British" (Rathbone 2007: 314, emphasis added).

As if subconsciously aware of his narrative bias, in Chapter 49 Rathbone shifts to the non-human, bird's eye view of a scavenging kite above Delhi, perhaps to mimic what LaCapra describes as "the dominance of an impersonal or 'voiceless' voice" that characterises claims to objectivity in historiography (LaCapra 1985: 117). Yet while depicting the arbitrary killings of civilians by British relieving forces, Rathbone cannot resist interjecting subjective viewpoints from (conveniently) ethical British witnesses who condemn the slaughter, as when Lieutenant Farquar bawls out his squaddie: "What the fuck, George, what the fuck did you do that for? That was simply fucking murder" (Rathbone 2007: 339). Indeed, the whole opening section of the chapter, presented as 'historical' description, at times approaches apologia. It explains "the traditions that governed siege warfare", under which only cities that surrendered where accorded mercy, and considers the extent to which British brutality was a direct "consequence of bitter hand-to-hand street fighting" involving counter-insurgency forces driven to the edge by three months of

---

sexually violated and tortured by Indians. Farrell wholly deconstructs the same motif since, as Erll notes, "the only attempt to defile an Englishwoman is made towards the end of the novel by an Englishman – the misanthropic magistrate", who assaults the 'fallen' Lucy Hughes (Erll 2006: 176).

[17] Divergent spellings of historical persons' names reflect alternative spellings adopted by different writers.

"appalling heat, under constant if not overaccurate [sic] bombardment, plagued by cholera, heatstroke and fever" (Rathbone 2007: 338). Much like Rodney's murders, British atrocities are here attributed to temporary insanity, as men break under intolerable strain. No such mitigating circumstances are adduced for Indian acts of barbarism. In contrast, *The Devil's Wind* positions subaltern extremism within a context of insidious trauma and the endurance of years of exploitation and humiliation at the hands of the British. Eventually, the pent-up sense of grievous injustice and "rage of slaves" explodes into violence, as at Meerut: "God knows [the sepoys] had had enough provocation. It was almost as though their officers were putting them through some test to find out how far they could go on bending human material before it would snap" (Malgonkar 1988: 58, 124).

In spite of his overtly sympathetic and subjective portrayal of Nana, Malgonkar's witness-bearing could be said to be *more* objective than that of Farrell, Masters, or Rathbone. He resists the temptation to lighten the burden of violent deaths, whether Indian or British:

> Once you have seen men struck down by modern weapons of war and reduced to mounds of torn, blackening flesh, [...] such sights are branded with fire upon your brain. Your vision is crowded by the dead or dying: fingers clawing the stone-hard earth in a shudder of death, as though to drown pain by greater pain; the mouths of men and animals forced open by unbearable agony and the blood flowing in spasmodic gouts from holes in contorting bodies ... these remain in focus [...]. The screams of the dying are like shards of steel wedged deep in your skull. (Malgonkar 1988: 188, unbracketed ellipses in the original)

Nana's reference to "men" democratically encompasses both Indian and British trauma, while his appeal to "you" seeks to draw the reader into the witnessing act. In Butler's terms, no frame delimits the recognition of human precariousness, preserving it for one race but denying it to the other.

Partisanship is restricted to stressing the Indian perspective with regards to how such deaths are subsequently (re)configured. Nana wonders whether mastering "the capacity to erase at will these horrors" and become "immunized" against them, as he suggests the British have succeeded in doing, constitute "the distinguishing mark[s] of the warrior", ensuring victory "as the master race" (Malgonkar 1988: 188).[18] Implicitly, he indicts the victors' privileged retrospective framing of certain aspects of the events – and the erasure of others, as evidenced by the memorials to the Cawnpore violence. Though thankful that the Bibighar inscription blames his followers without crediting him outright with the killings, Nana notes the spitefulness of including his name: "On the same principle, should not Queen Victoria's name be inscribed on a thousand monuments in India to suggest that she instigated the atrocities perpetrated by her subjects?" (Malgonkar 1988: 298) Malgonkar's stinging censure of the relativity of cultural memories of violence goes hand in hand with a demonstration of how the neo-Victorian Mutiny novel can serve as a cultural space for symbolic redress, as Nana imagines a comparable commemorative tablet for the Indian village of Daryaganj:

> A VILLAGE STOOD HERE.
> IT WAS BURNED DOWN BY THE MEN OF
> QUEEN VICTORIA'S ARMY
> ON THE 12TH DAY OF JUNE 1857.
> THE MEN, WOMEN, AND CHILDREN WHO RAN OUT
> WERE THROWN BACK INTO THE FIRE.
> (Malgonkar 1988: 299)

His fictional compensation testifies as much to the occluded, lost, and repressed testimony of Indian suffering, as to the suffering itself. Simultaneously, Nana's counter-memorial signals the postcolonial revisions of Indian cultural memory in the future of the texts' temporal setting.

4.   The Pit(falls) of Unrepresentability

Yet even Malgonkar's achievement is compromised somewhat by his refusal to imagine the Bibighar massacre, even as its barbarity is admitted. While not denying "the fact [...] that every single woman

---

[18] His contemplation of battle trauma resonates eerily with today's preferred depersonalised warfare, so often waged at great distances, and with public desensitisation from over-exposure to images of extraordinary violence.

and child in the place was killed", Nana restricts himself to a bare outline of the "horrifying details", which "may or may not be true" (Malgonkar 1988: 218), emphasising the contestability not of the massacre itself, but its (im)possible representations in cultural memory. Mukherjee notes that "[t]he very way in which the massacre was carried out eliminated the possibility of any direct witness, since it was in a closed room", and cites Lieutenant-Colonel G.W. Williams's 'Synopsis of the Evidence of the Cawnpore Mutiny' to the effect that "all seem instinctively to shrink from confessing any knowledge of so foul and barbarous a crime", so that all "[e]vidence [...] suddenly ceases on the fatal day" (Mukherjee 1990: 114). Malgonkar too, then, comes up against the unspeakable as regards Indian history's own Others. As Farrell's 'Afterword' asserts, "[t]he reality of the Indian Mutiny constantly defies the imagination" (Farrell 1999: 314). Farrell's British survivors too are haunted by recurring "dreams of the terrible days of the siege, which were like the dark foundation of the civilised life they had returned to" back home (Farrell 1999: 311). This black hole of the unimaginable already opens up earlier in the text with the arrival of the shocked survivors of the Captainganj revolt:

> [T]hey seemed to be having trouble telling [...] what it had been like. Each of them simply had two or three terrible scenes printed on his mind: an Englishwoman trying to say something to him with her throat cut, or a comrade spinning down into a whirlpool of hacking sepoys [...]. It was hard to make any sense out of what had happened, and after a while they gave up trying. (Farrell 1999: 94-95)

At the end of the novel, Farrell turns away from India, following the Collector back to England, where the one-time outspoken, would-be world reformer succumbs to a sense of futility, resigns his membership on cultural and philanthropic committees, and immures himself in his club, falling into silence like the Captainganj victims: "one might have thought that he himself had entirely forgotten about the siege" (Farrell 1999: 312). His case exemplifies how, to borrow Birgit R. Erdle's resonant formulation, "[t]he phantasm of illegibility" or indecipherability can conspire to arrest the "forgotten within forgetfulness" (Erdle 1999: 45).[19]

From one point of view, then, Farrell and Malgonkar's novels surrender to the desire for oblivion. As Luckhurst reminds us, "the impossible, aporetic or melancholic response" is sometimes *too* readily deemed "the only appropriately ethical condition for individuals and communities defined by their post-traumatic afterwardness" (Luckhurst 2008: 211-212). Yet it may also result in an (unethical) refusal to make the effort to bear witness in the first place, or the denial of the authenticity of alternative kinds of witness-bearing, turning unspeakability into a get-out clause. From another perspective, however, the novels stubbornly resist testimony's contrary function "as a form of forgetfulness, a 'flight forward', towards the word, and a dive into language", which is in part "also a search [...] for liberation from the traumatic scene" (Seligmann-Silva 2003: 153). Denied representation, trauma cannot be exorcised like an unwanted ghost,[20] what David Lloyd calls "letting the dead slip away without the trace of a wake behind them" (Lloyd 2000: 221), rendering their lost lives ungrievable once more.

> Mourning is no redress, if mourning the dead entails coming to terms with their loss, a loss [...] not ours to move on from, when our very capacity to move on is predicated on the progress that judged the dead dispensable. (Lloyd 2005: 153)

---

[19] Erdle makes the point with reference to Daniel Libeskind's contentious proposal to renovate the memorial at the former concentration camp Sachsenhausen. The full sentence reads: "Das Phantasma der Unlesbarkeit, das sich mit dem Einsatz des Trauma-Begriffs im deutschen Erinnerungsdiskurs verbindet, hält dieses Vergessene im Vergessen." ["The phantasm of illegibility, which is connected with the introduction of the trauma-concept in German memory discourse, holds back this forgotten [subject] within forgetfulness."] (Erdle 1999: 45, own translation)

[20] The lack of ghosts in neo-Victorian Mutiny fiction confounds reader expectations, habituated to tropes of spectrality – of rendering visible the unthinkable – from so much other neo-Victorian literature. Hence the genre contrasts with other historical fiction set in the period, such as US neo-slavery narratives, which deploys the spectral trope to address traumas denied cultural representation (see Brogan 1998). In Mutiny fiction, the subaltern wounded body, rather than the liminal ghost, reflects the lesser visibility (or outright invisibility) of non-white people's suffering in the mainstream.

In the Collector's case, the "dark foundation" of trauma becomes the *idée fixe* of his future existence.[21] In closing, Farrell's narrator suggests that rather than being formed in the image of its most noble ideas, "a people, a nation" may instead be "shaped by other forces *of which it has little knowledge*" (Farrell 1999: 313, emphasis added) – 'progressing' blindly, traumatically, if at all.

Trauma's unrepresentability thus also permits a more ethical reading, namely as an acknowledgement of unequally recognised suffering and a refusal to appropriate and consume others' trauma. It may signal a disavowal of the right(ness) to presume to speak with authority for persons of other cultures and their traumas, much as in J.M. Coetzee's *Foe* (1986), a postcolonial re-vision of Daniel Defoe's *Robinson Crusoe* (1719), with its rendering of the enigma of the subaltern Friday as literally tongueless and voiceless. In one sense, neo-Victorian Mutiny fiction *de-legitimates* the trauma paradigm as always being in the service of the *more* rather than *less* powerful – not least because those in power construct the systems of meaning, within which opposing claims for traumatic subjectivity and grievability are judged and made to compete with one another. Even those neo-Victorian Mutiny fictions predating the institutionalised rise of trauma studies in the 1990s anticipate trauma's twenty-first-century role as the keystone of cultural politics, as various individual and collective traumas vie for precedence on both national and global bases, and populations of different kinds of trauma victims/survivors contend for recognition and compensation. Mowitt touches on something similar in his resonant formulation of the Anglophone world's deployment of "the forensic strategy of comparative trauma calculation" (Mowitt 2000: 283).

The topos of unrepresentability retains an ambiguous position vis-à-vis the Mutiny. In part the motif reinforces the destructive binary roles of self and Other, by re-inscribing the opposite side's trauma as a de-realised and unimaginable form of suffering. In the case of Western writers especially this approach resonates strikingly with the Orientalist version of India and the "sublime ignorance" that, according to Douglas Kerr,

---

[21] As he remarks in a chance re-encounter with George, "Culture is a sham, [....] a cosmetic painted on life [...] to conceal its ugliness" (Farrell 1993: 313).

besets Western writing about the experience of the
Orient, punctuating it with blind spots, indecipherable
signals, untranslatability, impenetrable thickets of the
unknown,   beyond   representation,   gestured   at
throughout colonial and Orientalist discourse with
helpless   capitulations   to   the   mysterious,   the
inscrutable, the ineffable, the veiled East. (Kerr 2008:
238)

India at the time of the Mutiny becomes the quintessential trope of
(Western-defined) trauma, simultaneously its source and site, cause
and symptom. I have argued elsewhere that the re-imagined nineteenth
century has today become the 'new' Orient in a multi-cultural global
economy where the self-determining modern nations of the 'East' can
no longer serve as unmapped dark areas for the projection of
Eurocentric erotic fantasies (Kohlke 2008: 67-69). This may prove
equally applicable to fantasies of suffering, though working in both
directions. Neo-Victorian Mutiny fictions may serve the invidious
function of attempting to recover a lost sense of radical 'Otherness',
against which subjects of trauma-cultures, West *and* East, might
redefine themselves once more.

Bibliography

Arias Doblas, Rosario. 2005. 'Talking with the Dead: Revisiting the Victorian Past
        and the Occult in Margaret Atwood's *Alias Grace* and Sarah Waters'
        Affinity', *Estudios Ingleses de la Universidad Complutense*, 13: 85-105.
Bennett, Jill, and Rosanne Kennedy (eds.). 2003. 'Introduction', in *World Memory:
        Personal Trajectories in Global Time*. Houndmills, Basingstoke & New
        York: Palgrave Macmillan: 1-15.
Binns, Ronald. 1986. *J.G. Farrell*. Contemporary Writers Series. London & New
        York: Methuen.
Boccardi,   Mariadele.   2009.   *The   Contemporary   British   Historical   Novel:
        Representation,   Nation,   Empire*. Houndmills, Basingstoke: Palgrave
        Macmillan.
Booker, M. Keith. 2000. *Colonial Power, Colonial Texts: India in the Modern British
        Novel* [1997]. Ann Arbor: The University of Michigan Press.
Brogan, Kathleen. 1998. *Cultural Haunting: Ghosts and Ethnicity in Recent American
        Literature*. Charlottesville & London: University Press of Virginia.
Butler, Judith. 2009. *Frames of War: When Is Life Grievable?* London & New York:
        Verso.

Caruth, Cathy. 1996. *Unclaimed Experience: Trauma, Narrative, and History*. Baltimore & London: The Johns Hopkins University Press.

Chakravarty, Gautam. 2005. *The Indian Mutiny and the British Imagination*. Cambridge: Cambridge University Press.

Crane, Ralph J. 1992. *Inventing India: A History of India in English-Language Fiction*. Houndmills, Basingstoke: Macmillan Academic and Professional.

Craps, Stef, and Gert Buelens (eds.). 2008. 'Introduction: Postcolonial Trauma Novels', *Studies in the Novel*, 40(1-2) (Spring & Summer): 1-12.

Erdle, Birgit R. 1999. 'Die Verführung der Parallelem: Zu Übertragungsverhältnissen zwischen Ereignis, Ort und Zitat', in Bronfen, Elisabeth, Birgit R. Erdle, and Sigfrid Weigel (eds.), *Trauma: Zwischen Psychoanalyse und kulturellem Deutungsmuster*. Köln: Böhlau Verlag: 27-50.

Erll, Astrid. 2006. 'Re-writing as Re-visioning: Modes of representing the "Indian Mutiny" in British novels, 1857-2000', *European Journal of English Studies*, 10(2) (August): 163-185.

——. 2009. 'Remembering across Time, Space, and Cultures: Premediation, Remediation and the "Indian Mutiny"', in Erll, Astrid, and Ann Rigney (eds., in collaboration with Laura Basu, and Paulus Bijl*)*, *Mediation, Remediation, and the Dynamics of Cultural Memory*. Berlin & New York: Walter de Gruyter: 109-138.

Farrell, J.G. 1999. *The Siege of Krishnapur* [1973].London: Orion.

Goonetilleke, D.C.R.A. 2003. 'J.G. Farrell's Indian Works: His Majesty's Subjects?', *Modern Asian Studies*, 37(2) (May): 407-427.

Greenberger, Allen J. 1969. *The British Image of India: A Study in the Literature of Imperialism 1880-1960*. London: Oxford University Press.

Hartman, Geoffrey H. 1995. 'On Traumatic Knowledge and Literary Studies, *New Literary History*, 26(3): 537-563.

Herbert, Christopher. 2008. *War of No Pity: The Indian Mutiny and Victorian Trauma*. Princeton and Oxford: Oxford University Press.

Islam, Shamsul. 1979. *Chronicles of the Raj: A Study of Literary Reaction to the Imperial Idea towards the End of the Raj*. London & Basingstoke: Macmillan Press.

Kerr, Douglas. 2008. *Eastern Figures: Orient and Empire in British Writing*. Aberdeen and Hong Kong: Hong Kong University Press.

Kohlke, Marie-Luise. 2008. 'Sexsation and the Neo-Victorian Novel: Orientalising the Nineteenth Century in Contemporary Fiction', in Kohlke, Marie-Luise, and Luisa Orza (eds.), *Negotiating Sexual Idioms: Image, Text, Performance*. Amsterdam & New York: Rodopi: 53-77.

——. 2009. 'Nostalgic Violence? Neo-Victorian (Re-)Visions of Historical Conflict', in Guggisberg, Marika, and David Weir (eds.), *Understanding Violence: Contexts and Portrayals* [eBook]. Oxford: Inter-Disciplinary Press: 25-37. Online at: http://www.inter-disciplinary.net/wp-content/uploads/2009/07/vchue15e.pdf.

LaCapra, Dominick. 1985. *History and Criticism*. Ithaca & London: Cornell University Press.

——. 2001. *Writing History, Writing Trauma*. Baltimore & London: The Johns Hopkins University Press.

Lloyd, David. 2000. 'Colonial Trauma/Postcolonial Recovery?', *Interventions*, 2(2) (July): 212-228.

——. 2005. 'The Indigent Sublime: Specters of Irish Hunger', *Representations*, 92 (Fall): 152-185.

Luckhurst, Roger. 2008. *The Trauma Question*. London and New York: Routledge.

Malgonkar, Manohar. 1988. *The Devil's Wind: Nanau Saheb's Story* [1972]. New Delhi: Penguin Books India.

Masters, John. 1988. *Nightrunners of Bengal* [1951]. London: Sphere Books/Penguin.

Morey, Peter. 2000. *Fictions of India: Narrative and Power*. Edinburgh: Edinburgh University Press.

Mowitt, John. 2000. 'Trauma Envy', *Cultural Critique*, 46: *Trauma and Its Cultural Aftereffects* (Autumn), 272-297.

Mukherjee, Rudrangshu. 1990. '"Satan Let Loose upon Earth": The Kanpur Massacre in India in the Revolt of 1857', *Past and Present*, 128: 92-116.

Narayanan, Gomathi. 1986. *The Sahibs and the Natives: A Study of Guilt & Pride in Anglo-Indian & Indo-Anglian Novels*. Delhi: Chanakya Publications.

Perusek, Darshan. 1992. 'Subaltern Consciousness and the Historiography of the Indian Rebellion of 1857', *NOVEL: A Forum on Fiction*, 25(3) (Spring): 286-301.

Rathbone, Julian. 2007. *The Mutiny*. London: Little, Brown.

Rawat, Ramesh. 1998. '1857 and the "Renaissance" in Hindi Literature', *Social Scientist*, 26(1-4) (Jan.-Apr.): 95-1112.

Rothberg, Michael. 2008. 'Decolonizing Trauma Studies: A Response', *Studies in the Novel*, 40(1-2) (Spring & Summer): 224-234.

Roy, Tapti. 1994. *The Politics of a Popular Uprising: Bundelkhand 1857*. New Delhi: Oxford University Press.

Rubin, David. 1986. *After the Raj: British Novels of India Since 1947*. Hanover & London: University Press of New England.

Rushdie, Salman. 1992. 'The Raj Revival', [*The Observer*, April 1984], reprinted in John Twitchin (ed.), *The Black and White Media Show Book: Handbook for the Study of Racism and Television* [1988]. Stoke-on-Trent: Trentham Books: 130-133. [GOOGLE Books]

Seligmann-Silva, Márcio. 2003. 'Catastrophe and Representation: History as Trauma', *Semiotica*, special issue: *The Crisis of Representation* 143(1-4): 143-162.

Thompson, Edward. 1928. *Suttee: A Historical and Philosophical Enquiry into the Hindu Rite of Widow-Burning*. London: George Allen & Unwin.

Veena, R. 1999. 'The Literature on the Events of 1857: A Postcolonial Reading', in Pandey, Surya Nath (ed.), *Writing in a Post-colonial Space*. New Delhi: Atlantic Books: 1-9.

Vickroy, Laurie. 2002. *Trauma and Survival in Contemporary Fiction*. Charlottesville and London: University of Virginia Press.

Whitehead, Anne. 2004. *Trauma Fiction*. Edinburgh: Edinburgh University Press

Yaeger, Patricia. 2002. 'Consuming Trauma; or, The Pleasures of Merely Circulating', in Miller, Nancy K, and Jason Tougaw (eds.), *Extremities: Trauma, Testimony and Community*. University of Illinois Press: 25-51.

——. 2006. 'Testimony without Intimacy', *Poetics Today*, 27(2) (Summer): 399-423.

Contributors

Vanessa Guignery is Professor of English Literature at the École Normale Supérieure in Lyon, France, with special interest in contemporary British and postcolonial literature. She is the author of several books and essays on the work of Julian Barnes, including *The Fiction of Julian Barnes* (Palgrave Macmillan, 2006), and *Conversations with Julian Barnes* (University Press of Mississippi, 2009), co-edited with Ryan Roberts. She has published a monograph on B.S. Johnson, *Ceci n'est pas une fiction* (Sorbonne University Press, 2009), and articles on Anita Desai, Jeanette Winterson, David Lodge, and Michèle Roberts, and she is editor of the collections *(Re)mapping London* (Publibook, 2008) and *Voices and Silence in the Contemporary Novel in English* (Cambridge Scholars Publishing, 2009).

Christian Gutleben is Professor at the University of Nice-Sophia Antipolis, France, where he teaches nineteenth- and twentieth-century British literature. His research focuses on the links between these two historical periods and traditions, and he is the author of one of the earliest critical surveys of neo-Victorian literature, *Nostalgic Postmodernism: The Victorian Tradition and the Contemporary British Novel* (Rodopi, 2001), as well as co-editor of *Refracting the Canon in Contemporary British Literature and Film* (with Susana Onega, Rodopi, 2004). He has also published books on the English campus novel and Graham Greene, as well as numerous articles on postmodernism in British literature.

Ann Heilmann is Professor of English at the University of Hull, UK, where she directs the Centre for Victorian Studies. The author of *New Woman Fiction* (Palgrave Macmillan 2000), *New Woman Strategies* (Manchester University Press, 2004) and (with Mark Llewellyn) *Neo-Victorianism: The Victorians in the Twenty-First Century, 1999-2009*

(Palgrave Macmillan, 2010), she has also (co)edited a critical edition of George Moore, four anthology sets on Victorian and Edwardian (anti)feminism, and three essay collections, including *Metafiction and Metahistory in Contemporary Women's Writing* (Palgrave Macmillan 2007).

Marie-Luise Kohlke lectures in English Literature at Swansea University, UK, with research specialisms in trauma narratives and neo-Victorian fiction, as well as gender, sexuality, and violence. She is the General and Founding Editor of the peer-reviewed journal *Neo-Victorian Studies* (www.neovictorianstudies.com) and co-editor (with Luisa Orza of *Negotiating Sexual Idioms: Image, Text, Performance* (Rodopi, 2008). Her articles on women's historical fiction and trauma writing have appeared in *Feminist Review* and *Women: A Cultural Review.*

Georges Letissier is Professor of English at Nantes University, France. He has published articles both in French and English on Victorian literature, covering the work of Charles Dickens, George Eliot, Christina Rossetti, William Morris, and on contemporary British writers, including Peter Ackroyd, A.S. Byatt, Alistair Gray, Allan Hollinghurst, Graham Swift, and Sarah Waters. His most recent publication is the edited volume *Rewriting, Reprising: Plural Intertextualities* (Cambridge Scholars Publishing, 2009).

Mark Llewellyn is Senior Lecturer in English and Director of Postgraduate Research (Humanities and Social Sciences) at the University of Liverpool, UK. He is Honorary Secretary of the British Association for Victorian Studies (BAVS), Editor of the *Journal of Gender Studies,* and Consultant Editor of *Neo-Victorian Studies.* Mark has published widely on the work of the Anglo-Irish novelist George Moore, including an edition of Moore's *Collected Short Stories* (with Ann Heilmann; Pickering and Chatto, 2007). Working with Ann Heilmann, he has also co-edited *Metafiction and Metahistory in Contemporary Women's Writing* (Palgrave Macmillan 2007) and co-authored *Neo-Victorianism: The Victorians in the Twenty-First Century, 1999-2009* (Palgrave Macmillan, 2010). He is currently working on a monograph entitled *Incest and English Culture, 1835-1908.*

Kate Mitchell is a Lecturer in the English programme at the Australian National University. Her research is focused on nineteenth- and twentieth-century literary and cultural history, with a particular interest in neo-Victorian fiction and historical recollection in fictional narratives. She has just published *History and Cultural Memory in Neo-Victorian Fiction: Victorian Afterimages* (Palgrave Macmillan, 2010), and her articles on historical fiction have appeared in *Neo-Victorian Studies*, *antiTHESIS,* and a number of edited collections. She is currently co-editing a collection (with Nicola Parsons) entitled *Reading the (Re)Presented Past: Literature and Historical Consciousness, 1700-present.*

Catherine Pesso-Miquel is Professor of English Literature at the University of Lyon, France. Her research focuses on the contemporary novel in English, exploring questions linked to narratology, intertextuality, postcolonialism, and gender. Her two most recent monographs are *Salman Rushdie: L'écriture transportée* (Presses Universitaires de Bordeaux, 2007) and *Anita Desai, In Custody*, Atlande, 2009).

Elodie Rousselot is Senior Lecturer in English Literature at the University of Portsmouth, UK, where she teaches contemporary women's writing, postcolonial literature, postmodern historical fiction, and the neo-Victorian novel. Elodie has published essays on Francophone and Anglophone Canadian literature, Margaret Atwood and myth, and contemporary female writers and history. Her book entitled *Re-Writing Women into Canadian History: Margaret Atwood and Anne Hébert* is contracted to be published with Editions de l'Instant Même.

Dianne F. Sadoff is Professor of English at Rutgers, The State University of New Jersey, New Brunswick, USA. She has just published *Victorian Vogue: British Novels on Screen* (University of Minnesota Press, 2010) and has previously published *Sciences of the Flesh: Representing Body and Subject in Psychoanalysis* (Stanford University Press, 1998) and *Monsters of Affection: Dickens, Brontë, and Eliot on Fatherhood* (Johns Hopkins University Press, 1982). She has also co-edited (with William E. Cain) *Teaching Contemporary Theory to Undergraduates* (Modern Language Association, 1994) and (with John Kucich) *Victorian Afterlife: Postmodern Culture Rewrites the Nineteenth Century* (University of Minnesota Press, 2000).

Celia Wallhead Salway is Senior Lecturer in the Department of English and German Philology at the University of Granada, Spain, where she teaches courses in English, American and postcolonial literature. Her recent publications include *A.S. Byatt: Essays on the Short Fiction* (Peter Lang, 2006) and *Washington Irving and Spain: The Romantic Movement, the Re/Creation of Islamic Andalusia and the Critical Reception* (Academica, 2008). She has written further books and articles on writers including Thomas Pynchon, E.L. Doctorow, Salman Rushdie, Iris Murdoch and John Fowles. Her research group focuses on Utopian narratives, which is a thread that unites her work on all these writers.

Elisabeth Wesseling is affiliated as an Associate Professor to the Department of Literature and Art of the Faculty of Arts and Social Sciences, Maastricht University, the Netherlands. Her current research focuses on the cultural construction of childhood in narrative fiction (including children's literature) and science (developmental psychology and anthropology), as well as cultural repertoires for constructing the 'adoptable' child in global adoption. She also researches national and regional Gothic literatures. She is author of *Writing History as a Prophet: Postmodernist Innovations of the Historical Novel* (John Benjamins Pub. Co., 1991) and has published articles in *International Research in Children's Literature*, *Children's Literature in Education*, and *Science in Context*.

Julian Wolfreys is Professor of Modern Literature and Culture, with the Department of English and Drama, at Loughborough University, UK. The author or editor of over 40 books, his most recent publications include *Thomas Hardy* (Palgrave Macmillan, 2009) and *Literature, in Theory: Tropes, Subjectivities, Responses, Responsibilities* (Continuum, 2010). He is currently working on *The Derrida Wordbook* and *Dickens's City: A Topoanalysis in 26 Episodes* (both for Edinburgh University Press). He is the Editor of the newly established *Victoriographies: A Journal of 19th-Century Writing, 1790-1914*.

Index